MW01042979

Shifting the Meaning of Democracy

Shifting the Meaning of Democracy

Race, Politics, and Culture in the United States and Brazil

Jessica Lynn Graham

UNIVERSITY OF CALIFORNIA PRESS

University of California Press, one of the most
distinguished university presses in the United States,
enriches lives around the world by advancing scholarship
in the humanities, social sciences, and natural sciences. Its
activities are supported by the UC Press Foundation and
by philanthropic contributions from individuals and
institutions. For more information, visit www.ucpress.edu.

University of California Press
Oakland, California

© 2019 by Jessica Lynn Graham

Library of Congress Cataloging-in-Publication Data

Names: Graham, Jessica Lynn, 1974- author.
Title: Shifting the meaning of democracy : race, politics,
    and culture in the United States and Brazil / Jessica
    Lynn Graham.
Description: Oakland, California : University of
    California Press, [2019] | Includes bibliographical
    references and index. |
Identifiers: LCCN 2018048808 (print) | LCCN 2018051818
    (ebook) | ISBN 9780520966932 (Epub) |
    ISBN 9780520293755 (cloth : alk. paper) |
    ISBN 9780520293762 (pbk. : alk. paper)
Subjects: LCSH: United States—Race relations—Political
    aspects. | Brazil—Race relations—Political aspects.
Classification: LCC E185.61 (ebook) | LCC E185.61 .G738
    2019 (print) | DDC 305.800973—dc23
LC record available at https://lccn.loc.gov/2018048808

Manufactured in the United States of America

28 27 26 25 24 23 22 21 20 19
10 9 8 7 6 5 4 3 2 1

In loving memory
of my sweet and brilliant father,
Odell Graham,
and my sugar and spice grandmother,
Dorothy Yolanda Reid

Contents

Illustrations

Acknowledgments

They say it takes a village to raise a child. In many ways, this book has been my child over the last several years, and it certainly has taken a transnational village to bring it to adulthood. Whether it was moral support, academic guidance, research assistance, writing partnerships, or housing during my research travels, I have relied upon innumerable people to publish this book. Unfortunately, it is impossible to include here all the names of those who have assisted me in ways big and small. To those of you who do not find your name in the following pages, please accept my gratitude for helping to see this project to fruition.

It was my great fortune to study with and be trained by amazing scholars at UCLA, Cornell University, and the University of Chicago. At Cornell, Robert Harris Jr. supervised my first stab at graduate-level research and writing, and James Turner served on my committee. The faculty and master's students at Cornell's Africana Studies and Research Center created an incredible sense of academic and social community. I would especially like to remember the late Don Ohadike, who was like a father away from home. My dissertation co-chairs at the University of Chicago, Tom Holt and Dain Borges, provided priceless support, advice, and guidance, and they are models of academic and teaching excellence. Their wonderful encouragement, vast knowledge, and sharp intellect enabled me to believe that I could take on such a big project. This book and my trajectory as a scholar would simply have been impossible without them. I also thank them for all the letters of recommendation they've written for me over the years! I was thrilled when Kesha Fikes agreed to join my committee, despite our different disciplines, and share her prodigious brilliance and time. Gail Bederman was a mentor while I was a dissertation fellow at the University of Notre Dame, and she also was kind enough to join my committee. Gail's kindness and generosity gave me confidence at vulnerable moments, and the time and effort she put into reading, copyediting, and providing detailed comments on my work are indicators of the kind of scholar and mentor she is. I would also like to thank Julie Saville, Mae Ngai, George Chauncey, Ralph Austen, Ana Maria Lima, and Pedro Pereira for being great teachers.

Many people provided assistance or feedback on this book. Research assistants Alessandra da Silva, Priscilla Garcia, Patrícia Marcos, and Abner Sótenos each gave a helpful hand at crucial moments, and Mychal Odom made excellent historiographical suggestions. A special thank-you goes to Vineeta Singh, who was my research assistant during two summers and whose contribution to chapter 4 is especially appreciated. UC Press editor Kate Marshall secured amazing readers for my manuscript whose observations, critiques, and suggestions made this book infinitely better. Two of them, Barbara Weinstein and Marc Hertzman, revealed their identity to me, and I cannot begin to articulate the gratitude I feel for the exhaustive reports they produced. In addition to her perceptive theoretical, historical, and historiographical comments, Barbara even made copyedits to the draft. The care that all the readers put into the review of my manuscript amazes me. Maggie Smith and Juliana Froggatt provided their copyediting and developmental editing talents, and they were vital resources in some crunch moments. Allyson Hobbs generously offered to read several chapter drafts and gave me great feedback. Margrit Frölich read and made wonderful suggestions for chapter 3. Sales Augusto dos Santos made an insightful comment during a conversation with a group of scholars, including the wonderful Keisha-Khan Perry and Seth Mitchell, that completely altered the way I chose to employ racial terminology in this study. I would like to thank Petrônio Domingues, Flávio dos Santos Gomes, Mônica Raisa Schpun, and Jean Hébrard for giving me the opportunity to publish articles and sharpen my ideas.

Historian Ana Raquel Minion suggested that I contact Kate Marshall at UC Press because she had heard fantastic things about her. I am more than pleased that it is UC Press that is publishing this book. Everyone I have worked with at the press—Kate, Bradley Depew, Sabrina Robleh, Tom Sullivan, Enrique Ochoa-Kaup, Erica Olsen, Professor Margaret Chowning, and Emilia Thiuri—have made what can be a painful process less stressful. They were kind and supportive when tragedy struck my family and forced me to push back the publication date, and patient when fatigue and burnout slowed me down.

The knowledge, assistance, and kindness of many archivists over the years have been invaluable resources. Among these archivists are Renan Marinho de Castro, Daniele Chaves Amado, and Bianca Silveira at the CPDOC, Elisa Larkin Nascimento and the IPEAFRO team, Luis Antonio at the Museu da Imagem e do Som, Luis at CEDEM, Zezé at IPHAN, Joyce at APERJ, and Charlotte Sturm at the RAC. I made many, many trips to the National Archives in College Park, Maryland, and I would be remiss if I did not express the utmost gratitude to the late, phenomenal archivist John Taylor, whose influence is all over this study. I appreciate Lynda Claassen at UC San Diego's Special Collections and Archives, Ricardo Santos at the APESP, Richard Peuser at NARA, and Jaime Pensado at Notre Dame for scanning images that are reproduced in these pages.

A number of grants and fellowships made this book a reality. A Fulbright-Hays fellowship funded an extended research trip to Brazil. The Rockefeller Archive Center Grant-in-Aid supported my research in Sleepy Hollow, New York, and a number of internal grants at the University of Chicago got the project off the ground. I spent four years at the University of Notre Dame, first as an Erskine Peters Fellow and then as a Moreau Postdoctoral Fellow. The benefits I gained from these Notre Dame fellowships have been incalculable, and I met incredible people who contributed tremendously to any success I have enjoyed thus far. I am particularly indebted to Richard Pierce and Dianne Pinderhughes, who are natural, selfless, and extremely dedicated mentors. Heidi Ardizzone, Jason Ruíz, Mark Hauser, Hugh Page, Jacquetta Page, and Darren Davis gave much of their time and energy to the Peters Fellows. I was lucky that Susan Ohmer and Don Pope-Davis created the Moreau Postdoctoral Fellowship while I was finishing my dissertation. My Peters and Moreau co-fellows Denise Challenger, Seth Markle, Marques Redd, Laurence Ralph, Nicole Ivy, Jean Beaman, Samantha Noel, Sekou Remy, Cameron Hill, Anne Garcia-Romero, Vanesa Miseres, Percival Matthews, Patrick Chiyo, Getachew Befekadu, Anne Baril, Laura Hunter, and honorary fellow James Ford all made South Bend enjoyable and interesting. History Department and O'Shaughnessy Hall colleagues Jaime Pensado, Gail Bederman, Karen Graubart, John Deak, Rebecca McKenna, Jaimie Bleck, Ricardo Ramirez, Sebastian Rosato, Paul Ocobock, Rory Rapple, Julia Adeney Thomas, Catherine Cangany, Lauren Faulkner, Thomas Noble,

James Turner, John McGreevy, Daniel Graff, Brad Gregory, Patrick Griffin, Alexander Martin, Ted Beatty, Father Miscamble, Linda Przybyszewski, and Deborah Tor treated me more like a colleague than a short-term visitor. After I arrived at UC San Diego, I was also fortunate to receive a Ford Foundation Postdoctoral Fellowship, which would not have been possible if Kim Butler had not generously agreed to be my faculty mentor. Professor Butler also introduced my work to Petrônio Domingues, which resulted in the chance to publish in the *Políticas da Raça* anthology. The Faculty Career Development Program grant at UC San Diego provided me with much-needed course relief so that I could dedicate more time and attention to the writing of this book.

Many friends and colleagues have helped sustain me during the past several years. Fellow graduate students at the University of Chicago made the demands of the doctoral program and the bitterness of Chicago winters tolerable. I would like to thank Atiya Khan, Meredith Oda, Sarah Potter, Gwennan Ickes, Alison Lefkovitz, Elizabeth Todd-Breland, Janette Gayle, Arissa Oh, David Spatz, Jonathan Rosa, Jonathan Levy, Ellen Wu, Debra Michaud, Beth Cooper, Kim Hardy, Molly Hudgens, Timothy Stewart-Winter, Gautham Rao, Denise Bouras, Thomas Adams, Kelly King-O'Brien, Jessica Neptune, Sarah Osten, and Ronen Steinberg for being such an important part of my intellectual and social experience in Chicago. I learned from their intelligence and knowledge immensely. My friendships with Nicole Mottier, Jaime Pensado, Jenny Morales-Pensado, Pablito Ben, and Julia Young have brought me happiness, laughs, and good times. David Martin Ferguson is like family, and I could not have survived Chicago without him. My dear friend Nancy Buenger was an amazing roommate, research buddy, and finder/provider of free housing, and she is an incredibly kind soul. I was thrilled when Allyson Hobbs ended up in California, giving us the chance to be in closer contact again. Quincy Mills always has your back, and he and his wife, Gail, graciously allowed us to stay at their home when I was in town for research. Fellow Brazilianist Ann Schneider and I were roommates in Rio de Janeiro, and her kindness and work ethic always inspired. I also fondly remember the great food, conversation, and fun that I shared with Leora Auslander and Shoshana Holt-Auslander.

Friends outside of my academic life have made me feel like a balanced person. I feel as if Rachel Weiss (who always visited me no matter where I was), Brandon del Campo, Natalie and Jerold Mitchell, Diana Grill, Stephanie Friedrich, PJ and Carrie Dickson, and Jennifer Marshall are with me even when they are not. I'm glad to still have Katherina Kechris,

Erica Kan, Mebrahtom Keflezighi, Bahghi Keflezighi, Thabiti (John) Willis, Cathy Lee, Anna Ramirez, and Carolyn Griffin in my life after all these years. Research (as well as a free couch!) was an excuse and opportunity to spend time with Sandra Ohadike, Wendy Dolce, and Jamila Piracci, my girls from Cornell. Wendy's sister and brother-in-law, Marjorie and Jean, allowed me to stay in their home for several weeks while I conducted research at the Rockefeller Archive Center. My dear childhood friend Kerry Richmond and my godsons, Christian and Dillon, put me up during a two-week research trip in Fresno. Julia Young's father, Frank (some call him Malcolm), let me live in his Washington, DC, apartment for two entire months when I was conducting research at the National Archives. The late Nick Blatchford allowed Nancy and me to stay in his home for several weeks. The hospitality of these great people made my research possible; their friendship made it fun.

The friends and family I made in Brazil (*brasileiros* and *norte-americanos* alike!) have made that country feel like home. Thaís Xavier Krause, Betty Mattos, roommate Patrícia Acerbi, Okezi Otovo, Edson Moreira and family, Clarisse Teixeira, Edilson Teixeira, Cecilia McCallum, Cecília Azevedo, Divya Balakrishnan, Lauren Willy, Dora, Raissa, Babette, and Valerie Belanger have added so much to my life on so many levels. My family on my husband's side, *a família* Conceição, has welcomed me into their homes and into the family with heartfelt love and warmth. Marise, Theo, Israel, Fernanda, Dilza, Daniel, and their families have hosted me the most. I was shocked when my niece Melina actually slept in a recliner chair because her mother, Marise, wanted me to use her room. Marina, Neymar (no, not that one), Francisco, Kris, J.R., Tia-Tio, Tio Júlio, and all their children made me feel like family the instant I met them. My late mother-in-law, Dona Benedita, was one of the strongest women I have ever known. I am so grateful to have spent so much time in her presence and to have had a special connection with her. The experiences and bonds that I have forged in Brazil greatly contribute to why I like to go back!

I was extremely fortunate to have landed in a department that is friendly and supportive. I can genuinely say that I have always felt that everyone in the History Department at UC San Diego has been cheering and hoping for my success. There is so much that I could write here about my brilliant and kind colleagues that I hope it suffices to say a heartfelt and sincere thank-you to Nancy Kwak, Mark Hanna, Todd Henry, Jeremy Prestholdt, Cathy Gere, Simeon Man, Frank Biess, Uli Strasser, Hasan Kayali, Matthew Vitz, Ben Cowan, Eric Van Young,

Natalia Molina, Paul Pickowicz, Karl Gerth, Sarah Schneewind, Ed Watts, Bob Westman, Deborah Hertz, Rebecca Jo Plant, Claire Edington, Dave Gutierrez, Denise Demetriou, Wendy Matsumura, Bob Edelman, Michael Provence, Mark Hendrickson, Tal Golan, Weijing Lu, Patrick Patterson, Nancy Caciola, Tom Gallant, Nir Shafir, Andrew Devereux, Mira Balberg, Micah Muscolino, Michael Monteón, Michael Parrish, Cynthia Truant, Judy Hughes, David Goodblatt, Bill Propp, and the late John Marino. I do need to make special mention of a small handful of my colleagues. Pamela Radcliff was chair of the department from the time I was hired until the moment I received tenure, and I am grateful for the guidance she gave and the compassion she showed, particularly in difficult times. Luis Alvarez was my faculty mentor; his advice and willingness to answer any and all questions helped me move through the tenure process with less stress and anxiety. Rachel Klein was the lead reviewer for my tenure file, and I was reassured and calmed by the way she carried out that task with such dedication. Dana Velasco Murillo and I were hired in the same year, and her friendship, support, and advice have made a big impact on my life. Danny Widener was chair of my search committee, and he made me feel confident that this is a welcoming environment that would allow me to thrive. I also want to thank the hardworking staff for all they do to run the department. A special thank-you goes to Leah Tamayo-Brion and Susan Bernal for going above and beyond so that I could be there for my family when they most needed me.

Other friends and colleagues on campus have added so much to my experience here in San Diego. First and foremost are good friends and writing partners Gloria Chacón and Jillian Hernandez. It is not an exaggeration to say that I would not have finished this book without our writing sessions. My Black Studies Project co-conveners, Dayo Gore and Sara Clarke Kaplan, are amazing and inspiring partners and friends. I have grown intellectually and professionally through my work with them. Thandeka Chapman, Dennis Childs, Kirstie Dorr, Jin-kyung Lee, Boatema Boateng, Zeinabu Davis, Makeba Jones, Bennetta Jules-Rosette, Daphne Taylor-Garcia, Sara Johnson, Mya Hines, and Chelsea Richmond are among the many colleagues across campus with whom I have collaborated or interacted. Although she is not at UC San Diego, I am happy that Erika Robb Larkins is director of San Diego State University's Program on Brazil. It is nice for Ben and me to have another friendly Brazilianist in town. I feel the same way about Kenneth Serbin at the University of San Diego.

Finally, I would like to thank my family. I know my husband, Paulo, has often felt as if he is married more to this book than to me. His genuine concern and support have helped sustain me. During the difficult nose-to-the-grindstone days of finishing this book, I would often wake up to sticky notes around the house with words of encouragement and love. He is a beautiful soul with a gigantic heart, and I am thankful he is in my life every day. The arrival of my teenage children, Víctor and Andreza, here in San Diego was a life-altering occasion for us all. I thank them for trusting me to be their mother and for all the laughter, love, and personal growth we have experienced together. I would also like to thank Andreza for the few weeks she committed to helping me with some research several years ago. Gabi and her daughter, Dudo, remain in Brazil, and I thank them for the sweetness and love they have shown me. My sisters, Karyn and Cynthia, are my heroes. As my parents' health became of increasing concern, they did everything in their power to care for them and to protect me and my time so that my career could stay on track. These have been extremely challenging and difficult years, and my sisters have risen to the occasion like champions. They have sacrificed so much, and I can never begin to thank them for being such loving and committed sisters and daughters. Although my mother's condition will not allow her to appreciate the accomplishment of this book, I still feel her love for me, and that is everything. To Paulo, Mom, Karyn, Cynthia, Víctor, Andreza, and Gabi, thank you, and I love you.

This book is dedicated to my grandmother and my father. My grandmother, Dorothy Reid, almost lived to see her youngest grandchild receive a PhD. I still miss her, but I feel her presence. She was a spirit that death could not conquer. My father almost lived to see his youngest daughter publish her first book. It saddens me that he will miss this big milestone in my life, but I take solace in the fact that he knew I was accomplishing my professional goals. I am happy that in these acknowledgments, it will forever be documented that Odell Graham was an incredible man, a genius, kind, sweet, and gentle. This book is a part of my father's legacy.

A Note on Terminology

The translation of Brazilian racial categories into English is a challenge for all English-language scholars who write about race in the South American nation. There is no straightforward way to convert Brazil's more numerous racial terms to English, and one always risks showing a bias toward US classifications and nomenclature.[1] For instance, although "black" is the safest translation for *preto* and *negro*, using the same word for these two Portuguese terms loses the nuance between them, as Paulina Alberto reminds us. For much of the nineteenth and twentieth centuries, it was an insult to call someone *negro*, and *preto* was more acceptable as the term that simply referred to the color black. Blacks and mestizos who used *negro* in the twentieth century did so "as an emblem of racial unity," one that included *pardo* (literally, "brown" mestizos) and moved away from the tendency to characterize mestizos as an identity separate from the black race.[2]

For US blacks, *African American* is widely accepted today, but it relies on the US-centric and hegemonic use of the term *American*, which ignores all other populations of North, Central, and South America.[3] Blacks in Brazil rarely used *afro-brasileiro* ("Afro-Brazilian") during most of the twentieth century, and Alberto expresses discomfort with its connection to the exoticizing gaze of anthropologists early in the century.[4] In the United States, *people of color* is more prevalent, and it refers to all nonwhites, whereas in Brazil it usually applies to those who appear to be of African descent.

xx | A Note on Terminology

Despite its emergence as a popular term among black antiracist campaigners in the 1970s, black activist and scholar Sales Augusto dos Santos objects to *Afro-descendant* because of its political consequences for the contemporary black movement. Post–affirmative action racial politics seem to have validated this point. These policies have implemented racial quotas to reverse the exclusion of blacks in higher education and certain areas of employment. Sociologist Marcilene Garcia de Souza has argued that Brazilian racial quotas should target the populations that experience racial discrimination, but in many cases, the quotas do not. Unlike in the United States, being "black in Brazil is by phenotype, not by origins." However, many people who are "socially white"— those who would not otherwise identify or be perceived as black— successfully claim to be of African descent to benefit from racial quotas. Indeed, *Afro-descendant* and its focus on African origins can obfuscate how race as a social construct functions in Brazil, and the term can be manipulated to subvert the agenda for racial equality.[5] Aforementioned objections aside, many scholars, including historians, in Brazil continue to use *afro-brasileiro* and *afrodescendente*.

Each of the English terms presented here is somehow problematic, misleading, or confusing. Nonetheless, without other options, respected scholars writing in English have used and continue to use them all. I prefer the term *black,* but a refusal to incorporate other terminology would result in unbearably repetitive prose. I observe the Brazilian understanding of the term *people of color* when writing about Brazil and the US understanding when discussing the United States. Because this could lend itself to confusion, I use the term sparingly. With Santos's observation in mind, I have chosen to be thrifty with *Afro-descendant,* and when the term appears, it is typically as a catchall for blacks, regardless of nationality. I use it only occasionally in the Brazilian context to vary the terminology. As in many contemporary studies of race in Brazil, in this book, *black* and its synonyms refer to all those who would identify as *negro, preto, mulato, pardo, mestiço,* and a number of other mixed-race categories.

Abbreviations and Acronyms

ABB	African Blood Brotherhood for African Liberation and Redemption
ACLS	American Council of Learned Societies
AIB	Ação Integralista Brasileira / Brazilian Integralist Action
ANB	Associação do Negro Brasileiro / Association of Black Brazilians
ANL	Aliança Nacional Libertadora / National Liberation Alliance
ANLC	American Negro Labor Congress
CLT	Consolidação das Leis do Trabalho / Consolidation of Labor Laws
COMINTERN	Communist International (The Third International)
CPNNDP	Committee on the Participation of Negroes in the National Defense Program
CPUSA	Communist Party of the United States of America
DEOPS	Departamento Estadual de Ordem Política e Social/ State Department of Political and Social Order (Political Police)
DESPS	Delegacia Especial de Segurança Política e Social / Special Office of Social and Political Security (Political Police)

DIP	Departamento de Imprensa e Propaganda / Department of Press and Propaganda
DNP	Departamento Nacional de Propaganda / National Department of Propaganda
DOPS	Departamento de Ordem Política e Social / Department of Political and Social Order (Political Police)
ECCI	Executive Committee of the Communist International
FEPC	Fair Employment Practices Committee
FNB	Frente Negra Brasileira / Brazilian Black Front
FTP	Federal Theatre Project
GPNR	Governo Popular Nacional Revolucionário / National Revolutionary Popular Government
HCUA	House Special Committee on Un-American Activities
ILD	International Labor Defense
LSN	Lei de Segurança Nacional / National Security Law
LSNR	League of Struggle for Negro Rights
MES	Ministério da Educação e Saúde / Ministry of Education and Health
MID	Military Intelligence Division
MOWM	March on Washington Movement
MPSA	Motion Picture Society for the Americas
MUT	Movimento Unificador dos Trabalhadores / Unifying Workers' Movement
NAACP	National Association for the Advancement of Colored People
OCIAA	Office of the Coordinator of Inter-American Affairs
OSS	Office of Strategic Services
OWI	Office of War Information
PCB	Partido Comunista do Brasil / Communist Party of Brazil
PSD	Partido Social Democrático / Social Democratic Party
PTB	Partido Trabalhista Brasileiro / Brazilian Workers' Party

SPHAN	Serviço do Patrimônio Histórico e Artístico Nacional / National Artistic and Historic Patrimony Service
TEN	Teatro Experimental do Negro / Black Experimental Theater
UDN	União Democrática Nacional / National Democratic Union
UNE	União Nacional dos Estudantes / National Union of Students
UNIA	Universal Negro Improvement Association
WP	Workers Party of America
WPA	Works Progress Administration

Introduction

In 1943 a map titled "Brazil . . . A Stepping Stone for Invasion . . . East or West" sounded the alarm that Adolf Hitler reportedly planned to use Brazil to attack the United States.[1] The map of the Americas, Africa, and Europe included two-way arrows that showed how close both Vichy-controlled West Africa and the Cape Verde Islands were to Natal, Brazil. Another two-way arrow began in Natal, swept into the northern South American countries, and pointed directly toward the United States. The full spread map and its ominous title communicated a clear message from the US Office of the Coordinator of Inter-American Affairs, the publisher of the booklet, to the US public. The booklet, *Brazil: Introduction to a Neighbor,* relayed the importance of the South American giant—with its convenient geographic location, huge German population, and five thousand miles of largely unprotected coastline— to US safety and interests during the war. Just as the two-way arrows on the map suggested, the significance of this relationship was also felt in Brazil; however, whereas the United States' wartime influence on Brazil is well known, the reverse is a generally forgotten story in US history.[2]

If Brazil's wartime influence on the United States is overlooked, so, too, are the racial issues at play in the Brazil-US alliance. During the Second World War and the 1930s, which had been a tumultuous and polarized decade, Brazilian and US authorities regarded each nation's racial image as a critical component in the efforts to solidify their alliance and, relatedly, to create goodwill between the multiracial citizens

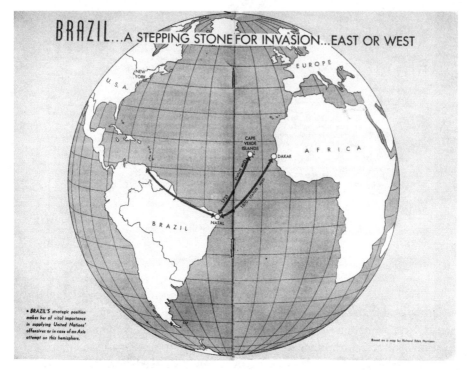

FIGURE 1. The map that appears in the booklet *Brazil: Introduction to a Neighbor.* The US Office of the Coordinator of Inter-American Affairs published the booklet in 1943.

of both countries. With so much at stake, including a possible Nazi occupation of the Americas, these racial considerations took on a sense of urgency and contributed to a prominent twentieth-century trend: the unsteady replacement of nationalisms that openly excluded people of color with those that emphasized the theoretical inclusion of all races.[3] Although this multiracial nationalism manifested differently in Brazil and the United States, in both countries the doctrine not only helped mainstream the acceptance of racial pluralism but also construed it as patriotic. *Shifting the Meaning of Democracy: Race, Politics, and Culture in the United States and Brazil* is a transnational and comparative study that explores and seeks to explain this historical sea change in official US and Brazilian nationalist ideals.

This book analyzes the co-constitutive emergence of racially inclusive nationalisms as Brazilian and US state doctrine between 1930 and 1945 in relation to blacks, who were, according to census data, the most populous nonwhite racialized group in both nations at the time.[4] It probes why and how this shift occurred, the modes through which it was expressed, its explicit relationship to notions of democracy, and the role of and consequences for US-Brazil relations. Indeed, political nationalism in these countries was tightly linked to ideas of democracy, even in Brazil during the Estado Novo dictatorship (1937–45). As a result, this study exposes the new, inclusionary ways in which Brazilian and US political conceptions became racialized during the Great Depression and World War II. Because of the significance of democracy, I refer to the articulations of inclusive, race-based nationalism as "racial democracy," an extremely common term in Brazilian literature and one, I contend, that pertains to the United States as well. This study assesses the international forces that most significantly precipitated racial democracy's newfound utility to the US and Brazilian states during this period: communism, fascism (especially Nazism), and World War II.

The stock market crash of 1929 and the Great Depression generated many skeptics of capitalism and the system of government considered to be its natural partner—liberal democracy.[5] This environment was ideal for leaders and advocates of movements that challenged capitalism, liberal democracy, or both. Fascist and communist groups seemed to be the biggest winners; their attacks on the economic and political status quo drew support from multitudes of disaffected and disillusioned people in Brazil and the United States. In Brazil the Far Left and Right grew polarized: large numbers of partisans began to clash fatally in the streets, justifying a repressive national security law in 1935.[6] In the United States, the 1930s was the heyday for communists and "fellow travelers," and contrarily, the fascist-like, anti-Semitic messages of Catholic priest and radio host Father Coughlin also produced a huge following.[7] Protests against the political and economic establishment from the Left and Right set up a unique labyrinth of political rhetoric that authorities in both countries had to navigate.

Heightened black activism in Brazil and the United States meant that politicized black populations influenced these political phenomena. The situation was dire for blacks in both countries during the Great Depression, as they were among the most economically vulnerable groups, trapped in low-paying jobs and kept out of many industries even when the economy had been strong.[8] In the United States, the national average for black unemployment in 1932 hovered around a whopping 50 percent, and many African Americans doubted that traditional black rights organizations like the National Association for the Advancement of Colored People (NAACP) held real potential to ameliorate their situation. Black radicalism grew significantly, and communism attracted many adherents, especially in black urban hubs like Harlem.[9]

Afro-Brazilians were also drawn to the Left and Right. José Correia Leite—a black activist and journalist—made it clear that Afro-Brazilians were not immune to the national politics at the time. Leite recalled that in those days, "you were either communist or fascist," and he stated that both political movements had taken "blacks to their death or to jail."[10] Blacks had grown weary of a government that, since the formation of the First Brazilian Republic in 1889, largely had disregarded their political, social, and economic rights. For example, similar to blacks in the US South, many Afro-Brazilians were excluded from participating in electoral politics because of the bitter combination of literacy requirements and the state's refusal to address black demands for improvements to the school system that was failing them.[11] Instead of investing in Brazil's black workforce, states like São Paulo heavily invested in European immigrants. Thus, like distressed and frustrated citizens in all corners of the globe, large numbers of Brazilian and US blacks agitated for alternative economic and political models in an effort to redress their various grievances, including racial inequality.

This book argues that the struggle that occurred between the US and Brazilian states, black activists, the Left, and the Right was in part a theoretical tug-of-war over the meanings of democracy. Typically this was not how the struggle was framed. Political leaders, antiracist activists, academics, and average citizens alike tended to construct the conflict as one of triple opposites: communism versus fascism versus democracy. This study examines a parallel rhetorical dispute that was taking place. In this debate, communists and fascists were opposed not to the idea of democracy per se but to liberal democracy, loosely characterized as a Western-style capitalist form of representative government. Those who denounced democracy from the Left and Right, then, customarily did so to attack this Western-style liberal democracy. In fact, fascists and communists frequently claimed to be genuine democratic movements themselves—"nonliberal democracies"—defending their own particular interpretations that usually excluded Brazil and the United States.[12]

Democracy was arguably the most popular and widely interpreted political term during the 1930s and World War II. According to eminent political theorist C. B. Macpherson, this was not the case in the fifty-year era before the First World War, when democracy went hand in hand with the liberal capitalist state and its principles of individual rights and freedom. The Bolshevik Revolution and its notion of proletarian democracy helped diversify the concept of democracy after World War I. In those decades following the war, democracy was perceived as "a good thing— so much so that everyone claim[ed] to have it." Democracy became "ambiguous . . . with different meanings—even apparently opposite meanings—for different peoples."[13] That said, the prominent political viewpoints of this study's period did share a baseline definition of democracy as the system of government that best fulfilled the needs of the people and promoted their well-being. *Best* was the operative word here, as all parties asserted superiority in their ability to provide the most fruitful political, economic, and social conditions for their people. The ambiguity and disagreements between them rested on their values and on what scholar Bernard Crick described as "democracy as a set of institutional arrangements or constitutional devices."[14]

It is important to clarify that this study does not present fascism as democratic, nor does it validate Hitler's attempts to democratize Nazism. Although leading political theorists like Macpherson, Chantal Mouffe, and Ernesto Laclau have argued that democracy can exist in forms outside of the liberal framework, it is clear that none of them would classify fascist states—and especially the Third Reich—as democratic. For instance, Macpherson, who had been greatly troubled by the rise of Nazism, contended that a nonliberal regime can be deemed democratic only if it has the "moral" objective "to provide the conditions for the full and free development of the essential human capacities of all the members of the society."[15] Mouffe, Angela Davis, Charles Mills, Carole Pateman, and Michael Hanchard are among those who theorize about the historical failure of Western democracies to meet such a moral standard for all races and genders, but such criticisms never translate into support for the notion of a Nazi democracy.[16] Again, the inclusion of fascists in this study is not an endorsement of their democratic claims; rather, my intention is to assess and acknowledge their impact on the racial democratic debate.

As national, class, gender, ethnic, and racial definitions of "the people" clashed, the question of who constituted "the people"—that is, which groups should benefit from democracy and how—distinguished political rivals from one another. From the 1930s through the end of World War II, an obsession with the racial characteristics of the people emerged. The international community urgently prioritized and openly reconsidered the racial benefactors of a truly democratic society. This book examines the ways that the democratic war of words in Brazil and the United States often turned on the issue of race, as the racial criteria of democracy became one of the key elements that differentiated the Left, Right, and center.

Communists and fascists were among those who highlighted race to frame their own democratic formulations. Especially in the 1930s, communists argued that racial equality was a key feature of any real democracy and pointed to discrimination in the United States and Brazil as proof that those societies were undemocratic. As chapter 2 assesses, communist racial democracy led anticommunist authorities, even racist ones, to defend their governments with more inclusive language. The rise of fascism in the 1920s and particularly the ascension of Nazism in the 1930s also began to alter the global discussion about race and democracy. Fascism focused the spotlight of democratic debate squarely on questions of racial and religious rights, tolerance, and equality. Of course, European fascism's impact on US and Brazilian racial democracy was most radical during World War II, especially after both nations declared war. In chapter 5 we see that the Axis powers used the United States' racial record to call out its democratic hypocrisy. After all, racial illiberalism should have been anathema to a liberal state, particularly one in which abolition legally transformed the formerly enslaved into free and equal citizens. Blacks also took advantage of the war and its racial politics to advance their own equal rights agenda. This book also shows how Brazil, in the unique position of being an Allied dictatorship, relied upon its reputation as a racially tolerant society to justify its alliance with liberal democracies. Here the Estado Novo (New State) took advantage of the Allies' anti-Nazi, antiracism rhetoric to portray Brazil as a democracy.

In both Brazil and the United States, communism, fascism, black activism, and World War II created a complex ideological landscape that rendered racial inclusion as democratic and nationalist, and racial exclusion as undemocratic and unpatriotic. In this climate, I contend that US and Brazilian authorities articulated multiracial nationalism to ward off the undemocratic accusations and to prove that their governments were true democracies. Authorities deemed their accusers a threat to their political power at best and subversive elements that endangered the nation's entire political system at worst. Therefore, official racial democracy—propagated largely to mediate, control, and guard against these perceived threats—emerged as a national defense strategy for the Brazilian and US states. By the *state,* I mean federal-level government and its agencies, governmental bodies like Congress that had national reach, and the Brazilian state police that helped create and maintain the

Estado Novo. I do not suggest that the state was a monolithic entity or even that authorities acted with the same objectives; instead, I try to describe how influential authorities and agencies were a part of a major trend, not yet absolute, toward racial democracy in both countries.

The relationship between the United States and Brazil, driven by the Good Neighbor Policy and World War II, further stimulated their official advance of racial democracy and influenced the ways that both countries produced and circulated it as international propaganda for national security purposes. The Good Neighbor Policy, which Franklin D. Roosevelt announced during his first inaugural address in 1933, set out to tighten the bonds between the nations of the Western Hemisphere. In part, Roosevelt promised to reverse US intervention in Latin America and to spearhead programs of cultural exchange. The Good Neighbor Policy was particularly important during World War II, when Brazil would become arguably the United States' most critical ally in the region. Brazil also relied upon the US financial support it earned in exchange for its wartime partnership and cooperation.[17]

This book argues that officials in Brazil and the United States worked together to construct and legitimize one another's racial and democratic images largely to tighten their wartime alliance. The two states largely carried out this work by collaborating on cultural productions. Such messages of racial democracy precipitated a rise in the presence of black culture and multiracial nationalist rhetoric in state cultural productions, including government-issued literature and state-produced film and radio. In part, cultural propaganda broadcast visual and verbal representations of the national community's racial composition and specified that many races and cultures were included in and accepted as part of the nation. These states also placed an official stamp of approval on once disparaged black cultural expressions, marking them as authentic national culture. However, authorities simultaneously limited the ways in which blacks themselves could represent the nation. For instance, the states commonly employed white cultural mediators in lieu of black performers to transmit black culture as a sign of racial democracy.

US and Brazilian officials and nonstate actors deployed essentially four (often interacting and coexistent) forms of racial democracy. These categories do not necessarily reflect the intentionality of the historical actors examined in this book. However, they were not preordained, nor did I produce them arbitrarily. Rather, these four classifications became clear to me while I researched the functionality of racially inclusive democratic discourse in the historical documents. I was quite surprised by the heterogeneity of voices articulating racial democracy and the multitude of the often contradictory positions they endorsed. I soon realized that the debate did not revolve only around the case for or against racial democracy. In fact, even among those who claimed to be its champions, there was no consensus about what a racially inclusive democratic society should look like. Thus I developed these four categories to analyze this rhetoric in the aggregate, identifying common threads of thought and offering deeper meaning and some structure to a cacophony of racial political ideals.

The first category, *racial realism,* was advanced by those who acknowledged that racism existed in their societies and pushed for practical, concrete steps toward racial justice. Racial realists fought for tangible change that would bring about greater equality, articulating racial democracy as a goal, not as a fact. Most realists argued that the eradication of racism was necessary to realize true political democracy and to protect national defense interests. Black activists working within and outside of the state typically were the most ardent advocates of racial realism.

Racial denial was the variant of racial democracy contrary to realism; its spokespersons clashed with the realists and denied that a problem of racial prejudice existed. Denialists took this stance in order to fend off the dangers they identified in accusations from the Left, the Right, and black activists that racism was endemic to their societies. In opposition to the realists, denialists expressed racial democracy as a current truth, not a work in progress. Realism was more common in the United States and denial more common in Brazil, but both categories had proponents in each country.

Racial dissuasion was the use of racially inclusive language to dissuade blacks from joining any movement considered a national threat, including communism. Racial dissuaders also discouraged blacks from engaging in actions that undermined the state by exposing racial prejudice. In order to steer them in the desired direction, dissuaders often tried to convince blacks that supporting the political status quo was in their best interest. Dissuasion typically was not a stand-alone category; it usually functioned in tandem with realism or denial.

Racial obstructionism was the effort to obstruct racially inclusive messages. Unlike advocates of the other categories, many obstructionists were against any expression of racial democracy. The staunchest racists who spoke unabashedly against black inclusion—particularly in places like the US Deep South, São Paulo, or Rio Grande do Sul—were prime examples.[18] Other obstructionists may have subscribed to a form of racial democracy yet blocked and removed realist messages about the problem of racism from the public sphere. This type of obstructionism was common in Brazil, especially during the Estado Novo dictatorship when the political police confiscated literature, burned books, and imprisoned the "subversive" opposition. Racial realists were silenced routinely as a result. In fact, the Estado Novo's 1937 ban of political parties largely demobilized the nation's most successful and organized black rights organization, the Frente Negra Brasileira. In the United States, anticommunist crusader Martin Dies precipitated the downfall of antiracist state cultural materials and projects.

In creating these categories, I have borrowed heavily from the words and frameworks that the voices I researched deployed in their formulations. Yet just as no agreement prevailed as to what a racial democracy should be in the 1930s and 1940s, not all the historical actors that appear in the following pages would have embraced these classifications. Again, the categories are purposefully broad, not to oversimplify or collapse complicated and multidimensional phenomena occurring in two nations but to establish enough room for the complexity and nuance that existed within them.

A central premise of this analysis is that from 1930 to 1945, the Brazilian and US states privileged what I refer to as non-action-oriented forms of racial democracy. Action-oriented realists did not speak in glittering generalities like their non-action-oriented counterparts; they specified economic, social, and political inequities that frustrated blacks' quest for freedom, pressuring the state to enact measures that would reduce or eradicate them. These realists advanced a proactive antiracist agenda, not a passive one. I contend that action-oriented realists had a difficult time moving the state past verbal commitments to racial pluralism because of the latter's prioritization of the national security concerns outlined. This is not to suggest that there was no action inherent in official language of racial democracy, but rather that authorities did not focus on utilizing "coercive state power"—such as legislation or substantial social policy enforced by the state apparatus—to explicitly tackle the problem of racial inequality.[19] Contemporaneous realists such as Afro-Brazilian leader Abdias do Nascimento expressed their frustration with what they perceived as a failure to pursue antiracist praxis. Nascimento complained that during the 1930s, cultural racial democracy incorporated blacks into society as ethnographic material when their struggle for freedom "cried out for urgent practical action to improve radically their horrible existence."[20]

The action-oriented and non-action-oriented binary of this analysis speaks to linguistic turn scholarship and its emphasis on the power of discourse and language to make race. As theorist Robert Young has warned, the linguistic turn's focus on racial difference as a scientific fiction, or as only a set of manufactured and illogical criteria and concepts, led many to define racism primarily as a set of falsehoods that should be tackled on the rhetorical level. Accordingly, freedom was to be claimed through realigned and more egalitarian representations and language of human difference. "What [this literature offers] as emancipation," Young concludes, "is not equal access to economic resources but the pleasure of disrupting dominant and oppressive meanings."[21] In other words, for Young this form of liberation was problematic in that it could be disconnected from the tangible material changes that would improve the quality of and possibilities for black lives.

Young's argument has strong analytical parallels with this book. Indeed, despite the emergence of more racially inclusive rhetoric, the general defeat of action-oriented racial realism during this period left much work to be done in the eradication of racial inequality for subsequent generations. However, rhetorical change had its benefits, and racial democracy did create new nationalist attitudes in the United States and Brazil that future antiracists were able to utilize to their advantage.

RACIST AND EXCLUSIVE NATIONALISMS

In order to illuminate the historical circumstances that helped make the shift from racially exclusive to racially inclusive nationalisms possible, I will provide a short sketch of these transitions in Brazil and the United States. The discussion of the former focuses on but is not limited to the state, whereas the summary of the latter more fully includes the non-state actors that pressured the state to adopt racially pluralist rhetoric. Although earlier transformations around the ideals of race and national identity took place in both nations, particularly in relation to abolition, this overview concentrates on the twentieth century.

In the early part of the century, racist nationalism was dominant in the United States.[22] Racist nationalists were strongly informed by US Anglo-Saxonism, which Reginald Horsman has described as the belief in "the American Anglo-Saxons as a separate, innately superior people who were destined to bring good government, commercial prosperity, and Christianity to the American continents and to the world." Inferior races were "doomed to subordinate status or extinction."[23] Even early twentieth-century leaders who rejected Anglo-Saxonism, including "melting pot" advocate Theodore Roosevelt, often advanced a form of racist nationalism. At its inception, the melting pot comprised various white ethnic groups; people of color were excluded from the mix.[24] Segregation laws, which the US Supreme Court validated in the 1896 *Plessy v. Ferguson* case, exemplified the state's active marginalization and exclusion of people of color from a nation defined as white.

Racist nationalists, especially Anglo-Saxonists, believed that the fate of the nation depended on the maintenance of the United States' white heritage. Nonwhite races were labeled threats to the broader national good, possible antagonists capable of derailing the country's divine destiny by contaminating society with their inherent inferiority. Anglo-Saxonists, many of them nativist agitators, also opposed the immigration and naturalization of Eastern Europeans, whom they placed on the lowest rung of the so-called white races. Anglo-Saxonism dovetailed anti-European racism with xenophobia against Europeans of a "lesser stock." This mentality strengthened and was strengthened by the popularity of scientific racism and social Darwinism, which categorized and ranked all human races as well as justified racial and ethnic discrimination.[25]

Much of the Latin American intellectual elite did not subscribe to such Western pseudoscientific reasoning wholesale, but these ideas certainly were influential. At the turn of the century, Raimundo Nina Rodrigues made a huge impact on Brazilian scientific racism as a pioneer in the fields of criminal anthropology, medical law, psychiatry, and anthropology, among others. Nina Rodrigues's groundbreaking studies echoed North American and European thought with his theses on indigenous and black inferiority, the ability of blacks to psychologically pollute the more advanced white upper classes, and the ways that miscegenation led to degeneration.[26] As the twentieth century progressed, however, the Brazilian elite adopted a more nuanced perspective. Nancy Stepan shows that during the interwar period, Latin Americans rejected the racial and hereditary focus of the Mendelian eugenics most popular in Anglo-Saxon countries, adopting in its place a neo-Lamarckism that prioritized environment and amelioration through hygienic and sanitation reforms. Nevertheless, these Latin American eugenicists were still concerned about degeneration and "beauty and ugliness, purity and contamination, as represented in race."[27] These preoccupations led even neo-Lamarckian eugenicists to argue for the exclusion of those degenerative elements, racialized as mestizos, indigenous, and black Brazilians. Such ideas about who should and should not be included in the nation's populace provided "scientific" reasoning for authorities that pushed racist policies.

Most of Brazil's early twentieth-century elite had accepted the theory of Aryan supremacy yet, unlike Nina Rodrigues, simultaneously disavowed the bleak belief that racial mixing necessarily led to degeneration. Their hope and assertion was that through miscegenation, racial progress would occur. The Brazilian elite contended that Brazil was whitening or that continued racial mixing and increased European immigration would eventually whiten Brazil's people of color. Europeans were thought to be more energetic and industrious than Brazilians, and whitening supporters also hoped that their temperament would rub off on local populations. The government even recruited and subsidized the voyages of cheap European immigrant labor. Proponents of *branqueamento*, the whitening process, predicted an Aryan Brazil in a few to several generations, insuring a "civilized" future for the nation.[28] If they usually avoided explicit racial language, Paulista regionalists encouraged this tendency to link civilization with whiteness when they insisted that São Paulo—the most common destination for European immigrants— was the epicenter of Brazilian modernity.[29]

The Brazilian state demonstrated its opposition to black immigration many times. Shortly after Brazil's monarchy was overthrown, the provisional government's immigration law admitted noncriminal foreigners able to work, except Africans and Asians.[30] In the early 1920s, many authorities decided to revisit the issue after being alarmed by several developments. The Chicago-based Brazilian American Colonization Syndicate planned for US black immigration to Brazil, and rumors spread that land developers in the state of Mato Grosso were recruiting US blacks for this purpose. Opponents of black immigration caused such a scandal that the government reneged on the concessions that had been offered to the developers, and two congressional deputies introduced a controversial antiblack immigration bill. The bill would have outright prohibited "human beings of the black race" from entering Brazil. Of the 113 deputies in the Chamber, 94 voted to advance it to committee for debate. Deputies against the bill and black campaigners like Evaristo de Moraes, all appealing to a patriotic sentiment of racial tolerance, managed to defeat it. A similar and unsuccessful proposal emerged two years later when US black newspaper publisher Robert Abbott, who had traveled to Brazil in 1923, planned to arrange for black cotton farmers to immigrate to Brazil that same year. Brazilian authorities eventually chose to act more discreetly, mandating their consulates in the United States to deny visas to blacks. Conveniently, this option protected Brazil's long-standing reputation as a racially cordial society, especially in comparison to the blatant racism of US policies.[31]

Asian immigration caused dissension and controversy in Brazil as well. Japanese immigrants began to arrive in 1907, inciting heated debates inside and outside political circles. Much of the agricultural sector championed the immigration of the Japanese, who were respected by landowners for their perceived agricultural knowledge, while others vehemently disapproved. Immigration of the Chinese was completely out of the question because of their alleged vices and lack of energy, both of which were viewed as contagious.[32]

In the United States, anxieties about national progress and unity also greatly shaped immigration law around the turn of the century. Before the 1921 Johnson Quota and 1924 Johnson-Reed Immigration Acts, European immigration to the United States was relatively open, but many restrictions existed on immigration of other groups, especially Asians. The Chinese Exclusion Act of 1882 outlawed the immigration of Chinese laborers, and in 1907 Japan agreed to limit the number of Japanese immigrants to the United States. (This explains why Brazil became a destination for Japanese immigration that same year.) In 1917 Congress passed an immigration act that created a "barred Asiatic zone" that broadly excluded Asians from admission. The 1921 and 1924 immigration laws echoed these policies by declaring Asians ineligible to immigrate based on their prohibition from naturalized citizenship, which had been upheld in the Supreme Court. The 1924 law also discriminated against Southern and Eastern Europeans, although they were marked as assimilable ethnic white nationalities and never had their access to citizenship or immigration denied outright. Furthermore, as Mae Ngai shows, the law and the implementation of border patrol policies at the Mexican border permanently branded Asian and Mexican immigrants and their offspring as "aliens."[33]

One distinction to make between US and Brazilian immigration policies is that the United States had a protective approach to its racial heritage, whereas the Brazilian elite typically had a corrective stance to theirs. Unlike their counterparts in Brazil, US policymakers and other influential thinkers saw immigration not as the solution to their racial concerns but as a menace to the nation's larger white majority population. However, both states unabashedly relied upon immigration law to protect or increase the white character of the nation. In this attempt to racially engineer Brazil and the United States, authorities considered people of color a threat to national well-being and progress.

THE MOVE TOWARD INCLUSIVE NATIONALISM AND RACIAL DEMOCRACY IN THE INTERWAR PERIOD

Alluding to Benedict Anderson's canonical work, Thomas Holt has written, "nations are not imagined at one moment, once and for all, but must be periodically *reimagined,* even reinvented, often at moments of crises, precipitated by the need to determine who belongs and who does not."[34] The Brazilian and US reimagining of their racial-national identities was a result of many moments of crises that came to a head in the 1930s and during World War II. One of these major events was the First World War, which left a deep mark on the interwar generation.

As the first decade after World War I, the 1920s was a particularly active period during which major developments and changes occurred in racial ideals, political beliefs, nationalism, and cultural tastes. Micol Seigel has written that the war "spotlit global racial relations and questions of racial justice as the Allies' rhetoric of democracy . . . caught on the snag of their own racially stratified societies." The black Brazilian activist José Correia Leite remembered that the democratic framing of the First World War helped arouse black desires for a better life. The 1920s did prove to be a seminal period for Afro-Brazilian racial consciousness and activism, and the black press grew as never before in the nation's history, most notably in São Paulo. By the mid-1920s, Brazil's black press was more emphatic in its call for civil rights. The newspaper *O Alfinete* signaled this trend in 1918 when its director wrote that the racially harmonious "symbol of our democracy" was "a fiction and a lie."[35] A growing number of black Brazilians challenged the traditional narrative of racial harmony, which both ignored racism and embraced whitening, to push for one that exposed their struggles and supported their demands.

In the 1920s many blacks fought for public recognition of their critical role in Brazilian history, and they also founded important black social, political, and educational organizations. In cities like Rio de Janeiro, Porto Alegre, and São Paulo, Afro-Brazilians campaigned to erect monuments to the *Mãe Preta* (Black Mother), the famous wet-nurse figure who breastfed the nation's elite children during slavery. At times with, at times without white co-advocates, these black activists and journalists deployed various rhetorical strategies to lobby for the creation of the Mãe Preta statues. Some framed the Mãe Preta as the nation's symbolic mother, who sacrificed for white and black children alike. Others downplayed the notion that she embodied multiracial Brazil, insisting that she represented modern Afro-Brazilians generally or black women specifically as well as their myriad contributions to the country's formation. Many blacks also used the Mãe Preta as a way to shame the nation for its practices of racial prejudice, such as the policy to replace Afro-Brazilians with European immigrant labor.[36]

São Paulo's Centro Cívico Palmares, named after the famed seventeenth-century *quilombo* (Maroon society), also demonstrated black organizing during the interwar period.[37] Founded in 1926, the Centro adopted a holistic approach to serve Afro-Brazilians, opening a library, an educational theater program, and a medical clinic. The Centro's leadership developed a relationship with politicians to better fight for the issues important to racially conscious Afro-Brazilians. It also led protests against the Civil Guard for its refusal to hire blacks.[38] These forms of activism sent a strong message to politicians that they should not turn a blind eye to racial injustice if they hoped to attract black support.

US blacks fought to install a more racially inclusive and equitable post–World War I order domestically and globally. A group of US blacks decided that if the peace negotiations in Versailles excluded the racial question, they would be an illegitimate affront to the aims of the conflict that supposedly made the world "safe for democracy," President Woodrow Wilson's wartime mantra. They joined forces to send a representative to France, who worked with the Japanese to put forth a doomed proposal to add a racial equality amendment to the League of Nations covenant, which the United States did not support.[39] Although the unsuccessful amendment was a sign of intense resistance to their cause at home and abroad, US blacks remained resolved to make action-oriented racial democracy a reality. These events foreshadowed greater racial political campaigns in the decade to come, as did the ways that blacks were reinventing themselves.

US blacks used their actions and words of resistance to disabuse society of the misconception that acts of intimidation would easily subdue their demands for respect, freedom, and equality. In 1925 Alain Locke coined the term *New Negro* to label his generation of blacks, a generation that was vehement in its racial pride and confidence. The New Negro jettisoned the docile and subservient depiction of blacks that had been prominent during slavery. New Negro women and men could be found in any region of the country, but many associated the movement with the urban North. The large black presence in northern cities during the 1920s was the direct consequence of the war, as massive numbers of blacks migrated to take advantage of wartime employment opportunities and to flee the suffocating racial oppression of the South. The black cultural renaissances that exploded in the 1920s, most famously in the New York district of Harlem, represented the New Negro in visual art, literature, and music.[40] The bold and less accommodating New Negro had major repercussions for US racial political nationalism, in part because most black migrants could vote for the first time after leaving the South, a region where black disenfranchisement was customary.

Many of these black migrants joined Jamaican-born Marcus Garvey's widely popular Universal Negro Improvement Association (UNIA). Historian C. Boyd James has contended that Garveyism resonated with "alienated blacks" in US cities because "more than elsewhere [these cities] expressed most severely the post–World War I brutality and suffering of the black peoples—the race riots . . ., the lack of employment, the sociopolitical atrophy, the disappointment . . ., and the discriminatory experience towards black veterans." Millions were drawn to the UNIA's unabashed black pride, its "Back to Africa" and "Africa for the Africans at home and abroad" mantras, and its black economic independence platform.[41] Because the UNIA failed to see the mass relocation of blacks to Africa, the multitude of black nationalists it helped to create remained in the United States as advocates of radical racial politics in various forms.

The 1920s was also a time when US and Brazilian blacks looked to one another for inspiration, camaraderie, and solutions to their racial exclusion, even if from afar. Black journals in both societies—such as São Paulo's O Clarim d'Alvorada and Progresso, the Chicago Defender, the Baltimore Afro-American, and the UNIA's Negro World—exchanged, translated, published, and/or editorialized on each other's content. These activities made up part of a broader effort among blacks in Brazil and the United States to contextualize their domestic racial status quo, educate the black population, and in many cases, maintain a connection with the Diaspora. Afro-Brazilian activists wrote about the events that occurred in Brazil's neighbor to the north, including the race riots, lynchings, and the UNIA. The US black press reported favorably on the Mãe Preta campaign and other aspects of black life in Brazil. However, blacks in both nations often mistranslated and misunderstood elements of the racial politics in the other nation, and they also could be uninterested in such transnational solidarities.[42] Although blacks in Salvador da Bahia were proud of their African heritage, by the mid-1920s pan-Africanism actually countered the goals of some Afro-Brazilians in other regions who struggled against characterizations of blacks as foreigners in their own land. The attempt to represent themselves as Brazilian and not African made Paulista blacks more hostile to Garveyism, perceiving it as a movement with little relevance in Brazil.[43] Even though a rejection of certain Diasporic politics existed, transnational modes of interpreting racial realities and contemplating strategies for greater inclusion were a trademark of Brazilian and US black activism in the interwar period.

In both Brazil and the United States, many other events in the 1920s also marked an upsurge in the challenges to exclusionary racialized conventions or created space for alternative frameworks. For instance, in the early years of the decade, the anger and frustration of young Brazilian army officers *(tenentes)* against the country's oligarchic system led to violent revolts in the military barracks of Rio de Janeiro, São Paulo, and Rio Grande do Sul. The year of Rio de Janeiro's *tenente* revolt, which spilled out into the streets of Copacabana, coincided with the country's independence centennial and the birth of Brazilian modernism. São Paulo's Modern Art Week in 1922 was a series of shows and exhibits in music, visual art, poetry, and theater. As Oswald de Andrade later stated in his famous "Cannibalist Manifesto," Brazilian modernism ushered in a uniquely Brazilian cultural scene that selectively absorbed elements from abroad to create a new Brazil.[44] Many modernists were progressive and open to shedding the narrow, homogenous, old elite images of the nation.

Modernism and *tenentismo* were distinct yet very clear indications of a sea change in Brazilian racial political nationalism. The former rejected limited European-derived racial and artistic expressions, legitimizing multiracial representations of the nation. The latter, a sign of discontent with the closed political process, signaled the fact that the demand for the political inclusion of traditionally excluded constituencies was reaching a critical point.

Social, cultural, and racial trends in the early twentieth century set the stage for the Brazilian elite to acknowledge increasingly, if unevenly, the African heritage of Brazilian culture in the 1920s as well.[45] One of these trends was the burgeoning craze among Rio de Janeiro's writers and journalists to report on the capital city's "underworld," where Afro-Brazilians were developing the music and dance style of samba, among other activities. The journalists and editors introduced their readers to a culture that simultaneously frightened and fascinated them.[46]

Many foreign enthusiasts of Brazil's black and *mestiço* culture also affected this shift, bestowing validity on what was once an embarrassment in the eyes of the Brazilian upper class. Some of these foreigners hailed from France, where a "primitive" vogue and an infatuation with the musical forms of the African Diaspora flourished. Blacks in various countries also were attuned to Diasporic culture in the 1920s. For instance, Afro-Brazilians played and danced to US styles such as jazz and the Charleston, and in the United States, the Brazilian maxixe was briefly popular in the 1910s.[47] The high acclaim of US black entertainers living in France, such as Josephine Baker, and visiting black musicians, such as Brazil's Oito Batutas, fueled this more favorable reception of black culture. Although the Brazilian elite were far from unanimously delighted in having black musicians represent their nation in Europe, for many others it was a proud and welcomed stamp of approval.[48]

In the United States, Prohibition and the New Negro cultural and artistic renaissances encouraged whites to venture into black neighborhoods for exciting nightlife where moonshine flowed freely. In the 1920s, many went to hear the latest music, jazz, at segregated clubs like the Cotton Club in Harlem, where intrigued whites could enjoy the black performers without having to sit next to any blacks in the audience. Young, middle-class whites were often at the forefront of these pursuits as they turned to black cultural expressions in order to rebel against "the repressive moral codes" of their parents and grandparents. According to William Barlow, "jazz, blues, dances like the Charleston and the black bottom, black slang, and jokes all became fashionable with this subgroup of 'white Negroes' and symbolic of their generational revolt against the established order." Carl Van Vechten tapped into this movement with his controversial 1926 novel *Nigger Heaven*, set in Harlem.[49] The appropriation of black culture in the United States during the 1920s helped open the door for greater forms of inclusive cultural nationalism in the following decade.

In academic and intellectual circles, the United States saw the simultaneous decline of scientific racism and the rising influence of "cultural pluralism" during the 1920s. Advocates of cultural pluralism wanted to problematize the "race-based nativism and homogenizing assimilation" that had reached new heights during World War I. Horace Kallen first used the term to argue that European ethnics should not be forced to sacrifice their cultural heritage in order to be Americanized. Kallen's use of cultural language and his appreciation for cultural difference paralleled currents in the social sciences. Columbia University professor Franz

Boas, the "father of American anthropology," produced a generation of scholars who revolutionized analyses of race and culture. By focusing on culture and the impact of historical factors on human difference, Boas and famous protégés like Ruth Benedict, Margaret Mead, and Melville Herskovits challenged the traditional beliefs about innate racial superiority and inferiority. Cultural pluralism was not a hegemonic ideology in the 1920s, but it certainly helped plant the principles of tolerance and acceptance that would be able to thrive in the racial, social, and political milieu of the 1930s. As Kallen's book title *Culture and Democracy in the United States* suggests, some also argued that these values needed to be understood within the parameters of US democratic ideals.[50]

The demarginalization of black culture, or its move toward the mainstream, was a part of the shift to racially inclusive nationalism. US and Brazilian state cultural policy reflected and promoted demarginalization as a way to articulate racial democracy. For example, as the precursors to samba emerged in Rio de Janeiro during the late 1910s, Brazilian authorities associated it with vagrancy and other activities that were illegal or regarded as nefarious—especially *feitiçaria*, or "witchcraft."[51] However, by the mid-1930s the Vargas administration officially endorsed the music and dance as a national treasure through its sponsorship of Rio's samba-centric Carnival. At the same time, anthropologists and other intellectuals would follow in the footsteps of black artist and intellectual Manuel Querino by publishing rebuttals to Nina Rodrigues's pessimistic theses on the dangers of blackness. Arthur Ramos, Gilberto Freyre, Jorge Amado, and even US scholar Ruth Landes celebrated the constructive impact of northeastern black culture, defined as authentic national culture, which Getúlio Vargas would embrace to some degree.[52]

A similar change took place with US racial-cultural policy on the state level. In 1922 a US official criticized the idea of sending a jazz band to Brazil's Centennial Exposition; he insisted that it would be a "distinct injury and an act other than friendly ... to introduce this so-called music there and have it considered as typical of musical art in the United States."[53] It is remarkable that within three decades, cultural policy would make a complete reversal, as the State Department sent wildly popular jazz tours abroad, including to Brazil, to represent the best of authentic US musical culture and to project an image of a racially harmonious nation.[54] According to Barbara Savage, the US government's change in attitude toward black culture made a turn in the early 1940s, which was about a decade after the Vargas regime embraced samba. Savage points to the radio program *Freedom's People*—produced by the

US Office of Education and broadcast nationally—that "redefined American culture as being driven by and dependent on black cultural contributions."[55] As we will see in chapter 4, this official transformation was well underway in the 1930s. Thus, both governments began to accept black artistic expressions as national culture in this study's time frame, when racial democracy was on the rise.

The Brazilian and US states' ever-changing approaches toward immigrant populations greatly influenced evolving ideas of inclusion as well. In the United States, government-supported crackdowns on labor in 1919 and the 1921 and 1924 immigration laws drastically decreased the influx of Southern and Eastern Europeans, rendered them less a threat in the eyes of authorities, and enabled them to "Americanize" more readily in the 1930s.[56] For the most part, by the late 1930s the government no longer vilified these immigrants and instead proactively sought to educate the US public that all Americans had been immigrants and all immigrants were Americans.[57] This campaign, buttressed by notions of cultural pluralism, helped establish fertile ground for broader ideas of national inclusion based on ethnicity and race. Although racialized groups like Asians and Latinos would not be ideologically naturalized in the same way Europeans were, pluralist discourse increasingly began to include nonwhites after trends accepting white ethnics were firmly in place.[58] Thus, the state's campaign to unite the country and integrate immigrants inadvertently helped bring about its eventual rhetorical inclusion of non-Europeans into the national community.

The start of Franklin Roosevelt's presidency in 1933 marked the beginning of a new era in US race-based nationalism. Liberals influenced by pluralist values successfully pushed through a reform agenda that reflected a civic nationalism, ending the dominance, if not the presence, of US racist nationalism. Civic nationalism was based on the action-oriented idea of "political and social equality for all, irrespective of race, ethnicity, or nationality, and a regulated economy that would place economic opportunity and security within the reach of everyone."[59] Black pressure and activism were critical to this shift, yet the frequent battles with authorities indicated that many New Deal civic nationalists were non-action-oriented, despite the inclusive principles they preached. Many of the New Deal programs enacted to alleviate unemployment during the Depression did result in drastic employment benefits for blacks, and officials like Mary McLeod Bethune and Harold Ickes worked tirelessly to maximize the New Deal's impact on black lives. Nonetheless, they were fighting against the practices of racial discrimination and exclusion that marked these programs, and New Deal agricultural policies even led to the displacement of over one hundred thousand black farmers in the rural South. Because Roosevelt was "constrained and dominated by his political dependence on the 'Solid South' and thus on the white supremacist ideology that controlled politics there," Mary Stuckey has written, he was unwilling and unable to champion the black antiracist agenda. Still, Gary Gerstle's "Rooseveltian nation" (mid-1930s to 1960) had dethroned the more hardline, racist language that reigned in the beginning of the twentieth century.[60] Outside of certain regions, blatant verbal racist nationalism became less prominent and the ideals of civic nationalism became more mainstream, all while racism itself both changed and stayed firmly intact in the entire country.

In Brazil the state's position on European immigrants also fostered a more hospitable, if different, climate for the doctrine of racial democracy. The 1920s saw the last huge wave of European immigrants to Brazil, and the 1921 Expulsion of Foreigners Law showed that the government was not pleased with all that the Europeans brought with them to Brazilian shores. They had been quite active in the massive recent labor movement, and the law, overexaggerating their role, targeted European anarchists for deportation. During the 1930s the economic crisis and high rates of unemployment—which the government in part blamed on the large number of immigrants—led the Vargas regime to valorize the "national" worker. As a result, policies meant to favor homegrown labor and capital were established. Although groups like Afro-Brazilians still confronted firmly entrenched racial discrimination, these new policies did improve their employment possibilities, and in cities like São Paulo, blacks and *pardos* (mulattoes) excelled in government jobs more than in other sectors.[61] It may have been inadvertent, but the official veneration of national workers gave Afro-Brazilians an unprecedented ideological position in nationalist thought in the 1930s.

A DEPARTURE FROM FREYRE-CENTRISM

In 1933 Brazilian intellectual Gilberto Freyre published *Casa-grande & senzala* (The Masters and the Slaves), a tour de force that has been credited with reconfiguring national identity and racial ideologies in Brazil. The book was the first and most impactful of a trilogy on the topic of Brazil's racial, social, and political formation. Although Brazilian beliefs that the country was a harmonious mixed-race society emerged long before Freyre, early nineteenth-century nationalists typically excluded blacks, exalting white and indigenous mixture only. The end of the slave trade in 1850 and especially the abolition of slavery in 1888 threw the spotlight on blacks, and both pro- and antislavery advocates focused on Afro-Brazilians in the multiracial narrative. Slavery apologists pointed to Brazil's so-called interracial paradise to portray the institution as just, whereas abolitionists often promised that, unlike the United States, Brazil's lack of racial prejudice would engender peaceful coexistence after emancipation. Eventually Afro-Brazilians assumed a more prominent place than the "premodern" indigenous in racial nationalism.[62]

Such pre-Freyrian racial discourse validates historian Petrônio Domingues's observation that Freyre "did not originate the myth of racial democracy, but he did consolidate it." Yet Freyre did signal a twentieth-century transformation. Even as his work was not a complete departure from whitening, Paulina Alberto argues that Freyre "helped crystallize the transition, begun . . . in the 1920s, from a paradigm of 'whitening' to one that celebrated cultural hybridity, racial mixture, and racial harmony as uniquely Brazilian traits."[63] Freyre does appear to have been the key ideological architect of the historical, sociological, and anthropological framework that granted social scientific legitimacy to racial democracy.

Freyre debunked eugenicist notions that miscegenation in Brazil led to a degenerated populace. The supposed problems facing Brazilians, such as "unstable health, [the] uncertain capacity for work, apathy, and disturbances of growth," were blamed on what Freyre referred to as the pre-Republic tradition of latifundiary monoculture.[64] The overemphasis on slavery produced lazy masters, and the one-cash-crop system did not allow most Brazilians, including elite families, to have an assortment of foods and a balanced diet, leading to a sickly population.[65] Freyre identified syphilis as another historical health problem that led to widespread illness in Brazil, especially before abolition, and argued that syphilis had "deforming" effects in Brazil that "drained the economic energy of the Brazilian mestizo."[66] Freyre also believed that mestizos were the most affected by both syphilis and malnutrition, resulting in the slow growth of Brazilian civilization compared to Western counterparts. By introducing environmental and historical forces that "stunted" the development of Brazilian mestizos, Freyre undermined the belief that they were inherently inferior.

Freyre's interpretation of Brazilian history helped free nationalists from the stigma that racially mixed societies were culturally, politically, socially, and economically deficient. Freyre argued that unlike the famed

Nordic peoples, the Portuguese were able to adapt to the tropical climate because they were open-minded enough to mix racially and culturally with black and indigenous peoples.[67] Thus, the Freyrian perspective lauded Brazil's mixed-race society as a unique tropical civilization, one whose European base, the Portuguese, demonstrated an unusually impressive lack of bias and a great deal of racial enlightenment. Freyre would later term this "lusotropicalism," a nod to this narrative's Portuguese-centrism. Freyre would more directly embrace whitening as well, asserting that the effects of European immigration in Brazil's sexually liberal country were, in fact, causing the nation's population to whiten. Freyre's prowhitening statement did not transmit the kind of shame about Brazil's mixed-race heritage that earlier writers exhibited.

Freyre's respect for the unique nature of Brazilian miscegenation, which Hermano Vianna called "mestizo nationalism," took root in the 1930s and helped pave the way for widespread national pride and unity. Novelist Jorge Amado described the impact: "It was an explosion, a new fact of life, something like we had never had before, and right away there was a feeling that we had grown and become more capable. Nobody who didn't live through those times can know how beautiful it was."[68] Freyre's work reified Brazil's reputation as a racially tolerant nation, especially compared to countries like the United States.[69]

Freyre's disavowal of scientific racial determinations reflected US trends in the social sciences during the 1920s and 1930s. Freyre studied with one of the leaders of cultural determinism, Franz Boas, and other preeminent scholars while a student at Columbia University in New York. Freyre wrote that the German anthropologist led him to appreciate "the just value of blacks and mulattoes" and taught him "to consider the difference between race and culture as fundamental."[70] Although Freyre later admitted that he had overstated Boas's impact on his scholarship in comparison to other influential professors with whom he had worked, *Casa-grande* indicated a change in Freyre's analytical approach to race in ways that were in line with Boasian theory.[71]

It is virtually taken for granted that Freyre's mestizo nationalism permeated all sectors of society, including the government. Many scholars have found this presumption to be problematic. Historians like Dain Borges have criticized the tendency to "assume . . . rather than prove" that Freyre was the source of these concepts when they appeared in the political sphere. (Gustavo Mesquita's recent research has made huge progress by uncovering how the "bureaucratic elite of the federal government" read and was profoundly influenced by Freyre's work, but many questions remain.) Micol Seigel suggests that Freyre is disproportionately credited with the nation's adoption of racial democracy. According to Barbara Weinstein, the literature "hardly addresses how and why racial democracy emerged as a compelling element of national identity . . . and it does not consider the historical circumstances [that] allowed [Freyre's] ideas to flourish." Weinstein is also unsatisfied with the presumptions related to the disparity between racial democracy's discourse of inclusion and societal practices of exclusion. Emília Viotti da Costa has pointed to our lack of understanding about the function or work the doctrine of racial democracy performs. Paulina Alberto warns against the inclination to "collapse under the single term *racial democracy*" what should be recognized as "contested multiple meanings." Antonio Guimarães asks and begins to answer why the political metaphor of "democracy" was chosen to describe harmonious race relations in the first place.[72]

This book sheds light on many of these understudied aspects of racial democracy. It joins the growing scholarship that problematizes Freyre-centrism, probes other historical and social factors that have produced and sustained racial democracy, and looks beyond the "myth" paradigm.[73] The myth paradigm—to which this research is greatly indebted—emerged in the 1950s and 1960s when revisionist scholars such as Florestan Fernandes and Roger Bastide examined the reality of racial discrimination in Brazil. These and subsequent studies echo what many black intellectuals and activists have long insisted: Brazil is far from the racial paradise it has claimed to be.[74]

This groundbreaking work was necessary for scholars to revisit the racial democracy myth with original approaches. In terms of this study, de-emphasizing Freyre allows us to see that contrary to conventional beliefs, the United States was also propagating nationalist rhetoric of racial democracy in a manner that was both similar to and distinct from what materialized in Brazil. It turns out that the nation Freyre identified as the foil for Brazil's racial democracy was not against racial democracy after all. In addition, this book correlates communism, anticommunism, fascism, World War II, and black activism with racial democracy in ways that offer new perspectives on the nationalist doctrine. For instance, the fact that anticommunist rhetoric in the 1930s included racial democracy is virtually overlooked in the historiography of Brazil and the United States as well.

This analysis also departs from typical studies of Freyrian thought by shifting the focus to the idea of democracy, as most studies fixate on the racial and downplay the democratic implications of this doctrine. It does not seem coincidental that *democracy* was attached to this narrative at a time when the world was obsessed with defining and/or protecting it. Indeed, both Freyre and Arthur Ramos chose democracy as the concept to describe Brazilian racial tolerance; Freyre had referred to it as "social democracy" before Ramos came up with the term "racial democracy" in 1941. Freyrian discourse distinguished between social democracy—which the Iberians, especially the Portuguese, mastered—and Western-style "political democracy." The former, of course, emerged from historical Portuguese practices and experiences coexisting peacefully with, borrowing generously from, and respecting other cultures. In contrast, Freyre stated that Western liberal democracies managed vacuous de jure and political equality on paper but produced toxic and divisive social and racial relations in actuality.[75] In other words, the Freyrian discourse constructed political democracy and social/racial democracy as polar opposites. Although the Estado Novo also hailed the unique benefits of Brazilian racial customs, I argue that the regime contradicted Freyre on this point and did not fully separate the two democracies. Instead, the Estado Novo utilized the racial dimensions of Brazilian social democracy to make claims to political democracy, particularly during World War II.

CHAPTER BREAKDOWN AND A NOTE ON SOURCES

Chapter 1 assesses how the Communist International (Comintern) and its US and Brazilian branches—the Communist Party of the United States of America (CPUSA) and the Partido Comunista do Brasil (PCB), respectively—deployed racialized rhetoric to depict the communist movement as democratic. Through the self-determination policy, attacks on black organizations, Brazilian support of the Scottsboro Boys, and the defense of PCB leader Luís Carlos Prestes in the United States, communists derided both governments as undemocratic oppressors of the proletariat while promoting communist regimes as the only path for workers of all races to experience real democracy. Chapter 2 is an examination of the states' responses and counterattacks to communist and black anticommunist provocations, demonstrating the manner in which racial democracy became a staple of official anticommunist rhetoric in the 1930s. The analysis focuses on the committees that US congressmen Hamilton Fish Jr. and Martin Dies established, Estado Novo anticommunist literature, and the case of Isaltino Veiga dos Santos, an Afro-Brazilian activist jailed for communist activity. Chapter 3 assesses fascists in the 1930s—specifically Adolf Hitler, Brazilian integralists, and leading US fascist intellectual Lawrence Dennis—who made race-based challenges to Brazilian and US claims to democracy. Chapter 4 analyzes state cultural production and black cultural demarginalization in the 1930s.

The final three chapters examine World War II, demonstrating how the concerns during the 1930s, especially in regard to fascism, intensified exponentially as Brazil and the United States became crucial to each other's wartime and economic imperatives. Chapter 5 teases out the role that race played in US-Brazil relations, including the way that German and Japanese propaganda in Brazil highlighted racism in the United States to gain sympathy for the Axis powers. Chapter 6 provides a detailed look at how racial democracy was broadcast in the exchange of cultural propaganda between these countries, often relying on white cultural mediators like Carmen Miranda and Orson Welles to do so. Here Brazil and the United States were collaborative partners, each helping the other create its racial and democratic image through radio programming, musical shows, and published literature.

After the transnational analyses of chapters 5 and 6, chapter 7 examines how blacks in Brazil and the United States utilized the war in an attempt to implement action-oriented racial democracy in their own countries. The responses blacks garnered from these states—the Afonso Arinos Law outlawing racial discrimination in Brazil and the US Fair Employment Practices Committee (FEPC)—can and should, in some sense, be deemed successes. However, a closer look at these apparent concessions shows that despite the language of racial democracy, they were not structured to bring about racial equality. The book concludes with a brief assessment of action-oriented and non-action-oriented racial democracy in the Cold War.

Black activism is integral to most of the chapters in this study. Nonetheless, the focus on blacks and black culture should not be taken as a generic narrative, one that is evenly applicable to all nonwhite races, for that is not the case. Neither is it the case that international circumstances and US-Brazil relations tell the entire story of how and why racial democracy came about on the state level in the two nations. Despite the importance of this relationship and global forces in the move toward racial democracy, it is my hope that future research will illuminate parts of this historical process that this and other studies have sidelined.

Transnational, comparative, and international studies are imperfect. One major challenge in conducting this research is that the archives, records, institutional infrastructure, and/or secondary literature are not always even in quantity, scale, scope, or content. Similarly, the literature and/or the sources are often vaster for one country than they are for the other, or the documents are different in nature. However, studies such as this one offer unique perspectives on human history. In this case, examining Brazil and the United States in relation to one another disabuses traditional misconceptions and lays bare unrevealed historical phenomena. One of the most important of these is this book's invalidation of the belief that racial democracy was a nationalist narrative that completely distinguished Brazil from the United States.

The transnational links between Brazil and the United States do not always drive this study. In order to respect the history of each country, often it is necessary to discuss them separately or comparatively, so as not to overstate their contacts and mutual influences. Certainly everything that occurred in Brazil did not relate to the United States, and vice versa. Thus, this book treats the histories of the United States and Brazil as if they were a set of train tracks, and indeed, this analogy accurately portrays the relationship between the two countries from 1930 to 1945: at times the histories run parallel, at times they diverge, and at times they intersect dramatically.

CHAPTER 1

Communist Racial Democracy in the 1930s

Workers, farmers, Negro and white, the lynching bosses we
    must fight.
Close your fists and raise them high, Labor Defense is our
    battle cry.
The Scottsboro boys shall not die, the Scottsboro boys shall
    not die,
Workers led by I.L.D. will set them free. Set them free! Set
    them free!

—"The Scottsboro Boys Shall Not Die," US communist song of the
    people, ca. 1937

The wind of revolt sweeps America
Blacks, Indians, pariahs; . . .
Miners, woodcutters, and seamen
Indeed, all proletarian masses
Wake up, workers

—"Anthem of the Poor Brazilian,"
    Brazilian communist
    revolutionary song, ca. 1935

In the 1930s the Communist Party USA (CPUSA) and the Communist Party of Brazil (Partido Comunista do Brasil, or PCB) declared their struggles to be part of an interracial movement that was invested in the ideals of racial equality.[1] Communists in both countries also claimed to represent the only political and economic philosophy that promised true, popular, and authentic democracy. Communists interlocked their ideas about race and democracy, arguing that only a genuine democracy—

which, they contended, the Soviet system exclusively produced—could bring about racial egalitarianism. I refer to this doctrine as communist racial democracy, and its advocates not only praised the Soviet system but also spurned racist societies as inherently *un*democratic. In other words, communists labeled racial equity as an essential litmus test for genuine democracy, a test, they asserted, that the Brazilian Republic and the United States were failing unequivocally. At certain moments, communists pointed to this failure as proof of these regimes' unworthiness to govern, insisting that the proper response was revolution. In fact, in 1935 language of racial democracy was part of the rallying cry for attempted communist coups in three Brazilian cities. Brazilian and US authorities responded with an anticommunist nationalist ideology of their own that promoted racial inclusion.

These phenomena are signs that the Moscow-based Comintern (Communist International), with branches in the United States and Brazil, was perhaps the most influential international organization to directly equate ideals of democracy with racial justice in the 1930s. And, contrary to contemporaneous beliefs, democracy was a central component of the Comintern's political philosophy throughout the entire decade, even during the organization's radical Third Period (1928–1935, officially). It was during the Third Period that the Comintern advanced its self-determination policy, promising blacks (and the indigenous in Latin America) the right to form their own separate states. On the face of it, the controversial policy was quite radical, but it was actually less a workable plan for black and indigenous independence and more a message of racial democracy and solidarity with communities that bore the yoke of oppressive states.

Communist efforts to embarrass the United States internationally for its record of racial injustice forced a proactive response by state anticommunists, as we will see in the next chapter. The comparable cold war story is well known and debated: the international outcry over the violent repression of US black freedom fighters aided in the passage of cold war civil rights legislation. This chapter shows a similar tendency decades earlier, as the Soviet Union claimed to be free of racial discrimination while it humiliated its US adversary by exposing racial inequities in the North American power. For instance, in the 1950s and 1960s, the Soviets invoked images of police hosing down blacks and mobs attacking defenseless activists in the United States.[2] This Soviet strategy had precedent—in the 1930s local communists led protests in Brazil and other nations over the young black men in Scottsboro, Alabama, wrongly charged with rape.[3] The international scandal the communists helped to generate out of the Scottsboro case was but one example of their attempts to paint the United States as backward and undemocratic on the question of race.

The national mobilization in defense of the Scottsboro Nine in the United States, particularly among blacks, is also evidence that antiracist activism on the ground was robust, a phenomenon that made the communist strategy viable. Furthermore, Glenda Gilmore's observation that "African Americans always used geopolitics to fight domestic racism" meant that Moscow's internationalist strategy naturally resonated with the many US blacks who had long rejected domestic boundaries for the freedom struggle.[4] The presence of black radicals who were born outside the United States, especially in the Caribbean, but lived in the country had a huge impact, as their transnational lives manifested in their politics and overall worldview. Indeed, these black radicals hoped to use communism as a way to advance their own global liberation agenda.[5]

Although Brazilian communists certainly discussed race less systematically and frequently than their North American counterparts, they did express revolutionary racial sentiments and even promoted racial consciousness among blacks. During this decade, especially in the first few years, the PCB maintained perhaps the most radical racial position in the country. The advent of communist racial democracy also marked the first time that the PCB directly theorized the issue of race.[6] The PCB attacked Brazil's reputation as a racially tolerant nation and constructed historical narratives that praised blacks as national heroes and agents to a much greater degree than the official state accounts. While a few scholars have acknowledged that in the 1930s Brazilian communists were among the rare groups to spotlight racism in Brazil and to stray from its racial utopia myth, very little has been written on Brazilian communists' racial discourse.[7] In fact, as Pedro Chadarevian has pointed out, the literature has generally stated just the opposite: that the PCB refused to engage the racial question and blamed classism as the sole cause of the hardships that Afro-Brazilians confronted.[8]

Despite his familiarity with the communists' Scottsboro campaign, contemporaneous black activists like José Correia Leite also advanced the oversimplified idea that communists failed to distinguish between race-based discrimination and class oppression.[9] This perspective ignores important evidence, such as black anthropologist and communist Édison Carneiro's discussion of racial oppression at the First and Second Afro-Brazilian Congresses in 1934 and 1937, as well as the PCB policy and literature assessed below.[10] Still, there is something revealing in what Leite and others have said. We cannot assume that the change in policy during the 1930s accurately reflected the lion's share of opinions and attitudes within the PCB, especially since its leadership argued that antiblack racism was not a problem in Brazil until the early 1930s.

According to Aruã Silva de Lima, the slower adoption of the policy in Brazil compared to the United States may have been because Afro-Brazilian "organizations were relatively free of leftist influence, not having had the organic closeness [with] communist groups in the 1920s" that was common in the United States.[11] Presumably such contact would have made white leftists knowledgeable enough about racial discrimination to disabuse them of the racial paradise myth. Nonetheless, US black communists complained that the CPUSA ignored Comintern directives to prioritize the "Negro Question." In addition, few US black communists fully agreed with the most radical of the Comintern's Negro resolutions, particularly the self-determination policy.[12]

What becomes evident in this chapter is that the global antiracist Left, and even less progressive black activists, transformed the Comintern into a conduit that spread radical racial consciousness and politics internationally, particularly in the first half of the 1930s. In other words, the Comintern helped to establish a new international political milieu, in which racial awareness and attention to racial injustice were elevated worldwide. We see signs of this in Brazil and the United States. Communists in Brazil used the US Scottsboro case to pull blacks into their political orbit, and these discussions seem to have inspired a greater investment in racial politics among Afro-Brazilians. US communists portrayed Brazilian political prisoners, including the famous communist leader Luís Carlos Prestes, as antiracist Brazilian freedom fighters in a way that naturalized the place of race in the overall struggle for political and economic democracy. The development of these parallel rhetorical commitments to racial egalitarianism created and solidified a transnational camaraderie of sorts between these two nations and many others as well.[13]

Finally, this chapter shows that the debate over the relationship between racial inclusion and systems of economy/governance that ensued between communists and anticommunists in both countries was largely a debate about democracy, as the next chapter will also demonstrate. Communists and the states under Getúlio Vargas and Franklin Roosevelt battled over democratic ideals. Both sides claimed to defend and represent true democracy, and the racial qualities of democracy

played an important role in this conflict. Therefore, we should not cat-
egorize *communism* and *democracy* as mutually exclusive terms. In the
1930s the contest was not communism versus democracy per se, but
how to define democracy, and in the course of this dispute, even anticommunist US and Brazilian authorities absorbed communist racial
rhetoric.

In order to contextualize the communist viewpoint on race and
democracy, we must appreciate how and why communists vigorously
sought black support. To a great extent, communist racial democracy in
Brazil and the United States materialized in order to recruit Afro-
descendants. Just as communism pulled the state into formulations of
racial democracy, communist rhetoric was similarly yanked and tugged
by race-conscious organizations. In essence, the period was a discursive
mosh pit in which language and ideas about race and democracy were
flying from all directions, hitting one another head on. All parties, it
seemed, had something at risk.

COMMUNISM AND THE COMPETITION
FOR BLACK SUPPORT

As the 1920s progressed, the Comintern's focus on blacks and the
importance of their role in the communist struggle increased. By the
early 1930s, Comintern theses unequivocally stated that, in order to be
victorious, the revolution in Brazil and the United States depended on
the active participation of blacks. At the same time, communists looked
with alarm at the success of racially conscious black movements that
were opposed to socialism and steered their members away from the far
Left. These and other factors caused the Comintern to adopt new policies in the 1920s that, for the first time, specifically addressed the Negro
Question and were largely driven by the perceived necessity to attract
blacks to the communist cause. In these efforts, communists paid special
attention to Afro-descendants who were already active in black-
identified organizations.

The Comintern considered "reformist" black movements to be direct
competition, for their tactics and teachings countered the notion that
proletarian revolution was the only path to equality. If these organizations were deemed advantageous to the movement, communists tried to
obtain support from their leadership, especially those with a determined
likelihood of converting to communism. Otherwise, communists
attempted to either discourage entry into or recruit black workers from

the rival organizations that they concluded were hopelessly void of revolutionary potential. Alternatively, new recruits could also conduct a communist takeover of such organizations and grab the reins of the leadership.[14]

Many factors developing in the United States, Brazil, and the Soviet Union led the Comintern and both domestic parties to target blacks in this new way. The rapid urbanization of blacks in the United States and Brazil by 1930 was one critical change that rendered them important potential members of the communist movement. In Brazil the massive move of formerly enslaved blacks into the urban labor force shaped early twentieth-century processes of industrialization and the labor movements that accompanied them, including communism.[15] Similarly, US historian James Grossman defines the World War I Great Migration as the "second emancipation," during which Southern rural blacks sought to take advantage of new job opportunities in urban areas.[16] The urbanization of blacks mattered greatly, as Comintern policy reflected the Marxist-Leninist judgment that the industrial and urban proletariat was the vanguard of the revolution.[17] In places like São Paulo and Harlem, Afro-descendants' vibrant social and political movements, even their participation in mainstream politics, seemed to bear witness to the urban thesis and the fact that black city dwellers were ready to mobilize. Because the epicenter of communist activity was in the cities, black urban movements were also more visible to party leaders. Therefore, for the Comintern, the proletarianization of blacks in the United States and Brazil represented a transformation of Afro-descendants into important revolutionary players.

In neither national context did these early twentieth-century migrations epitomize the overall black experience at the time. Under the leadership of senior Japanese member Sen Katayama and others, the Executive Committee of the Communist International (ECCI) did recognize that most of the world's people of color remained in rural areas. Communists in Brazil and the United States also understood this. In 1928 the PCB reported to the Comintern that there were four times as many rural workers as industrial counterparts in Brazil (eight million and two million, respectively), and in 1931 the Executive Committee of the Comintern's International Red Aid reminded the Brazilian chapter that the majority of agrarian workers were black and indigenous.[18] In 1928 a Comintern resolution calculated that 86 percent of US blacks lived in the South, with 74 percent of that number residing in rural zones.[19] Katayama (who had witnessed and experienced racism while studying in the United States during the 1890s), Ho Chi Minh, and black CPUSA member Otto Huiswoud helped spark the fresh interest in people of color and rural labor in the Comintern that culminated in its Third Period.[20] However, the Third Period's newfound radical racial policies and attention to the rural sector did not mean that the Comintern jettisoned its partiality for the urban proletariat.

At times making explicit links to the significance of their urbanization, Third Period resolutions asserted that blacks held the key to communist success. Around 1930 the CPUSA's Negro Department argued that the historic migration of blacks into the urban market signaled the "rapid growth of the most important driving force of the [US] national revolution." In part citing ECCI resolutions, the Negro Department added that the new black proletariat had a "special duty to perform in the leadership of the Negro masses" (including the "peasantry") and reiterated their significance as leaders in the entire struggle. The freedom of white workers, it was argued, could not be achieved without them.[21] Although it did not mention black migration, the Comintern's South American Bureau articulated a similar warning in its thesis on Brazil that was issued about the same time. After noting that the "majority [of Brazil's] population is made up of mestizos and blacks," the bureau declared: "Without pulling the black and Indian masses into the struggle, no revolution of the masses is possible in Brazil." The South American Bureau chided the PCB for not doing more on this front.[22]

These racial theses largely reflected the ways in which US-based blacks influenced the Communist International. There were many reasons for the disproportionate attention and stature that US black residents received in Moscow during the 1920s and 1930s compared to others in the African Diaspora. One explanation was that some high-ranking Comintern leaders had interest and experience in US race relations, as was the case with Katayama and even Vladimir Lenin. Another was the perception that US blacks—including the numerous radicals of Caribbean origin, with their transnational politics—were "the most advanced by virtue of their location at the center of the American empire," in the words of the historian Minkah Makalani.[23] Certainly, the language of the Comintern's 1928 Resolution on the Negro Question reflects this sentiment: despite attempts that some black radicals made to broaden its scope, the adopted resolution focused on the United States. One paragraph did acknowledge that the "Negro race everywhere is . . . oppressed by foreign or native imperialism"; however, the passage also specified that "the Negro worker of the USA [should be] the vanguard of the Negro struggle all over the world." A 1930 resolution abandoned the vanguard clause, which had been the Comintern's stance since at least 1922, but not the overall thesis on black liberation that was crafted with the United States in mind.[24] Therefore, the efforts to ignite a black proletarian revolution in the United States dominated how the Comintern handled the Negro Question internationally.

The CPUSA's predecessor, the Workers Party of America (WP), began concerted efforts to recruit radical blacks in 1921—a year before the Comintern first addressed the Negro Question—and this had huge impacts on both the WP and the Communist International. That year, the WP targeted the African Blood Brotherhood for African Liberation and Redemption (ABB), a relatively small, self-defined nationalist, secret, paramilitary group that was founded in Harlem in 1919 and considered itself part and parcel of a broad interracial movement to end racial oppression for people of color everywhere through armed defense and an international coalition of organizations.[25] Brotherhood members felt the Comintern was well positioned to help execute their agenda, largely because its policies on the national question and on racial and colonial oppression resonated with the ABB's platform. This drove the Brotherhood's willingness to collaborate with the WP, despite the ABB's major skepticism about the WP's dedication to the Comintern's racial resolutions. Thus, many ABB members did recruit for and officially joined the WP over the next few years. By the end of 1923, the Brotherhood was running the WP's Harlem branch, and when the ABB dissolved two years later, many of its members, especially the leadership, continued their work in the WP. Brotherhood members became central to the ways in which racial policies developed in Moscow and thus globally.[26] They would bring their radical racial politics into the communist movement at a time when communists were still reducing racial inequality to a matter of class.

The Comintern drafted its first "Theses on the Negro Question" in 1922, with the critical involvement of ABB leader Huiswoud and member Claude McKay, who had traveled to Moscow to become the first black radicals ever to participate in a Communist International Congress. The Brotherhood's reputation preceded their arrival; communists typically upheld the ABB as reassuring proof that the socialist cause could compete with racial movements for black support. However, McKay and Huiswoud disabused Fourth Congress delegates and observers of the idea that the ABB separated the two, and they argued that Comintern policy should follow suit.[27]

Although granted only a second-class delegate status of sorts, McKay was among the most vociferous spokespersons for the revolutionary promise of racial consciousness at the Comintern's Fourth Congress. The Jamaica-born writer argued vehemently that black organizations could be invaluable partners in the communist movement, serving as key components in an interracial, intercontinental coalition against racism and imperialism. Much to the chagrin of the US delegation, McKay also publicly decried the lack of commitment and indifference to racial equality at best and bigoted attitudes at worst that flourished among WP members. As "possibly the first black person in Russia since the revolution," according to Makalani, McKay was treated like a celebrity and asked to give a lecture on these subjects to the Fourth Congress by none other than the then head of the Communist International, Grigory Zinoviev.[28]

Huiswoud, an official US delegate, was elected the chair of the Comintern's Negro Commission. He was much more discreet in his criticisms than McKay, but he also used his position to ensure that the Brotherhood's broader racial politics found their way into Comintern resolutions. That black antiracist organizations thrived was both natural and advantageous to the communist movement, he argued: these organizations oriented blacks against imperialism and/or created significant international alliances. The Comintern was swayed, and for the first time, it resolved that black-identified organizations could be revolutionary players in the anticapitalist struggle and that communists should support such groups deemed worthy partners. Copying the language of the Brotherhood's own program, the Comintern's resolution also declared racial equality a goal and articulated the need for organized black labor in the face of white unions' exclusionary practices.[29]

As the delegates debated the value of black organizing, they attempted to determine the implications of one very popular black movement in particular: the Universal Negro Improvement Association, or UNIA. Marcus Garvey—the black Jamaican leader who successfully promoted the mantra of black emigration to Africa, black enterprise, and black pride—had brought the UNIA to the United States in 1916 and moved its headquarters to Harlem two years later. Garveyism attracted attention from communists and black activists of all backgrounds when the UNIA quickly overshadowed every other black group in the United States with its unprecedented number of followers, who reached the millions and typically hailed from the black working class.[30] Garvey's "Back to Africa" mantra claimed that blacks would achieve true freedom only if they returned to a free African continent that was liberated from European colonialism. Garvey believed that blacks in the West should lead their African brethren, placing himself at the helm, and argued that the success of this venture depended on the economic independence and cooperation of African Diasporic communities. Combining the economic and return-to-Africa agendas, he founded the Black Star Line in 1919, a shipping line with a mission to promote international black trade and migration to Africa. Many ABB members had supported or even joined the UNIA at one point, respecting Garveyism's proactive spirit of black pride and political awareness.[31] By the early 1920s, however, the admiration for Garvey had turned into sharp disapproval when he made a conservative turn and began to denounce black militancy. ABB members still continued to evoke his movement to convince the Comintern and the WP that black organizing and the antiracist struggle carried impressive revolutionary power.[32] After years of being targeted by the US government, Garvey was accused of mail fraud, imprisoned from 1925 to 1927, and deported in 1927.

Communist theses reflected the Brotherhood members' love-hate relationship with Garveyism, which exposed the fact that they were encouraged yet concerned by its success among the black working class. Three years after the Comintern's Fourth Congress, the 1925 Workers Party of America Convention simultaneously derided the UNIA's brand of black separatism and expressed the belief that the group was redeemable. Like Huiswoud in 1922, the WP felt that the UNIA had the potential to transform into "an organization fighting for the class interests of the Negro workers" alongside the interracial communist movement.[33] Brotherhood members in particular had hopes of redirecting the Garvey movement toward a racially informed, anticapitalist class consciousness, and ABB founder Cyril Briggs even reached out personally to Garvey. Garvey balked at the gesture, and attempts to push the UNIA to the left failed.

As both the UNIA and the ABB declined in the mid-1920s, the Comintern approved the US black communist Lovett Fort-Whiteman's campaign to form the American Negro Labor Congress (ANLC), an all-black nationwide revolutionary labor organization of various industries and trade unions that functioned in local branches.[34] Communists had many goals for the ANLC, including the absorption of members of both the UNIA and the ABB. Indeed, after the ABB disbanded in 1925, many of its members helped lead the ANLC, and some former Garveyites did join the communist movement, although apparently not in large numbers.[35] The ABB and Garveyism also continued to impact the Comintern after their falls, as its 1928 racial theses mirrored and retooled the variants of black nationalism (or internationalism) that these groups expressed.

In 1928 the Comintern's debate on the Negro Question centered on how to characterize African Americans and what steps should be taken to bring about their equality. Were US blacks an oppressed racialized nation with the right to self-determination, or were they an oppressed racialized minority? Although the former ABB member Harry Haywood was the only US black delegate to support the first position, he helped draft the resolution that the Comintern ultimately adopted, marking the move to the Third Period, which affected official communist racial policy in the United States, Brazil, and elsewhere. The oppressed-nation theory branded the historical legacies of slavery and racial discrimination, hatred, and notions of hierarchy as too entrenched and divisive for a racially integrated "'pure' proletarian revolution" to produce black liberation. In order to achieve that liberation, blacks had the right to self-determination, or control of their own society, government, and land distribution. Because it was drafted to address the problem in the United States, the resolution stated that US blacks would exercise their right to self-determination in the so-called Black Belt of the South, where African Americans remained the majority and could create a "Negro Soviet Republic."[36]

The resolution included one often ignored clause that briefly validated "the Negro woman in industry," stating that women's lot as the "most exploited" population of the working class rendered them "a powerful potential force in the struggle for Negro emancipation." Having actively participated in the racial and political debates and movements of their generation, some black women radicals, like Audley Moore, were drawn to the Black Belt thesis because it resonated with Garveyism: others, like Pauli Murray, could not approve of a policy that seemed to resemble Jim Crow. Many "black left feminists," to use Erik McDuffie's term, took advantage of the pithy reference to black women to demand CPUSA support for their definition of self-determination—grassroots work that secured tangible results and dignity for black women and their families. However, the Comintern's theses on the Negro Question remained masculinist in nature.[37]

Even with Garvey in exile after 1927 and the UNIA a skeleton of its former self, Garveyism's impact on Third Period communism appeared as strong as it had been in the early 1920s. Of course, the Comintern found fault with Garveyism when it settled on the self-determination policy, asserting that the "Back to Africa" slogan "impede[d] the movement of [the black] masses towards a revolutionary position."[38] However, around 1930 the CPUSA's Negro Department, housed in the party's Central Committee, credited Garveyism's "tremendous success" to its utilization of "the national sentiments prevalent among large sections of the Negro toilers" and argued that the UNIA "glaringly emphasized" the "national character of the Negro liberation movement." The problem with Garveyism, it claimed, was that the "Negro bourgeoisie" attempted to manipulate and contaminate the black working class's innate nationalism for its own "class aims."[39] The message was that communists would be wise to tap into the power of black nationalism and rescue it from the grip of the corrupt black bourgeoisie, which, apparently, could only be achieved under communist leadership. The party hoped that its self-determination policy would induce and facilitate this outcome.

ABB members had a complicated history with the self-determination policy. On the one hand, several years before the Comintern followed suit, Briggs had campaigned for a black nation—a "colored autonomous state"—and argued that it should be located in the United States or one of several other parts of the world, including South America. On the other hand, it seems that the ABB never officially adopted Briggs's idea, nor did the majority of the Brotherhood support the thesis, drafted by former member Haywood and Charles Nasanov, that became the Comintern's self-determination policy.[40] But regardless of the black radicals' judgment, self-determination remained the Comintern's policy during the Third Period.[41] And specifics aside, the Comintern's stated commitment to Afro-descendants and to an explicitly race-based policy granted black leftists a privileged position in the party, at least nominally.

Armed with the Comintern's new endorsement of a racial worldview, black communists led the CPUSA in the mission to recruit African Americans and steer them away from other black organizations. US communists appear to have felt more threatened than their Brazilian counterparts by a larger array of black organizations, since their records indicate an obsession with many more black groups. Black churches, in the United States and elsewhere, were among the organizations that drew communist contempt. The 1928 Resolution on the Negro Question advised that in "the work among the [US] Negroes, special attention should be paid to the role played by the churches and preachers who are acting on behalf of American imperialism."[42] In 1930 the Comintern's International Trade Union Committee of Negro Workers contended that the church's promise of "compensation in heaven" for black workers' miseries "befogg[ed]" their minds and rendered them "helpless prey to capitalism and imperialism."[43] Many CPUSA members issued similar warnings. James S. Allen, the son of Russian immigrants and a prominent party journalist and author, was particularly drawn to the "Negro Question" and sought to generate mistrust of black churches. In his 1932 pamphlet "The American Negro," Allen gave multiple examples of black preachers, "race leaders," who, he argued, "to advance their own position as middle class and at the same time gather in what dollars they can, . . . lick the boots of the white ruling class and stoop to the lowest forms of treachery and betrayal," advising African Americans against labor organizing and strikes.[44]

Black feminists in the CPUSA also strove to topple the conservative black bourgeois politics of respectability that dominated African American church culture in the United States. Black women radicals—such as African Blood Brotherhood founding member Grace Campbell—employed many methods to do this, including "stepladder" orating on the streets of black communities, espousing a black feminist atheism, and helping to found and sustain churches that advanced socialist politics, like the Harlem Unitarian Church. The leading black leftist Louise Thompson Patterson also worked with traditional black churches to organize rallies for common causes like that of the Scottsboro Nine (discussed later in this chapter). Still, the Comintern had resolved that Marxism and atheism went hand in hand, and, as the Harlem Unitarian Church communist Richard Moore discovered, the party did force members to renounce church affiliations. Even Huiswoud, Moore's friend and a frequent attendee of the Harlem Unitarian Church, cautioned that "the church [is] an instrument of imperialism" and wanted the focus of communist activism to remain the workplace.[45]

Communists perceived the National Association for the Advancement of Colored People (NAACP), the Pan African Congress, the National Association of Colored Women, the National Urban League, the UNIA, and other such groups as they did US black churches and the Brazilian Black Front (Frente Negra Brasileira, or FNB): counterrevolutionary, petty bourgeois organizations that led the entire race astray. Black leftists were reminded of their responsibility to spread the communist message: "Negro communists must *clearly dissociate* themselves from all bourgeois currents in the Negro movement, [and] must indefatigably oppose the spread of the influence of the bourgeois groups on the working Negroes."[46] Harry Haywood—who became the head of the CPUSA's Negro Department in 1931—spoke and wrote in extremely scathing terms about these organizations. His favorite target seemed to be the NAACP, which he rightfully considered the most influential of the "Negro reformist" groups in the early 1930s. "Negro reformists," he wrote in a 1934 report to the CPUSA, believed that the "Negro question can be solved within the confines of the present capitalist imperialist social order without revolutionary struggle." Haywood provided the example of the Costigan-Wagner antilynching bill, which the NAACP fought to enact. He felt it misguided to deduce that such a law would, or was even intended to, stop all forms of lynching, particularly those "frame-ups" that were sanctioned by an unjust and racially biased legal system. Worse yet, he found the bill outright dangerous, insisting that its true purpose was to pacify and "disarm" the working class and to under-mine the communist revolution, the only real solution to the problem. His unforgiving conclusion: "Under the guise of a fight against lynching, the NAACP leaders, in effect, give practical support to the lynchers."[47]

In addition to ridiculing their lack of class consciousness and an uncritical attitude toward capitalism, the CPUSA challenged the so-called reformists by forming bodies that competed with their work and fought with them to secure the best talent and the allegiance of African Americans.[48] For instance, the CPUSA organized the International Labor Defense (ILD) in 1925 to provide legal representation and advo-cacy for workers. As the ILD became involved in high-profile black rights trials, especially the Scottsboro case in the 1930s, it deprived the NAACP of the chance to increase its legal prominence and secured more attention for the Communist Party as an organization dedicated to racial justice among potential black recruits. And recruit it did. For instance, McDuffie argues that the Scottsboro case was among the three major factors that brought a second generation of black women into the CPUSA.[49] Due to its lack of success, the party replaced the ANLC with the interracial League of Struggle for Negro Rights (LSNR) in 1930, which also organized support for the Scottsboro Boys. Haywood was eventually appointed its general secretary and the writer Langston Hughes its honorary president. The LSNR drafted a comprehensive and audacious program that aimed to put an end to racist practices, includ-ing lynching, residential and military Jim Crowism, racial barriers in labor unions, sharecropping, racial stereotyping in media, and anti–interracial marriage laws, to name a few.

The LSNR hoped to pull black women and men concerned with a vast array of issues into the Communist Party and to radicalize activists who may have found organizations like the NAACP or the National

Association of Colored Women appealing. In its program, the LSNR called for blacks to "disown the dallying, hesitant, groveling methods of those who have been in the past and are today hailed by the powers-that-be as the leaders of the race." Specifically, it determined the NAACP, the Tuskegee Institute, and leaders such as Walter White and W. E. B. DuBois to be in the "line of betrayers of the best interests of the Negro people [that chained Negroes] to the chariot of American imperialism."[50] In a report to the CPUSA (which the party published and sold as a pamphlet), Haywood laid out the exact steps that the LSNR needed to take to defeat the so-called betrayers: "The Party and the LSNR should undertake to build up opposition within all important reformist and petty bourgeois nationalist mass organizations, the setting up of LSNR fractions [sic] within them, in this way, establishing positions inside from which to carry out the struggle against and exposure of the misleaders and rally the masses under our leadership."[51]

Haywood was eventually disappointed that the LSNR—like the ANLC and unlike the rival NAACP—ended up largely ineffectual, unable to evolve into a movement with functioning and well-funded local branches. Harlem organized an active, successful chapter in which black women were prominent and flourished,[52] but otherwise the LSNR and the ANLC seemed to demonstrate the CPUSA's inability and unwillingness to contribute the human and financial resources necessary to inspire a large black following. In Haywood's assessment, it operated as if the LSNR was the "Negro Party" and thus carried the burden of addressing black-related issues for the entire party, providing the CPUSA with an "excuse for failing to tackle head-on the Afro-American question and white chauvinism," even within the party itself.[53] But if the CPUSA's actions exposed a weak determination to fight for racial equality, the party's official racial rhetoric and policy, emanating from the Comintern, did not.

As stated earlier, black leftists residing in the United States had a massive impact on the ways that the Comintern revamped its racial theses. Official Comintern branches, including the Communist Party of Brazil (PCB), were obliged to adopt these new policies. Yet it would be completely erroneous to assume that internal factors did not lead the PCB to realize that black recruitment and a strong antiracist posture would be important for the future of the domestic party. In fact, developments within Brazil's borders dovetailed with external pressures to produce a PCB that was more racially conscious and compelled to take black participation in the party seriously, at least in theory. That the

PCB espoused such militant racial policies in the 1930s was almost completely overlooked until very recently, as contemporaneous and historical writers alike have claimed that the party denied the existence of racial discrimination. This image may be due to the PCB's lack of commitment to the Comintern's new guidelines, exposing a disconnect between Comintern directives and practice on the ground, similar to what occurred in the United States.

Although communist self-determination policy originated in response to the situation in the United States, the Comintern clearly intended for it to operate in other nations too, including Brazil. The Sixth Congress, in 1928, did not specifically address self-determination in Latin America, but this did not signify its inapplicability to blacks worldwide.[54] As a report of the Sixth Congress's Special Negro Commission explained, the "Negro question in the United States must be considered in relation to the Negro question and struggles in other parts of the world."[55] This language underscored the Comintern's internationalist strategy, which in part reflected the Pan-African perspective of many black communists and the global approach of Asian radicals.[56] We know that the black leftist Cyril Briggs had considered South America as a potential location of an autonomous black state, and the Comintern's 1922 resolution on the Negro Question had linked the struggles of South American blacks to their brethren not only in the United States but also in places like China and India.[57] The year 1928, however, was the first time the Comintern systematically addressed the racial issue and Afro-descendants in Latin America.

If the Sixth Congress marked a new phase in Comintern racial theory, it also signaled Moscow's newfound interest in Latin America, two simultaneous occurrences that resulted in discussions about implementing the self-determination policy in the region. The Sixth Congress was the first time the Comintern delegated a chapter dedicated to Latin American strategies, and in the following year, the Comintern convened the first Latin American Communist Congress.[58] The Swiss Jules Humbert-Droz—the first head of the Comintern's Latin American Secretariat, who also served on the Sixth Congress's Negro Commission, which approved the self-determination policy—played an essential role in connecting the policy to Latin America. The Comintern appointed Humbert-Droz as ECCI representative and head of its Commission to Draft Latin American Theses, and in 1929, just months after the Sixth Congress ended, he attended the first Latin American Communist Congress in Buenos Aires.[59] Historian Manuel Caballero called this "the most important meeting of the Latin American sections of the Comintern" and said it gave the racial issue "disproportionate importance." He concluded that the Sixth Congress's prioritization of the black question had seeped into the consciousness of the congregants in Buenos Aires, who, after much deliberation, followed Humbert-Droz's suggestion and proposed national self-determination as the solution to the racial problem in Latin America.[60]

Although the PCB's original statutes mandated adherence to Comintern directives, the Brazilians did not immediately adopt the self-determination policy, and it took a couple of years before evidence of it appeared on Brazilian soil. In fact, in 1929 PCB leaders in Brazil and Buenos Aires denied that racial injustice warranted special attention in their country at all. When Humbert-Droz traveled throughout South America to survey social realities a month before the conference, he noted Brazilian communists' perspective on race in their country. The Swiss leader wrote from Pernambuco, "According to information from our comrades, racial prejudices do not exist in Brazil."[61] At the conference itself, the four registered Brazilian delegates offered a racial analysis that was attentive and sympathetic to the plight of the indigenous but much less so to that of their black counterparts: "The status of blacks in Brazil is not of such a nature as to require that our Party organize campaigns that make demands for blacks with special watchwords."[62]

The heated debate about racial discrimination in Brazil often hinged on comparisons made to the United States. Using the alias Ledo, PCB leader Astrojildo Pereira stood his ground in Buenos Aires, complaining that the Negro question in Brazil was being misdiagnosed. In the United States, blacks and whites fought in labor unions and even in the CPUSA, Pereira said, leading some "to believe that in Brazil the same thing is produced, to believe that in the Brazilian worker's movement there is also a fight between black and white workers. All this is false." As proof, Pereira claimed that there were black leaders in the PCB and that there was no social difference or tension between black and white urban or rural workers. Humbert-Droz and other Comintern militants like Abraham Heifet, a.k.a. Guralsky—who would soon take over as leader of the secretariat— and Venezuelan leader Ricardo Martinez agreed that the Brazilian racial situation was not identical to that of the United States and other countries in the Americas. However, they noted that fact was immaterial to whether or not racism plagued the South American nation.[63]

Ample evidence that racial discrimination did mark Brazilian society generated tremendous frustration with the Brazilian leadership's stubbornness on the issue, particularly when, as Guralsky said, in Latin America "we cannot have and lead a revolution without giving a clear and obvious response" to the racial question.[64] Despite what comrades said in Brazil and Buenos Aires, Humbert-Droz could not help but note Brazilian racial disparities during his visit to the country. On docking in Pernambuco in May 1929, he wrote: "[T]he men who do the heavy work are all men of color, while the commissaries, the supervisors, those who handle penalties, and the civil servants, the well-dressed women, etc., are all white. Perhaps there are some whites among the former group and some [people of color] among the latter, but this doesn't change the proportions, and if there are exceptions, they are tiny and do not change the general rule."[65]

These observations clearly colored his argument that the self-determination policy was appropriate for Latin America. Other participants in the Buenos Aires meeting similarly disagreed with the Brazilian leaders. A Cuban delegate argued that, "in Brazil, contrary to the information from the comrades from that country . . . the problem [of prejudice] exists" for blacks.[66] Among other things, Comintern leaders cited reports of a white worker strike against black workers at the Fordlândia rubber plantation in Pará, disproportionate levels of black illiteracy, the legacy of slavery, and racial exclusion in higher military ranks.[67]

Since 1923 Comintern had requested information about the racial status quo in Brazil, inviting PCB members to participate in debates on the topic, to little avail.[68] In October 1931, Octávio Brandão, who had been a PCB leader in the 1920s, wrote to the party's Political Bureau in Brazil from his new home in Moscow, mentioning the "great interest in current [Brazilian] blacks and Indians" there but adding that despite his attempts to study these populations, "materials [about them] are rare." Unsatisfied with the lack of existing literature, Brandão, a self-labeled *caboclo* (a person of mixed indigenous and European heritage), attempted to conduct his own study of Afro-Brazilians by sending a list of research questions to his PCB comrades two days later. The list began with the statement, "We ask that you inform *us*," affirming that other parties sought the data as well, and continued with a set of twenty questions. The questions sought, in part, to determine how many blacks were in Brazil; the overall percentage of blacks in the population; information about blacks in all areas of work; details about black women and child labor; the relationship between black and white workers; the historical role of blacks in Brazil; and black participation in the PCB. (At the First Afro-Brazilian Congress three years later, black communist

Édison Carneiro would state that it was "well-known" that the PCB ranks included "a huge contingent" of blacks.) The questionnaire ended with one brief instruction, which also helped clarify the purpose of the survey: "We need to dedicate the greatest attention to black workers."[69]

Within several months, the PCB partially yielded to such appeals and criticisms as it competed with the Frente Negra Brasileira and even the fascist integralist movement for Afro-Brazilian support, advertising self-determination as a way to guarantee black economic, political, and cultural sovereignty. In doing so, the party officially relinquished the portrayal of Brazil as a convivial, racist-free society. Clearly the PCB's policy reversal could not have been more drastic. It rejected the position that Afro-Brazilians relatively benefited from the country's benign racial characteristics. In a dialectical turnabout, the party then subscribed to the viewpoint that those very characteristics were so structurally oppressive that blacks could not achieve liberation through integration but rather had to seek refuge in liberated, autonomous societies.

On the one hand, communist self-determination was an import into Brazil, but on the other hand, Comintern policy did not seem to drive the PCB's new antiracism entirely. It is certainly true that the autonomous-black-state thesis that the PCB advertised was drafted at the Sixth Congress. It is also correct that the Comintern was pressuring the PCB and insisting that the Brazilians execute "a systematic and serious effort . . . among oppressed races."[70] Nonetheless, Moscow's agenda worked in tandem with domestic circumstances that, in many ways, provide a more compelling explanation for the PCB's antiracist turn. The PCB was aware of the increase in post-1930 black racial consciousness and political engagement in the country, and Brazilian communists attempted, at least verbally, to harness these phenomena. Self-identified black Brazilians in the broader communist movement must have influenced the policy shift as well, but unfortunately we know very little about the extent of their impact.

Like other segments of Brazilian society, blacks were galvanized by the so-called Revolution of 1930—the coup that brought President Getúlio Vargas to power. He and his co-conspirators promised a new era and a departure from the patterns that Brazil's traditional oligarchy had established. Specifically, Vargas vowed to end the widespread corruption, unpopular economic policies, and electoral fraud associated with Brazil's oligarchic rule. He also pledged to address major social ills through reforms like comprehensive labor codes. This generated a new sense of opportunity for those who had long felt marginalized politically, economically, socially, and racially under the Old Republic. Afro-Brazilians experienced and contributed to the spirit of change and possibility that washed over the country in 1930. The black leader and journalist José Correia Leite said that "with the 1930 Revolution, blacks gained a new sense of enthusiasm and came to regard it as the solution to all their hardships." Historian Flávio Gomes made a similar observation: "In the debate about the inclusion of various segments of society, the black population and its leadership perceived that moment as important to politicize the racial issue."[71] Especially in urban settings, Petrônio Domingues has noted, blacks praised the revolution and "began organizing themselves collectively, taking to the streets and occupying the public space."[72] The FNB, founded in São Paulo, emerged out of this explosion of black activism. It was not the only black organization in Brazil, but it quickly became the largest and had the greatest political influence. Most important for the purposes of this analysis, it was also the black group to garner the most attention from the Communist Party.

The founders of the FNB—including Leite, Arlindo and Isaltino Veiga dos Santos, Jayme de Aguiar, and Gervásio de Moraes—were veteran journalists and advocates of the Afro-Brazilian cause. They began the FNB in 1931, taking advantage of the hopeful postrevolutionary moment. Black activists had already been organizing with growing levels of participation in the 1920s, and the FNB could be seen as an inheritor of these earlier efforts. Kim Butler has shown that Afro-Brazilians had already developed new collective identities by 1930, and the FNB constituted part of the decades-long evolution of black self-determination strategies in Brazil. Distinct from yet with some similarities to the communist model, the FNB ideology of self-determination manifested as separatist black cultural, social, educational, and political services and activities, driven by the idea that "we separate to unite."[73] In other words, black solidarity, vis-à-vis separatism, was to be the entrée into broader social integration. FNB self-determination called upon people of color to perceive blackness in novel ways, particularly as an identity around which to develop a racial political agenda and, for the first time in history, to form an official Afro-Brazilian political party.[74] Clearly this form of self-determination resonated, as about seventy thousand blacks[75] joined the FNB in multiple cities and states before the Estado Novo government banned the organization in 1937.

The impact of the Frente Negra, largely an urban phenomenon, on the Communist Party was significant. As Pedro Chadarevian has written, "the emergence of an organized urban black movement" was an important factor that "drove the change in the Party's [racial] doctrine" in Brazil.[76] The PCB was tremendously concerned with the success of the anticommunist and integralist-linked FNB, both fearing that it would undermine communist work among the Brazilian proletariat and coveting this reservoir of politically engaged blacks, whom it foresaw as valuable party members. In fact, as we will see in the following chapter, FNB leaders did work to impede the growth of communism among Afro-Brazilians, and denunciations of communism were regular features of the Frente Negra's newspaper, A Voz da Raça (The voice of the race).[77]

PCB literature shows that the party employed the strategies toward black organizations that were outlined earlier and discussed in the US context: it attempted to prevent blacks from joining the FNB, pilfer from the FNB's existing membership, and incite a communist takeover of the organization. The PCB appealed to Afro-Brazilians by expressing solidarity with racially conscious blacks and with the antiracist struggle that led them to join forces with groups like the Frente Negra. Communists hoped that blacks would look to the Communist Party and the Soviet Union, not the FNB, as role models and leaders of racial equality. Thus, what developed was an outright fight between communists and the Frente Negra for black support.

The official PCB journal, A Classe Operária (The working class), contributed to the party's anti–Frente Negra propaganda and participated in the black recruitment crusade. The 1931 article "Blacks Are Expelled from the Bourgeois Rinks" lambasted the "bourgeoisie of São Paulo" for blocking the entrance of blacks into the city's skating rink. While the communists agreed that the practice should end, A Classe Operária also ridiculed the way that the Frente Negra's leadership protested this case of racial exclusion.[78] The article labeled the FNB a "society founded by the bourgeoisie to cheat our black comrades" and declared that its appeal to General Rabelo, the governor of São Paulo, was wrongheaded: "Rabelo was placed in government . . . by people who serve the American bourgeoisie, the same people who lynch [US] blacks in the streets." The article implored "oppressed blacks" to "take charge of the 'frente negra'" and fight alongside the PCB, "the only party that . . . recognizes for blacks the same rights held by whites [and that] fights in defense of all the oppressed, white or black!"[79] The PCB's reference to the United States in this very domestic story was an early attempt to spread communism by internationalizing both the black struggle and black identity politics, encouraging Afro-Brazilians to identify racially with blacks in other parts of the world.

The article's description of the PCB as a party that "does not distinguish race or color" shows that the color-blind philosophy that the Comintern officially retired during the Third Period remained intact in Brazil at least into the early 1930s. The PCB was, in effect, then a party in transition on the racial question. The fact that most of the *Classe Operária* article deprecated the Frente Negra rather than the custom of racial exclusion and discrimination suggests that the party considered the FNB the greater problem of the two. At the same time, the FNB's campaign awakened the party leadership to the new organization and its stature as a powerful force among Afro-Brazilians. In its concern over the FNB, the Communist Party became aware of the opportunities that Brazil's urban black base presented. Shortly after the FNB's foundation, the PCB radicalized its racial policies and discourse, including embracing the self-determination policy, which emboldened party members to label the FNB as weak on racial equality.

Throughout its racial campaign, the PCB disparaged the Frente Negra and praised the communist and Soviet devotion to the "black race." For example, the PCB's pamphlet "To All the Black Workers and to the Proletariat in General!" showcased its commitment to the black cause in no uncertain terms: "In the struggle for their total liberation, black workers and the black race in general only have one guide—THE COMMUNIST PARTY." The pamphlet claimed that the Soviet Union was the sole country on earth where blacks were truly granted all their rights, challenging the comparable Brazilian narrative. The PCB-linked Socorro Vermelho do Brasil (International Red Aid of Brazil), the Brazilian branch of the Comintern's International Red Aid, published a flyer that was addressed to "Black Workers" and encouraged Afro-Brazilians to defend the Soviet Union as the "only country" that fought for "all workers—black, white, indigenous, and of all colors!" Painting a picture that starkly contrasted the PCB to the FNB, these publications also insisted that the FNB was no ally of black labor. The PCB pamphlet referred to FNB leaders as "traitors to the black race" and contended that the black battalions that many *frentenegrinos* enlisted in and helped form in 1932[80] called upon blacks to "die in the interests of the oppressors and exploiters, both national and foreign," of the working class. The Socorro Vermelho flyer echoed this sentiment, pointing to the Frente Negra's combatants as a sign that the group's leaders were "under the influence of the feudal-bourgeoisie and the imperialists," not black workers.[81]

Self-determination became the mantra meant to signify that the PCB better understood the struggle for racial equality and was more dedicated to the black working class than the nation's largest and most influential Afro-Brazilian organization. A PCB manifesto explained that this policy was meant to return "all the land [that] had been robbed" from blacks and the indigenous and to grant them the right to govern those territories themselves. The Socorro Vermelho urged blacks to work within the "Frentes Negras" to fight "concretely" for these self-determination rights and to bring about their own self-governed state, where blacks could also practice "the religion they desired."[82]

Other Comintern bodies and sources also contributed to the dialogue about the FNB. The Comintern's Secretariat of South and Central America told the PCB's Central Committee that "workers of color" were "deceiv[ed]" by the false leftism of the Black Front. A confidential, unsigned Spanish-language letter may also have been from the Secretariat of South and Central America. The letter, written in 1935, was likely addressed to the PCB and/or its leaders. It reiterated the importance of working among blacks and suggested that the communist-led National Liberation Alliance (ANL) ally with the "frente negro [sic]" only if the FNB "openly broke with the reactionary Vargas government and merged its activities with the revolutionary objectives of the Alliance."[83]

The Communist Party assigned its youngest members the task of targeting frentenegrinos (FNB members) to promulgate the PCB's revamped antiracist policy and message among blacks. Communist groups instructed the Federation of the Communist Youth of Brazil (Federação da Juventude Comunista do Brasil)—which the US ambassador to Brazil referred to as an effective organization "coming to be a matter of concern"—to prioritize black recruitment.[84] In virtually the same language, the South American Bureau of the Communist International Youth (in 1931) and the Fifth Plenum of the Communist Party of Brazil (in 1932) outlined the responsibility of the Federation of the Communist Youth of Brazil in their resolutions, acknowledging that racism, not just class oppression, must be addressed. As the bureau put it: "We must devote special attention to young black and indigenous workers, fighting for their demands as oppressed races." The bureau and the plenum reminded the Communist Youth that these Brazilian racial groups "constitute a very serious revolutionary force that the Federation must harness." Specifically, they resolved that the Communist Youth of Brazil should "work within organizations of the black masses, such as the Frente Negra, those of the indigenous, etc., to organize the revolutionary opposition there and to promote our policy of self-determination for oppressed races."[85]

In light of the vitriol that many communist organizations hurled at the Frente Negra and its leaders in the early 1930s, it is unlikely that the party planned to nurture any meaningful cooperation or partnership with the FNB. At times the PCB appeared to want to trigger a communist coup within the FNB. In the words of the article discussed above, the PCB attempted to persuade "oppressed blacks . . . to take charge of the 'frente negra.'" In its title and again in its text, the Socorro Vermelho flyer quoted above also implored black Brazilians to "conquer the leadership of the Frentes Negras in order to fight for your self-determination."[86] In other instances, the PCB hoped to motivate like-minded frentenegrinos to abandon the Black Front for the Communist Party. In both cases, one thing is clear: in order to appeal to frentenegrinos and other black workers, the PCB and the Comintern were compelled to publicize a program of black racial consciousness and to acknowledge racism in Brazil.

Like their North American counterparts, however, PCB leaders showed resistance to and a failure to understand the Comintern's new racial policy, even as the PCB itself appeared to adopt it. In a 1933 letter to the PCB's Central Committee, the Comintern's Secretariat of South and Central America applauded the PCB's "serious examination" of the national question during its August 1932 plenary session as a "definite step forward." Yet for the most part, the compliments stopped there. The secretariat was concerned and dismayed by the ways the plenary exposed "with total evidence how weakly the leadership of the party knows even the basic principles of [the] Leninist national policy" that buttressed the new racial theses. In fact, the secretariat noted that "certain participants of the plenary expressed opposition to the self-determination principle," unfavorably comparing it to legalized racial segregation in the United States. The secretariat complained that "every possible variety of bourgeois 'racist' theory [was] spread widely throughout the party" and observed a "refusal to fight for the self-determination" of even indigenous groups, whose plight received a relatively substantial amount of sympathy within the PCB. As a result, the letter continued, the party had "still not worked much at all among the workers of oppressed nationalities," or blacks and the indigenous. The secretariat told the PCB to fight decisively "against the underestimation of the national question and in defense of the Leninist principle of 'self-determination of the nationalities, even separation.'"[87] Thus, although PCB racial rhetoric and policy did make a sudden reversal, verbally conceding a problem of racial prejudice in the nation and proffering likely the most militant policy on the matter, communists' opinions and beliefs proved much more obstinate.

In Brazil and the United States, black organizations—such as the African Blood Brotherhood and the Brazilian Black Front—attracted communist attention. In both nations, the Communist Party fought to recruit from the same pool of members as black-rights groups: politically minded black workers. Communists certainly had much to lose, for the Comintern declared Afro-descendants indispensable collaborators for the movement's success. Therefore, as communists crafted their discourse of capitalist democracy's class exclusion and exploitation, it would have been disadvantageous for them not to engage parallel rhetoric based on racial exclusion and exploitation, which myriad black leaders and groups were already articulating. There is ample evidence in both nations that this revolution in rhetoric did not translate into a revolution in communist thought or action on the ground. In fact, it seems that in Brazil and in the United States, self-determination functioned less as a blueprint for black liberation and more as a recruiting slogan, sending the message to blacks that the parties were emphasizing their struggle and racial injustice in new ways. Thus, the self-determination policy is a clear indication that black recruitment had become a critical issue and that racial politics had radicalized, all of which manifested in sharp democracy-based charges against the US and Brazilian states.

COMMUNISM VERSUS THE STATE: DEMOCRACY AND ITS RACIAL MEANINGS

In the 1930s, communism was a powerful factor in constructing the ideological milieu about democracy and race through which Brazilian and US state authorities were forced to navigate. Communists may have ridiculed many black organizations and labeled them incapable of redressing racism, but they blamed the origin of said racism on capitalist states. Thus, even as communists tried to strip those groups of their antiracist credentials, they also shined a bright light on racial inequalities in these two countries, citing capitalist and political structures, such as forms (or lack thereof) of democracy, as the root cause. In Brazil, communists consistently disputed President Vargas's claims that a new, politically and socially responsible democratic era had been born with his 1930 coup d'état.[88] For parts of the decade, US communists similarly decried the social welfare programs of President Roosevelt's New Deal as incapable of remedying inequalities. Communist critiques of these societies framed the democracy debate in terms of inclusion/equality versus exclusion/exploitation, racial and otherwise. Racial injustice was framed not only as undemocratic class oppression but also as a distinctly unique and special category within it.

Communists employed three key strategies based upon democracy and race to argue that the US and Brazilian economic and political systems spawned inequitable societies. Naturally reflecting Marxist theory, these rhetorical tactics sharply contrasted communism with the economic, political, and racial status quo in both countries. The first strategy characterized the definitive element of the US and Brazilian capitalist states as bourgeois exploitation of the proletariat, or "bourgeois democracy." The second strategy denounced racism, or "white chauvinism," in the United States and Brazil. The third strategy merged the first two, contending that racism itself was a product of and innate to all bourgeois democracies. Here communists intertwined the problems of racism and classism to drive home their principal point: capitalist democracy was founded upon the exclusion and oppression of the majority by the privileged minority. The contrary was supposedly the case with communist democracy, as proven by the policy of self-determination. What emerged was a tale of contrasts: the traits stamped onto the US and Brazilian states—undemocratic and racist—were simultaneously framed as antitheses to communism, which its adherents labeled as intrinsically democratic and antiracist. The racial question and democracy were inextricably linked, and the former, it seemed, would help the people distinguish the fraudulent democracies from the real ones.

In 1919 the theses on democracy of the First Congress of the Comintern emphasized economic equality and declared capitalism and democracy as irreconcilable contradictions. Indeed, the idea of democracy, one of the pivotal notions to shape Comintern philosophy, was omnipresent in its theses and resolutions. The theses, largely composed by Lenin, rejected the notion that self-proclaimed democratic societies were actually inclusive democracies, positing that "in no civilized capitalist country does 'democracy in general' exist; all that exists is bourgeois democracy." The theses defined bourgeois democracy as "a purely rhetorical and formal recognition of rights and freedoms, which are in fact inaccessible to the working people . . . on account of their lack of material means." Thus, "so-called democracy, i.e., bourgeois democracy, is nothing but the veiled dictatorship of the bourgeoisie."[89]

The Comintern embraced proletarian revolution and dictatorship as the initial steps toward dismantling bourgeois democracy and building a democracy that included the working class: "History teaches us that no oppressed class ever did, or could, achieve power without going through a period of dictatorship." The proletarian dictatorship, however, was described as fundamentally democratic in that it provided "an unparalleled extension of the actual enjoyment of democracy [for] those oppressed by capitalism—the toiling classes." Still, the platform promised that "the dictatorship of the proletariat [is] a temporary form of government" and that the end goal was a stateless and classless "genuine democracy" in which everyone would enjoy "liberty and equality." In other words, the proletarian dictatorship would instigate and oversee the process that would collapse the hierarchical class structure, producing a united, free, and democratic society in which the workers controlled the means of production. Comintern leaders promised that "the Soviet system makes possible [this] genuine proletarian democracy—a democracy for the proletariat, by the proletariat."[90] Therefore, even though communists spoke frequently of revolution and dictatorship, the final new world order they projected was not authoritarianism but bona fide democracy, a point examined by state bodies like US congressional committees and the Brazilian political police, as we will see in the next chapter.[91]

Engaging the second strategy, communists also provided innumerable examples to make the case that the United States and Brazil were lands of racial inequality. For instance, Brazilian communists habitually commemorated abolition to indict the legacies of slavery persistent in the 1930s and also denied the traditional narrative that Princess Isabel was primarily responsible for freeing the slaves. The PCB asked its followers not to believe the common tale that a benevolent Princess Isabel had eradicated slavery from Brazil, calling this history "forced [on the people] by the enslaving capitalist regime." Instead, they contended, pressure from the "black masses," industries "that required 'free' whites" (presumably to replace the less desirable black labor), and "English imperialism in search of a new consumer market" brought about the Lei Áurea (Golden Law). The PCB also detailed the suffering and horrors of the transatlantic slave trade and slave life, revising accounts that tended to hail Brazil's slavery as more humane than that of other societies, like the United States.[92]

The PCB did celebrate the 13 de maio (Thirteenth of May) abolition anniversary—not as the day on which the burdens of slavery were lifted but as a time to honor how the enslaved, through their resistance and agency, had brought about emancipation in their *quilombos* (Maroon societies) and in the mass abandonment of plantations *before* Princess Isabel signed the Lei Áurea.[93] Furthermore, communist literature distributed around the 13 de maio framed communism within the tradition of Zumbi and the quilombo he defended and died for—Palmares, the famous seventeenth-century Maroon society that had up to twenty thousand inhabitants and survived for about one hundred years. Conjuring the image of the Comintern's black self-determination strategy, the PCB described Palmares as "the first Republic of Black Workers" and, more tellingly, as a "republic that had the seeds of primitive communism."[94] Such statements both resonated with and buttressed those we have already seen in Brazil that naturalized communism as a race-based freedom struggle.

When black communist Édison Carneiro and PCB pamphlets challenged national memory on the meanings and aftermath of slavery and abolition, they used powerful language meant to confront the state. One PCB pamphlet insisted that "the black slave liberated in 1888 is, with very little difference, the black worker of today." As chapter 4 will discuss, Carneiro was even more critical of postemancipation Brazil. In the paper he presented at the 1934 Afro-Brazilian Congress, Carneiro said that after blacks were "proletarianized," they were forced into the "other slavery that was capitalism," which was "even worse than [the original form of] slavery." PCB pamphlets made numerous proclamations that backed these statements about the false promises of abolition: "For a 13 de maio of struggles for the true liberation of the entire black race . . . !," "the devious bourgeois judges do not consider the violation of black women a crime," and "lying discourses about the 'complete emancipation of the black race.'"[95] The Special Delegation of Social and Political Security confiscated copies of these pamphlets in the Federal District, Rio de Janeiro, signaling the state's awareness of and opposition to this discourse, as well as its organized attempt to suppress it.

In the United States, communists' attacks on the state's perpetuation of societal racism, which they deemed democratic infractions, also invoked the tropes of past and current slavery. In 1930 the ECCI resolved that "the yoke of the Negroes in the United States is of a peculiar nature and particularly oppressive. This is partly due to the historical past of the American Negroes as imported slaves, but is much more due to the still existing slavery of the American Negro." The Comintern pushed the latter issue, citing the plight of black tenant farmers and sharecroppers in the South: "It is only a Yankee bourgeois lie to say that the yoke of Negro slavery has been lifted in the United States." But northern slavery persisted as well, especially in the "whole system of 'segregation' and 'Jim Crowism,'" which originated in the "Yankee arrogance towards the

Negroes [that] stinks of the disgusting atmosphere of the old slave market."[96] The CPUSA repeated this message to adults and children alike. For instance, the communist-controlled youth publication *New Pioneer* echoed the Brazilians' stance on Princess Isabel in its articles about Abraham Lincoln, who, they argued, transferred the slaves from feudal to capitalist oppression.[97] An early CPUSA Negro policy primer contained entire subsections dedicated to US black history that explained why the US "Civil War did not achieve the complete liberation of the Negro slaves." Referring to the end of Reconstruction and the rise of sharecropping as an oppressive regime, the document stated that the formerly enslaved had been relegated to a "semi-serf position" that continued to be "strongly felt at the present time."[98]

The CPUSA's Negro Department mocked the United States as a "so-called enlightened capitalist civilization" with a list of damning grievances that unveiled the stark reality of racial inequality and firmly placed the United States in the class of decidedly unenlightened racist societies. Communists identified blacks North and South, rural and urban as "the weakest section of the working class, i.e., the section with the least rights." The document labeled black factory workers as "the lowest paid wage slaves," stated that black farmers "still exist[ed] in bondage but little removed from chattel slavery," and enumerated various other injustices, including the growing crisis in lynching, mob violence, and "police terror," as well as "overcrowded Jim Crow districts," where "high rents" and "foul and disease-breeding housing" were the norm. The CPUSA also launched devastating condemnations about the political obstacles US blacks confronted: "All over the country they suffer from political oppression and in the South especially they are denied the most elementary democratic rights—rights to vote, freedom of speech and assembly."[99] By centering racial injustice as a defining characteristic of the US political economy, communists utilized the condition of US blacks to render "enlightened" and "capitalist civilization" as inherently paradoxical. In this and other instances, communists used the word "democratic" to subvert the common belief that "enlightenment" and "capitalist society" were synonymous with "democracy."

The question of democracy defined the third strategy, as communists spotlighted contemporary racism in both nations and argued that it encapsulated a brutal, entirely undemocratic historical relationship between the state and blacks. Such circumstances opposed the racial characteristics communists ascribed to real democracy and unequivocally marked the racial issue as a democratic question. From the outset,

the Comintern made explicitly racial guarantees about its own democratic program and counterposed it to capitalism: "The equality of citizens, irrespective of sex, religion, race, or nationality, which bourgeois
democracy everywhere has always promised but never effected, and
never could effect because of the domination of capital, is given immediate and full effect by the Soviet system, or dictatorship of the proletariat."[100] In other words, only communism, and certainly not capitalism,
could realize racial egalitarianism.

The CPUSA and the PCB championed the self-determination policy as
a way to spread their democratic theory in the United States and Brazil.
Indeed, self-determination became a rhetorical linchpin of communist
racial democracy. In 1930 the Comintern's Negro Commission issued a
resolution to clarify that self-determination was a "free democratic right"
for blacks.[101] Harry Haywood explained the policy in an article published in the *Communist* magazine. Blacks could be neither forced into
forming their own state nor cajoled into opting against it.[102] Haywood
alluded to the fact that many in the party were confused by the policy,
particularly since the CPUSA also maintained a position against "white
chauvinism"—or white racism against nonwhites, especially blacks[103]—
in the party: backing black self-determination seemed to capitulate to the
ideas of racists who would prefer a separation of the races. The party
deployed its democratic theory to defend self-determination from these
leftist detractors. The CPUSA insisted that although the "liberation struggles of the Negro masses are part and parcel of the proletarian revolution," the revolution "must necessarily contain within itself a national
revolutionary, democratic current—the struggles of the millions of
Negroes for democratic rights, special equality and the right of national
self-determination."[104]

In order to clarify why self-determination constituted a logical option
for African Americans, CPUSA documents articulated black oppression as
a lack of democracy, offering self-determination as a cure for this political,
economic, and social ailment: "American imperialism tends to deny
democracy in general—freedom of speech, assembly, equality of sex,
etc.—and the democratic rights of the Negro in particular. Hence, the
struggles of the Negro masses for Social Equality and self-determination is
[sic] directed at the very foundation of the imperialist dictatorship in the
United States."[105] James Allen—whom the scholar Roderick Bush called
the party's "leading theoretician of Negro Liberation during the early
1930s"—echoed this Negro Department outline when he wrote in 1932
that "so-called democratic rights—participation in primaries and elections,

holding office, and jury service—are denied the Negro in the South." He continued with a discussion of poll taxes, voter intimidation (which he termed "terrorism"), literacy tests, all-white primaries, and statistics of low black voter registration as justification for the policy.[106] Such statements support the historian Mark Solomon's assessment that more than anything, self-determination should be seen as a democratic slogan.[107]

Although there is less documentation about self-determination in Brazil than in the United States, the Brazilian communists also explicitly formulated the policy as a way to promote democracy. For black communist Édison Carneiro, self-determination was emblematic of communist "worker's democracy." If the communist revolution succeeded, Carneiro believed it was possible that blacks would not feel the "desire to separate from the white proletariat." However, it was important to Carneiro that the PCB honor this option. His writing parallels Harry Haywood's explanation of self-determination in that it demonstrates how choice itself represented a fundamental democratic freedom for blacks.[108] One PCB Program Manifesto further explored the issue of land rights that the policy redressed for blacks and the indigenous, beginning with a rhetorical question: "What democracy [exists in the Brazilian] regime for the millions of workers, peasants, blacks and Indians[?]" It went on to denounce the racial oppression that blacks and the indigenous faced as evidence of the democratic abyss, detailing how they had been torn from the earth they had nurtured over generations with their hard labor.[109] Here the PCB conceived of self-determination as a democratic intervention that could exercise radical agrarian reform to remedy racial injustice in many shapes.

As this section has shown, communist discourse about racial democracy did three significant things. First, it declared it impossible for racial inequality to exist in a genuine democracy. In other words, communism deemed racism a canary in the coal mine of democracy. Second, communists put self-proclaimed democracies on the defense, or at least foregrounded their race relations. This was particularly true of racially plural societies like the United States and Brazil. Finally, communists insisted that their system was the only way for people of color to experience democracy on the same level as whites. In the early 1930s, they typically advertised the communist model as a proletarian revolution, which was to be the indirect route to democracy. As we will see later in this chapter, a new phase of communist racial democracy emerged when the Popular Front era began around 1935, as language of democracy increasingly dominated communist rhetoric.

THE SCOTTSBORO NINE AND LUÍS CARLOS PRESTES:
BRAZILIAN–US COMMUNIST SOLIDARITY AND RACIAL
DISCOURSE

Communist parties' internationalist perspective, which the Comintern's global scope facilitated, resulted in transnational support and recognition of one another's efforts and struggles. If the effects of capitalism and bourgeois democracy were truly borderless, communists would have to demonstrate common bonds in their suffering. This section shows how Brazilian and US communists often chose to highlight racism in both nations as evidence of their shared plight, countering the narrative that US-style racial oppression was foreign to Brazilians. In fact, the commonalities articulated between South and North Americans and the protests they generated led the US and Brazilian authorities to collaborate in their surveillance of communist activities and publications.

In 1931 communists worldwide found an ideal event around which to demonstrate their commitment to the end of racism—the Scottsboro, Alabama, case of nine black teenagers falsely accused of raping two white women.[110] It was largely the communist press that made the case infamous around the world, as they declared the Scottsboro "Boys" exemplars of the oppressed black proletariat in the United States. They pointed out the hypocrisy of US democracy and humiliated the nation through a relentless exposure of the institutionalized racism that the Scottsboro ordeal so aptly represented. Of course, attorneys from the communist International Labor Defense had taken on the case, which gave the communists access to material that allowed them to present it as a riveting epic. The US criminal justice system, identified as an offspring of the state's oppressive bourgeois regime, was cast as the racist antagonist. The innocent victims were the Scottsboro Nine, whose protracted, unimaginable suffering symbolized the dire straits of the exploited proletariat worldwide. The equality-seeking protagonist/hero was played by the tenacious ILD, a freedom-loving child of the Communist International.

The case and its dramatic appeal became a liability to the US government, as shown by State Department documentation of the ways in which it compromised the United States' standing as a democracy and by records of the outcry over the situation in countries around the world. Brazil was no exception. As Roger Bastide and Florestan Fernandes's seminal *Brancos e negros em São Paulo* documented years later, the Scottsboro case was one of the critical recruitment tools that communists and socialists used to mobilize the "proletariat of color." However, it appears only briefly and as "Scotbar" in the study, which may have limited scholars' examination of the case's impact in Brazil. Bastide, who wrote the chapter on the case, credited it with being a key element in the consciousness-raising process among Afro-Brazilians that occurred after the First World War. José Correia Leite's memory of the vigorous communist "Scotbar" campaign among the black population corroborates Bastide's conclusion. Furthermore, because the *Brancos e Negros* study was a cumulation of interviews with and questionnaires filled out by Afro-Brazilians, the recollection of "Scotbar" likely came from the testimony of blacks highlighting the factors that had prompted individual or communal racial awareness.[111] But well before Bastide and Fernandes, US and Brazilian authorities had chronicled the ways in which Brazilian communists contributed to the international protest over the Scottsboro Nine.

In a leaflet distributed by the Brazilian Socorro Vermelho, communists insisted that a coordinated global response was the Scottsboro defendants' singular hope: "Only the solidarity of the proletariat of every country, protesting with every means against this 'class justice,' can save the nine young Scottsboro workers, victims of the bourgeoisie."[112] Brazilian communists did not stop at the distribution of leaflets. In 1933 the US ambassador to Brazil, Hugh Gibson, reported to Secretary of State Cordell Hull that for the second time in as many years, communists protesting the incarceration of the Scottsboro "Boys" had defaced the embassy with tar. Gibson wrote that in 1932, "on the occasion of one of the Scottsboro trials, tar was thrown over the Embassy, and . . . other embassies and legations (outside of Brazil) have also been subjected to the same treatment." In 1933 the embassy's guard on duty was tarred along with the building, and the assailants left literature signed by the International Red Aid of Brazil that connected the plight of the "Negro workmen of Scottsboro" with the Brazilian people suffering under Vargas.[113]

As these incidents demonstrate, Brazilian communists used the Scottsboro case to internationalize Brazilian racism to dislodge Brazil's longstanding narrative of interracial exceptionalism and to validate the argument that capitalism naturally begot racism. Similar language appeared in 1935 when the US communist journal the *Daily Worker* published, under the title "Brazilian Toilers Express Solidarity with American Workers," a letter from an interracial group of ten self-described Brazilian political prisoners in a Rio de Janeiro jail. Like the communists who had vandalized the embassy, the signatories to this indictment, addressed to the Alabama Supreme Court, aligned their struggle with that of the Scottsboro Boys and declared common, fraternizing enemies. They identified their own oppressors as "the government of Brazilian plantation owners and bourgeoisie, allied with foreign bankers, including those of North America." They told the Alabama Supreme Court that these same US bankers "are your bosses," vowed their "strongest opposition and the deepest repugnance," and warned that "you may be sure that your rule of terror will not prevent the oppressed Negro masses from demanding their rights. The torture to which you are submitting the young Negroes of Scottsboro cements still more firmly the unity of Negro and white workers of all continents and all races for the common struggle."[114] By linking their oppressors, these Brazilian communists facing political persecution became natural allies with the Scottsboro defendants. They also erased the line that many had drawn between supposed Brazilian racial tolerance and US racial bigotry, squashing the notion of Brazilian interracial exceptionalism.

Brazilian communists also invoked the Scottsboro defendants frequently in their abolition-awareness campaigns, analyzed above. As one PCB pamphlet declared, "We connect, on this *13 de maio*, our demonstrations to the black Scottsboro workers' fight for liberty."[115] In its direct appeal to black comrades, another pamphlet insisted that abolition's anniversary was a day to honor and remember black heroes of the past and black martyrs of the day, including the Scottsboro Nine and Zumbi.[116] In this sense, nationality did not circumscribe the celebrated champions of this national holiday, and race was the common denominator uniting them.

Communists in the United States mobilized on behalf of their Brazilian counterparts as well. Like the Scottsboro case, that of the white Brazilian communist leader Luís Carlos Prestes was splashed across communist literature globally, including in the United States. His story presented another opportunity to dramatize the communist struggle with an intriguing plot line. Prestes, the so-called Cavaleiro de Esperança (Knight of Hope), had been an army lieutenant when he led a popular revolt in the 1920s. Already a legendary figure before becoming a communist, he was launched into international communist stardom by his role in the failed November 1935 communist coups in three Brazilian cities and subsequent arrest. In Harlem, black communists were enjoined to rally behind Prestes and black Brazilian communists, and the State Department filed clippings of the *Daily Worker*'s coverage of these events. They were spearheaded by the black communist James Ford, the division organizer of the Communist Party in Harlem and a CPUSA vice presidential candidate, who urged: "We must demand the release of Prestes and general amnesty for all political prisoners, including . . . Negro leaders." Although thousands of miles separated the United States and Brazil, event organizers suggested that the distance and borders were irrelevant: "We American Negroes must come to their assistance."[117]

At least three articles in March 1936 issues of the *Daily Worker* rallied readers, especially blacks in Harlem, to come together and object to the imprisonment of black political prisoners "perhaps" tortured and murdered by the Brazilian state. James Ford specifically named Isaltino Veiga dos Santos, a founder of the Brazilian Black Front, as one of the blacks persecuted by the Vargas regime. (Ironically, Santos vehemently expressed his staunch anticommunist politics in his prison writings, as chapter 2 will discuss.) Harlem communists also gathered to protest the death of the white US communist Victor Barron, who had been arrested by Brazilian authorities in Rio de Janeiro after the 1935 coup in that city and subsequently died while in their custody. Barron's father, Harrison George, met with Ford and other leaders in Harlem where black communists also expressed outrage over the death and the incarceration of black political prisoners.[118] As proof of the vibrancy of black Brazilian communist activity, an article on this meeting exaggerated that "millions of Brazilian Negroes, who make up over 40 per cent" of Brazil's population, were active in the communist leader Prestes's movement.[119]

In 1936 the US communist press published a thirty-nine-page booklet on Prestes that characterized him as a natural leader of the people whose actions had always been guided by the values of racial democracy. The reader was informed that even at the military academy, "Prestes was reckoned as an especial friend of the oppressed Negroes and mulattoes[, which] brought him into conflict with the aristocratic elements among the officers, who looked down with contempt upon these plebians [sic]." However, Prestes had been obstinate, making yet "firmer contacts with the democratic circles in the army."[120] Indeed, the 1924 revolt in Rio Grande do Sul that Prestes had led and the subsequent Prestes Column—a group of up to fifteen hundred rebels that had spent two and a half years marching through the Brazilian backlands in hopes of mobilizing the people to rise against the state oligarchies—were described throughout the booklet as part of the fight for "democratic liberties." And in this democratic movement, "Negroes, mulattoes and Indians fought like brothers at the side of their white comrades." The Popular Front National Liberation Alliance (ANL) that Prestes headed at a later point was also framed as a vanguard of racial democracy. For instance, as the booklet noted, the ANL's demands included "democratic popular liberties [and] complete abolition of all special rights and privileges in favor of individual races, colors and nationalities."[121] This US publication about the Brazilian Prestes was one more instance of the communists' efforts to define democracy racially and to criticize those countries with "special rights and privileges" based on a racial and color hierarchy.

POPULAR FRONT POLITICS AND COMMUNIST RACIAL DEMOCRACY

When the Seventh Congress of the Comintern met in 1935, world observers noted that the organization made a decided rhetorical shift "from global proletarian revolt and dictatorship to a defense of peace and democracy."[122] This was the formalization of a major transformation in strategy that had been occurring for the previous year or so—the implementation of the Popular Front. The Popular Front was a response to the rise of Nazi fascism, when Moscow determined that Hitler posed a threat to its very existence and that collective security was the best plan to counter this threat. As a self-protective measure, Comintern resolved to prioritize anti-Nazi/fascist activity and commanded communists worldwide to form alliances with other organizations and political groups. Thus, ironically, communists allied with groups they had previously and condescendingly referred to as "reformist," "bourgeois," or "social fascist" during the militant Third Period (1928–1934/35), in order to defend the also once despised liberal democracies.[123] As a result, during the Popular Front period, communist language abandoned discourse that promoted proletarian revolution and dictatorship in favor of rhetoric that praised liberal democracy. During the Seventh Congress, the Bulgarian Comintern leader George Dimitrov articulated the party's new strategy about communist democracy: "We are the adherents of Soviet democracy of the working people, the most consistent democracy in the world. But in the capitalist countries we defend and shall continue to defend every inch of bourgeois-democratic liberties, which are being attacked by fascism and bourgeois reaction, because the interests of the class struggle of the proletariat so dictate."[124]

While speaking more frequently and generously about democracy, communists continued to advance racial equality ideals, but they were less radical and even more directly linked to democratic values. By the time of the Third Conference of South American and Caribbean Communist Parties, held in Moscow in October 1934, the Comintern had largely embraced the Popular Front strategy, although it would not be official until the Seventh Congress the following year.[125] At this conference, it was clear that racial justice was still a major consideration in the tactical shift underway. For instance, Luís Carlos Prestes, in exile in Moscow and not a member of the PCB's leadership at the time, was specifically asked to address the question of blacks in Brazil at the meetings. He spoke about the problem of "racial oppression" in Brazil and concluded that the party should "raise before blacks the issue of equal rights. We communists are against any form of racial oppression of the masses."[126] Despite these remarks, the black leader Abdias do Nascimento found the former's grasp of the fight for racial equality lacking. Nascimento wrote of his encounters with Prestes years later that "in classic Brazilian fashion, [Prestes] 'sympathized with' or could even declare 'support' for our movement, but definitely he did not understand the specificity of our struggle."[127]

The US government recorded the events at the South American and Caribbean conference and noted how Comintern mandated that "special attention must be paid to the task of drawing into the national liberation, anti-imperialist front the widest Indian and Negro peasant masses." Comintern singled out these groups in large part because "more than half" of the population of "100 millions" in South and Caribbean America were "oppressed Indian and Negro peoples." The US report also documented the conference's statement that "steps have been taken, but only the first steps [to draw] the widest masses of the oppressed Negro Indian [sic] masses" of Brazil into the PCB.[128] The racial agenda and the principles that Prestes expressed at the conference found their way into the manifestos of Brazil's main Popular Front and self-defined democratic movement, the ANL.

As did most Popular Front groups worldwide, Brazilian communists joined forces with other antifascist parties, and they formed the ANL in 1935; unlike most Popular Front groups, the ANL attempted to overthrow the government just months later.[129] The PCB's influence in the organization was immense, and it greatly shaped the ANL's rhetoric of racial democracy.[130] "Democracy" was the ubiquitous catchphrase of the ANL, and the group claimed to admit anyone who was willing to fight "for democratic rights." The ANL's "Anthem of the Poor Brazilian"—in this chapter's epigraph—was one example of its multiracial perspective, as it both hailed the revolutionary contributions of "blacks, Indians, and pariahs" and urged their further participation in the movement.[131] In another instance, Luís Carlos Prestes's affiliation with the ANL was first publicly announced to a crowd of almost ten thousand during the group's May 13, 1935, rally in Rio de Janeiro, resonating with the PCB's past abolition commemorations.[132]

In Prestes's 13 de maio letter, read at the Rio gathering in his absence, he reaffirmed his commitment to the PCB, lauded the democratic mission of the ANL, called for the ANL to install a National Revolutionary Popular Government, and reminded its members that the movement should refuse all racial distinctions.[133] Prestes's racial rhetoric was noticeably less militant and revolutionary than the earlier PCB pronouncements that promoted self-determination. Certainly during the Popular Front the PCB maintained a softer language of racial democracy to avoid alienating its liberal allies. However, the fact that racial democracy remained part of the National Revolutionary Popular Government platform—the agenda that the ANL hoped to secure during the 1935 insurrections—rendered the ideology dangerous and subversive, despite the toned-down language.

Perhaps the most emphatic expression of the ANL's racial democracy was its celebrated manifesto, signed by Prestes and read in 1935 by Carlos Lacerda to a crowd commemorating the 1922 army revolt. The section dedicated to the theme of race stated: "With the Alliance will be all the men of color in Brazil, the heirs of the glorious Palmares traditions, because only ample democracy, of a truly popular government, will be capable of forever ending all the privileges of race, color, or nationality, and can give to the blacks in Brazil the immense prospect of liberty and equality, free from any reactionary prejudices, for which they have fought with bravery for more than three centuries."[134] Similar to the other communist abolition literature we have seen, the ANL Manifesto presented its movement as a natural continuation of the struggle waged by the powerful Maroon society Palmares. Like the PCB, the ANL promised that its democratic vision was the only feasible road to the racial equality for which generations of blacks had crusaded. The Popular Front organization's efforts among blacks were duly noted by top black leaders such as José Correia Leite, who wrote that the ANL actively "looked to involve blacks," even if Abdias do Nascimento was less than impressed with the leadership's knowledge of their problems.[135]

The ANL also educated its members on racial issues. Two days after May 13, 1935, the ANL sponsored a free educational workshop led by the renowned Brazilian scholar Arthur Ramos on "Racial Problems in Brazil."[136] One ANL newspaper printed an entire series on João Cândido, black hero of the 1910 naval revolt against white officers' practice of whipping sailors of color. (Ironically, Cândido associated with the fascist integralists.) University branches of the ANL addressed the topic of equality for Afro-Brazilians in a few journal issues, while some students even launched unsuccessful attempts to organize a black front. The students' evident failure to mobilize after the police confiscated the newspapers carrying Cândido's story raises important questions about the commitment of many communists to the antiracist cause.[137] Still, there can be no doubt that the communists played a critical role in making rhetorical racial democracy salient.

In the United States and Brazil, state authorities documented the communists' revised democratic message. Various authorities in cities like São Paulo and Rio de Janeiro shared their confidential reports and intelligence on communist activity with the staff of the US embassy. One such confidential report of the São Paulo Departamento de Ordem Política e Social (DOPS), or the political police, compiled data on the city's communist activities in 1939, a year after the PCB declared support for Vargas. It in part outlined communist tactics among the masses and found that recent PCB publications included only "propaganda revolving around democracy," with "communism" having virtually disappeared from this messaging.[138] The government was, however, less than comforted by the PCB's apparently conciliatory politics and relative endorsement of Vargas.

In the same year, US authorities also took notice of the change in communist rhetorical strategy. A confidential report on inter-American activism among suspected communists reflected these officials' distrust of anything termed "Popular Front." The report argued that Comintern's Seventh Congress, "realizing that communists could not make any headway with their antiquated, aggressive, and direct slogans and actions, called for indirect methods by promoting their movement, including the advocacy of the extension of 'democracy' according to their interpretation of the term."[139]

Anticommunist congressional leaders in the United States tried to grasp the communist notion of democracy and its new Popular Front. In 1938 Congressman Martin Dies, the chairman of the House Special Committee on Un-American Activities (HCUA here; also known as HUAC), referred to the Dimitrov speech that signaled the birth of Popular Front politics and called Comintern's claims to democracy "famous." Many of the HCUA's witnesses were asked to discuss the communist shift to the Popular Front. Witnesses, such as former communist journal contributor Ralph De Sola, explained how the Popular Front policy materialized in the party, like in the communist youth publication *New Pioneer*. De Sola observed that the pre–Popular Front *New Pioneer* subscribed to the then communist position that Abraham Lincoln "was nothing more than a middle class lawyer [who] really created a situation which . . . removed the slaves from a feudal ownership and transferred them to an economic ownership." But with the Popular Front transformation, De Sola testified that the new party line compared Lincoln to Lenin, both men constituting "great heroes of the American people."[140]

In the United States, the Popular Front era occurred sans uprising, and the revolutionary jargon of the previous movement, including its racial message, was toned down tremendously. In addition to the shift away from self-determination that we also saw in the ANL, the US Popular Front ushered in a period that altogether de-emphasized black issues. Popular Front politics demanded a platform with a broader appeal, and with antifascism as the priority, even the lip service paid to black concerns decreased. In black communist hubs like Harlem, the CPUSA largely ceased addressing local problems, like segregation in hiring practices, in order to keep in good favor with white workers. In Alabama, the black leadership of the state's formerly black-dominant party was replaced by whites who generally abandoned black issues. Racial sensibilities complicated coalition building with white liberals in all parts of the country. Such changes in the party dovetailed with events like the Nazi-Soviet Pact to curtail black support of the party as the decade came to a close.[141]

Despite the CPUSA's relative devaluation and mainstreaming of its racial politics during the Popular Front, national political rhetoric and policies continued to highlight racial democracy. In 1938 the Communist Party election platform called for "Jobs, Security, Democracy, and Peace," while the party's vice presidential candidate, James Ford, incarnated the racial underpinnings of this mantra. Ford, the party's leader in Harlem, was the first African American candidate for US vice president in history. Under Ford and presidential candidate Earl Browder, the party reminded the public that it still stood for "socialism, the highest form of democracy," like that which existed in the Soviet Union, "where democracy triumphs." However, the platform simultaneously conceded that in 1938, "the issue is not socialism or capitalism—the issue is democracy or fascism." Thus, the party submitted its platform "for the consideration of the American people as the basis of the democratic Front." Among the items on the platform's agenda were "full rights for the Negro people," including "equal rights to jobs and education, equal pay for equal work," the abolition of segregation, and anti-lynching legislation. Some points were reiterated in the platform's proposal to "safeguard American democracy." Under the actions approved to safeguard democracy were the abolishment of poll taxes and other infringements on voting rights, the release of "the Scottsboro boys and all other political prisoners," and the prohibition of propaganda and activities against Jews, Negroes, and other groups.[142] Thus, in spite of the more relaxed racial policy and a significant scaling down of party activities in the black community, the CPUSA did not abandon racially inclusive democracy in theory.

In the 1930s Brazilian and US communists argued that true democracy was antithetical to racial exclusion, and they promised that their model of democracy reflected their commitment to racial justice. This issue became one of the communists' main rallying cries, in large part to recruit the huge black working class, and at times to justify an overthrow of the government. The Scottsboro defendants and Luís Carlos Prestes became communist causes célèbres and opportunities to portray communist racial democracy as integral to a powerful international movement. The Popular Front period saw the deradicalization of racial politics in both countries, yet communist antiracist language continued. We will now examine the ways in which these strategies provoked state nationalist responses that utilized racially inclusive democracy as self-defense.

CHAPTER 2

Embattled Images of Racial Democracy

State Anticommunism in the 1930s

In the United States and Brazil, authorities in the 1930s attacked head-on the communist claims that their governments represented not democracy, freedom, and racial inclusion but racial and other types of exploitation and oppression. Indeed, democracy was at the epicenter of the debate, as both communists and anticommunists professed adherence to the ideal and embedded racial justice in its very definition. In the process of refuting communist assertions and accusations, Brazilian and US state anticommunists generally agreed with their adversaries' racial terms and conditions of democracy. Black leaders and journalists, typically the most vocal advocates of racial realism as a form of effective anticommunism, had a huge impact on these discussions. This chapter describes the two states' deployment of racially inclusive nationalist and democratic rhetoric in response to the communist challenge during the 1930s and, when possible, assesses their motives, among them the need to dissuade blacks from joining communist ranks and strengthening the movement. What resulted in both instances were official doctrines of racial democracy that emerged as tools of national defense.

Official anticommunism in Brazil and the United States diverged greatly during the 1930s, however. During this decade, the Brazilian president Getúlio Vargas and his supporters used both real and fabricated communist schemes to warrant the expansion of federal power and a more repressive government. In 1937 Vargas discarded the 1934 Constitution and replaced it with one that outlined the Estado Novo dictatorship. Vargas justified the Estado Novo with references to the foiled communist-led uprisings of the National Liberation Alliance (ANL) that took place in the military barracks of Natal, Recife, and Rio de Janeiro in November 1935.[1] The government's reaction to the insurrections was prompt, and agencies like the Comissão Nacional de Repressão ao Comunismo (National Commission for the Repression of Communism) were created to suppress the movement in all sectors of society, including the workplace, politics, and culture. Although the Estado Novo outlawed all political organizations, presumed communists were the most tenaciously hunted down, being arrested in the thousands. Many were tortured and some were killed at the hands of the police. Political police records show that the Estado Novo targeted blacks as well.[2] In this context, racial obstructionism—or the crackdown on the people and literature advertising communist racial democracy—became an important component of Brazil's tough anticommunist policy. This chapter in part analyzes the state's obstructionism through the case of Afro-Brazilian political prisoner Isaltino Veiga dos Santos, whose incarceration was protested by black communists in the United States.

Whereas anticommunism was the official position of state nationalism in Brazil, the vigorous US anticommunist activities only occurred in certain sectors of the government during the 1930s. Franklin Roosevelt was opposed to red-baiting, publicly denouncing and ridiculing congressional anticommunist tactics. For its part, the Communist Party shifted to its Popular Front strategy in 1935–39 and supported Roosevelt's New Deal, especially the 1935 Wagner Act, which provided collective bargaining rights to labor organizations. Indeed, as Ellen Schrecker has observed, in many ways the CPUSA "served as the unofficial left wing of the New Deal."[3] Many liberal congressional members' viewpoints reflected that of the Roosevelt administration, judging what would eventually be called McCarthyism distasteful, abusive, and un-American. However, as the Depression produced a lack of confidence in capitalism and an upswell of support for communism, anticommunism ascended in tandem. Congressional anticommunist committees and hearings, brutal police repression (especially of labor organizing), teacher loyalty oaths, and state anti-sedition statutes all constituted effective official anticommunist actions that intended to elevate communism to national security enemy number one.[4]

Getúlio Vargas and his propaganda machine asserted Brazil's reputation for racial harmony, redefined democracy, and labeled a farce the communists' claims for Soviet democratic superiority. Because of

Brazil's international prestige in race relations, Vargas was more confident than US authorities in confronting communists head-to-head on
the racial question. On the other hand, anticommunist officials in the
United States were more self-assured on the issue of democracy than
the Brazilians because Brazil spent most of the 1930s in democratic
limbo or heading swiftly toward dictatorship. The anticommunist language that developed in these countries bears out this difference.
Regardless, US officials also lambasted communist democratic claims,
and notwithstanding their insecurities about spotlighting race relations,
they repackaged US democracy with distinctly racial attributes.

In response to communist attacks on the United States' poor racial
record, US state anticommunists forged nationalist frameworks prem-
ised on race and democracy.[5] Certainly, as communists racialized their
dispute with anticommunists over capitalism and governance, US anticommunists were obliged to counter in kind. The latter aimed to create
an alluring image of the United States far preferable to the Soviet Union
and the communist model, which painted the Soviet Union as a racial
utopia free of discrimination. They knew that they were in a battle for
black hearts and minds, and they hoped African Americans could be
dissuaded from choosing communism. This chapter highlights the
House special committees that anticommunist congressmen Hamilton
Fish Jr., a racial realist, and Martin Dies, a denialist, spearheaded, as
well as the debates they generated.

Brazilian anticommunism in the 1930s remains relatively understudied, as scholars have tended to focus on excavating the history of Brazilian communism during this period.[6] This historiographical gap is beginning to be filled by academics such as Carla Luciana Silva and, most
notably, Rodrigo Patto Sá Motta, but this scholarship does not point to
racial democracy as a characteristic of state anticommunism. The following pages reveal that this was indeed the case. Brazilians scrambled
to classify the freshly implemented Estado Novo dictatorship as a
uniquely Brazilian democracy. Estado Novo agencies and representatives admitted that the dictatorship was dissimilar from other democracies, but they argued that it was one more suitable for the Brazilian
people. Authorities argued that Brazilian communism rendered Estado
Novo–style democracy necessary because the failed Popular Front coup
required an aggressive state comeback. In terms of democracy's racial
features, the communist impact on the Estado Novo was both indirect
and direct. Indirectly, communism legitimized the regime's new "militant democracy" language that added democratic nuance to the myth of

Brazilian racial harmony.[7] Directly, Brazilian authorities and agencies referred to race in their anticommunist attacks, although to a lesser extent than the North Americans.

This chapter also complicates traditional Brazilian-US comparative scholarship by demonstrating that nationalist claims to racial democracy occurred both in Brazil and in the United States, and as early as the 1930s. In addition, Brazilian racial democracy was constructed not only by using the United States as the national "other" but also in opposition to the Soviet Union. Here the Vargas regime competed with the communists to prove that Brazil, not the Soviet Union, was the true racial utopia. Despite their country's more blatant forms of legalized racism, many US authorities followed a similar strategy.

US CONGRESSIONAL LEADERSHIP IN ANTICOMMUNIST RACIAL DEMOCRACY

In the United States, the reaction to communism varied from one branch of government to another during the 1930s. In a controversial move, Franklin Roosevelt officially recognized the Soviet Union during his first year in office, and he felt that much of the anticommunist fervor was unnecessarily alarmist and extreme. Especially by the end of the 1930s, Roosevelt was much more disquieted by Nazism than communism, and this position reflected that of his administration in general. Bureau of Investigation (later FBI) director J. Edgar Hoover, along with influential members of Congress and military leaders, believed that communism was a serious national security concern. The State Department also kept a watchful eye on communist activities. Numerous devout anticommunists were suspicious of persons and programs associated with Roosevelt and the New Deal. Many of them launched communist accusations against the administration, and some even systematically examined the government. The United States had more heterogeneous state voices than Brazil at the time, which made official anticommunism and opposition to it much more fragmented.

Legalized racial disparities in the United States caused its anticommunist officials to feel more anxious, more vulnerable, and at a greater disadvantage in countering communist racial policy than their South American counterparts. US anticommunists also had to deal with frequent black mobilizations around racial politics and well-established African American organizations and institutions, a great source of concern. US authorities that advocated racial realism agreed in some ways with communist criticisms about racism in the country, but they resolved that the United States must present itself as a democracy more appealing to blacks than the communist model. Realists supported a racial democracy that was primarily action oriented, guided by the desire to eradicate the causes and effects of racial inequality, stripping communists of fodder for their propaganda. Racial denialists, on the other hand, granted little or no credence to communist claims about the severity of racism in the United States. However, denialists did acknowledge the gravity of the accusations themselves and recognized, even prioritized, the need to counter such criticisms with a defense of US democracy. Denialist racial democracy maintained a rhetorical, non-action-oriented position, however, and was not structured to work toward redressing the injustices people of color faced.

US state agents troubled by communism among blacks also relied upon dissuasion—paternalistic warnings issued directly to blacks that Soviet racial democracy was a fallacy, and reminders that they were US, not Russian, citizens. Dissuaders attempted to convince blacks that the racial status quo in the United States was better than that in the Soviet Union. Finally, US anticommunist obstructionists were opposed to US racial democracy of any kind, rhetorical or action oriented. Most unabashedly promoted in the South, obstructionism insisted that the best way to curtail black communism was to put black leaders and all interracial activists under surveillance, using any means necessary to undermine their efforts for racial justice. Even though the state figures I focus on here did not fit into this latter category, it is important to note that obstructionists were especially quick to label any race-rights and/or interracial organization as communist and foreign instigated.[8] Thus, they played a significant role in augmenting state agencies' hypersuspicion of such groups as communist. Anticommunist state actors often used a combination of these reactions in their attempts to squash black communism.

Two of the highest-profile and most organized US anticommunist efforts in the 1930s were special congressional committees that investigated US communist propaganda and activities—the 1930–31 Fish committee and the 1938–44 Dies committee.[9] The investigations, files of communist documents, and testimonies presented at the committee hearings demonstrate the ways in which anticommunists elevated the racial problem as a key democratic issue. And problem it truly was, for it became clear that racism was an enormous national security liability. The committees felt that opportunistic communists loyal to a foreign government were exploiting US racism with their discourse of racial democracy in order to recruit blacks to execute a coup. In other words, the communist ideal of racial democracy was an existential threat to the form of democracy practiced in the United States, and those involved in or responding to these congressional committees generally addressed the issue with one or more of the four racial democracy strategies.

In 1930 Congress authorized and funded a House Special Committee to Investigate Communist Activities, spearheaded and chaired by the Republican representative Hamilton Fish Jr. of New York. Fish strongly believed that the government was not doing enough to understand the extent of the domestic communist threat, so he proposed the committee with the purpose of investigating communist propaganda, literature, and activities in educational institutions, the CPUSA, and its affiliates.[10] Fish made it a point to educate Congress on what he perceived to be the lack of concerted anticommunism in the broader government, and he even blamed Congress for the growth of communism "through its do-nothing policy."[11] Fish was likely the government's most recognizable expert on communism nationwide for most of the 1930s, and he stood atop the anticommunist soapbox for many years.

Fish understood that communists conceived of their movement as democratic, and he wanted to ensure that US citizens did not. In an article he published just after his committee's final report, he wrote: "They want you to believe . . . that there is some connection between Liberalism and Communism." He argued that in reality, the current Comintern leaders had overthrown the post-czar Provisional Government, "the first democratic government that Russia had ever known," to establish "their dictatorship, which is the worst form of autocracy the world has ever known." If Fish contended that the link between communism and liberal democracy was imaginary because the Soviets did not honor "civil rights, freedom of speech, of assembly, and of the press, trial by jury, and so on," he certainly understood that the issue of racial equality favored communist democratic assertions: he felt that the Soviet Union's racial policy (if not practice) was one of communism's more convincing democratic features, whereas racial discrimination was the United States' most conspicuous democratic offense.[12]

While Fish lambasted the communists' depiction of their self-proclaimed democracy—he mocked the Soviet Union as a "great peaceful nation where everybody is rich and happy and sublime" and praised the United States as truly "the soundest, the fairest, the most honorable, and the wisest form of government yet devised by the mind of man"—he acknowledged that racism complicated this binary. Testimonies from his committee's black witnesses reassured the public that blacks were "loyal to their country, their flag, [their] governmental institutions," and their religion, yet Fish notably added, "*in spite of* inequalities." He acknowledged that "[w]herever there is a Communist meeting, the white and the colored people assemble together and dance together. The Communists mean just what they say, so their [racial] propaganda [does have] some little appeal."[13] These three points—that blacks were loyal to the United States, that blacks experienced racism in the United States, and that communists were much more open-minded in all things racial—formed the basis of Fish's realist anticommunism. He found the Soviets' general democratic claims contrived, but he did believe that communist racial democracy was stronger than its US counterpart, and he understood that many blacks thought so as well.

In his June 1930 closed testimony to the committee, J. Edgar Hoover focused on communists' efforts "to incite revolutionary activity [and] racial antagonism" among blacks.[14] The later testimonies of Matthew Woll, John Lyons, and William Z. Foster provided proof of Hoover's warning. Woll, the vice president of the American Federation of Labor, and Lyons, a New York police inspector, said they had seen blacks and "men of all races dancing with pretty white girls at Communist affairs" in Chicago and New York.[15] (The committee's final report indicated that white men danced with black women as well.)[16] Lyons stated that this form of social equality in the CPUSA was very appealing to blacks, and problematic in light of his evidence that Soviets specifically targeted blacks to overthrow the US government.[17] When asked during his subsequent testimony if he believed in complete social equality between whites and blacks, black self-determination, and interracial marriage, CPUSA executive secretary Foster responded: "I do, most assuredly."[18] Fish's aforementioned reference to such communist racial views and practices showed that he understood why they would be alluring for blacks, even if he felt that blacks would not fill communist ranks en masse.

Perhaps the most influential group to mold Fish's racial realism was the black leaders his committee called to testify, especially A. Philip Randolph, a socialist critic of communism. Randolph harnessed the fear of black communism while simultaneously assuaging it, nimbly striking a precarious balance between identifying racial justice as a national security issue and painting blacks as a deserving, patriotic lot. The black journal *New York Amsterdam News* accurately expressed Randolph's strategy with its front-page subtitle: "Congressional Committee Told Communists Have Made Little Headway, but Have Fertile

Soil in Racial Discrimination."[19] Randolph, the leader of the Brotherhood of Sleeping Car Porters, reported to committee members that "the number of Negroes in the Communist party is very small, [but] I should say there has been an increase in Communist sympathy among Negroes." Randolph attributed said increased sympathy to intensified communist activities in the black community and US discrimination, particularly lynching and disenfranchisement. Randolph insisted that the best way to conquer the spread of communism was to eradicate racial inequality. He took great pains to reassure the Fish committee that despite all the odds, blacks were committed to fighting for their rights within the US system.[20] Thus, there was no reason to panic for the time being, but if the country did not get its act together and do right by blacks, it might concede future victory to the communists. Fish embraced a form of Randolph's calming yet pessimistic racial realism.

Like Randolph, NAACP secretary Walter White and former black southern communist leader R. C. Miller located the so-called red menace not in the black community but in racism and in the state's role in protecting racial injustice. Miller said that "our condition is miserable and the Negro will . . . join anything to better himself." White made similar claims, worth quoting at length:

> One lynching in Mississippi stirs more unrest among Negroes than all the Communist propaganda which can be spread in a year. . . . The greatest pro-Communist influence among Negroes in the United States is [those who indulge] in lynching, disfranchisement, segregation and denial of economic and industrial opportunity. The thing that can best stop the spread of Communist propaganda among Negroes in this country . . . is drastic action by the United States government [to end] lynching, segregation, disfranchisement, and other forms of brutal bigotry. . . . The way to open the minds of American Negroes to propaganda from abroad is to convince them that they have no stake in their own land, that they have no rights. . . . How can Communism fail to make progress among Colored people . . . when Negro newspapers broadcast the recent expulsion from Russia of two Americans, not for lynching, but for beating a Negro worker?[21]

Making the case for action-oriented racial realism, White challenged the state to match what he depicted as Soviet racial democracy and to regard this act as an important national security measure against the communist threat. He thus portrayed the NAACP's antilynching campaign not as a potential communist tool, as many charged, but, contrarily, as a guard against communism. Similarly, he openly criticized the very nature of the Fish committee inquiry: why was it investigating communism and not the Ku Klux Klan, a group whose organized terror had handed over scores of blacks to the communists?[22] A *Pittsburgh Courier* editorial agreed: "We are not averse to an investigation of Red activities since we hold no brief [for] the Reds . . . but it seems to us that the commission could do much more valuable work by investigating anti-Negro activities." Furthermore, the editorial maintained, "there are but 20,000 Communists . . . endeavoring to undermine the foundations of our 'democratic' government, [whereas] there are tens of millions of whites who are actively or passively fomenting prejudice . . . and actually undermining the foundations of real democratic government by indiscriminate hanging, broiling, and baking of Negroes."[23] This echo of White's action-oriented racial realism suggested that only concerted steps against racism could remove the quotation marks deemed necessary around "democratic."

More-radical blacks, such as Cyril Briggs, the African Blood Brotherhood leader-turned-communist, used the Fish committee investigations as an opportunity to condemn US racism as systemic to capitalist, bourgeois democracy and to boast that Soviet racial democracy was converting many blacks to its side. Briggs's 1930 *Pittsburgh Courier* article "Lynch Terror Haunts Congressional Probers" documented the visit by Fish committee investigators to New York workers' camps. Their arrival at Camp Nitgedaiget was met by protesters, including the communist leader Jack Perilla, who specifically addressed the two southern committee representatives, Robert Hall of Mississippi and Edward Eslick of Tennessee: "The gentlemen from the South may be hurt to know that there are no lynchings or pogroms in Soviet Russia," he proclaimed proudly. Briggs reported that Richard Moore, the CPUSA candidate for New York comptroller, added: "All this talk of democracy is a joke. Democracy in this country is but a brutal capitalistic dictatorship." Racial violence was central to what he meant by the "brutal" reminders that US democracy was nonexistent.[24]

Hamilton Fish was not hostile to the viewpoint that the United States deserved to be faulted for racial injustice, even before the start of his committee. A complicated figure, he championed certain issues critical to blacks, most notably antilynching legislation, which he fought for during his entire tenure as a congressman (1922–45). Furthermore, during World War I, Fish had been the captain of the all-black 369th Infantry Regiment, the so-called Harlem Hellfighters, known for their role in holding back German advancement during the Battle of Meuse-Argonne. After he accumulated a relatively progressive profile on racial matters, his political career ended in scandal when he was accused of being a Nazi sympathizer, which he denied until his death. Thus, Fish is simultaneously remembered as a possible anti-Semite and as an antiracist advocate whom blacks considered a friend.[25] Fish seemed to subscribe to the notion that the United States was an incomplete democracy due to its racism, writing in his memoir that he told the members of the 369th upon their return to the United States, "You have fought and died for freedom and democracy. Now, you should go back home to the United States and continue to fight for your own freedom and democracy."[26]

Fish also used democratic language in the effort to enact his antilynching bill in order to back action-oriented steps. Reflecting upon the valor and patriotism of the 369th Infantry Regiment, he said on the floor of the House: "Let me tell you something that perhaps members of the House do not fully appreciate, and that is that the colored man who went into the war had in his heart the feeling that he was not only fighting to make the world safe for democracy but also to make this country safe for his own race." Fish later wrote about his disgust with Roosevelt for not backing the antilynching measures, arguing that Roosevelt "told the American people that they had to fight a world war to protect democracy in Europe [while] he refused to support my efforts to extend the blessings of democracy to American blacks."[27] It is consistent, then, that Fish conceded a certain validity to the communists in comparative racial democracy. His personal sense of racial democracy had long been action oriented—he merely developed another perspective, anticommunist realism, when his committee's investigations seemed to uncover how high the stakes were in the black community.

But Fish was also a dissuader, paradoxically urging blacks to look past the injustices they faced and to agree that the United States was, despite it all, a racial democracy. Years after his committee's end, he warned blacks "not to compromise with Communism, Fascism, or Nazism." Although "radicals and Communists will tell you that the Constitution is a scrap of paper, [it] is the greatest charter of human liberty ever devised by man," he promised. He elaborated on the last point to show why it was of special interest to blacks: "The colored people have more at stake than any other group in upholding and defending the Constitution from the attack of those foreign termites who would undermine and destroy [it] to set up a dictatorial form of government and leave the colored citizens like the Jews in Germany, to the mercy of the Southern Congressmen who opposed the anti-lynching bill." Fish even conjured the Scottsboro Boys, arguing that it had been the Supreme

Court's function as established by the Constitution that had upheld the young men's civil rights against the tyranny of the South.[28]

Fish's dissuasion underscores an important characteristic of his racial democratic ideology: unlike many blacks, he did not frame action-oriented racial realism as a requirement of anticommunism. Part of his legacy to US anticommunism was the notion that black communism could easily pose an existential threat to the United States, although blacks in general were a loyal, God-fearing people, a message his committee included in its final report. This is not to suggest that Fish never made the connection between antilynching legislation and anticommunism, as Walter White did, but his committee did not make policies to undo racial discrimination an official aspect of its reports' proposed state-sponsored anticommunism. Future state anticommunists interpreted Fish's findings to mean that dissuasion and racial denial, not realism, were the logical approaches to combat black communism. This was the attitude of Martin Dies.

Hamilton Fish Jr. was sympathetic to blacks' complaints about the United States, but Martin Dies, a Democratic representative from Texas, was not, and neither was his House Special Committee on Un-American Activities (HCUA, later HUAC). Dies detested labor radicalism, the state's growth, and its economic and labor interventions under the New Deal. Communism topped his list of concerns; Dies seemed to find the communist threat in almost everything, accusing the labor movement, the New Deal, and many "Trojan Horse organizations" of being tools for communist subversion. His dislike of the labor movement was closely related to his anti-immigration roots; in the 1910s and 1920s his father had led efforts to restrict immigration. As Gary Gerstle has written, the "younger Dies, though not indulging in the eugenics-inflected talk that had been popular then, blamed eastern and southern Europeans for the nation's problems and declared them unfit for membership in his American nation."[29] It is not surprising that Dies dismissed the problems of racial discrimination in the United States. At the same time, perhaps his apparent rejection of scientific racism explains why he was at least open-minded to the ideals of racially inclusive nationalism.

The HCUA was established to investigate "un-American" and subversive domestic and foreign-originated propaganda. By 1938, when the committee began its investigations, it was aware of communist racial democracy, and Dies linked most forms of antiracism to communism. That said, the HCUA did embrace the general idea of racial inclusion. In fact, the committee's list of un-American activities included not only communism, Nazism, and fascism but also racial hatred and intolerance. As Dies said during an HCUA hearing in November 1939, "[t]he Chair believes that any organization in this country which is disseminating propaganda of a class, racial, or religious hatred character is un-American; or at least the question of un-Americanism is raised sufficiently to warrant this committee's consideration of such organizations."[30] Thus, Dies did espouse racial democracy as nationalist ideology, defining racial hatred as antithetical to Americanism. A few years later, he said that he had always "preached the fundamental doctrine of American tolerance" and that he believed the United States to be "the home of all of us—Gentiles, Jews, Negroes."[31]

A 1938 *Pittsburgh Courier* article might have been a sign that the journal held out hope for the Dies committee, although the piece could also be read as sarcastic. The *Pittsburgh Courier* reported that Dies spoke "wisely" when he said that "the essence of Americanism is [the] class, religious and racial tolerance [that] constitute the three great pillars on which constitutional democracy rests." The *Courier* opined, "after such a liberal statement, Mr. Dies may be expected to leave no stone unturned to make racial tolerance a reality in Texas."[32] The tone of incredulity here exposes the fact that Dies's racial democracy was not action oriented: he typically placed the activities of racial equality agitators in the same racial hatred/intolerance category as white supremacist organizations, narrowing the space for criticism of racism.

The HCUA's communist propaganda investigation gave its members a firm comprehension of communist theories and policies, and members knew that the Comintern and the CPUSA based many of their arguments, racial and otherwise, upon the fundamentals of democracy. Part of Dies's mantra in his many speeches and publications was that the CPUSA, through its "front" organizations like the American League for Peace and Democracy, carried "false passports under the aliases of peace and democracy."[33] The committee studied Comintern and CPUSA resolutions, speeches, and literature, which guided their interrogations of witnesses such as William Z. Foster, then CPUSA national chairman. Questioning Foster about his 1932 book *Toward Soviet Russia*, J.B. Matthews, committee counsel and director of research, asked, "when you wrote this book . . . was it your understanding that the democracy of the United States was a dictatorship of the bourgeoisie?" Foster responded yes. Matthews and Dies continued to drill Foster on the point of democracy, essentially asking whether or not he still held the opinion, in that Popular Front era, that the "dictatorship of the bourgeoisie [was] masked with hypocritical democratic pretenses." Foster found it difficult to reconcile Comintern's more radical Third Period politics, reflected in his 1932 book, with its newer Popular Front policy, and he responded that a simple yes or no answer was impossible. Matthews cited parts of Comintern's Fifth Congress that explained how the "Soviet form of state, being the highest form of democracy, namely, proletarian democracy, is the very opposite of bourgeois democracy."[34] The committee also examined materials concerning the communists' platform on blacks. Presenting a 1929 issue of the communist journal the *Daily Worker*, Matthews pointed to and read from an article that reprinted Comintern's Resolution on the Negro Question.[35] Foster verified the statements.

Many witnesses, such as Sallie Saunders, a Federal Theatre Project actress, were called to testify on the racial practices of communists. Saunders, referred to as a "pretty blonde" by the *Chicago Defender*, was asked to recount the events surrounding a telephone call she received from a black coworker asking for a date. When asked if she had reported the call to her supervisor, Saunders replied yes, adding, to evident dismay, her recollection of the supervisor's response: "Sallie, I'm surprised at you. He has just as much right to life, liberty, and pursuit of happiness as you have. . . . It is in the Constitution." Chairman Dies wanted clarification whether the supervisor actually said that he was "in favor of social equality." Saunders answered yes. Furthermore, Saunders reported that a secretary expressed her disappointment that Saunders had rejected the black man's offer because, as Saunders recalled, she "personally encouraged Negro attention on all occasions and went out with them or with any Negro who asked her to." Asked if this secretary had said that interracial dating was policy, Saunders replied that she did not, "but she is a representative of that [communist] party, and they hobnob indiscriminately with [blacks], throwing parties with them left and right." Saunders confirmed that "social equality and race merging" were indeed elements of the communist program.[36] Saunders's testimony supports historian Dayo Gore's analysis about the manner in which communist interracialism focused on black men and white women, "leaving black women as marginal figures in the process."[37]

At a different hearing, the pamphlet *The Negroes in a Soviet America* caught Chairman Dies's attention because of its assertion that true racial equality could only be realized with the Soviet model and because of the way it underscored the importance of blacks to the communist movement.[38] Chairman Dies's first book, based upon the HCUA's hearings, quoted from the pamphlet—written by black communist James Ford and his white comrade James Allen—in his chapter dedicated completely to communism among blacks. Dies's chapter began: "Moscow has long considered the Negroes of the United States as excellent potential recruits for the Communist Party." He estimated that Russians were spending incredible sums of money on black recruitment and training, principally because "Moscow realizes that it can never revolutionize the United States unless the Negro can be won over."[39] Clearly Dies believed that black communism could and should be framed as a national security issue.

Like his predecessor Hamilton Fish, Martin Dies realized that communist racial discourse was, in fact, an attempt to praise the Soviet Union as the world's only authentic racial democracy. Dies believed the communists' efforts were responsible for igniting "racial hatred" in black communities. Blacks were taught, Dies wrote patronizingly, "that the only country which recognizes [their] rights is Soviet Russia, and that the only political party which will battle for [their] emancipation is the Communist Party." Dies dwelled on the "social equality" blacks experienced among communists, especially between black men and white women: "Communist girls have been sent among Negroes to practice 'social equality.' Thus, by profession and practice, the Communists encourage the Negro to demand 'social equality' with the whites."[40] Dies invoked testimonies like that of Sallie Saunders, who implied, and from whom the committee inferred, that communists made virtual prostitutes out of white women in order to encourage interracial courtship and prove the verity of communist racial democracy. Clearly distressed at the gender dynamics of communist racial democracy, Dies later stated outright that he "deplored" this movement for social equality among blacks.[41]

Dies considered absolutely baseless the premise that Soviet racial democracy shamed US democracy in comparison. Dies's denial largely ignored US discrimination while reversing the communist narrative: blacks experienced racial democracy in the United States, not Soviet Russia. Dies placed blacks who spoke against racism under a shroud of suspicion because, as he wrote, "Communists believe that an appeal to racial prejudice and an *exaggeration* of grievances will gradually separate the two races into hostile camps (resulting in) a sort of auxiliary to the class struggle and civil war." Therefore, he almost invariably determined black protests and resistance to be communist instigated: "The Negro *is told* that he is persecuted and maltreated; that his lot in the United States is unbearably hard; and that he is, in fact, a peon or slave of his white masters," Dies wrote. With hard racial denial, Dies protected

the reputation of his southern region and ignored the possibility of racism in the North: "Under our free institutions, the Negro has made great
progress in the United States. Despite propaganda and misrepresenta-
tion, he lives in peace with the white people of the South." Furthermore,
"lynching has practically disappeared," and he claimed that blacks and
whites got along splendidly, despite those "in both races who are exceptions to this rule." In fact, "there is no other country on the face of the
earth where two distinct races enjoy such friendly relationships."[42]

Martin Dies deemed the black "exceptions" as un-American because
they challenged his nationalist image of racial democracy, promoted
"racial hatred," and/or validated communist claims. He blamed black
activists, not racial discrimination, for causing disequilibrium in the
harmonious race relations he described. Black communists were among
the worst offenders, and Dies felt that they carried out the party's agenda
"under the guise of social and economic programs," in preparation for
"bolder [revolutionary] efforts in the future." He indicated that black
communists were also responsible for indoctrinating often-clueless
blacks working alongside them with the conviction that "the Negro is
mistreated and that he must demand his social and economic rights."
Dies even went so far as to deduce that blacks in the struggle actually
adopted the strategy of the Nazis. The HCUA had concluded that the
communist-influenced National Negro Congress used the "identical
motive that Hitler has exploited so successfully, namely, that of racial
hatred," he wrote.[43]

Despite Dies's and the HCUA's vast interpretation of racial hatred
activities, they did not seriously investigate the Ku Klux Klan or similar
groups—perhaps not to compromise their denial—and many blacks
protested this lack of investigation vociferously.[44] Just as they did in
reaction to the Fish committee, black journalists attacked the HCUA on
this point, exploiting the committee's professed objective to probe all
"un-American" activities by making a nationalist case for their opposition to the KKK, stressing that a true US racial democracy would label
the infamous white supremacist group as un-American *and* undemocratic. These action-oriented racial realists identified the Klan as fascist
and pushed the Dies committee to assess such native-born movements
along with those of foreign origin. The black journalist Cliff Mackay,
who penned the "Globe Trotter" column in the *Atlanta Daily World,*
was particularly incensed at the HCUA's failure to study the KKK and
characterize it as a threat. "Klannish Americanism" was a problem,
Mackay insisted, and he accused Dies of being slow to recognize in

rightist extremists "as grave a danger to things democratic as those movements to the left." Reminding Dies that the Klan had only recently threatened southern blacks who dared to vote, Mackay and black journalists like the *Pittsburgh Courier*'s P.L. Prattis pointed out that the Klan freely dismissed constitutional rights and thus US democracy. The *New York Amsterdam News* stated that the Klan "does more to tear down democracy in the United States by flaunting law and order than the [German American Bund] and the Red Party combined."[45]

After the Dies committee failed to act on these multiple requests to investigate the KKK, similar groups, and lynch mobs for more than a year, the NAACP urged Congress to consider withholding funds from the HCUA until it agreed to do so. By ignoring these racist groups, the NAACP contended, the Dies committee was refusing to acknowledge their un-Americanism and therefore was giving them the "'go' signal." The *Pittsburgh Courier* took a bolder tack when it discussed these criticisms of the HCUA: "Here, it would appear, the critics err. Since when have the activities of the Ku Klux Klan been un-American?"[46]

To many in the black community, the Dies committee's unwillingness to take on the Ku Klux Klan qualified Dies as a racial obstructionist who blocked racial democracy from blossoming in the United States and veiled racism with anticommunism. The *Chicago Defender* reported that many black leaders interpreted the HCUA's failure to inquire into the KKK as evidence of the committee's racist agenda, criticizing it for being "more interested in throttling and killing any organization that has among its aims opposition to race prejudice . . . than it is [in] Communism or un-American activities."[47] In another article, the *Defender* condemned Dies as "un-American" for his approach to the Klan: "We declare that violation of the constitutional rights of black Americans lays the basis for the destruction of our democracy as a whole." Unfortunately, wrote the *Defender,* "Mr. Dies seems not to know this truth." The article was certainly a pitch for action-based, racially inclusive nationalism, determining that "democracy for the man farthest down" was "democracy for all."[48]

The *Chicago Defender* contributor Adam Lapin criticized the Sallie Saunders testimony and the committee for expressing shock that her supervisor felt that the US Constitution guaranteed racial equality. "Thus a belief in the Constitution and a refusal to discriminate against the Race was added to the 'un-American activities' to be investigated by the witch-hunt Dies committee," he lamented.[49] Lapin and the other black writers and leaders who most aggressively complained about the

Dies committee on these and similar points accused Dies of obstructing racial democracy, "perhaps consciously," as the *Defender* charged.[50]

While it is certainly the case that Dies effectively labeled anyone who so much as muttered "racial equality" as communist and therefore un-American, many of his black contemporaries seemed to overlook the ways in which he reflected an important element of what was becoming US racial democracy. Dies's attempt to block racial equality was not a barrier to the development of racial democracy as a doctrine, for such an assessment denies him a voice in its formation. It also assumes that racial democracy had to be more than denial or rhetoric. In fact, Dies and thinkers like him played a critical function in shaping racially inclusive nationalism in the United States—one that often privileged those uninterested in and even opposed to racial equality, and one that proved ill-equipped, even unable, to redress racial discrimination.

Because Dies concurred with the Fish committee's conclusions on the threat posed by black communism—that blacks were generally loyal but a potential red hotbed—racial dissuasion became one of his preferred anticommunist tools. Writing what could easily be confused with the words of Hamilton Fish, Dies was reassuring on the so-called slow progress of the CPUSA among blacks, declaring it "a tribute to the patriotism, loyalty and religion of the Negro" that the communists had not "succeeded to the extent expected." Indeed, Dies felt it important to "acknowledge with gratitude the refusal of the great majority of Negroes to be duped by the agents and ideologists of the ruthless dictator, Stalin." Still, he believed that vigilance and counterefforts were of the utmost importance: "Nevertheless it is undoubtedly true that much misunderstanding has been brought about by communist propaganda and activity among the Negroes. We cannot view with unconcern the future consequences of this destructive program of Moscow."[51]

Fearing increased communist headway in the black community, Dies tried to dissuade blacks from accepting communist doctrine. He cautioned that communist success in the United States "would plunge the Negro into slavery" and would reverse "the great gains he has made in the past century." Dies warned, "Communists take great pains to conceal from the Negroes the fact that Communism is materialistic and atheistic and opposed in principle and practice to Christianity. The Negro is told that Communism is the application of Christian teachings, and that he can embrace Communism without sacrificing his religion."[52] On the contrary, conversion to communism entailed converting to a political religion and relinquishing spiritual beliefs, Dies wrote.

Many in the government, including President Roosevelt, opposed the anticommunist inquiries of the Dies committee, and the heated debates about it often revolved around one of the few issues on which the committee and its opponents were surprisingly united: rhetorical racial democracy.[53] Yet there was no consensus on how to define racial democracy. Racial denialists like Dies characterized it loosely as "cooperation and a spirit of tolerance and good will," excluding, of course, terrifying notions like actual "social equality."[54] Several others, politically and/or morally against Dies's red-baiting, invoked the issue of racial democracy in their objections to the HCUA.

Referring in part to the committee's investigation of racial justice groups, Representative Joseph Shannon of Missouri argued from the House floor that the HCUA tried to "camouflage its racial prejudices and anti-labor feelings by going 'hog wild' on the subject of communism."[55] Representative Kent Keller of Illinois accused the Dies committee of arousing "suspicion, fear, resentment, distrust [and] prejudice" among the people, which was contrary to the country's needs: "What we do need . . . is the broadest possible tolerance along all lines [including] tolerance of religion[,] tolerance of race [and] tolerance of economic proposals."[56] By the end of the 1930s, the intense disputes over anticommunism frequently were about the nebulous notion of racial democracy, as anticommunists used it to defend against the communist menace, and opponents of anticommunists employed the doctrine to shield organizations that fought racism from the red-baiters. It is difficult to pinpoint exact, common features among the various visions of US racial democracy, except that they all articulated some ideal of racial inclusion and they all loosely defined racism as un-American.

High-profile anticommunists such as J. Edgar Hoover, Hamilton Fish Jr., and Martin Dies placed communist racial democracy as a top concern, since they understood that black recruitment was critical for the Comintern's revolutionary goals. Serious anticommunists like them found it difficult to exaggerate the danger this posed, for they believed, as Fish would write, that the communists' "stated, official intent was to overthrow our constitutional government through violence, [making] them a special—and worrisome—group."[57] State authorities in other agencies participated in anticommunist efforts as well. For instance, Fish's claims about CPUSA missions to collect confidential data on the army and navy led to a Justice Department and New York City Police raid on the alleged leader of this operation. Members of the military also attended Fish's official speech in which he summarized the state of

US communism and his committee's final recommendations to curb that threat.[58]

Dies, who constantly sought the limelight in his efforts, gladly carried on Fish's work, and despite the controversy surrounding his tactics, the press's coverage of his committee kept the fear of a red menace in the US psyche. A few months into the HCUA's hearings, 41 percent of those polled had not heard of the committee; that figure dropped to 28 percent the following year. Furthermore, when the committee came up for renewal in 1939, a Gallup Poll found that 53 percent of the public believed it should continue, including 74 percent of those who had an opinion on the subject and/or knowledge of the committee's work. A year later, 65 percent were in favor of continuation, or a whopping 91 percent of those who were neither undecided nor unfamiliar with the committee, showing the effectiveness of Dies's desire to convince the nation that communism should be taken seriously.[59]

By extension, if communism was public enemy number one, then Soviet racial democracy, which was meant to buttress the communist movement, was integral to the threat. Even the racist sensibilities of an anticommunist like Dies did not prevent him from recognizing that the outright rejection of the communists' racially inclusive ideals would play right into their hands. Those who countered anticommunist tactics also often used a nationalist perspective on race and democracy to do so, whether they set out to defend antiracism groups under siege or to engage the committees' stated position on racial questions. Thus, communism as an international conduit of racial democracy and perceived existential threat not only pulled the United States toward ideological racial democracy but also made odd bedfellows of many with otherwise very distinct racial beliefs.

In these debates on communism in the United States, many parties participated in shaping racial democracy. From those who believed in racial equality and pushed for the state to intervene on their behalf, to those who cringed at the thought of its repercussions, all fought for a voice, and the resulting rhetoric of racial democracy was nondescript enough for them all to use, progressives and conservatives alike. Anticommunism gave many racial conservatives a powerful stake and influential role in this process, allowing their denial and rhetorical positions to fit under the wide rubric of racially inclusive politics. People like Martin Dies were not obstructionists in the sense that they did not work to prevent racial democracy from becoming a part of national identity. Dies battled to help define racial democracy, and he was successful. In other words, although Dies was a racist, he promoted a vision of the nation that was racially inclusive but with severe limitations.[60] My intention is not to exonerate Dies but instead to critique the weakness of the ideology that he helped to develop. In large part, the rhetoric- and dissuasion-focused form of racial democracy overpowered action-oriented realism, reflected in the failure to pass antilynching legislation, for example. What materialized was a national identity that espoused racial pluralism but maintained the racist reality. At its core and through this process, racially inclusive theory became bound to racially exclusive practice.

ANTICOMMUNISM, DEMOCRACY, AND RACE UNDER VARGAS AND THE EARLY ESTADO NOVO

Brazilian state anticommunists did not wrestle with the racial implications of democracy on such a national and public level as their counterparts in the United States. Yet articulate racial democracy they did, even if the racial component of anticommunist discourse was much more subtle in Brazil during the 1930s. This subtlety cannot be confused with a lack of urgency, however, as the gravity of the national security question was much greater in Brazil after three serious communist insurrections in November 1935. Consequently, anything perceived as a benefit to the anticommunist cause took on significant weight in ways that Dies and Fish never experienced. The regime relied on denial to reinforce its democratic claims, and black anticommunists pressed authorities to adopt action-oriented realism. Regardless, the Vargas regime gave more attention to defending itself democratically than to defending itself racially.

In Brazil the year 1930 signaled the beginning of sustained, organized, and growing anticommunism. Before Getúlio Vargas's Revolution of 1930, anticommunists usually framed the threat of communism as foreign and exotic, one that had little chance of succeeding on the national scene.[61] However, after 1930 the coalition of conservatives and leftists that supported Vargas's coup began to look suspiciously upon one another. Conservatives in particular feared that the influence of leftists would overwhelm their own leverage. Debates over issues such as the potential recognition of the Soviet Union were heated and often resulted in red-baiting. Accusations that Vargas's regime was communist were clearly off the mark, which became abundantly clear after the repressive state response to the communist coups of 1935.[62]

The buildup to the 1935 insurrections and the state's subsequent crackdown were apparent at least by the second half of 1934, when leftists were clashing violently with the Brazilian fascist integralists and the police. The government attempted to control the *extremistas* and restore order through its National Security Law (LSN), submitted as a bill to Congress at the beginning of 1935 and signed into law on April 4. The National Liberation Alliance (ANL) emerged in part to oppose the LSN, and within months it had grown to more than one hundred thousand members.[63] The ANL was outlawed after expressing the desire to implement a National Revolutionary Popular Government. The government's reaction to the communist-led ANL military uprisings in Natal, Recife, and Rio de Janeiro in November of that year led to even harsher reprisal, thrusting the nation into a state of siege and vigorous political repression.[64]

The uprisings politically benefited the president, who was in a power struggle with the state oligarchies and was, as the Constitution of 1934 established, ineligible to run for president in 1938. In order to avoid leaving office at the end of his term, President Vargas exploited the revolts and a fabricated communist plot to manufacture a patriotically framed, fear-based, and oppressive anticommunist frenzy that made his eventual dictatorship a seemingly natural and sensible step. This anticommunist campaign introduced expanded federal powers, hardened the LSN, and initiated back-to-back states of national emergency, culminating in Vargas's Estado Novo (New State) dictatorship in 1937.[65] After the 1935 insurrections, Vargas called the first ever meeting of a president's cabinet to deal exclusively with communism. During a series of meetings, officials suggested that improving living conditions and addressing social discontent would weaken the leftist movement. The proposal to create a propaganda organ also came out of these historic meetings.[66] Thus, the propaganda machine that subsequently cranked out the state's message was meant to tackle the social issues the communists and ANL had capitalized on, which included racial concerns.

In its efforts to address the people's social grievances, the Brazilian government frequently invoked the language of democracy. Depicting the dictatorship as democratic was a top priority for many of its authorities and propagandists. It would be misleading, however, to suggest that communism was the only important factor that led the Vargas regime to espouse democracy while the state grew dictatorial. For instance, Francisco Campos—author and ideological architect of the Estado Novo Constitution, who also served as minister of education and then as minister of justice under Vargas—was writing about his authoritarian vision of democracy for Brazil well before the Bolshevik Revolution.[67] Nonetheless, as the state blamed the rollback of rights on the communists, it simultaneously reflected the latter's message that economic well-being must guide government policy, or what the communists defined as "authentic democracy."

The Estado Novo embarked on an anticommunist offensive that published and distributed pamphlets, books, magazines, and other literature directly to the public and through the press to discredit the movement and its democratic claims.[68] The Federal District Police Department's Serviço de Divulgação (Publicity Service) published a book about its "intense propaganda work . . . against subversive ideologies," bragging that the service had distributed "articles and communiqués" to its network of about 1,300 newspapers "spread throughout the entire national territory."[69] The Departamento Nacional de Propaganda (DNP, or National Department of Propaganda) also worked with "thousands of journals" and promised that "[e]ven in the most distant [Brazilian] land . . . the anticommunist campaign is felt in all its intensity." Bemoaning how the rosy narrative of communism had "deluded" a large number of Brazilians for years, the DNP believed this task of countering communist rhetoric and exposing the Soviet "reality" was critical for national security interests.[70]

The DNP's media blitz typified Brazilian propagandists' response to communist claims that Russia was the "freest of all democracies" and an egalitarian, inclusive society. In *Twenty Years of Tragic Experiment: The Truth about Soviet Russia,* the DNP lambasted the "falsity of red 'democracy'" and mocked Russian leaders who attempted to "demonstrate the 'democratic' character" of Russian elections. Not once did this chapter fail to place the word *democracy* in reference to Russia in quotation marks to suggest its fallacy. In the book, the DNP also scoffed at "red revolution" literature that presented Russia "as an earthly paradise, where men live happily, in equal conditions under the protection of an exemplary government [in] a country without . . . conflict of interests."[71] The central thesis of *Twenty Years of Tragic Experiment* was that such a vision of the Soviet Union was an absurd lie. The DNP children's book *O Brasil é bom* (Brazil is good) similarly engaged in the campaign to discredit the idea of a Soviet paradise. "What is communism?" the book asks. "Communism is evil. . . . It is a regime of slavery that reduced Russia to misery. Russia is an unhappy country," not heaven on earth.[72]

State anticommunists not only attacked the concept of Soviet democracy but also argued that Brazil itself was democratic, leading up to and during the dictatorship. In a 1936 speech on the Dia da Pátria (Day of the Homeland), which the DNP published as the pamphlet *Ordem e democracia* (Order and democracy), Vargas seemed to prepare the nation for the imminent dictatorship, already framing it as a necessary, new democratic order. Democracy, Vargas announced, could not be "rigid and immutable," impervious to change. Instead, Vargas insisted that democracy should be malleable, "reflecting social progress [and] aggressive resistance in order to defend itself when its legitimate fundamentals are threatened," especially by communists.[73] Even as rights and liberties were being rescinded, Vargas stressed that the state was always to be understood as preserving Brazilian democracy from the communist forces that he said sought to tear it down.

Another one of Vargas's 1936 speeches, also distributed as a pamphlet, warned the public that if the state failed to act decisively in the name of democracy, dire consequences would result. He recounted the outcry over the LSN and suggested that such acts had come to be justified by the "brutality" of the communist uprising. "Democracy is, certainly, the regime of liberty. But it would not even be a regime if this liberty could transform itself into an instrument of its own destruction." He added, also foreshadowing the Estado Novo, that the "fundamental task of the state is, today more than ever, its defense."[74] As he moved his government toward authoritarianism, Vargas argued that dangerous times mandated new rules. He maintained that democracy for democracy's sake threatened its very existence and that expanded state power at the cost of civil liberties was the only way to protect the Brazilian democratic way of life, its "regime of liberty," from communism.

Even after the Estado Novo dismantled Congress and the electoral process in 1937, the state continued to present the new government and the never legally ratified constitution as democracy at its best. Rodrigo Patto Sá Motta's pathbreaking study of Brazilian anticommunism shows how the dictatorship limited liberal-democratic and antiauthoritarian criticism of the Soviet Union in order to circumvent similar criticism of the Estado Novo.[75] However, it is also true that the state did not shy away from the idea of democracy; it actively used the term to characterize the Estado Novo. Claiming that classic liberalism was passé and no longer critical for a democratic society, Vargas's regime commandeered the communist viewpoint that true democracy rested on economic liberty, specifically, as well as equality and freedom for all, more generally. Labeling the Estado Novo as new and improved democracy, the dictatorship sustained this rhetorical contortionism as part of its anticommunist discourse until redemocratization in 1945.

The author of the Estado Novo Constitution, Francisco Campos, invoked communism in his defense of the 1937 coup and swore that Brazil had been on the verge of a civil war largely due to skyrocketing tensions that communists had caused. Campos argued that the old liberal democracy was incapable of confronting these challenges, whereas the Estado Novo's more modern, "substantive," and less "formal" variation of democracy could. The 1937 constitution instituted democratic values more broadly than the previous constitutions, Campos maintained, and he also said that the essence of democracy rested not in systematic procedures like universal suffrage or in rules like term limits but in the fulfillment of the people's social needs. Campos—who articulated these ideas in an interview that was reported in the newspapers—believed that the older Brazilian democracies had failed to recognize this and had prioritized democratic methods over democratic realities, a flaw the Estado Novo had corrected.[76]

The 1939 Estado Novo Exposition boasted about everything new the dictatorship represented: the New State and the new constitution with its "new democratic character," including the "new concept of democracy" that had abandoned "the formalism of the old liberalism." Through the exposition, authorities hoped to clarify the "confusion" that existed "even among eminent journalists" about the difference between a "representative regime and (a) democracy," contending that "popular consensus," a democratic benchmark, manifested "not only through full elections." The exposition presented the Estado Novo as more democratic than liberalism in that it respected "the creative initiative of individuals" by interpreting their feelings directly instead of through the banned political parties. In fact, the Estado Novo told the public that it served the "common good" and that the former "individualistic democracy['s]" failures had made Brazil susceptible to "class strife."[77] *Brazil Is Good* advanced a similar argument; the new constitution "conserved the democratic spirit in Brazil," suppressed the "old evils that were threatening" the country, and realized national unity "as was never before possible."[78] In other words, the Estado Novo message was that the dictatorship more successfully embodied popular consensus, the heart of democracy, than formal representative government.

The 1939 Estado Novo Exposition also interlaced its populist democracy propaganda with communist-like notions of economic liberty while claiming to guarantee these ideals more fully than communism or Brazil's traditional liberalism. Indeed, pre-coup individual market competition had "translated into, in fact, the subjection of the weakest (in favor) of some privileged classes." To demonstrate the Estado Novo's abolition of these past injustices, the exposition highlighted the dictator's labor interventions and social legislation as democratic actions that had "stripped many pretexts of communist agitation."[79] Similarly, *Brazil Is Good* claimed that under the Estado Novo, there were "no more class divisions, because *equality* between capital and labor, between the boss and the worker was established with the creation of the Justice of Labor."[80] And equality, the Estado Novo Exposition confirmed, was the concept upon which "the essence of democracy reside[d]."[81]

Although the Estado Novo appropriated the communists' economic message, the dictatorship also mirrored the US nationalist narrative and its "pull yourself up by your own bootstraps" ideology. The same chapter in *Brazil Is Good* that portrayed communism as evil also described Brazil under the Estado Novo as a country of self-made men, where economic opportunity was unlimited for anyone with the drive and desire. The book juxtaposed the "misery" in Russia—a land of no prosperity, where a boy who wanted to be an engineer could be forced to work as a coal miner—with the freedom in Brazil, a nation whose people chose their professions. "Brazil is a rich country [where] any man can become wealthy with honest work, initiative, and creative capacity. . . . For this reason, Brazil is good," young readers were told.[82] Therefore, the DNP advertised the Estado Novo's economic democracy as an unusual combination of the competitive, liberal, capitalist economy with the communist-leaning "*equality* between capital and labor" paradigm seen above.

The Brazilian state also responded directly to communist discourse of racial democracy, entering into a propaganda battle over which nation was the real racial paradise, the Soviet Union or Brazil. The Brazilians countered communist racial declarations with three main strategies, which overlapped in many ways with those of the United States. Racial denialists rejected communist assertions that Brazil was anything less than a racial utopia vastly superior to the Soviet Union. As other chapters in this study show, when racism was exposed in Brazil, officials often singled out foreign perpetrators, complaining that they did not know or respect the Brazilian way. This explanation branded racial prejudice as just as alien to Brazilian culture as communism itself. Thus, racial denialists in the 1930s did not bother prescribing solutions to racist practices since they did not regard them as a Brazilian problem. Operating in tandem with denial was racial obstructionism, which in Brazil typically constituted blocking communist racial democracy propaganda from entering the public sphere. Obstructionism involved confiscating or banning so-called communist literature with racial emphases and the arrest of persons perceived as advocates of communist racial propaganda. Finally, anticommunist authorities attempted to dissuade Afro-Brazilians specifically from joining communist ranks, and they collaborated with black leaders to do so. With these components of official anticommunism, the Brazilian government tried to protect the country's reputation as a racially tolerant society.

In its promotion of racial denial, the Estado Novo maintained that the economic equality and liberty its democracy secured better than past regimes assured Brazilian racial justice as well. Estado Novo propaganda did not always state outright that racial inequalities were more pronounced in the former Brazilian democracies, but it certainly made the suggestion. For instance, *Brazil Is Good* praised the dictatorship for ending "class divisions" and argued that under the Estado Novo, Brazil tolerated "no racial divisions, since only merit grants the privilege of social ascension."[83] Because the Estado Novo claimed to have corrected the past economic subjugation of the masses, the possibility of upward social mobility among all races based on meritocracy alone must also have been a new phenomenon of its making. Here, state anticommunist literature reflected the manner in which communists defined democracy as an economic structure that was racially inclusive.

Getúlio Vargas himself invoked denial and a defiant image of Brazilian racial democracy as part of his anticommunist message. In a telling 1936 speech given weeks after the communist uprising, Vargas used racial democracy as a way to declare Brazil's society and government superior to that of its Soviet counterparts. The speech—reprinted as a pamphlet and excerpted on a poster—compared the two countries. Likely in a broadcast over state radio, Vargas said that communism enslaved its people by "treat[ing] man as an instrument" whose sole purpose was to work. "The contrary should be our objective," Vargas continued. "Our objective prepares man to be useful to himself and to society so that, living jointly with other men, he loves them without egotisms and without prejudices of class or racial superiority."[84] In this speech, Vargas constructed Brazilian racial democracy in opposition to an oppressive Soviet and communist "other." He classified the lack of racial prejudice as an anticommunist characteristic, as evidence of the freedom that people experienced in a nation that respected them as humans and not merely as labor. According to Vargas, then, racial democracy was a Brazilian "objective" that was "contrary" to communist goals. By locating Brazilian ideals within an antiracist value system in this important speech, Vargas's anticommunism presented those attracted to the communist platform of class and racial democracy with an appealing alternative. In doing so, he also repaired Brazil's image that had been damaged by the communists' unflattering racial portrayals.

Another important aspect of the state's anticommunist racial democracy was obstructionism. Censorship of all things communist was not the only goal here; the regime also demanded a positive image of the government. The administration believed that voices of opposition threatened homogeneity of thought, an Estado Novo priority. Thus, the Department of Press and Propaganda (or DIP), the Department of Political and Social Order (the political police, or DOPS), and the Ministry of Education were all charged with the tasks of "ideological sanitation" and the control of knowledge.[85] For example, Brazilian citizens could be incarcerated simply for distributing communist literature.[86] The state clearly understood the power of the word to manipulate worldviews and principles, and since authorities persecuted communists most doggedly, communist racial discourse was targeted as well. In fact, every communist pamphlet or flyer with racial content cited in the previous chapter was confiscated by the state in an attempt to remove the communists' racial propaganda from society.

Among the racially charged literature that the state confiscated were lyrics to "subversive" communist hymns that mentioned the plight of blacks in Brazil or hailed communism as the only way to bring about true racial democracy. The majority of lyrics seized called upon the people to unite against the ruling "tyrants" and preached that equality and liberty should extend to everyone in, as one song placed it, a "free land of free brothers!"[87] Some communist songs specified that "free brothers" (and sisters) were multiracial, such as the "National Anthem of the Poor Brazilian" quoted in the epigraph to this chapter. Calling all comrades to join the battle against exploitation and for "bread, earth, and liberty," which was the communist slogan, the second stanza described the racial vision for the movement: "The wind of revolt sweeps America; Blacks, Indians, pariahs; . . . Indeed, all the proletarian masses." Set to the tune of the Brazilian national anthem, the hymn represented the nationalist and multiracial character of the communist movement.[88]

Brazilian authorities also obstructed the dissemination of fiction that they considered to have communist racial subtexts. This was especially the case with the books of prolific young novelist Jorge Amado, whose leftist politics penetrated his stories about the struggles of typically black or *mulato* workers and highlighted their cultural practices. Amado's valorization of Afro-Brazilian culture, his exposure of the injustices workers faced, and his sometimes socialist themes led to the government's infamous 1937 burning of his books, which had been determined to be communist propaganda. Among these Amado books were 808 copies of *Capitães da areia*, 223 copies of *Mar morto*, and 267 copies of *Jubiabá*, all of which focus on the lives of the subaltern classes in Bahia, a hub of Afro-Brazilian life and culture.[89]

Perhaps the most severe acts of racial obstructionism were not the state's removal of literature from the streets but its removal of people who advocated communist racial democracy. Isaltino Veiga dos Santos—who had helped to launch the FNB with his brother Arlindo and other black activists in 1931—likely was the highest profile black prisoner in this regard. Santos briefly served as FNB secretary-general, the second highest-ranking position, and he met with Getúlio Vargas on behalf of the organization in 1933.[90] As we saw in chapter 1, blacks in the United States knew of Santos's imprisonment and rallied for his release. Santos was a political prisoner for over a year, and he remained under the state's surveillance after his liberation.[91] During his incarceration, Santos, his family, and a police deputy friend wrote letters to authorities declaring his innocence. These letters and the political police's reports on Santos's leftist activities provide a window into the anticommunist campaign targeting the black population as well as the relationship between state and black anticommunism.

In 1933 Santos was expelled from the FNB. Although scholars have not pinpointed the exact reason for this, it seems he was at odds with the other leaders.[92] Soon thereafter, this black activist who had espoused conservative views and collaborated with police on communist repression was himself in communist circles, working as a journalist for the leftist paper *A Platéa* and signing the Popular Front for Liberty's manifesto.[93] The São Paulo State Office of Political and Social Order (DEOPS), or the political police, reported that Luís Carlos Prestes founded the Popular Front for Liberty after the ANL had been abolished.[94] Authorities also said that Santos established the Federação Nacional dos Negros do Brasil (National Federation of the Blacks of Brazil), an organization about which little is known, but one that

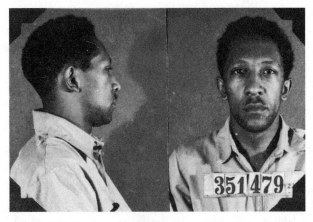

FIGURE 2. Mug shot of political prisoner Isaltino Veiga dos
Santos, taken in 1936. Courtesy of the Arquivo Público do
Estado de São Paulo.

officials believed merged his racial politics with his leftist affiliations.[95]
Alienated from the right-leaning FNB, Santos may not have become a
genuine communist or sympathizer, but he did turn into an enemy of the
state because of his ties to the Left.

Santos was thrown into the infamous São Paulo jail for political prisoners, Maria Zélia, on November 28, 1935—the day after state militias
quelled the nation's communist insurrections.[96] Santos was detained for
signing the manifesto, posting communist propaganda in the streets, and
working among union activists for the communist cause, claims that
historian Petrônio Domingues finds suspect.[97] Most significant for the
purposes of this analysis, the DEOPS accused Santos of trying to recruit
Afro-Brazilians to communism and the ANL. The São Paulo political
police told DOPS, the federal office in Rio, that after joining the ANL,
Santos had "soon tried to regiment *all of the elements of color* around
that [Communist] Party, organizing, to better meet his goals, the Federation of the Blacks."[98] Another undated memo stated that he organized
the federation with the "intention to maneuver the elements of color,
carrying them" to the ANL.[99] For the political police, then, Santos represented blacks' potential susceptibility to the ANL. As a result, the
state's racial anticommunism manifested as obstructionism, demanding
that Santos and his so-called communist agenda be removed from the
streets in order to protect national security. The accused repeatedly
stated that he was not a communist, and he wrote multiple letters to different authorities declaring his innocence.

The prisoner's letters and those of his family are important reminders that the state's racial anticommunism did not develop without the input of blacks, who both validated and challenged it. Preeminent black anticommunist leaders helped construct the state's narrative about the spread of communist influence among the Afro-Brazilian population, and they were proactive racial dissuaders. However, black activists' realist interpretation of Brazilian racism and its role in adding to communism's appeal contradicted the regime's denial.

In their letters to authorities, Isaltino Veiga dos Santos and his brother Arlindo vindicated the need for the state's racial obstructionism, which ironically had led to Isaltino's arrest, by detailing energetic communist recruitment tactics among a vulnerable black population. The brothers' defense of Isaltino relied upon his portrayal as a dedicated anticommunist soldier in a milieu that required his dissuasion. Isaltino wrote: "I am not a communist, very much the opposite, I always combated and will continue to combat [communism]."[100] In another letter, he told the political police superintendent that since 1932 he had worked with Arlindo and others "in the repression of communism" through their short-lived League against Communism. He added that the group continued "this patriotic campaign" through the FNB, its journal *A Voz da Raça* (The voice of the race), and various events they set up to show "the perniciousness of such a repellent creed."

Isaltino indicated that the police were active contributors to some of these efforts as well. Although he never worked in the police department, despite his desire to, Isaltino stated that he "provided [them with] reports of the names and addresses of people that we suspected exercised extremist activities," adding that the majority were foreigners—in other words, not black.[101] (This last point is reminiscent of A. Philip Randolph and Walter White's discursive gymnastics about communism among blacks, implying that it simultaneously was and was not a matter of serious concern. Similar to US black anticommunists, Isaltino also emphasized his own Catholic faith and that of Afro-Brazilians as another barrier to communism.) To verify his claims that he had, in fact, worked with the police to repress communism, Isaltino urged the superintendent to contact São Paulo's Deputy of "Vagrancy Repression," a longtime family friend.[102]

When his letter-writing campaign failed to secure his release after more than two months in the miserable prison, Isaltino wrote directly to the friend and deputy, offering additional information about his situation. In his letter, Isaltino explained that his alliance with the Left had everything to do with patriotism and racial pride and nothing to do with communist sympathies. He told Deputy Armando Caiuby that although his plan had failed and backfired, his leftist pursuits were a plot to infiltrate the communist movement. He stated that he had signed the Popular Front manifesto "for the defense of my race, and consequently my country, precisely because the majority of the elements of the race, [are always lured by] those who want to exploit their eternal discontent, and therefore I infiltrated, to take a position in order to benefit the race, as I always have."[103] After receiving Santos's letter, Caiuby wrote to DEOPS superintendent Botelho to corroborate the story about their partnership in racial dissuasion. Caiuby wrote: "Isaltino and Arlindo helped me a lot in the repression of communism. They were combative elements of the 'League Against Communism' in 1932 and 1933. . . . I know he is not communist."[104]

In his petition for his brother's release, Arlindo Veiga dos Santos, former FNB president, wrote that Isaltino's work in dissuasion had frustrated the work of communists desperate to enlist blacks into the movement. Arlindo reported that the brothers had disseminated "anti-socialist and anti-Bolshevik propaganda, through the Frente Negra Brasileira," bragging that their actions "were great refractors to [communist] ideas seeking to infiltrate the national Black People." He explained that communists, anxiously in search of "an agent for the blacks," had become "disheartened" because these dissuasion efforts were successful. Arlindo maintained that the "agent for the blacks" was not Isaltino, declaring emphatically, "HE IS NOT A COMMUNIST."[105]

By presenting themselves as experts on the communist status quo, Arlindo, Isaltino, and like-minded blacks forged a space for their voices to be heard by those who determined both state anticommunist and racial policy. The Santos brothers and other members of the FNB worked with police on multiple occasions, allowing them to educate authorities on the state of communism among the black population, and giving them an upper hand in their rivalry with black leftist radicals. Black anticommunist dissuaders provided accounts that underscored the need for obstructionism and a vigilant eye among blacks, even when they characterized Afro-Brazilians as generally patriotic. Anticommunism gave these blacks an opportunity to affect not only how authorities perceived black communism but also what they knew about Afro-Brazilian organizations and politics.

We see evidence of the Santos brothers' and especially Arlindo's influence in Deputy Caiuby's letter when he explained that the FNB's program "was patrianovismo. As a 'patrianovista' Isaltino, his brother Dr. Arlindo and all the blacks"—including the entire Santos family, whom he knew "well"—wanted the return to power of the imperial family, Caiuby wrote. He reassured the superintendent that this was "a conservative program."[106] However, even though he was president of the Frente until 1934 and, according to Paulina Alberto, he continued to "set the tone for . . . the Frente's projection of its ideology to members nationwide," Arlindo's passionate *patrianovismo* was controversial among FNB leaders and apparently was incomprehensible to the rank and file.[107] In just one of many indicators of the organization's ideological schisms, Isaltino told the police in his postarrest statement that he had left the FNB because he disagreed with his brother on reinstating the monarchy. Cauiby may not have gotten all the details right or he may have fibbed to help a friend, but his presumed awareness of the entire Santos family's political beliefs shows that he discussed politics with them and learned about their viewpoints. Arlindo, cofounder and onetime president of the Ação Imperial Patrianovista Brasileira (Brazilian Imperial Patrianovista Action), appears to have been particularly influential as Caiuby demonstrated an Arlindo-centric grasp of the FNB's political philosophy. Due to his level of professional and social intimacy with the family—he also wrote that Isaltino and his family often frequented his home—it is impossible that Caiuby's interactions with the brothers did not shape his impressions of FNB politics specifically and black politics in general.[108]

The manner that Isaltino approached his relationship with Deputy Caiuby reflects the classic patterns of Brazilian patronage. A ubiquitous practice throughout the nation, patronage was key to Brazilians' survival or upward mobility, especially for those in economically and socially precarious positions. For many blacks struggling with financial instability, building relationships with more powerful people who could offer assistance in times of need was essential.[109] This seems to have been the case with Isaltino and Deputy Caiuby. We know that Isaltino was in an extreme predicament after leaving the FNB because the Frente had provided much of his livelihood, perhaps even housing. His brother wrote that Isaltino "was in an awful economic situation; unemployed, suffering from the consequences of that." Caiuby mentioned that when Isaltino left the FNB, he "looked for me every month for work." Isaltino reminded Caiuby in his letter that he had requested a post with the political police "to better develop my repression of communism work."[110] Evidently such a job with the police did not materialize, which may explain why Isaltino moved to leftist ranks where he was able to secure employment.[111]

These letters offer a glimpse into the world of anticommunist-based patronage that other blacks also must have inhabited, allowing them to contribute to the state's anticommunist racial democracy as well. Isaltino utilized anticommunism to strengthen his bond with would-be *patrão* (patron) Caiuby, hoping the deputy would come through with a job when he was desperate, and asking him to intervene with the DEOPS superintendent when he was in trouble. Although we do not know the scale of such practices of patronage as it relates to black anticommunism, Isaltino could not have been the only Afro-Brazilian who attempted to use the communist scare to establish comparable partnerships as a means of survival. Whether these blacks adopted similar lines of dissuasion or contradicted the Santos brothers is uncertain, but it is inconceivable that other blacks—including those on the state's payroll— did not influence official racial anticommunism in many ways.

If the Santos brothers' dissuasion validated the state's need for obstructionism, the family's racial realism diverged greatly from official denial and even questioned the government's democratic promises. Both Isaltino and Arlindo were unequivocal in their assessment that it was blacks' unique material and social circumstances that rendered them dangerously susceptible to communist racial democracy. In a letter cited briefly above and quoted more fully here, Isaltino wrote that "the majority of the elements of the race, failing to possess necessary instruction, much less a broad vision from a political-social point of view, [are always lured by] those who want to exploit their eternal discontent." Arlindo's defense of his brother made a similar observation but identified Isaltino as the misguided soul. Isaltino was among communists, Arlindo insisted, because he was "equipped with precarious self-taught knowledge" that made him "[in]capable of distinguishing between good and bad principles when they present themselves." Thus, the brothers chronicled a deficient educational system that underserved the black population and facilitated the communists' ability to "deceiv[e] so many," in Arlindo's words.[112] The solution, Arlindo and Isaltino implied, was that the government's anticommunist plan had to eradicate institutionalized inequalities that disproportionately affected blacks.

Arlindo also detailed Isaltino's compromised "psychological state," triggered by his unemployment, to show how racial discrimination and its deleterious economic impact played into the hands of communists. Arlindo wrote that after Isaltino left the FNB, he had been hired for "a job in a large <u>foreign</u> company" based on a friend's reference, "without, however the bosses having personally met him [and therefore not] knowing that he was black." Continuing his Freyre-esque rhetoric that outsiders were responsible for racism in Brazil, Arlindo quipped, "[c]ertainly the illustrious Aryan guests of our country did not want a black person in their offices. They made up an <u>excuse</u> and they did not take him." According to Arlindo, this disappointment and the other misfortunes he was suffering made his naïve, patriotic, and desperate brother powerless to the communists who "would easily deceive one more." If Isaltino really was performing a mole operation, his brother seemed to have been left in the dark, as Arlindo argued that Isaltino did not know he was engaged with communists.[113]

Isaltino's wife, Filena, added to the family's realism as its boldest voice, holding the government accountable for ameliorating black socioeconomic woes and therefore for fulfilling its responsibilities as a democracy. Filena protested her husband's detention and claimed that the political police had no concrete evidence against him. She told of the "moral and material harm [and] distressing deprivations" that her husband's imprisonment was causing the family. Beyond Isaltino's wrongful incarceration, she implicated the government in her grim situation: "[C]omplete abject poverty is closing in, something a modern state that has as its principle function the protection of large and poor families [such as ours] cannot allow to happen." In fact, so ominous were Filena's circumstances that the following words were added at the bottom of the letter she had dictated: Sent "[w]ithout a stamp since the supplicant finds herself without resources."[114] Filena's sharp assertions that the shame for her predicament fell in the government's lap undermined the state's racial denial as well as its democratic proclamations leading up to the dictatorship. Democracy under Vargas was supposed to have disproved communist accusations about the inadequacies of the regime and assertions of the superiority of communist racial democracy. Filena's realism seems to have proved the communists right.

Like Filena, Isaltino also guilted authorities in his letters to them, specifically racializing Filena's demands that the government honor its democratic promises. On the anniversary of abolition, he evoked emotionally the "mãe negra, who cradled infant Brazil [and] represents my own [mother], who cries inconsolably every moment to see me" in prison. In a letter to the prison director, Isaltino described himself as "a black Brazilian who has never lied to his country, [a nation that] has already cost the blood of his grandparents," a clear reference to slavery.[115] Isaltino contended that blacks deserved and required special attention because of their historical sacrifices and the fragile place in

Brazilian society that made them vulnerable to communism. It was not just the state's democratic duty; it was the job of a regime that advertised national security as its top priority.

The Santos brothers' dissuasion offensive was based on the narrative of an ever-present communist threat in the black community, a narrative that they and likely other black anticommunists shared with the police. This is to suggest not that Afro-Brazilians brought about the state's suspicion of blacks but rather that they sought and, in at least a few instances, obtained access to authorities, providing input on the situation. Yet whereas the Santos family painted a raw and uncensored portrait of Brazil's racial reality, the state told a cheerfully denialist story and obstructed communist messages and messengers that said otherwise. The Santos family argued that racial dissuasion as an anticommunist tactic would be impotent if it remained unaccompanied by an action-oriented economic and social policy to reverse the effects of racism. More specifically, the Santos brothers felt that adequate education and strong occupational opportunities to elevate the quality of life for blacks must be assimilated in the state's anticommunist agenda. They implied that such an action-oriented plan would help generate a natural immunity to communism among blacks.

Ironically, education, economic improvements, and labor laws were keystones of the Vargas regime's self-defined democracy before and during the Estado Novo.[116] Black realism subverted the democratic image Vargas constructed in opposition to the communist model, and blacks pressured the state to bring action-oriented democracy to fruition in a racially conscious way. Wherever the state wavered, the Santos family warned, communists could strike.

During the 1930s, state agents of anticommunism in Brazil and the United States perceived communism as an interracial revolution intent on overthrowing the government. As a result, they viewed communist portrayals of Soviet racial democracy and their focus on racial inequality in each country as subversive propaganda. Authorities countered with varying strategies of anticommunist racial democracy of their own, ranging from action-oriented calls for true racial justice in the case of Hamilton Fish Jr. to Martin Dies's and the Vargas regime's statements that denied the existence of a racial problem altogether. The anticommunist state under Vargas was especially keen to manufacture a democratic ideology to cloak his dictatorship, telling Brazilians that Vargas's new, modern democracy brought greater security as well as social and economic equality for all. In the United States, the society's point of weakness was its infamous and violent racial discrimination, which proved to be a huge thorn in the side of the anticommunist campaign. Finally, despite the realism of blacks who inextricably linked antiracist policy and anticommunism, the non-action-oriented strand of denial dominated official anticommunist racial democracy in these countries. These racial nationalisms embraced inclusive ideals even as they failed to incorporate racial justice as a goal.

CHAPTER 3

Presaging the War

Racial Democracy and Fascism in the 1930s

For the proponents of liberal democracy who fought communism in the 1930s, fascism was another sign that the only democratic model they acknowledged was in crisis. While they deemed fascism an existential threat to democracy, fascists, like the communists, begged to differ and presented what they claimed was a better democratic paradigm. Thus, this chapter provides more historical evidence to support political theorist C. B. Macpherson's observation that democracy became "ambiguous [with] opposite meanings" for several decades after the First World War.[1] As discussed in the introduction, Macpherson did not regard fascist regimes as democratic, and the following pages do not legitimize the notion of fascist democracy in the least. Yet fascists were important interlocutors in the conversations about democracy at this volatile moment, and their words and actions radically altered the way that it was defined, especially in terms of race.

Adolf Hitler's relationship to the idea of democracy and the racial order in the United States was quite complex. Hitler said that democracy was worthless, but he defended his National Socialist German Workers' Party as a democratic movement, one that was more fitting for countries like Germany and Brazil than the US counterpart. And these declarations were not just about advancing nonliberal democracy; at times the Third Reich catered to liberal sensibilities as well. For instance, Nazis chose to hold numerous referenda, only to rig the vote, in order to construct a democratic facade in the liberal mold.[2] Hitler also frequently referred to the Western nations' racial discrimination and inequality as liberal democratic hypocrisy at its best, while his government's jurists respected and researched US race legislation for their deliberations over drafting Nazi exclusionary laws.

Prominent US fascist Lawrence Dennis, a black man passing as white, also pointed to the state-sanctioned mistreatment of people of color in the United States to declare that the democratic emperor had no clothes. As an advocate of multiracial fascism, Dennis may have been unique among his US political cohort, but this position was a mainstay in Brazil's very popular fascist movement, the Ação Integralista Brasileira (Brazilian Integralist Action), or AIB. The AIB's racial philosophy contained strong anti-Semitic and anti-Japanese strands, but integralism did not propagate racist doctrine broadly, and the party condemned Nazi "racial imperialism."

In both the United States and Brazil, blacks intensified the spotlight on German fascism to upgrade and centralize racial considerations in the political debates.[3] Before the Nazis' genocidal nature became common knowledge, blacks expressed their dissatisfaction with the status quo by suggesting that the United States and Brazil were at least as racially oppressive as Germany. For example, as Glenda Gilmore has shown, the writings of the US black press in the early 1930s belie the common belief that US citizens were ignorant about Nazi persecution at the time. The US black community fought to sound the alarm about the increasingly horrific developments in Germany. In addition, US black journalism elucidated the African American strategy to compare "Jim Crow with Nazi oppression to unsettle white supremacy's place in a democratic system."[4] In Brazil the black community's analysis was more varied, with at least one controversial but powerful and influential leader actually looking to Nazism for solutions to Brazil's entrenched racial discrimination. Overall, the indictments that these black democratic theorists issued undercut the moral standing both states sought during the escalating racial political crisis.

Fascism's reverberations upon the racial meanings of democracy—particularly in regard to state rhetoric—predictably were stronger after the United States and Brazil entered the war, as we will see in chapters 5 through 7. Neither the Vargas nor the Roosevelt administrations made many specific public pronouncements about racial democracy in relation to fascism during most of the 1930s, which may seem surprising in retrospect. While these states were slow to respond with words, domestic and international racial political discourse was changing rapidly nonetheless. This chapter focuses on fascism's impact on the shifting rhetorical landscape of the 1930s, reserving the examination of the states' responses to fascism for the chapters that examine the 1940s, when the Brazilian and US governments joined the debate in earnest. It is in those chapters that the fascist-related deployment of the four racial democracy categories will be discussed. For now, we begin with the first several years after the twentieth century's most infamous fascist came to power.

HITLER SPEAKS ON RACE AND DEMOCRACY IN EUROPE, THE UNITED STATES, AND BRAZIL

The speeches of Adolf Hitler demonstrated how the world's dominant fascist leader tackled the issue of democracy. In addition to the obvious, such as his dictatorial reign and the Third Reich's execution of six million Jews, an assessment of Hitler's speeches in the 1930s makes it easy to understand why he has been viewed as an opponent of democracy. In fact, to a large extent, Hitler was a self-labeled antidemocrat. He freely referred to what would become the Allied nations as "the democracies" and marked his National Socialist government as antithetical. For instance, in a 1932 speech perceived as one of Hitler's "greatest triumphs" in his quest for power, Hitler assured the German public that "democracy will in practice lead to the destruction of a people's true values." The "rule of the people" was problematic because it barred a nation's intelligent minority, the "most capable individuals," from governing in order to create space for "the chance majority." In Hitler's view, this system of government guaranteed "the rule of stupidity, mediocrity [and] inadequacy." In 1936 Hitler would, as he did incessantly, reiterate this interpretation of liberalism: "the principle of democracy . . . wherever it is allowed practical effect, is the principle of destruction."[5]

Ironically, as Nazis vilified other nations' embrace of democracy, Hitler simultaneously praised his National Socialism as more democratic than the Western regimes. There are many examples of these assertions in Hitler's speeches. In some of them, Hitler appealed to the very liberal democratic standards of representative democracy that he labeled as destructive to make his case. In 1935—after adding the title of president to his chancellorship, roles that should have been held by two people—Hitler addressed the German Parliament. He conveyed his weariness of hearing the "Anglo-Saxon countries [express] regret that Germany should have departed just from those principles of democratic government which such countries consider as specially sacred." Referencing the fact that he and the National Socialist Party originally took legal steps to attain power, Hitler derided this opinion as being "based upon serious error," for "Germany too has a 'democratic' constitution. The present German Government of the National Socialist State has also been elected by the people and feels itself in the same way responsible to the people." At the end of 1938, Hitler again reminded the public that "[u]nder the rules of Parliamentary Democracy I obtained the absolute majority of votes and today," he exaggerated, "I have the unanimous support of the German people." This, he said, was "Democracy in our eyes."[6]

Echoes of this populist sentiment, consciously framed as democratic, abound in other speeches. In 1934 Hitler insisted that if "democracy should be but the executor of the will of the people, then we are better democrats than our opponents in most of the so-called democracies in the world." In 1935 he proclaimed that "people talk of democracies and dictatorships, and they have completely failed to realize that in this country an upheaval has taken place the result of which—if democracy is to have any meaning at all—must be called in the highest sense of the word democratic."[7] Part of this nominal democratic upheaval was the replacement of Germany's deadlocked and malfunctioning Weimar parliamentary system with the Führer state that Hitler promised better served Germans. The omnipresent Nazi motto, *"Ein Volk, Ein Reich, Ein Führer"* (one nation/people, one empire, one leader), symbolized Hitler merging with the homogeneous, "pure" Aryan race.[8] With this merger, the Führer represented the will of the German people and, according to Nazi ideology, a new and better democratic paradigm. Historian Nicholas O'Shaughnessy has written that the five rigged referenda Hitler held before the war also helped construct the myth of the Führer as the "medium who divined the deeper thoughts of the masses and embodied them in dynamic action." O'Shaughnessy argues that both the referenda and the myth were "part of a new concept of acclamatory democracy," one in which rhetoric, mass rallies, and the Führer as "seer of the public will" were elements of a novel Nazi democracy far superior to the Weimar Republic and other liberal regimes.[9]

To those who disputed Nazi democratic assertions, Hitler asked, "What is democracy then after all?" He questioned the authority of Western powers to unilaterally define democracy and claim it as their own: "Who has the right to speak in the name of democracy? Has the good God handed over to Mr. Churchill . . . the key to democracy?"

Hitler disturbed antifascists around the world with his description of the Third Reich's annexations of Austria and Sudetenland (a German-majority area of Czechoslovakia) as evidence of his title as "Arch-Democrat." He contended that as "Arch-Democrat" he had "not over-thrown two democracies but [had] overthrown two dictatorships," after failing "to persuade [them] to introduce for their subjects the right of self-determination by the way of Democracy." In other words, the annexations were Germany's effort "to establish Democracy in these countries, that is, to give freedom to the oppressed."[10]

Another nation that Hitler allegedly targeted as the perfect candidate to be "freed" by Nazi rule was Brazil. Hitler supposedly rendered untenable the relationship between the United States and Brazil and argued for Nazi influence in Latin America's largest country. Nazi exile Hermann Rauschning's 1939 book *Hitler Speaks*—widely cited by con-temporaries as a glimpse into Hitler's private thoughts and plans—included a conversation between the Führer and a "trusted, leading member of the S.A. [paramilitary group who] had just returned from South America" in 1933. In his book, Rauschning testified that Hitler asked many questions about Brazil and articulated his intentions to "create a new Germany there."

In *Hitler Speaks,* the Führer was confident that the Brazilians not only "will need us if they are going to make anything of their country" but also were "fed up with" the unreliable United States that only sought to "exploit" them.[11] Whereas the North Americans simply offered "invest-ment capital," Germany could also furnish the more useful "spirit of enterprise," "organizing ability," and Nazi "philosophy." Accordingly, the Brazilians would be emboldened to renounce an obligatory accep-tance of US-style government. "If ever there is a place where democracy is senseless and suicidal," Hitler allegedly stated, "it is in South America." The Führer was quoted as saying that with German support, Brazilians would develop the strength to follow "their own instincts" and "throw both their liberalism and their democracy overboard"; otherwise, Brazil-ians would continue to "think they must still give lip-service to democ-racy." Regardless of the veracity of Rauschning's account, his influential book constructed a narrative in which Hitler framed the United States and its democracy as completely ill-suited for the Brazilian (and South American) context.[12] Both US and Brazilian officials would take note of Rauschning's exposé during the war, and as we will explore in chapter 6, a more racialized version of this message would make up a critical ele-ment of Nazi wartime propaganda in Brazil.

Hitler had strong opinions about the racial ideals that undergirded liberal democracy. In the 1932 speech referred to earlier that was credited with helping to secure his political base, Hitler was shocked that democracy did not account for any "essential difference in value," at least in theory, "between negroes [sic], Aryans, Mongolians, and Redskins." Hitler was dumbfounded that democratic and internationalist beliefs were "carried to such lengths that in the end a negro [sic] can sit as president in the sessions of the League of Nations." For Hitler this constituted distressing proof of the denial of and disrespect for the innate "differences in value" that should distinguish the races from one another.[13]

As he derided these principles of racial equality, Hitler also used them to expose the pretense of Western countries, especially the United States. In 1939 Franklin Roosevelt sent telegrams to Hitler and Mussolini appealing for peace, in part expressing dismay that Ethiopia had lost its independence. Hitler's response was to recall the history of the African continent: "As for the fact . . . that one nation in Africa is alleged to have lost its freedom—that too is but an error—for . . . practically all the previous inhabitants of this continent have been made subject to the sovereignty of the other nations by bloody force, thereby losing their freedom. Moroccans, Berbers, Arabs, negroes [sic], &c., have all fallen a victim to foreign might, the swords of which, however, were not inscribed 'Made in Germany,' but 'Made by democracies.'"[14] Hitler often stated that racism and democracy historically had gone hand in hand.

The Nazis questioned the United States' democratic standing because of its racial record, even while the regime studied and admired US racist legislation as a model for the infamous Nuremberg Laws that delineated Nazi racial policy. The Nazi secret police's newspaper sarcastically justified segregating Jews on public transportation with the claim that Germany would be "follow[ing] a democratic example [set by the United States,] the world's freest country." The 1939 article went on to characterize the US meritocratic ideal as a myth, pointing out that even esteemed black national heroes could not so much as legally sit next to a white "sewage worker."[15] As legal historian James Whitman has written, it is important to note that Nazi statements about the hypocrisy of US racial illiberalism were not merely propaganda stunts; Nazi lawyers examined, drew lessons from, and frequently cited US race law in private settings where policy was being decided as well.

Whitman does not suggest that US racial code led to Nazism, but he does show that Nazi jurists perceived the United States "as the innovative world leader in the creation of racist law," and they turned to this legislation—which they knew countered liberal democratic values—for ideas. The Nuremberg Citizenship and Blood Laws established second-class citizen status for the Jewish population and outlawed marriage and sex between Jews and "Aryans." The restrictive US immigration laws summarized in this book's introduction declared certain nonwhite national/racialized groups unfit for US citizenship in a manner that res-onated with Nazi goals to legally marginalize German Jews. The Third Reich also considered the US western expansion policy and its annihila-tion of the indigenous to be useful and helpful. Another inspiration was the 1896 *Plessy v. Ferguson* Supreme Court decision that legalized seg-regation and codified second-class citizenship for blacks and other peo-ple of color. Furthermore, after searching for cases worldwide, the thirty US states banning interracial marriage provided the only antimiscegena-tion laws the Nazis could find as precedent for their Blood Law.[16]

The Nazi *National Socialist Handbook for Law and Legislation*, pub-lished in late 1934 or early 1935, contains ample references to the dis-connect between US principles and these racist policies. The handbook—which, Whitman writes, "was intended to mark out the path for future Nazi lawmaking"—in part utilized US racial code to universalize and naturalize Nazi racial philosophies. In light of the "abundance of statu-tory racial regulation in the" United States, the handbook found it "incomprehensible" that the Third Reich and its political ideology had "been the targets of serious attacks." These laws, the book continued, validated "the necessity of segregating humans according to their racial descent . . . even where a political ideology stands in the way." In fact, US "liberal and democratic" beliefs about "the equality of everything that bears a human countenance" did not prevent the United States from being an excellent model for Nazi laws, the handbook added.[17] The Third Reich's desire to emulate aspects of US racial legislation was far more damaging to the United States' democratic image than the Nazis' condemnations, but both undermined the authority of US democracy in ways that eventually would require a racial response from the state.

In spite of lambasting democracy as the key to a people's destruction, Hitler and the Nazis also claimed to embody its basic tenets, advertising German National Socialism as a democratic form of government. Their discourse also highlighted the racial double standard of liberal democ-racies, especially the United States. Hitler's messy constellation of racial and democratic statements had global impact and was a sign that race was becoming a more prominent component of democracy. However, not all fascists admired or sought to imitate Hitler's racial political rhetoric. In Brazil, the massive integralist movement appreciated Nazi authoritarianism but rejected its overt racist ideology.

BRAZILIAN INTEGRALISM

Although Brazil possessed the world's largest official Nazi party outside Germany—with about twenty-nine hundred members in at least seventeen states—another national group quickly became the biggest and most influential fascist organization in the country.[18] In 1932 Brazilian journalist Plínio Salgado founded this group, the Ação Integralista Brasileira. According to preeminent scholar of fascism Roger Griffin, integralism was "[b]y far the most significant case of fascism in Latin America."[19] The AIB also became the first nationwide political party of the masses in Brazilian history, with branches in every state. Integralism dwarfed Brazilian Nazism considerably: in 1936 the so-called green shirts boasted between six hundred thousand and one million members.[20] Despite its status as a political party, historian Rosa Feiteiro Cavalari has written, "[i]ntegralism always presented itself as a movement of culture," one with a spiritual essence that was concerned less with political power than with bringing literacy, education, art, philosophy, and science to the people. Integralists also agitated for corporatism and economic nationalism, and opposed liberal democracy as well as, of course, socialism/communism.[21]

Both national and foreign personalities and movements inspired Plínio Salgado to create the AIB. In his public and private writings, Salgado cites conservative Brazilian thinkers such as racist jurist and sociologist Oliveira Vianna and Alberto Torres, the politician and nationalist writer who argued against biological racial determinism. Internationally, it was not Adolf Hitler but Benito Mussolini who most influenced Salgado. Before founding the AIB, Salgado had traveled to Italy and had the opportunity to interview Mussolini, and he returned to Brazil immensely impressed with the state of Italian society and governance under Mussolini's rule. The Italian government later aided the AIB, both providing propaganda materials for integralists to disseminate and, it seems, regularly depositing funds into AIB coffers.[22] Although there were certainly many cases of collaboration between Brazilian Nazis and integralists, the Third Reich itself was not open to working with the AIB. The Nazi regime could not reconcile its policy with integralism's distinct racial philosophy; its Brazilian, not German, nationalism (which the Nazis derogatorily referred to as "Lusitanian nativism"); and the perceived competition between Brazilian Nazism and the AIB for adherents. Indeed, scholar Ana Maria Dietrich describes the Third Reich's approach toward the AIB as one of "non-acceptance, non-collaboration, and even contempt."[23]

Like the communists, integralists articulated their own racial vision for a political democracy and delineated a place for blacks in the integralist proposal for a new Brazil. The AIB actively attempted to recruit Afro-Brazilians, competing with communists for black support.[24] In this contest, the AIB had one great advantage: its relationship with Arlindo Veiga dos Santos, Frente Negra Brasileira cofounder and president. At the forefront of these efforts were the party's continuous attempts to downplay the role European fascism may have had in and on the movement. Integralists wanted the public to see the AIB as a fiercely autonomous party composed of uncompromising patriots who were fixated on solving Brazilian problems and serving the country's populace. The AIB's unique racial political nationalism helped create this desired profile. Together, the above factors qualified integralists as one of the most influential groups in the national debate about race and politics. The organization's uneven and incomplete rhetoric of racial inclusion combined with its ideas about genuine democracy to generate a marketable model of racial democracy that resonated with Brazilian realities.

Integralists perceived Brazil as a mixed-race nation and sought to unify the various populations to achieve "true social synthesis," giving the often-isolated European element the task of whitening the populace.[25] Indeed, the AIB did not deviate from the idea that whites were at the top of the racial hierarchy, and integralists imagined whiteness as the dominating element in the new, consolidated Brazilian race. In addition to Christian whites, the other races included in the integralist vision were blacks and the indigenous (especially the Tupi, who were in many ways considered the national cultural base). Natália dos Reis Cruz argues that the language of miscegenation only hid the integralist's intolerance for cultural plurality and other forms of difference that they defined as traditionally un-Brazilian.[26]

Integralism sought the "ethnic and cultural homogeneity of the Brazilian population which should be obtained through assimilation or the amalgamation of the diverse races and cultures that exist in Brazil," but not all races and cultures were welcome to join the mix. Cruz suggests that some exclusionary racial ideas of the Sociedade dos Amigos de Alberto Torres—founded the same year as the AIB—migrated with participant Plínio Salgado into the integralist movement. The Sociedade honored

Torres in part by lobbying against Jewish and Japanese immigration. The Sociedade and the AIB attempted to cast their anti-Semitism as a mere concern with the so-called refusal of Jews to assimilate into Brazilian society. Gustavo Barroso—head of the integralist militia, AIB "principal theoretician," and a party leader "second probably only to Salgado"—helped in this framing of integralist anti-Semitism as antiracism.[27]

Barroso was a polygenist who believed that whites (namely Aryans) had emerged as the dominant race in the history of racial conflict, yet he argued that their Christianity and moral code of "altruism" caused them to reject a "rivalry of classes and races, [calling] all men brothers and declar[ing] them equal." Barroso insisted that this project of human equality through spiritual unity was never achieved in large part because of the Jewish people and their "materialism." Thus, as Marcos Chor Maio has pointed out, Barroso and the integralists founded their anti-Semitism on the idea that Jews were responsible for global racism.[28] This argument allowed the integralists to echo statements that many at the time associated with Nazism, while separating the movement from the kind of racist attitudes that would render Brazilians an inferior people and nation.

AIB leaders berated German immigrant communities for a lack of satisfactory assimilation as well, yet this criticism was motivated by the leadership's desire for Germans to properly Europeanize other groups, including Jews. Both groups' perceived unwillingness to partake in Brazilian racial and cultural homogenization made it impossible to produce the desired result. Integralist leaders and writers also espoused anti-Japanese sentiment, in spite of the support integralists often expressed for the Axis powers. For instance, in 1936 the AIB paper, *A Ofensiva*, complained that the Vargas regime's new immigration laws did not show the "courage to declare frankly, openly, that Japanese immigration does not suit us." Such notions were in part based on the belief that the Japanese brought disrespect for the law into the country.[29]

The AIB's racial framework connected antiracism to anti-Semitism, equating a racially egalitarian world with the rejection of Jewish values, and allowed integralists to claim that the AIB was separate and independent from European fascist systems. The question of whether or not the AIB was a fascist movement—and in particular, one that was European derived—did plague the party during the 1930s and remained central in the future scholarship about integralism. Carlos Henrique Hunsche produced the first academic study of the movement in 1937 and determined that the party was in fact a fascist movement with strong

ties to and influences from European counterparts.[30] Integralist leader
and lawyer Antonio Gallotti's letter to a fellow green shirt, written in
August 1937, indicated that such assessments were widespread. Gallotti
complained about accusations that the AIB advanced a foreign fascist
doctrine and acted as "an instrument of Hitler." The writer pointed to
the "democratic popular front" as the source of what he clearly considered to be malicious rumors.[31]

One of the AIB's key strategies to counter the charges that it was a
European puppet organization was to align integralist racial theory
with Brazil's eminently recognizable nationalist ideal of interracial harmony and tolerance. Integralist writer Hélio Rocha explained how
Nazism directly countered the AIB's philosophy and was unappealing to
Brazilian integralists: "as Christians, how could it be possible for us to
accept racism and the sanctioning of Germanic mythology substanti-
ated by a frenzied Nationalism and an idolatrous paganism 'corrupted
by the Boss's religious paranoia,' as Plínio Salgado stressed well?" AIB
national secretary of doctrine Miguel Reale endorsed the sentiment:
"European nationalism thrives on falsehoods and aggressions. . . . We
can and should be nationalists, without the need to base our unity on
hate or fear. This is why the racist struggle does not seduce us."[32]

The AIB's racial nationalism preached pride, not shame, in Brazil's
racial makeup. In the AIB's founding manifesto of October 1932, a section was devoted to the question of integralist nationalism, a central
theme in the movement. Issued on the heels of São Paulo's Constitutionalist Revolution, which constructed a European/white and modern versus black and "backward" regionalist discourse, the manifesto decried
the lack of nationalist pride among Brazilian city dwellers.[33] Striking a
similar tone to that of racialist thinkers like Gilberto Freyre, the manifesto stated that "Brazilians in the cities do not know the national thinkers, writers, or poets. They are ashamed of the caboclo and the black
man of our land. They acquire cosmopolitan habits." The document
made it clear that cosmopolitanism's call for the rejection of *caboclos*
and blacks was a foreign concept that had no place in the integralist
vision of Brazilian nationalism. The following year, the Doctrine Department of the AIB published another pamphlet signed by Salgado and
others that, among other things, explained the purpose behind integralist educational policy. A critical function of schools, the text informed,
was to create national unity in places where "racial unity [did not
already] exist."[34] In other words, the former type of unity was predicated on the latter.

Like the PCB and the Frente Negra, AIB leaders advocated a vision of self-determination that relied upon racial ideas to reject foreign influence in Brazil. For the integralists, self-determination was the right of the people *(o povo)*—the united, multiracial, national "social synthesis"—to manage their own affairs and control their own destiny without the intervention of foreign entities. Self-determination was constructed as the antithesis of racial and cultural imperialism, which the AIB argued undermined world peace in part by fostering territorial expansionism and materialism.[35] AIB racial political theory characterized integralism as a staunchly nationalist movement for which foreign influence, including European fascism, was contrary to its core mission.

The AIB's language of racial inclusion composed one part of integralist racial democracy; its claims to democracy constituted another. Historian of integralism Marcus Klein has identified a shift in the leadership's position on democracy in the last few years of its existence. As late as October 1934, Salgado and other AIB leaders continued to advocate for the toppling of the Brazilian democratic regime, with Salgado declaring that integralists "despise [the Constitution] so much that [they] will use it to destroy it. Oh! The integralistas will go to elections. Why? To put an end to the right to vote, to elect men who raise their voice in congress so that . . . parties and liberal democracy are definitely abolished." Miguel Reale identified Adolf Hitler's acquisition of power through the electoral process as a prime model.[36] Then, in January 1935, the Brazilian Congress passed the repressive National Security Law, which mostly targeted communists but was also a reaction to the violent integralist-communist street clashes that climaxed in 1934. In response to the law, Salgado "denied, in open contradiction to earlier statements as well as acts of his followers, the revolutionary intentions of the organization. . . ." Salgado "suddenly" argued that integralists sought to subvert neither the regime nor Vargas. As a reflection of this new policy, the AIB revamped its statutes, which began to champion reform within representative democracy over revolution. During this period, the AIB began to refer to itself as "genuinely democratic" and "expressed its adherence to democracy."[37]

Klein's observation that the AIB began to support democracy in 1935 is quite accurate in the sense that the integralists retired their more militant program for one that sought to work with, instead of against, the government. Yet it is also true that virtually since its inception, the AIB embraced the discourse of democracy and gave it a uniquely integralist definition. Well before the LSN's passage and the AIB's accommodationist tone, its Doctrine Department's 1933 *Primer of Brazilian Integralism* intended to educate the public on integralism's basic principles in a question and answer format. The pamphlet—signed by Reale, Salgado, and others—used the word *democracy* at least twice as a way to describe the AIB.[38]

Before declaring the AIB a democratic movement, the primer set out to debunk the idea that the Brazilian government (before the 1934 constitution was ratified) was a democracy at all, an accusation that had racial resonances. In the section titled "What Is True Popular Representation?," the pamphlet argued that liberalism was not the answer: "This Democracy is a lie." Here the fact that political parties and not the people chose the candidates (which is still the case in Brazil) was cited as proof that the nation lacked democracy. The AIB's demand that the people choose their candidates was accompanied by a catchphrase that reverberated with communist literature: "Only the representation of the worker is popular representation." Continuing to lambaste the political party system, the pamphlet pushed for corporatism, contending that through labor unions "economic representation was realized." Political parties, poorly disguised "organizations of economic character," were a sham. Therefore, as the pamphlet read in all capital letters, "INTEGRALISM IS THE REALIZATION OF SOCIAL DEMOCRACY." The pamphlet ended with an elaboration of the sentiment: "Integralism is the realization of social democracy through the progressive identification of the state with society and with the nation." It is worth noting that this same primer that categorized the AIB as democratic also identified "racial unity" as a function of the integralist school system, making this document a modest edict of the AIB's racialized notion of democracy.[39]

Black integralist Coronel Newton Braga also defended the AIB on the question of democracy, using racially inclusive language to reinforce his claims. In July 1937 the integralist *Anauê!* journal published an article titled "The Candidate of the People," written by Braga in support of Plínio Salgado's temporary candidacy for the presidency. Braga disagreed with those who characterized the AIB as antidemocratic. He asserted that the AIB was "installing a true democracy in Brazil" for Brazilians of all professions, social categories, and ethnic origins. Next to the article appeared an image of a black *integralista* doing the party salute, clearly a nod to the fact that "ethnic origins" included Afro-Brazilians.[40] Braga's article was undoubtedly a part of the AIB's efforts to recruit the Afro-Brazilian vote for the election, which will be touched upon later in this chapter.

Salgado was sensitive to accusations that the AIB was an antidemocratic movement and fought to convince the public otherwise. *A Ofensiva* published one of his articles on this point in 1936. In the piece,
Salgado responded to questions that journalists and the public in general always asked about the integralist movement, including "whether
or not integralists want a totalitarian state, and whether or not [the
AIB] is antidemocratic." Salgado replied "no" to both questions and
insisted that the AIB wanted to usher in "the democracy that does not
already exist in Brazil."[41]

Integralists constructed a distinctive form of fascist racial democracy,
one that justified anti-Semitism by subsuming it under racial tolerance
and allowed them to battle claims that the movement was an antidemocratic and racist pawn of European fascists. Thus, racial democracy
was an effective tool to frame the AIB as antiracist, nationalist, and
democratic—a bona fide movement for *all* the Brazilian people, by the
Brazilian people.

LAWRENCE DENNIS AND US FASCISM

In the United States, an unlikely figure emerged as a proponent of fascism in the 1930s, a man that secretary of the interior and Roosevelt
confidant Harold Ickes referred to as the "brains" of the fascist movement in the United States. It was certainly Lawrence Dennis's intellect
that made him stand out from the other fascist sympathizers that
appeared in the United States during this decade. Historian Arthur
Schlesinger Jr. referred to Dennis as the "one intellectual [who] brought
to the advocacy of fascism powers of intelligence and style [with]
Goebbels-like qualities." "America's No. 1 Intellectual Fascist" (from
Life Magazine) and the "prophet of 'intellectual fascism'" were other
designations Dennis's contemporaries gave him. He was likely the best-
known fascist in the United States, and not just in intellectual circles. In
the 1930s his writings, especially his book *The Coming of American
Fascism*, acquired a large readership, his name often appeared in the
pages of newspapers, and his voice was familiar to many who listened
to debates and commentary on the radio and/or attended public
speeches. Indeed, his biographer Gerald Horne has written that Dennis
became "the authentic domestic voice of fascism."[42]

Dennis's life and career attracted much attention. The Italian Ministry
of Foreign Affairs invited him to visit Italy as its guest, and Dennis met
Mussolini. He later traveled to Germany and hobnobbed with Minister

of Propaganda Goebbels and even met the Führer. Dennis claimed that he was never a fascist, only a student of what he had believed to be the "wave of the future," an assertion Gerald Horne finds "hard to swallow." His activities and profascist stance garnered Dennis the attention of the FBI, and eventually he was charged with sedition, accused of scheming to trigger a military-based coup in order to replace the US government with a Nazi regime. In the context of these experiences, what makes Dennis's biography even more exceptional is the fact that, by US standards, he was a black man passing as white. As shocking as his racial roots were, they shed light on his strong race-oriented views, which he deployed both to discredit US democracy and to promote a more racially inclusive form of fascism.[43]

Lawrence Dennis, born to a black mother and an unknown father, spent his childhood in segregated Atlanta and Washington, DC, identifying as black. When he was ten years old, he traveled the world as a well-known Negro child evangelist. After enrolling at Phillips Exeter Academy in his early twenties, Dennis began to pass as white. As Horne suggests, Dennis likely chose this path because he realized that his race would always overshadow his intelligence and limit his life possibilities.[44] Dennis's time at Exeter and later at Harvard permanently shaped his worldview. So, too, did his military service during World War I (it seems he was officially identified as white), his work in the diplomatic service and on Wall Street before the 1929 economic crash (which he forecasted), and evidently, the New Dealers' rejection of his attempt to obtain a position in the administration. He rejected the New Deal as well, refusing to support not only Roosevelt but also the very system of government practiced in the United States.[45]

Like Hitler and the Brazilian integralists, Dennis was less a democratic contrarian than a dissenter to the idea that liberalism was functionally democratic. Dennis's 1936 book *The Coming American Fascism* analyzes this issue. In it he stated, "if democracy means the rule of the people, it must mean that rule under some efficient formula of political organization. The people do not rule by legal definition but by efficient political machinery." On this point, Dennis contended that the "efficiency of public administration in controlling the conditions of life in a country is the measure of popular rule." Dennis found the belief that liberalism assured such efficiency "a distorted sense of reality." Furthermore, he argued that "most of the rules of liberalism which are most touted as safeguarding popular rule merely insure the rule of the rich, powerful, irresponsible, and selfish who, under liberalism, can produce expressions of popular will and opinion to suit their selfish interests." According to Dennis, the better alternative was fascism, which "would rationalize our scheme of political organization." At this point, Dennis called for the end of what he termed the "confederacy of sovereign states" and instead recommended a "highly centralized government which would exercise the powers of a truly national State."[46] Thus, only with fascist centralization would the United States achieve the "efficient political machinery" that Dennis considered fundamental for the "rule of the people" to truly occur. In this sense, fascism, and not liberalism, met his standards of democracy.

Lawrence Dennis's 1940 book *The Dynamics of War and Revolution* expanded upon this discussion of democracy and explained in greater detail why, using his guidelines, the US liberal state was not democratic.[47] In *The Dynamics of War and Revolution,* Dennis devoted four and a half pages to defining democracy and capitalism, which he described as "two aspects of the same social system." In these pages, he teased out the notion of democracy, clarifying that he used the term "in the sense in which it is currently employed in popular speech [which] refers to a certain pattern or ways and institutions which may be further identified by the phrases, parliamentary government, liberalism . . . all of these terms meaning a governmental system in which the rights of minorities to oppose the majority in certain approved ways is respected." Dennis noted that in the United States, there was no flexibility on this interpretation, as people in the United States "are apt to assume that nowhere can the people govern themselves unless they do so in the particular way we are used to and like." Again, Dennis took issue with such a monopoly over what constituted democracy, opining that "an entirely different pattern of ways and institutions may with equal propriety and etymological correctness be termed democratic."[48]

Dennis quoted Abraham Lincoln to counter the line of thinking that constructed rigid practical and philosophical boundaries around what did and did not qualify as a democracy. If "of the people, for the people and by the people" was "the essence of democracy," Dennis wrote, "it may, I think, be fairly held that a socialist dictatorship . . . is as democratic as the government" of the United States. Moreover, Dennis held that "all governments and societies . . . have to be democratic. That is to say, they must be more or less of the people, by the people and for the people." If this were not the case, he wrote, the disaffected populace would quickly overthrow their leaders in armed revolt. Despite his opposition to the ways that the term *democracy* was understood and used, however, Dennis found it easier "to restrict the application of the term *democracy* to social systems the American people consider democratic."[49] His concession here obscured his embrace of the "etymological" sense of democracy and the way in which he clearly characterized fascism as a democratic system.

Fascism as democracy, à la Dennis, preferably would exclude the racist underpinnings manifested in Nazi concentration camps or Italy's invasion of Ethiopia. Dennis believed that the United States was too heterogeneous to adopt a policy similar to Hitler's exclusive nationalism: "The American racists would have to blacklist not only the Jews, but also the Roman Catholics, the Irish and the Southern Europeans," who accounted for "nearly one third of our total population. [Thus, in the United States] racism could never become the plank of a successful political program."[50] Whatever the form of fascism to be "inevitably" taken up in the United States, Dennis hoped that it would reflect different racial values from those of the Nazis, even as, tellingly, he allowed for the possibility of their being the same:

> If it be assumed that one of our values should be a type of racism which excludes certain races from citizenship, then the plan of execution should provide for the annihilation, deportation, or sterilization of the excluded races. If, on the contrary, as I devoutly hope will be the case, the scheme of values will include that of a national citizenship in which race will be no qualifying or disqualifying condition, then the plan of realization must, in so far as race relations are concerned, provide for the assimilation or accommodation of race differences within the scheme of smoothly running society.[51]

On the one hand, Dennis's words on a prospective future US model of fascism painted a classic vision of racial democracy, even deploying multicultural phraseology with expressions such as "assimilation" and "accommodation." On the other hand, he rendered racial exclusion, annihilation, deportation, and sterilization thinkable. As Horne has argued, the precarious line Dennis attempted to walk between possible racial persecution and antiracism was irreconcilably tense.[52] Dennis also tried to act as interpreter of Nazi racism, implying that Hitler "blame[d] everything on the Jews" as a "good political strategy . . . since the moronic public mind is not capable of assimilating abstract ideas." If the Nazis insisted on persecuting Jews, Dennis felt they should be more subtle and treat them "more or less as we treat the Negroes in America." That way the Nazis could still "practice discrimination and all that, but [avoid] conflict with American opinion."[53]

This last statement is a window into Dennis's perceptions of the fallacies of US democracy vis-à-vis race. He found it ironic that "White America . . . cannot tolerate European oppression of minorities but we have never been without" oppression. Dennis linked this racist behavior to the ideal of democracy directly: "Democracy, when it flourished, when it was revolutionary, militant and successfully imperialistic, never respected the rights of the weak except as it suited capitalist or nationalist interests." As examples, he referred to "the African slave trade [and] the extinction of the Indians in North America to make it safe for white democracy."[54] (The latter point mirrored one made by Nazis who invoked Native American history to reject US "ethical maxims" in 1938. Nazis argued that these righteous attitudes had not been "part and parcel of American practice.")[55] This excerpt is a sign that Dennis was more hostile to US racism than he was to that of European fascism, largely because of what he saw as US hypocrisy. He used the experience of oppressed racial and ethnic groups to drive home his contention that democracy in the West was a myth. At the same time, Dennis argued that fascism was genuinely democratic, appealing for a racially inclusive fascist democracy.

BLACKS ON FASCISM, RACE, AND DEMOCRACY

Like Lawrence Dennis, Brazilian and US black activists paid special attention to the advent of fascism and the evolving racial policies of the Third Reich in the 1930s. Black writers and activists were among the first to discuss the domestic repercussions of Hitler's racial politics in the United States and Brazil, and blacks incorporated Nazism into their theories about race and democracy. Among some of the most prominent Afro-Brazilian activists, liberal democracy did not appear to be the dominant model upon which they attached their greatest hopes for racial justice. Although the Frente Negra Brasileira leadership met with Vargas and would praise him at times, the FNB also denied the Vargas administration the moral racial standing it would claim increasingly as the Nazi/ Axis crisis engulfed the world.[56] By highlighting the problem of serious racial discrimination in Brazil, the black activists belied the state's forthcoming wartime propaganda that Brazil was a world leader on this matter. FNB leader Arlindo Veiga dos Santos even favorably portrayed Nazism as an undemocratic nationalist paradigm that could promote racial equity in Brazil more effectively than the Brazilian system of government. It is no surprise then that the FNB had some connections to

Brazil's fascist integralist movement. US blacks appeared to overwhelmingly refuse to recognize hope or potential in fascism. Nonetheless, like Arlindo Veiga dos Santos, US blacks in the 1930s similarly depicted racism in their own country as equal to or worse than that of Nazi Germany in order to shame and question US democracy, especially as they pushed their antilynching agenda.

In retrospect, the challenges US and Brazilian blacks launched against their societies may seem hyperbolic until one remembers that for most of the 1930s, few predicted the impending mass murder of Jews. Furthermore, searches of both leaders' public proclamations during the 1930s show that neither Vargas nor Roosevelt emphasized racial persecution in Germany publicly for the majority of the decade. In fact, James Whitman has written that Roosevelt "cautiously refrained from singling out Hitler" altogether in his rhetoric against dictatorships until sometime between 1937 and 1939.[57] Thus, blacks helped to spotlight Hitler's racial nationalism before the world truly came to terms with the consequences of Nazi totalitarianism. Black perspectives also forewarned US and Brazilian authorities of the racial political issues that would concern both governments during the war and impact the Brazil-US wartime alliance as well.

The Ação Integralista Brasileira and its links with the FNB intensified fascism's racial significance in Brazil, although the extent and depth of this relationship have been debated. The integralists had a natural champion in Arlindo Veiga dos Santos, who was politically conservative and identified with the AIB's anticommunist, Christian, and illiberal nationalism. Santos and AIB founder Plínio Salgado had a personal and ideological bond as cofounders of the Sociedade de Estudos Políticos (Society of Political Studies), an important AIB antecedent. Salgado even sought Santos's official endorsement for the AIB but never received it. Former FNB leader José Correia Leite would later claim that when Santos was still FNB president, he promised Frente support and exaggerated Frente member numbers at the AIB's first conference. The FNB's newspaper *A Voz da Raça* also published one of Salgado's articles, and Salgado himself attended a Frente Negra meeting in the city of Santos.[58] There may even be evidence of an FNB "recruitment effort" in aid of the AIB during the 1937 election campaign before Salgado dropped his bid to run for president.[59] When AIB journal *Anauê!* commemorated abolition during the 1937 campaign, its "May 13" article promised politically engaged blacks, like the frentenegrinos, that the party sympathized with and was committed to understanding their grievances: "we want to stress the deep interest in the blacks' problematic situation in Brazilian society."[60]

The AIB did not call for the return of the monarchy as did Santos, but both movements did advocate for replacing the existing political regime and doubted the efficacy of liberalism. The two groups also "shared nationalism characterized by the ideas of national unity and the formation of a *Brazilian race* (approached, of course, in a different way, perhaps contradictorily so); anticommunism; and the objective of generating a moral revolution in order to 'reorganize' Brazilian society."[61] Perhaps these organizations' slogans are the best indication of their philosophical closeness: the only difference between the FNB's "God, Country, Race, and Family" motto and that of the AIB was the former's inclusion of "race."

Arlindo Veiga dos Santos spoke against democracy using the illiberal political lens through which he observed the status quo, and he was not alone in the Afro-Brazilian activist community. In a 1934 issue of *A Voz da Raça,* Santos wrote that countries like Italy and Germany "take pride in themselves [and] do not permit the jokers of liberal democracy," socialists, communists, or others, "to preach their stupidity freely." He conceded that Hitler's "defense of the German race [had] even reached the extreme," but he blamed the "meekness" of the previous democratic Weimar regime for creating the "toughness of a man who knows what he wants and executes it."[62] Black activist and journalist José Correia Leite may have exited the FNB in its early days and used his paper, *O Clarim d'Alvorada,* to attack the Frente Negra, but he also recognized that in a way, the FNB and Santos were a product of the times. Leite would recollect that Brazil's deep political divisions and extremism in the 1930s did not yield a liberal democracy–friendly ambiance in the country. Leite said that for most politically conscious people, "the democratic idea, republican[ism], these ideas were out of the question." He pointed out that Afro-Brazilians were no exception to the rule and that black activists did not tend to organize around the tenets of liberal democracy in the 1930s.[63]

If Arlindo Veiga dos Santos's antiliberalism was relatively ordinary among many black Brazilians, Santos's positive racial interpretation of Nazism must have been on the extreme right of Afro-Brazilian political thought. In an *A Voz da Raça* article, Santos stated that Brazil could learn a great deal from the Germans, giving as an example Hitler's burning of the books that "diminish[ed] German pride." Santos believed that because Hitler sought the "affirmation of the German race," the book burning was a "logical" act. Santos went on to denounce the "infinity" of Brazilian books that disparaged the "black-luso-indigenous Brazilian race ... namely its black element," denying the major contribution Afro-Brazilians had made to the formation of the nation. "When Brazil has a real nationalist government," Santos added, it would set fire to such "infamous books" as well.[64] In another article in the FNB's newspaper, Santos conveyed his awareness that Hitler's German pride meant he would not be welcome in Germany as a black man. Santos was not offended, as he saw this as another sign of healthy racial nationalism, something he strove to achieve in Brazil. In fact, he celebrated Hitler's valorization of the racially defined national worker and lamented the failure of Brazil to protect black and *mestiço* Brazilians in a similar fashion. The FNB, he stated, was uninterested in "foreign blood" on Brazilian soil.[65]

Santos's comments must be placed in the proper Brazilian and global context to be understood. First, it is hard to imagine Santos making these statements during the 1940s once their full import and significance would become clear. In the earlier part of the decade, Santos felt that it sufficed merely to label Hitler as extreme while reducing Nazism into a lesson of successful nationalism. Such an analysis must have been impossible several years later. Before then, however, Santos considered it appropriate to look to Nazism for potential solutions to the historical racist practices that black Brazilians confronted. After slavery's abolishment, many industries in the commercial capital, São Paulo, locked out black applicants, instead hiring from the European immigrant populations that many Paulista businesses had promoted and sponsored. Santos also worried about the prospect of Brazil whitening and losing its mixed-race and black heritage, and all these concerns led him to push for a twenty-year moratorium on immigration. Arlindo Veiga dos Santos joined other FNB writers, including his brother Isaltino, in expressing contempt for the prioritization of white arrivals over the unappreciated black nationals that treated the latter as if they were the foreigners in Brazil.[66] Thus, Santos's reaction to Hitler had much to do with his anger at a Brazilian immigration policy that had openly, proactively, and purposefully replaced black workers with European labor.

Santos's illiberalism, which informed his evaluation of Nazism in its early years, was a recipe for his realist racial democracy and challenged both Brazil's narrative of interracial harmony and the strength of the pre–Estado Novo Vargas government. Santos was convinced that a strong, centralized, nationalist state was necessary to create genuine Brazilian racial pride, which would respect the indispensability of Afro-Brazilians and expunge antiblack discrimination. Showing that such pride was not the case in Brazil, despite nationalist accounts to the contrary, was integral to the FNB's mission. As one *A Voz da Raça* article indicated, the FNB was dedicated to attacking the "color prejudice that whites say does not exist in Brazil."[67] In Santos's estimation, liberal democracy would not produce the race-based patriotism he deemed critical to eradicate this antiblack racism. By using the Third Reich as a possible solution to Brazil's racial discrimination, Santos preemptively problematized the Vargas regime's declaration that Brazil was an international leader of racial tolerance during the war. Santos argued that the opposite was true, and the FNB generally discredited Brazilian claims to extraordinary interracial relations as well. The devaluation of Afro-Brazilians also allowed Santos to characterize the state as weak. After all, Nazi Germany proved that a strong government produced strong racial nationalism. Of course, Vargas would implement his own dictatorship in a few years, and in a bitter turn of events for frentenegrinos, the Estado Novo would ban all political organizations, including the Frente Negra and the AIB, in 1937.

The Frente Negra's brand of conservative illiberalism, particularly under Santos's leadership, was too far right for many Afro-Brazilians' taste, resulting in avoidance of, dissensions within, and defections from the FNB. The FNB's links to the AIB were one problem for blacks who associated integralism and fascism with racism, regardless of the AIB's language of racial tolerance. The Afro-Brazilian leftist activist Júlio Romão reflected on his local integralist leader's attempt to recruit him into the AIB when he was just fifteen years old. Romão burned the green shirt the leader gave him and refused to join the movement, later explaining his rationale: "I didn't believe in Aryanism. I couldn't accept it!"[68] Abdias do Nascimento—who became arguably the most celebrated Afro-Brazilian activist of the twentieth century—formed a friendship with Salgado but later left the AIB after confronting racism in the organization.[69] Leite and *O Clarim d'Alvorada* were the FNB's best-known rivals. They had many criticisms of the FNB, including its conservative patrianovismo. Other leftists who were upset by the prevalence of right-leaning politics in the FNB fractured from the group to form the Frente Negra Socialista, which, in Leite's words, was "not able to progress." Its statutes revealed the group's dissatisfaction with the FNB's autocratic leadership structure, which gave the president a great deal of power. The Frente Negra Socialista's governing model was much less hierarchical.[70]

It is difficult to know what the majority of Afro-Brazilians thought about the relationship between racial democracy and Right-leaning movements like fascism, integralism, and Nazism in the 1930s. Blacks had a notable presence in the integralist movement, as photographic documentation shows, but we know little about what drew them to it.[71] Abdias do Nascimento stated that before he left the AIB, he benefited from the ways the movement educated him on social, political, and economic realities.[72] As part of a community woefully underserved in education, many other politically minded Afro-Brazilians must also have been attracted to the AIB for the educational opportunities it offered. What the average Frente member believed about this question is similarly difficult to uncover. Invoking the arguably elitist notion that Santos's charisma, intelligence, and eloquence enchanted the majority-illiterate FNB base, Leite for his part did not sense a genuine interest among them in the monarchist beliefs that made Santos so sympathetic to extremely strong government and fascism. Historian Kim Butler also has argued that the rank and file mainly were drawn to the organization for its services, not its political ideology.[73]

Regardless of their opinions on fascism and racial democracy, black Brazilians in the 1930s politically organized around racial injustice in unprecedented numbers, which was, in itself, a statement on the matter. This mobilization reinforced the FNB's attacks on Brazil's narrative of racial harmony. Therefore, even when they did not mention fascism outright, the efforts of blacks resonated with the snowballing global fascist crisis and the Vargas regime's eventual utilization of race to differentiate itself from fascist governments. Black activists rendered that line of division untenable at best.

In the United States, blacks framed their struggle for equality in democratic terms during the 1930s before the rise of national antifascist sentiment. This trend culminated in World War II when the *Pittsburgh Courier,* a popular black newspaper, famously launched a "Double V" campaign, calling for victory against fascism abroad and victory against racism at home. Even before the United States entered the war in 1941, blacks used *Nazism* and *racism* interchangeably to refer to a decidedly antidemocratic, "un-American" trope. Unlike the Double V campaigners, black antifascist, antiracist advocates in the 1930s were speaking to a nation that had not declared war on the Axis powers and whose public was still probing how and why fascism contradicted US ideals of democracy. State officials played a major role here, using terms like *oligarchy* and *dictatorship* to decry fascist regimes as the antithesis of democracy. Blacks led the effort to ensure that *racism* was one of these terms. In other words, blacks inserted and prioritized race when debates about the dangers of fascism and totalitarianism engaged political rhetoric that excluded or sidelined race.

Joel Augustus Rogers—a well-known black author, international correspondent, and journalist—used Franklin Roosevelt's 1937 State of the Union address, in which the president never mentioned race, to make completely race-centered remarks. Just as Hitler had bristled at Roosevelt's reprimand of German and Italian imperialist ventures in the 1930s, Rogers and other US blacks dismissed Roosevelt's right to stand on the democratic high ground as he cast aspersions on Hitler. In a *Pittsburgh Courier* article, Rogers did applaud Roosevelt's "rap at dictatorships" during the 1937 State of the Union. Roosevelt did not mention Hitler or Mussolini by name, but Rogers interpreted the president's disapproval of oligarchies, which Roosevelt placed in opposition to democracy, as a direct attack on the German and Italian governments. However, he warned that Roosevelt's condemnation may have backfired and actually supported the fascists in believing that their form of government was valid. He explained that the ability to shame a party could occur only when "the reputation of he who makes the rebuke" is admirable. Rogers wrote that the reputation of the United States was far from it. In fact, European dictators looked poorly upon the United States and were justified in doing so, he added, especially when it came to racial issues.[74]

In January 1937—before the Third Reich's genocide began in earnest—Rogers positioned fascist Europe as morally superior to the United States on the question of race, declaring US racism much more entrenched and troubling than the discrimination found in Nazi Germany. He believed that African Americans, at least, "would generally meet nothing but courtesy in Germany . . . provided [they] shunned politics and behaved." As a result, Rogers insisted that US officials' outrage at the political developments in Europe had no leverage, particularly when "Nazis and Fascists are also well informed about [US] lynching." He claimed that fascists simply responded to such criticisms with questions such as "What about your lynching and burning alive of human beings?" or "What about your Scottsboro case?" Fascists could therefore ridicule "President Roosevelt's excellent defense of democracy" in the same way that US citizens balked at Hitler's speeches. Until

Roosevelt put an end to physical and legal lynching, starting with the release of the Scottsboro defendants, the United States would remain "a long way from true democracy."[75]

By this time, the Jamaican-born Rogers was acknowledged as an expert on world affairs in the black community, having spent a considerable amount of time traveling through Europe and Africa. He had published and would continue to publish books and articles about his research on blacks in the Diaspora. Rogers's article responding to Roosevelt's speech was not the first time that he published a piece about the nature of racism in European countries.[76] Because of his reputation as a specialist in such matters, we can assume that Rogers's viewpoint—that US racism softened fascism's image and rendered the United States a great democratic hypocrite—carried significant weight in the black community.

Rogers was certainly among the bolder black critics of US democracy at the time, but his article in one of the nation's most circulated black newspapers reflected common African American strategies in the 1930s. For instance, in October 1938, the year after Rogers published the above article, the black newspaper the *New York Amsterdam News* published a piece that in part made hay of another of Roosevelt's nonracial statements. The article, "U.S. Woos Negro Troops as Another World War Looms," also foreshadowed the line of thinking among blacks that so concerned US authorities once the nation entered the war three years later. It predicted that Europe was heading to war and that the United States would soon follow. The piece cited the recent letter Roosevelt had sent to Hitler in which the US president encouraged a letup in the rising tensions between the Third Reich and Czechoslovakia. Roosevelt, fretting about the possibility of the strains in relations leading to war, exhorted Hitler to do everything in his power to maintain global peace.[77]

The *New York Amsterdam News* reported that many blacks felt Roosevelt was "wrong in sending messages to Hitler and President Benes of the Czechs," invoking African Americans' past traumatic experiences with unkept democratic promises. The article implied that US blacks regarded Roosevelt's letter as a signal of US involvement in European affairs that could easily manifest militarily. This was against the "motto" of "the average colored citizen" that implored Roosevelt to "stay out of Europe." The reason for blacks' lack of enthusiasm for potential war was their disappointing experience after World War I, which had been trumpeted as the conflict that would "save the world for Democracy." However, for US blacks, "the world [was] no better off [in 1938] as a result of what happened in the world war a generation ago."[78] In other words, despite "winning" the war, US blacks were still awaiting the racial democracy for which they had fought, died, and killed.

The newspaper reported that the black community was already abuzz with war talk and that blacks "spen[t] most of their spare time talking about war, listening to the radio and reading war news in the papers." They believed that war was "inevitable" and the "consensus of opinion" in the black community was unequivocal: "If war comes and we have to go, we are going to make sure that we'll get real Democracy for our race when the war is over." Blacks would "not be used as pawns again to fight the white man's battle."[79] Democracy for whites only would no longer be tolerated. As we will see in chapter 7, the *Amsterdam News*'s forecast was tremendously accurate, as US blacks took a much more militant stance during the Second World War and predicated African American support on some kind of racial realist program.

In 1939 the *Baltimore Afro-American*, likely the highest-selling black newspaper on the East Coast at the time, published journalist Ralph Matthews's critique of democracy as a system of government that echoed Arlindo Veiga dos Santos's views.[80] In a piece titled "Is Democracy a Failure?," Matthews contended that the "basic weakness of representative government" explained the failure of antilynching legislation and other racial injustices. Drawing conclusions that paralleled those of Santos, Matthews pondered the possibility of a benign fascist regime. He admitted that history warranted a generous dose of skepticism among blacks when it came to the idea of authoritarian rule, especially after they witnessed "evil" in fascist Germany and Italy. Yet in theory a strong fascist government that held aloft the standard of racial equality and banished segregation and other forms of injustice could be more effective than US democracy, which he designated too weak and powerless to eradicate racial discrimination.[81] Therefore, in an odd twist, the authoritarian nature of Nazism, which made it possible for Hitler to carry out racial genocide, conceivably held the key to racial justice in a way that liberal democracy did not. Matthews did not have much faith that a government of the people would ever be able to overcome the prejudice that resided in those people's attitudes. The public would have to be forced into a more racially equitable society, and perhaps, he suggested, only a fascist government was strong enough to bring that to fruition.

Matthews aside, the black press generally played up the similarities between Nazi Germany and US-style racist democracy, another Rogers trope, as was the tendency to base the comparison on the Roosevelt administration's unwillingness to redress the problem of lynching. A short piece titled "Home Style Nazism" in the May 1939 issue of the *New York Amsterdam News* referred to a recent lynching in Daytona Beach, Florida, as being "as lawless and heinous as any employed by the hated Nazis. All because the victim was a colored American." The paper stated unequivocally that "Democracy can never spread from this country to another until democracy exists here: and democracy can never [be] obtain[ed] in the US until all groups of citizens receive equal protection under the law." Instead of trying to export democracy to foreign lands, the paper charged, the government should work to install action-oriented democracy in the United States. The article implied that a good first step toward action-oriented US democracy would be the ill-fated antilynching bill.[82]

Pastor and activist Adam Clayton Powell Jr. touched upon the US implications of European fascism in his *New York Amsterdam News* "Soap Box" column. Powell was particularly scathing in his treatment of the United States and its parallels with Nazi Germany in his post-Kristallnacht column published at the end of 1938. Of course, the soon-to-be congressman could not have known that the pogrom he wrote about would mark a watershed in the history of the Holocaust. Powell chronicled the fact that President Roosevelt both recalled the US ambassador to Germany and issued a damning statement of disbelief that "'this could happen in the 20th century.'" In lieu of praising Roosevelt for these protests, as timid as they were, Powell asserted that the president had "placed himself in a position that will take a lot of shrewd wiggling to get out of." The wiggling had to do with a Mississippi lynching that Powell connected to Kristallnacht. As Powell told at the article's outset, the lynching victim was a twenty-four-year-old black man who was assumed to have assaulted a seventy-eight-year-old white woman. The woman evidently did not know the man's name, "yet through some sort of intuition the mob went directly to [the victim's] home." Powell insisted that if Roosevelt did not denounce the lynching—as "fifteen million Negroes in America demand[ed]"—his words against the pogrom would be worthless. Worse, Powell believed that Roosevelt's refusal to condemn the lynching amounted to an endorsement of both the Mississippian and the German tragedies. "If Mr. Roosevelt remains silent, then we can only deduce the lynching of the Negro is an achievement of the 20th century. . . . What if a Jew is lynched in Germany . . . or a black boy [is] hanging from a tree in Mississippi? It is all the same [because] persecution is persecution." Powell conceded that the scale and nature of oppression varied, but he felt that by not expressing outrage at the lynching (a topic Roosevelt infamously ignored), the president supported, by default, the same twentieth-century world order that had produced Nazism. According to Powell, that new world order was undemocratic and signaled the fall of the West.[83]

Powell stated outright that the history of US blacks exposed the United States as a fascist state, not a democracy, and that US blacks played a special role in combating all varieties of fascism. His message to blacks emphasized their shared bond with Jews and other oppressed peoples of the world. "Just because we are members of a race that has known Fascism in one form or another since 1619," Powell wrote, there was no excuse for blacks not to also advocate for the cause of those in a similar situation. After all, "the Jew and the darker races of the world [were] the scapegoats of a rapidly dying western culture." Powell compared the ways Nazis blamed the "lousy Jews" for Germany's economic woes to the US South's complaints that "dirty Negroes" constituted too heavy a financial burden for the region to bear. These examples served as proof that the "theories of democracy [had] not gone beyond the blue print [sic] stage." Still, Powell did preach that blacks should insist that Roosevelt "clean up his own backyard of lynching and economic slavery" before he involved the country in dealing with another nation's racism.[84]

Blacks also used US attempts to assist the victims of Nazi Germany to highlight the similarities of these states. When the US government agreed to accept Jewish refugees from Germany and Austria, the Harlem Civic Association published an open letter to President Roosevelt in the *New York Amsterdam News* implying that this was democratic, Christian, and humanitarian. However, it also imagined the moment when the refugees would arrive in the nation, learn that "what has been printed relative to the abuses of Negroes in the Southern part of this democracy is true," and find "many, many Hitlers in the United States Senate and the South." The association surmised that the refugees, recognizing their own plight in the treatment of blacks, would not feel safe living in the United States. Pointing to Roosevelt's silence on antiblack violence, the Harlem Civic Association asked the president why he was interested in the predicament of "a persecuted race abroad before getting [his] own house in order." The letter ended with the strong proclamation that Roosevelt could very well have "his brothers' blood stains" on his hands.[85]

The Harlem Civic Association, Adam Clayton Powell Jr., and the other African Americans studied here harnessed the Nazi and fascist threat to deny the United States its democratic status. Their racial political lens allowed blacks to link Germany and the United States and rendered inadequate the Roosevelt regime's largely raceless political rhetoric against fascism and totalitarian rule. By comparing the Nazi mentality with that of US lynchers and the government that refused to suppress them, black political theorists maintained that both the United States and Germany had fascist tendencies on some level. This blurred the line the Roosevelt administration placed between the US and German political systems, a line that distinguished these regimes as mutually exclusive and wholly antithetical. By contrast, like the Brazilian Arlindo Veiga dos Santos, Ralph Matthews advanced what was perhaps the most surprising of all opinions in response to Nazism. In the 1930s Matthews's and Santos's confidence in liberal democracy was so minimal that they looked to fascist regimes, even Nazism, as a promising paradigm for forcing change in their societies, a change that could conceivably produce a nationalist pride in blackness and/or uproot racial injustice. Regardless of their specific argument, black US and Brazilian commentaries on developments in Nazi Germany helped to globalize tragedies like Kristallnacht in ways that the Vargas and Roosevelt regimes generally did not do in the 1930s. As such, blacks established early racial political frameworks that their societies would employ to grasp the domestic repercussions of Nazism in the years to come.

Despite the cacophony of opinions about fascism presented in this chapter, we can identify prominent themes that emerged from these debates in the 1930s. In the aggregate, the disparate voices analyzed here made it clear that the relationship between racial nationalism and democracy largely would define the ideological stakes of global and domestic fascist movements. *Democracy* became shorthand for a legitimate form of government, and profascists tried to appropriate and redefine the term, abandoning the tenets of liberalism or sometimes attempting to demonstrate the existence of liberal democratic traits in authoritarian regimes. The goal of profascists was to destabilize and compromise the liberal democratic model that had been dominant for several decades, and racial discourse was key. In addition to characterizing deep-seated and systemic racial discrimination as democratic deception, these rhetorical strategies extolled the so-called logics and benefits of exclusive racial nationalism or, contrarily, the potential of a fascist regime to bring about greater inclusion and equality than a "weak" liberal democracy. Black antifascists called to attention the domestic implications of European fascism, using the Third Reich to rebuke the lack of official action-oriented racial democracy.

State Cultural Production, Black Cultural Demarginalization, and Racial Democracy in the 1930s

Although the US and Brazilian states did enact policies that proactively framed their democracies as racially inclusive in the 1930s, these initiatives mainly operated in the cultural realm. For instance, President Roosevelt never supported the bills that were drafted to end lynching or voter disenfranchisement. He told his disappointed wife, Eleanor, that he considered such a civil rights agenda toxic to his political coalition, which depended not only on the black vote but also on the Southern white obstructionists who steadfastly protected Jim Crow. Instead, as historian Lauren Sklaroff has argued, the US New Deal relied on "art and media projects as viable forms of racial policy."[1] It was largely through culture that the Vargas regime specifically targeted black inclusion in Brazilian society as well.

During the 1930s the Brazilian and US states grew and expanded in groundbreaking ways, including in the area of cultural policy. After Vargas's successful coup in 1930, the federal government assumed many broad powers that municipal and state authorities had previously enjoyed, and it also branched out into uncharted territory. One of Vargas's signature novelties was the *brasilidade* ("Brazilianness") campaign meant to construct a strong national identity. Creating a sense of cultural nationalism was a crucial element of this campaign, particularly since Brazilians resolutely clung to regional identities, as São Paulo's 1932 revolution demonstrated dramatically.[2] Franklin Roosevelt and the New Deal also ushered in an "elephantine growth of the federal government"—as William Leuchtenberg argued in his classic study—largely because the state and municipal governments could not handle the crisis that was the Great Depression. Leuchtenberg contended that as a consequence, the years "1933 through 1938 marked a greater upheaval in [US] institutions" than any era prior to it, with the likely exception of the South in the wake of the Civil War.[3] During this period, US intellectuals and artists established a more formal relationship with the government, developing and producing Works Progress Administration projects and other ventures of a cultural nature. In fact, like the Vargas regime and its push for brasilidade, the large cadre of intellectuals and artists hired by the New Deal government constructed and reconstructed national culture as well as national identity.

The enlargement of the US and Brazilian federal governments generated cultural production juggernauts unprecedented in the history of each country, image- and message-making machines that crafted and disseminated their racial political doctrines. The cultural machines enabled these states to produce, manage, and/or help control the nationalist narratives about race and democracy that so concerned authorities in the 1930s. It was largely through cultural materials that the Vargas and Roosevelt states were able to represent Brazil and the United States as racially inclusive societies in the ways they found most advantageous. These cultural efforts were therefore an integral aspect of the shift to racial democracy in the 1930s, and they set the foundation for culture to serve an even greater official function during the Second World War.

This chapter analyzes state cultural activities in radio, music, theater, and literature as articulations of racial democracy. It describes the state cultural apparatuses in both countries and explains what their political purpose was as well as how they came to promote black culture. Indeed, the black cultural demarginalization to which these regimes contributed accelerated tremendously in the United States and Brazil during the 1930s. The process both pushed and pulled many black cultural forms from the margins of white(r) society and into the mainstream, and/or portrayed blacks as legitimate members of the nation. For instance, in the United States the New Deal's Federal Arts, Theatre, and Writers' Projects unveiled black stories, sounds, and characters that mainstream society often had disparaged, ridiculed, or ignored.[4] African American participants in these initiatives, like writers Zora Neale Hurston and Richard Wright, added to black efforts to dismantle long-standing negative stereotypes. Brazilian authorities considered early samba to be related to proscribed practices they deemed disreputable and antithetical to a "civilized" national culture, namely vagrancy and *feitiçaria* (commonly identified as Afro-Brazilian "witchcraft"). In the 1930s the local and federal governments began to subsidize Rio de Janeiro's Carnival and champion samba as authentically Brazilian.[5] Like some of the New Deal projects, Brazilian state cultural work also detailed blacks' place in Brazilian culture and history, as the cultural materials that formally commemorated the fiftieth anniversary of Brazil's abolition of slavery will show.

State-assisted, state-sanctioned black cultural demarginalization represented diverse imaginings of racial democracy. This was largely due to the vigorous disputes that occurred among those engaged in official cultural production, including the predominantly white government program directors and the artists and intellectuals they contracted. Daryle Williams has coined the term "culture wars" to describe the battle between Brazilian cultural managers who sought to control national canon formation and to dictate the visual and musical styles that would define brasilidade. Lauren Sklaroff has pointed to the war that US blacks waged for "cultural self-determination" in their collaborations with the overwhelmingly white liberal administrators of state cultural projects.[6]

The outcome of all this friction was a veritable racial democracy smorgasbord. At times demarginalization manifested as racial denial with authorities hailing the increased embrace of black culture and the fresh representations of blacks in cultural output as a sign of genuine democratic inclusion. It was also common for projects to make glowing claims about the nature of race relations in their society or to skirt the uncomfortable, more pressing issues that black activists raised. Demarginalization materialized as racial realism when cultural producers presented a nationalist image and narrative that candidly confronted the reality of racial injustice. As we have established, racial realism was more commonplace in the United States than in Brazil. US black writer Sterling Brown, director of the Federal Writers' Project Negro Affairs Division from 1936 to 1939, was one vocal advocate of racial realism, and he hoped that honesty and black representational agency would lead to greater equality.[7] Yet demarginalization also engendered racial obstructionism and resistance from authorities on the US Dies committee, in Brazil's Ministry of Education and Health (MES), and in other state agencies.

Demarginalization did have a very action-oriented result: it reduced racial economic disparity in the cultural sphere. The plethora of black-themed official cultural projects in the United States culminated in many job opportunities for African Americans during the difficult Depression years. Even when New Deal cultural offices failed to hire significant numbers of blacks, African American watchdogs both inside and outside of the government protested and were able to force some improvements.[8] In Brazil the local and federal governments' sponsorship of Carnival was perhaps the most reliable state-funded monetary benefit to accompany demarginalization.[9] In other words, apart from any realist messages that insisted on better circumstances for blacks, demarginalization actually boosted the economic prospects for many of them.

The extent to which demarginalization helped black artists and intellectuals was restricted, however. In the United States and Brazil, the reliance on white cultural mediators—who controlled, oversaw, produced, and/or performed what were recognized as black cultural expressions—minimized demarginalization's economic and racial political advantage.[10] Blacks sought roles as mediators and patrons themselves, but white mediators often enjoyed the lion's share of the wealth generated by black culture's growing popularity. The dependence on white mediators and the fact that demarginalization frequently functioned as racial denial, especially in Brazil, did stunt its action-oriented potential and regularly led to exploitation.

White cultural mediation in state projects operated differently in the United States and Brazil, particularly in the mid- to late 1930s when the New Deal's relief program for the arts, Federal One, was most active. Federal One contained black divisions that hired African American actors, dancers, writers, musicians, and other artists to create, participate, and in many cases direct projects that focused on black culture and experiences. In Brazil there was no equivalent nationwide program in place that set aside jobs in multiple areas of the arts specifically for blacks. Yet despite this advantage, blacks fought discriminatory hiring practices and struggled to attain fair employment representation in Federal One offices across the country. In addition, the predominantly white New Deal administrators and supervisors made the final decisions about which projects and content were approved, denying blacks the autonomy they needed to fully advance their realist agenda.[11]

The Brazilian and US states used cultural production to construct many of the messages and symbols that informed the public on how to maneuver through the convoluted labyrinth of racial political ideologies during the 1930s. Domestic politics and the need to secure public support for Vargas and Roosevelt were at the core of these efforts. Thus, before we assess how the cultural apparatuses became major sites of demarginalization and helped bring racial democracy to life for the US and Brazilian publics, we will examine these cultural production machines and how they worked politically.

TRANSFORMATIONS IN BRAZILIAN AND US STATE CULTURAL PRODUCTION

The expansion and evolution of state cultural work in the United States and Brazil during the 1930s did not mirror each other, despite striking commonalities. In Brazil the private sector entertainment industry was much smaller in scale and proportion and had fewer financial resources than that in the United States. On the one hand, this meant that the US government relied on and collaborated with a larger media industry, benefited from its more extensive infrastructure, and had fuller access to the necessary media equipment than its Brazilian counterpart. On the other hand, Brazil's more modest private entertainment industry granted the Vargas regime greater control. Nonetheless, the impulse that drove both states to become dominant cultural producers was deeply political. In the aggregate, these activities buttressed the Roosevelt and Vargas regimes' political agendas. The group of artists and intellectuals the governments employed to do this work typically tried to promote their own political visions, often with limited success.

The number of Brazilian state offices related to culture exploded in the 1930s with the creation of the MES, the National Artistic and Historic Patrimony Service (SPHAN), the Department of Press and Propaganda (DIP) and its predecessors, the National Institute of Educational Cinema, and the National Theater Service, among others. As Mônica Pimenta Velloso explained, it "was during the Vargas era that the relationship between intellectuals and the state defined the cultural domain as 'official business,' one that entailed its own budget and intervened in all sectors of production, diffusion, and conservation of intellectual and artistic work."[12] Although many government agencies were too understaffed and underfunded to be as influential as Velloso suggests, the state had a strong impact on the themes and the volume of national cultural production in the 1930s, particularly in comparison to what existed before Vargas took power.[13]

Together these agencies were responsible for executing Vargas's "ideological sanitation" crusade, which directly linked state cultural work to perceived national defense imperatives. Vargas may have desired a multiracial, multiclass, multiregional coalition, but he in no way wanted that diversity to translate into a diversity in political thought. Maria Luiza Tucci Carneiro has shown that "the control of culture" was essential for state offices like the DIP, the MES, and the DOPS (political police) to repress the circulation of "revolutionary" ideas. Officials in these and other agencies invoked the patriotic need to protect "national security" as justification for their efforts.[14] In fact, officials understood their cultural and security missions as so entwined that the MES—which privately informed Vargas in 1935 that it would "really be the Ministry of National Culture"—even had its own National Security Division.[15] According to Carneiro, communists and blacks were among the groups the state cultural body most targeted for repression or censorship in the name of national defense.[16] We have already seen the official anticommunist cultural approach, as some of the sources examined in chapter 2 were products of the cultural propaganda machine.

In the United States, the Works Progress Administration's Federal Project Number One (Federal One) drove this enterprise. Federal One was launched in 1935 largely in acknowledgment that artists and the intelligentsia also needed employment during the Depression. Federal One originally allocated $27 million to its divisions: the Federal Art Project, the Federal Music Project, the Federal Theatre Project, and the Federal Writers' Project.[17] At its peak in 1936, it employed almost forty-five thousand people in offices nationwide. As a result, the US government was transformed into a major employer of artists and intellectuals, who, in turn, became state-sponsored creators of the stories, sounds, and images that defined US society and culture. Despite the fact that Federal One funding was a small fraction of the overall WPA budget, these cultural projects had offices across the nation, "made a lot of political noise," and produced works that millions of people saw, heard, or read.[18]

The US state cultural machine was not as unabashed in its political repression and control as its Brazilian counterpart, yet it did often censor materials perceived as too challenging to the government and/or the desired national image. Cultural producers did not enjoy unrestricted freedom, as the experiences of Sterling Brown, the black Federal Writers' Project (FWP) national editor of Negro affairs, will show below. The WPA music unit's catalogue of the recordings in the Library of Congress Archive of American Folk Song—which excluded at least one song perceived as too politically embarrassing to the Roosevelt administration—is another example.[19] Some members of Congress also remained very vigilant about state cultural themes, particularly the anticommunist zealot Martin Dies, who was highly suspicious of Federal

One.[20] Federal One, then, was a battleground of ideologies as artists, intellectuals, and officials inside and outside the cultural machine fought to determine the political message it delivered to the public.

The most revolutionary and powerful state cultural activity, as well as a clear example of how this work functioned as political propaganda, occurred in the realm of radio. The political use of radio was controversial in both countries, and observers nervously commented on its potency as a political tool. Radio provided the first opportunity for presidents to speak directly to the people, most famously through Roosevelt's radio "fireside chats" and the frequent transmission of Vargas's speeches during his government's nightly *Hora do Brasil* radio program.[21] The ways that Vargas and Roosevelt supported and mobilized radio to communicate and promulgate propaganda boosted the medium's popularity in both nations. Radio was also the most effective mechanism through which Roosevelt and Vargas could transmit their racial democratic messages to the most expansive audience and in the most remote places. This advantage was especially helpful as Roosevelt and Vargas sought to mount extensive, pluralistic political bases to maintain power. In comparison to other media, such as print journalism or cinema, radio was cost-effective and relatively easy to spread throughout the country, and it did not exclude the illiterate.

The Vargas regime was fundamental in the ascension, influence, and content of radio in Brazil during the 1930s, when the medium became a prominent feature of national life. In 1931 twenty stations existed in Brazil; in 1941 that number had risen to almost one hundred. Radio units themselves also became more ubiquitous in Brazilian homes thanks to their increasing affordability. By the end of the 1930s lower-income households were able to purchase used radios or new units on installment.[22] In 1931 the government passed the first statute to specifically regulate radio broadcasting. In appreciation of radio's impact on a society that recorded an illiteracy rate of over 60 percent in 1934, authorities decreed that radio broadcasts be a "service of national interest and educative purpose."[23]

Brazil's 1932 radio law permitted radio stations to fund programming through the sale of advertising space. According to Othon Jambeiro and his coauthors, the introduction of commercials immediately converted radio from an "erudite, instructive, and cultural" medium into "a popular instrument of leisure and amusement" and mass communication.[24] The move to commercial radio mandated the transmission of material that would draw large audiences, including popular music. The state retained control, however, as the radio stations were obliged to submit their content for state censorship and to broadcast state propaganda. (As chapter 6 demonstrates, this included US state programming and propaganda during the war.) The nightly *Hora do Brasil* show was the centerpiece of Vargas's radio political propaganda.

Radio became one of Vargas's secret weapons to legitimate his regime and to inspire national unity around his leadership. In 1936 Lourival Fontes, head of Brazil's Department of Propaganda and Cultural Diffusion (a forerunner of DIP), said that the Vargas regime "cannot underestimate the work of propaganda and culture undertaken on the radio," citing the power of radio to reach "where the school and the press do not." Despite being a bitter rival of Fontes, minister of education and health Gustavo Capanema agreed with him about radio's potential, telling Vargas in 1936 that "radio has a role of inestimable value to play" in a country so vast. Capanema envisioned it as a means of teaching elite cultural, social, political, and moral aesthetics, practices, and values to the Brazilian masses. He encouraged Vargas to conceive of radio as much more than a mere source of entertainment and information.[25]

Although this process began earlier during Vargas's rule, the "symbiosis of radio and politics had its greatest expression" with the onset of the Estado Novo.[26] In a message he sent to Congress six months before dissolving it, Vargas identified the "pressing" need for the government to spread its broadcasting activities in "the diverse and distant zones of the hinterlands"—where he resented the local presses' focus on "news of a regional character"—in order to "reinforc[e] [the public's] knowledge of the democratic regime."[27] From Vargas's perspective, the government's radio policy was essentially a political project, and he turned to radio to facilitate his goal of transforming Bahianos, Pernambucanos, Cariocas, Paulistas, and Gaúchos into Brazilians.

In the United States, a struggle emerged between corporate interests and reformers over the use of radio. The business lobby prevailed in 1934 when federal law codified the "corporate- and advertiser-centered model for radio" that had been in existence for years. But the reformers, who envisioned radio as a medium for civic and educational purposes, were not entirely defeated. Their efforts convinced radio stations not only that noncommercial broadcasts would have an audience among the elite and others but also that adopting a public service mission (if only part-time) would increase the industry's respectability. Broadcasters made it clear to Franklin Roosevelt that they hoped he would both seriously consider their commitment to public interest radio and take advantage of the chance to disseminate his agenda broadly. Roosevelt and other politicians availed themselves of this opportunity, especially after discovering that without journalists present, they could maintain control over their message and avoid the need to subject themselves to questions or challenges.[28]

More than any other president in US history, Franklin Roosevelt benefited from radio, stimulated its popularity, and utilized the medium as an effective political tool. This would not have been possible without the advances in technology that made radio such an omnipresent device in the so-called golden age. As in Brazil, radio sets became more affordable, and even during the destitute days of the Depression, the number of radio owners grew precipitously. In the seven-year period between 1930 and 1937, the percentage of US homes with radios had doubled from 40 to 80 percent.[29] With the spread of radio, Roosevelt's intermittent, intimate fireside chats became a fixture in homes across the country as families gathered around the radio to hear the president explain New Deal policies, introduce new programs, provide war updates, and promote nationalism. Russell Buhite and David Levy have argued that the fireside chats "signaled to average Americans what attitudes and actions were unpatriotic [and] instill[ed] in listeners feelings of unity."[30] Of course, the feelings of patriotic unity were to be experienced vis-à-vis Roosevelt's leadership and were connected to his vision for the nation. The size of the audience gave Roosevelt incredible influence. In the early 1940s, before Pearl Harbor, nearly fifty-four million listeners, or about 72 percent of the US population, tuned in to one of Roosevelt's fireside chats.[31]

Radio allowed President Roosevelt to adopt a new mode of governing in which invisibility facilitated his leadership and coalition building across the country. First, throughout his presidency, Roosevelt visually hid his physical disability, caused by polio, from the public as much as possible to conceal what would have been perceived as weakness. Radio helped Roosevelt to do so without compromising his ability to maintain a strong political presence. He was perhaps the first president whose voice, separate from his physical form, garnered complete authority with so much of the public. Furthermore, before radio, members of the public were obliged to assemble in person to hear political speeches, which forced them to confront one another—and often uncomfortable alliances—in the flesh. But the commonly at-home or local consumption of radio broadcasts made it possible for strange bedfellows to avoid awkward interactions, enabling the "new urban political coalition [to] remain largely invisible to itself," as Barbara Savage has noted.[32] The benefit of invisibility was not just limited to Roosevelt's chats or formal speeches; it was also useful when New Deal cultural programming touched upon sensitive matters like racial nationalism.

In the United States and Brazil, politics converged with radio in the early stages of the medium's existence. Radio would turn into a fundamental mechanism through which black cultural demarginalization as an expression of official racial democracy occurred. All the appropriate factors were on hand for this situation to materialize. Two charismatic presidents appreciated and respected the power of radio and endeavored to maximize its political potential. In the United States, the commercial radio industry generally seemed to welcome and encourage the New Deal to take advantage of the medium. In Brazil, the Vargas regime's use of radio had less impact when the content was as blatantly political as the fireside chats. (In fact, the *Hora do Brasil* program was nicknamed *Hora de fala sozinho* [Hour of talking to himself] because its vapid content failed to draw a fan base comparable to that of the fireside chats.) The more muted political nature of artistic- and entertainment-focused programming met with greater success and therefore pleased the Brazilian commercial radio stations.[33] As a result, the transmission of black musical forms that could attract a larger listenership became a key component of the government's cultural brasilidade efforts. US audiences also enjoyed state-sponsored cultural content over the radio, which similarly advanced various expressions of racial political nationalism by bringing black culture into the mainstream. Although it was a crucial piece of the enormous cultural production machines in Brazil and the United States in the 1930s, radio was just one source of and medium for demarginalization.

BLACK CULTURAL DEMARGINALIZATION

The 1930s was the decade in which the US and Brazilian states began, in earnest, to recognize black music, dance, artistry, literature, and other such pursuits as national treasures. This was not a perfectly clean or linear trajectory in which full acceptance of black culture occurred, but it did mark a major turning point, especially in relation to state cultural production. In line with the message of racial inclusion, official demarginalization also entailed the greater presence of black subjects in cultural materials and validated their membership in the national community. Brazilian and US black artists and intellectuals had staked their claim to a rightful place in their societies for generations. Demarginalization was not something that merely happened to blacks as they passively observed: many of them actively worked to stimulate demarginalization, while others fought against it. Most blacks, however, sought a degree of control over their cultural representation. Blacks also struggled to benefit financially from the mainstreaming of the culture that largely had arisen from their neighborhoods when employment in cultural production often landed in the laps of white mediators. Disagreements erupted among and between blacks and state cultural managers about the ways that demarginalization should characterize the United States and Brazil in racial political terms that were relevant to contemporaneous challenges and debates.

Radio became the site of a fierce battle over black cultural representation.[34] US blacks aggressively asserted their voice in the debate about the purpose of radio, often crusading for racially progressive content and programming that carried an action-oriented social and political purpose. From both inside and outside the government, blacks pressed to use radio to educate the public on racial realities and to champion the cause of racial equality. US black activists protested radio and other media stereotypes that depicted blacks as a hopelessly feckless, farcical, and inferior (if at times harmless and even lovable) lot. In the 1930s activists targeted US commercial radio's first serial, the comedy *Amos 'n' Andy*, named for the two black male leads who rather incompetently ran their taxicab company. Launched in 1929 and voiced by white actors, *Amos 'n' Andy* quickly became a hit and attracted the lion's share of the radio audience, approximately forty million listeners daily. Although very popular among blacks, many concerned African Americans maligned *Amos 'n' Andy* for its portrayal of the black community as uneducated and naive. *Amos 'n' Andy* dissenters believed the show mocked their demands for social and political equality by painting blacks as ill prepared for and undeserving of those rights. The black *Pittsburgh Courier* newspaper derided the show as antiblack "propaganda" and organized a petition against it that accumulated 740,000 signatures.[35]

As the *Amos 'n' Andy* anecdote shows, US blacks did not always fight against invisibility per se in their push for demarginalization. Historically, blacks appeared in the majority of popular culture forms in the United States, even in absentia. *Amos 'n' Andy* followed in the footsteps of one such long-standing tradition: minstrelsy. One of the nineteenth century's most widespread and fashionable theatrical genres, minstrel shows included white (and sometimes black) entertainers who donned blackface to perform grossly stereotypical representations of blacks not dissimilar to the *Amos 'n' Andy* characters.[36] Thus, US blacks often focused on "cultural self-determination" and the right to have control over their community's image. African Americans wanted their cultural representation to reflect their worth as serious political agents and legitimate members of US society who deserved respect, not ridicule. They strove for black inclusion in spaces and narratives from which blacks tended to be excluded—those that bestowed political, social, and economic rights.[37]

African Americans had a few important allies in the Roosevelt administration that helped them launch a counterattack against the negative depiction of blacks and advocate for an action-oriented, realist racial democracy. In 1935 secretary of the interior Harold Ickes, who had been president of the NAACP in Chicago, launched the short-lived Radio Education Project at the Office of Education. Ickes explicitly stated that the primary mission of educational radio should be the eradication of racist attitudes in the United States. These early Office of Education radio initiatives provided African Americans and their allies with the first opportunity to use national radio as a platform to transform blacks' negative image.[38]

The Radio Education Project and the Federal One programs ensured black cultural visibility and included African Americans in mainstream narratives. These projects established a space for black and other racially progressive cultural producers to create and disseminate work that otherwise would not have existed. The nature of the cultural work attracted many intellectuals, artists, and activists who brought their visions and dreams into their positions. Furthermore, the Great Depression precipitated the economic collapse of many black cultural enterprises that had thrived during the 1920s, leaving blacks in most cultural industries jobless or severely underemployed. The state cultural machine, including what Lauren Sklaroff has termed its "black bureaucracy," helped alleviate this situation.[39]

Federal One institutionalized demarginalization with the formation of black divisions where so many of the cultural machine's black bureaucracy worked. One could certainly argue that the creation of separate units was a form of segregation and marginalization, and some southern states had Negro Writers' Units (NWU) because of Jim Crow laws and practices. Blacks like NAACP director Walter White took issue with these segregated bodies because they facilitated the firing of blacks whenever budget cuts occurred.[40] However, many blacks had the opportunity to experience a degree of cultural self-determination in these divisions. In fact, Rose McClendon, African American actress and leader in the black theater movement, was the first person to propose setting up so-called Negro Units to Federal Theatre Project (FTP) director Hallie Flanagan. McClendon strongly believed in the power of black theater to promote African American artists and themes that advanced an antiracist agenda, and her perspective shaped the direction of the Negro Units. As a result, the FTP created roles that diverged from the stereotypical tropes commonplace in mainstream productions. The Negro Units typically produced the least sanitized versions of black life as well, confronting the brutal realities of US racial history and fiercely challenging old clichés. McClendon would briefly serve as codirector of the New York City Negro Unit under her friend, white director John Houseman, before she tragically succumbed to cancer.[41]

Sklaroff has contended that black producers such as Carlton Moss, Sterling Brown, and Truman Gibson "displayed a more intense personal investment" in their work than their white mediator colleagues. Blacks believed that what Carlton Moss termed "cultural emancipation" could also translate into political, social, and economic emancipation, and they put the spotlight on issues that generally were ignored outside communities of color.[42] Even the popular intellectual radio programs *America's Town Meeting of the Air* on CBS and the *University of Chicago Roundtable* on NBC evaded topics about race at the time.[43] Thus, through the black divisions in particular, the government's cultural programming played a critical and unique role in the broad dissemination of images and stories that depicted blacks realistically and challenged what US racial democracy could and should be. As historian Catherine Stewart explains, the "special 'Negro projects' were intended to reflect the democratic spirit of the New Deal."[44]

If less personally invested in these projects than the members of the black bureaucracy, the white cultural mediators who ran most of the state programs often used cultural production to portray the United States as a racially plural society and democracy.[45] Rachel DuBois's work with the Radio Education Project epitomized this mission. Her disgust with the wildly popular and racist radio broadcasts of the Catholic Father Coughlin and her experience as a teacher and education reformer led her to contact John Studebaker, US commissioner of education. She pitched the idea that the US government should produce a radio series that countered Coughlin's message of exclusive white Christian nationalism. She hoped such a series would "reduce intergroup prejudice" by illuminating the ways that people of various racial, ethnic, and religious backgrounds were fundamental to US history, culture, and society. The idea eventually materialized in the Radio Education Project's signature program, *Americans All, Immigrants All,* which aired in 1938 and 1939 and was "a twenty-six-week nationally broadcast series that sought to create a state-sanctioned narrative of American history that made immigrants, African Americans, and Jews visible." Barbara Savage has written that this was a landmark project that developed "a new paradigm about ethnicity and race" in the United States, establishing a role for blacks and others based on a "myth of success."[46]

The *Americans All, Immigrants All* thirty-minute episode "The Negro" offered blacks "a rare opportunity to present a new image of 'the Negro' to a mass audience, black and white, that had been fed a steady diet of black buffoons and mimics in the media, especially on radio." Rachel DuBois fought for the inclusion of African American advisors on "The Negro" script, arguing for their importance as "our largest minority group [and] our most important problem, since our democracy, after all, will rise or fall according to the way we treat that group." Commissioner Studebaker appointed Alain Locke and W. E. B. DuBois as informal, unpaid consultants. Locke and DuBois may have been disappointed with many aspects of the final product, but their contributions to the episode resulted in a script that explained black experiences in ways unfamiliar to mainstream audiences. Listeners learned what was not found in most history books, such as the fact that the entire nation, not just the slaveholders, benefited from slavery. African Americans like Harriet Tubman and Sojourner Truth were emblems of black agency and resistance. Black voices were free of hyperbolic, theatrical dialect. The show even described how blacks were hit especially hard during the Great Depression due to the "last hired, first fired" phenomenon and abysmal housing conditions. Last-minute decisions caused the latter discussion to be cut from the live broadcast to accommodate a nine-minute song that Locke believed problematically invoked the feel of the old plantation slave as opposed to the bold New Negro. The official recording of the show sent out for educational purposes stuck to the original script.[47]

Music, dance, and other forms of black cultural expression were often key components of black state cultural productions, as in "The Negro." In fact, the FTP Negro Unit's Play Bureau, responsible for determining which plays would go into production, advised that black theatrical pieces incorporate music heavily to maximize mainstream appeal. Because of the FTP's objective to "democratize theater in America and to satisfy the interests of diverse communities," Sklaroff has written, "music that readers considered to be distinctly 'Negro' was significant in the evaluation of a production's potential success." Black dramaturgists understood that the FTP preferred plays that highlighted black music, and audience responses to such work indicated that the Play Bureau's assessment was accurate.[48] Furthermore, the commercial and academic folk movement and, relatedly, Roosevelt's advocacy of a populist "common-man ideology" infiltrated the WPA and Federal One projects. Jazz, understood to have emerged from black communities, was "swept up in this new populism," even if most of the popular bands had white bandleaders.[49]

The scholarship of official demarginalization in Brazil during the 1930s traditionally has focused on music, especially the government's approval of samba as national culture in ways that maintained strong and recognizable Afro-Brazilian roots. When the Vargas regime chose samba to assume the mantle of brasilidade, it did not just sponsor Carnival; samba also was broadcast across the nation as the epitome of Brazilian musical ingenuity, greatness, and autonomy.

One of the first, historically celebrated moments to mark the official endorsement of samba came in 1932, when Deixa Falar (the first samba school, or permanent parade band and group) received state subsidization for its participation in Rio de Janeiro's Carnival. From the outset, Deixa Falar illustrated how samba could be used on behalf of political causes. Its *enredo*, or the song repeatedly performed during Carnival, was "A Primavera e a Revolução de Outubro" (Spring and the October Revolution), referring to the Revolution of 1930 that had brought Vargas to power. Music journalist Sérgio Cabral wrote that this was "the beginning of the love affair" between Vargas and Carnival.[50] Vargas's team already had experienced the ways the lyrical content of popular music could be politicized and could quickly evolve as "an instrument of propaganda." During the 1929 presidential campaign, some pro-Vargas songs had been recorded, although those for his opponent, Júlio Prestes, may have been more commonplace.[51] At any rate, the first barrage of pro-Vargas popular songs appeared after the Revolution of 1930, and Deixa Falar seemed to ensure that samba was officially a part of the trend in politically oriented music.

Samba performed at least two critical functions for Vargas's brasilidade efforts. First, it was an effective way for Vargas to rally support among the overwhelmingly illiterate working class. Vargas hoped to build a broad political base, one that pulled supporters from groups traditionally marginalized as political actors. The incorporation of pro-Vargas lyrics in irresistible popular music could help achieve this end. Second, even though Vargas intended for his political constituency to be racially, socially and regionally pluralistic, he did not want it to be ideologically heterogeneous. Samba lyrics were used to communicate the values of brasilidade and to help dictate how proper Brazilians should think and behave.[52]

As the state pushed for nationalism, it set standards for the Carnival parade's samba school participants in ways that both advanced Vargas's political objectives and elevated an imagined, authentic Afro-Brazilian culture. The year 1934 signaled the beginning of the state's bona fide brasilidade efforts in the federal capital's Carnival, when the city government inaugurated three regulations. The first rule banned wind instruments in order to privilege the elaborate percussion sections that authorities decided was the African-derived signature style of samba from the *morro* ("favelas"). The second directive required each samba school to include an *ala das baianas* (wing of Bahian women). This wing constituted a group of women dressed in the traditional clothing associated with black Bahian practitioners of candomblé, a syncretic religion that combined West African religions with Catholicism. The look of these women was well known because they wore their signature long white dresses and head wraps to sell Bahian dishes in the streets. (Singer and actress Carmen Miranda appropriated elements of this look.) Their homes were also known as the venues of the early samba gatherings. The role of the Mãe Negra/Preta analyzed in previous chapters is relevant here. Bahian women were natives of the state that contained Brazil's first capital city and of the region that cradled the nation in its early stages. Baianas were therefore connected to the Mãe Pretas that nurtured Brazilian civilization, just as they had nurtured the birth of samba. Finally, Rio's government mandated that all Carnival lyrics reflect a "nationalist theme."[53]

Pianist Radamés Gnattali, from Rio Grande do Sul, remembered that when he arrived in Rio de Janeiro in the late 1920s, samba was limited to that city. "After the arrival of radio," he continued, "everyone started to hear it."[54] The government's support for and role in the shift to commercial radio accountable to listeners' desires were critical factors in the spread of samba from the nation's capital to the rest of Brazil. One radio producer said that "around 1935 and 1936 Paulista radio was obliged to acknowledge the music from Rio. It was no longer possible to disregard the pressure from the listener." Anthropologist João Baptista Pereira refers to this moment as carioca music's invasion of Paulista radio programming, the "infiltration of carioca music into São Paulo's carnival, and the surge of samba schools" that mirrored those in Rio. Similar things were transpiring in other regions, as posters were sent throughout the nation to advertise the carioca music played on the radio. It was, certainly, a reciprocal process in which the public's taste affected what was broadcast on the radio, and what was played on the radio helped determine the public's musical palate.[55]

Like US blacks, Afro-Brazilians were central to the demarginalization of their art and entertainment, as many proactively sought protection and backing from whites, broader recognition for their music as national culture, and economic benefit. Blacks in the early twentieth century helped lay the groundwork for the progress that occurred in the 1930s. For instance, the famous black *tias* (aunts) who hosted the multifaceted ceremonies at which samba was developed often solicited police approval for their parties. Women like Tia Perciliana (Perciliana Maria Constança), the mother of famous musician João da Baiana (João Machado Guedes), and the celebrated Tia Ciata (Hilária Batista de Almeida) also invited society's powerful and influential members into their homes.

Senator Pinheiro Machado was among the elite guests to enjoy live music at Tia Perciliana's house. Machado purchased and inscribed a tambourine for her son, João da Baiana, whose instrument had been confiscated by police while he was en route to Machado's house. (Machado had hired the musician to perform for his high society guests.) The tambourine, whose inscription indicated that it was from Pinheiro Machado, protected João da Baiana during his future interactions with the police.[56] Although these forms of patronage were not the norm among musicians of this period—the not-so-renowned musicians had lesser luck—the tias and the fortunate musicians helped to forge pathways toward demarginalization for what would become samba.[57] The patrons defended and financially supported their favorite Afro-Brazilian musicians, and they played a part in black music's marketability among those in their social circles whenever they contracted blacks to perform at private and public events alike.

In addition to cultivating patronage when possible, Afro-Brazilians also actively used journalism to enlarge their reputation, nationalize their music, and acquire greater financial security. In the early twentieth century, newspapers and journalists were major propagators of popular music, influencing society with their picks for up-and-coming artists, musical genres, and songs. Historian Marc Hertzman has described the ways that black artists shaped this process by seeking out journalists to provide them with information and interviews. Sinhô, the so-called King of Samba, even called journalists when he composed a new song. Newspapers also frequently invited *sambistas* to partake in various samba competitions. When the *A Nação* newspaper held a contest for the best samba composer of the favelas in 1935, Paulo da Portela (Paulo Benjamin de Oliveira)—black musician, community leader, and cofounder of the Portela Samba School—appealed to the public. His friends helped stuff the ballot box to ensure da Portela's victory.[58] Paulo da Portela and the other artists understood that their actions would spread their names as talented sambistas, which could translate into higher sales, more paying engagements, and longer careers.

Afro-Brazilian efforts to tap into the commercial potential of samba were controversial among many blacks. In his seventies, one successful black sambista and samba school composer looked back on the early years of samba with nostalgia, saying, "I miss those days: everything was pure. We suffered with the police but we sang what we felt. The samba of that time was authentic. Today you even have this bossa nova nonsense with the name of samba."[59] Afro-Brazilian journalist Vagalume (Francisco Guimarães) was a major critic as well. His 1933 book *Na roda do samba* cast aspersions on what he believed to be contaminating the music—its rapid commodification and commercialization. Vagalume argued that when samba remained "safe" in the mostly black hillside communities, it maintained its spiritual and cultural essence. When it ventured into the world of the depraved music industry, samba became unrecognizable.[60] Vagalume's assessment, echoed by the first testimony here, was that black cultural demarginalization should not be celebrated as an economic opportunity for blacks; rather, it should be lamented as a certain death of cultural authenticity.

Regardless of Vagalume's denunciations, black efforts to attain media endorsements could also grant the musicians a degree of authority in terms of how the public perceived and appreciated samba. In 1936 *A Rua* magazine crowned Paulo da Portela the foremost *Cidadão Samba* (Samba Citizen). In response to the honor, da Portela enumerated "decrees" that called upon "all the aristocrats of this extremely democratic Republic" to "realize that Samba is made from pieces of the soul, scintillations of the brain, much love, and big dose [*sic*] of patriotic love."[61] Da Portela was instructing Brazil's elite to embrace samba as an inherently patriotic art form, one that deserved its respect and backing. By describing the aristocrats as members of a democratic society in his appeal, da Portela suggested that there was a connection between democracy and their adoption of samba as nationalist music. It appears that he believed the "democratic" component was relevant to whether or not samba would continue to move into the mainstream.

RACIAL DEMOCRACY IN STATE DEMARGINALIZATION PROJECTS

The US and Brazilian states' mainstreaming of black cultural forms and the increasing characterization of blacks as deserving constituents conveyed numerous categories of racial democracy that frequently caused tension among those engaged in cultural work. Realism versus denial, white cultural mediators versus black performers, intellectuals/artists versus state managers: these were some of the ideas and actors that clashed in official demarginalization projects. They were also integral to the broader debate about what it meant to be a democracy in the United States and Brazil. This section's US analysis will assess several instances of demarginalization in Federal One projects in radio, theater, poetry, music, and more. The Brazilian analysis will focus on various events that commemorated the country's fiftieth anniversary *(cinquentenário)*, in 1938, of slavery's abolition. This discussion of state cultural materials is organized by category of racial democracy, not by country.

Before delving into the cinquentenário, we will take a quick detour with Gilberto Freyre to acknowledge his place in Brazilian state-sponsored cultural work and rhetoric. Freyre's valorization of blacks, racial mixture, and northeastern culture represented the regime's position when the Ministry of Education and Health published his lectures and paid for some of his trips abroad. Freyre also helped create the agendas and the historical, cultural, and regional foci of state institutions such as the National Artistic and Historic Patrimony Service (SPHAN). Finally, the federal government's cultural machine included bureaucrats who read and were tremendously influenced by Freyre's ideas. Many of these intellectual bureaucrats personally knew Freyre as well. Even though he did not use the term "racial democracy" at the time, many of them must have been aware of the manner in which Freyre linked Brazilian racial nationalism and democratic values by praising lusotropical "social democracy through the mixture of races" in 1936 and 1937.[62]

That said, Gilberto Freyre also illuminated how state agencies disagreed over brasilidade and how anticommunist concerns factored into this discord. While the federal government's cultural, historical, and statistical agencies tended to favor Freyre, the National Commission for the Repression of Communism accused him of being subversive. Furthermore, Agamenon Magalhães, the "Aryanist" *interventor* (Vargas-appointed governor) in Freyre's home state of Pernambuco, opposed his mestizo nationalism, and the rather politically conservative Freyre was detained by the Pernambucan political police for being a "communist" and/or "agitator" in 1935 and 1942.[63] To what must have been Magalhães's chagrin, Freyre's racial political nationalism already was quite popular by the 1938 cinquentenário.

The cinquentenário of abolition was a rare series of official (and unofficial) commemorations that specifically addressed the black population historically, culturally, politically, economically, and socially. Several state cultural entities and authorities were involved, including Minister Gustavo Capanema and his Ministry of Education and Health, as well as rival minister Lourival Fontes and his propaganda department. The official commemorations manifested in multifarious ways: academic conferences, music and dance performances, radio broadcasts (including the nationally broadcast radio play *A Lei Áurea,* commissioned by Fontes and named after the abolition law), official publications, political speeches, and local festivals were all included.[64] Olívia Gomes da Cunha has written that "the programs of the commemorative festivities were abundantly documented in newspapers across the entire country."[65]

Capanema asked Arthur Ramos—the distinguished white specialist on Afro-Brazilian culture and the scholar who would coin the term "racial democracy" in 1941—to organize the official celebrations. Ramos intended for the cinquentenário "to promote, give visibility to, and valorize aspects [of Brazilian society, culture and history] that were rarely made significant in official narratives," which was in accord with his scholarly modus operandi. Specifically, Ramos hoped to bestow dignity upon blacks and the labor they carried out and to stimulate research that analyzed the black race and its impact on Brazilian civilization. Some of the artists and intellectuals involved made it a point to assess the state of Afro-Brazilians in 1938, rendering the past event of abolition imminently present: as da Cunha argued, creating an official "national history" did lead to a reevaluation of the present realities. Although many other participants appeared anxious to glorify enslaved blacks' bygone function in constructing the nation, they also romanticized abolition as racial reconciliation and as the point of departure for national racial democracy without evaluating the status quo of the current black population. Even Ramos's plan to validate blacks "in a certain discursive territory [did] nothing to alter the breadth of [the state's] public policies" that could have benefited them more concretely.[66]

The abolition radio play *A Lei Áurea* (The Golden Law)—which famous dramatist Joracy Camargo penned and the Society of National Radio transmitted across the nation on the Thirteenth of May—pushed a denialist narrative, but it did contain one intriguing example of racial realism. In the play, two journalists led the listener through three historical episodes: Princess Isabel's pro-abolition speech from the throne, the abolition debates in the Senate, and the princess regent's signing of the Golden Law. None of the episodes highlighted the agency of the enslaved to overthrow the institution. The character Preta Velha, or Old Black Woman, appeared early in the play. When one of the journalists asked the enslaved woman whether she knew abolition was imminent, she replied that she did, but she seemed unimpressed. Her nonchalance on the issue and preoccupation with selling snacks was juxtaposed with the energy described in the streets. The journalist was clearly confused as to why this enslaved woman, who presumably had more to gain than many of the revelers, appeared the least joyous. She implied that she had seen it all before with the passage of the Law of the Free Womb in 1871, sixteen years earlier. In fact, its name was a misnomer, Preta Velha indicated; her children, she said, were "even more enslaved than I." The law granted slaveholders the option either to avail themselves of these children's labor until they turned twenty-one or to hand them over to the state and receive indemnity once they reached eight years of age. Very few chose the latter. Thus Preta Velha educated the public on the fallacy of the "free womb." She seemed to trust the reporter's insistence that slavery was truly ending only when he told her that black abolitionist José do Patrocínio was attending the princess regent's speech.[67]

Preta Velha's reaction reminded the listener that blacks' history with the state was wrought with betrayal and distrust. Her attitude was presented not as ignorant but as pragmatic about what blacks could expect from the government. As a black woman whose body had been codified and dissected into slave and free compartments, Preta Velha could best communicate this betrayal, especially after she presumably had nourished Brazilian civilization as a Mãe Preta. Preta Velha, whose namelessness gave her a symbolic quality, was the most poignant representative of the state's deception and its role in black oppression. This message was unlikely the intention of Camargo, whose account of abolition and Princess Isabel was otherwise exceedingly saccharine and sanguine. Ironically, his inclusion of the enslaved black woman—normally a comforting, unthreatening, and reassuring emblem of Brazilian interracial harmony—performed a subversive function in his tale of abolition.

Afro-Brazilian lawyer Evaristo de Moraes's participation in cinquentenário-related events added to Preta Velha's realist rhetoric, which touched upon the state's breach of trust with blacks. Moraes published a newspaper article that addressed slavery, abolition, and their legacies about two months before presenting his paper "Blacks as a Factor in Civilization" at the cinquentenário conference. Perhaps reflecting the analysis he would present at the abolition conference, Moraes's newspaper article extolled blacks' economic impact on Brazil's industrial epicenter. The article, "Before European Immigrants It Was Blacks That Made São Paulo Great," discussed "the black race's enormous contribution to the fortune of São Paulo," challenging the view that European immigration was the key to the city's industrialization. He reminded readers of the mainstream journal *Diário da Noite* that enslaved blacks had "given [the European immigrants] the economic advantages of which they are so proud."[68]

In general, Moraes's piece rebutted São Paulo's racially exclusive identity that located the roots of its so-called unique modernity in the contributions of whites, a central theme of its 1932 Constitutionalist Revolution. In particular, Paulista exceptionalist discourse and iconography highlighted the *bandeirantes*—characterized as the white pioneers who ventured into uncharted, inland territories and made possible the expansion of Brazil—and European immigrants.[69] More specifically, Evaristo de Moraes composed the article in response to an official's suggestion that the police employ racial profiling and target blacks to identify the unknown murderers of two Chinese citizens in São Paulo. Moraes reproached the official for deprecating the very race that had built the city, and he referred to the racial prejudice blacks continued to confront in Brazil. The lesson to the official and to the reader was that blacks deserved respect for the ways that their unpaid labor and tremendous sacrifice had created Paulista and Brazilian prosperity. Stereotyping blacks as murderers and criminals not only disrespected the legacy of slavery but also exposed the ignorance and callousness of those who failed to come to terms with the discrimination that explained blacks' precarious place in society.[70]

In the United States, official demarginalization materialized as racial realism with much more frequency, largely due to some of the intellectuals and artists whom the government hired to produce its cultural program-ming. African American writer and scholar Sterling Brown, Federal Writers' Project national editor of Negro affairs from 1936 to 1939, was one of the most forceful advocates of racial realism in state cultural pro-duction and he received a lot of pushback for it. As his biographers John Edgar Tidwell and Steven Tracy have written, Brown's work on the FWP's state guidebook series showcased his intention to reveal the "rela-tionship between social need and literary representation."[71] Brown fought against black stereotypes and hoped to redress the fact that, in his words, the "Negro has too seldom been revealed as an integral part of American life."[72] In showing that blacks occupied a meaningful place in US society and history, Brown did not want to skirt the harsh realities; instead, he sought to expose them completely. Officials in South Caro-lina, Florida, and Mississippi were among those that fought Brown's efforts to truthfully describe the status quo of the black community in their states.[73]

Brown wrote what is considered one of the most scathing and contro-versial portrayals to come out of the FWP's state guide series. His 1937 essay "The Negro in Washington" described in vivid and even poetic detail the conditions of the black community in Washington, DC. He later recalled that his essay "pointed out that in the shadow of the capital were some of the worst ghettoes and slums in the world [and it also] attacked the segregated school system. Nothing that strong had ever been written in a government publication."[74] After chronicling the dire hous-ing situation, Brown wrote about the Supreme Court's decision to uphold the residential restrictive covenants that prohibited blacks from moving into certain areas. In other sections of the report, his sharp prose often read like a dreary novel: "Around the corner there may be a squalid slum with people jobless and desperate; the alert youngster, capable and well trained, may find on the morrow all employment closed to him. The Negro of Washington has no voice in government, is economically pro-scribed, and segregated nearly as rigidly as in the southern cities he con-temns."[75] The incriminations of the US government as a force that con-structed and perpetuated black exclusion seem to have set "The Negro in Washington" apart from other FWP projects. Officials did not take kindly to Brown's government-subsidized raw realism, and Congress demanded that the second publication of the essay be "severely bowdlerized."[76]

A good example of the tamer racial realism that was more likely to appear in state cultural materials was the *Let Freedom Ring!* radio series. The Office of Education's short-lived educational radio project

produced the series "with the assistance of the Works Progress Administration" and broadcast it nationally over the Columbia Broadcasting
System (CBS) in 1937. The Office of Education also published the thir-
teen scripts, written by white couple Dorothy and Harold Calhoun, in
a volume that included lesson aids for classrooms. Dorothy was a writer,
and Harold was both a professor of political science at UCLA and an
assistant to the US attorney general from 1936 to 1945. The foreword
to the publication explained that the series' listeners would learn about
"the courage, the struggle, the triumph of men and women who fought
to win and safeguard the civil liberties expressed in the bill of rights."[77]
The last show in the series, "Right of Racial Equality," focused on
blacks and the indigenous and briefly mentioned Asians, and some of
the other scripts also contained racial themes.

The thirty-minute "Right of Racial Equality" episode tackled the ways
that race had informed US democracy throughout the country's history.
At the outset, the script somewhat absolved US racial inequality by
declaring that no civilization had forged "just relations" among different
racial groups. Ancient Egypt and ancient Rome were invoked as a part of
this tradition. The United States was then introduced triumphantly with
the statement that "America is one of the few countries even today which
have written the great ideal of racial equality into their fundamental law."
The script then mentioned the Thirteenth, Fourteenth, and Fifteenth
Amendments, which outlawed slavery, granted equal protection under
the law, and expanded/protected male suffrage, respectively.[78]

Just as the script appeared to be a denialist account of US history,
one of the narrators admitted that "these great Constitutional ideals are
ahead of actual practice even in America [as] ignorance, fear, economic
rivalry, human prejudice and antagonisms [explain why] public opinion
still lags behind the laws." The script outlined the troubled relationship
between indigenous nations and whites during US western expansion,
ending the tale sanguinely with the words of Commissioner of Indian
Affairs John Collier: "The Indian as a race must not die, but must grow
and live." The pithy discussion of Asians indicated that US whites originally accepted the Chinese but came to see them as rivals during the
gold rush and the Great Depression. African American history occupied
much more space in the script. The slave trade, Dred Scott, John Brown,
the white supremacist Black Legion, and Clarence Darrow all made an
appearance. Celebrated American Civil Liberties Union lawyer Clarence
Darrow's real words came near the end of the script, and a set of related

questions about racial equality followed. Darrow stated, "I believe the life of the Negro race has been a life of tragedy, of injustice, of oppression. The law has made him equal, but man has not." Darrow also stated that until humankind "loves his fellowman [sic], and forgets his color or his creed [w]e will never be civilized." Since the idea of an uncivilized democracy was a paradox, Darrow in effect was labeling US democracy a farce. Clearly Darrow doubted the announcer's claims at the top of each episode that US democracy gave its citizens rights that only kings previously enjoyed.[79]

Clarence Darrow's closing comments may have issued a challenge to US democracy, but the script was markedly distinct from Sterling Brown's "The Negro in Washington." "Right of Racial Equality" did educate listeners that the Supreme Court had refused Dred Scott's petition for freedom by holding that as a legal slave, he was "not a citizen and cannot come to court," but it was also an overwhelmingly redemptive narrative that draped US racism with justifications and exonerations. The state's sins had all occurred in the past, and it had taken action-oriented steps to correct them with Civil War and Reconstruction–era constitutional amendments. The problem was human prejudice, not the government.

However, as Sterling Brown pointed out, the government continued to legally reinvigorate black inequality, as when the Supreme Court declared constitutional the racial segregation he railed against, another fact "Right of Racial Equality" ignored. To hear the script tell it, one would never know that the courts and Congress had been upholding and strengthening the structures of racial inequality. Indeed, "Right of Racial Equality" presented all the heroes of racial equality as white. Dred Scott was only mentioned to segue into the white abolitionist John Brown's story, as Brown was outraged at the Supreme Court's decision in the case. In the script's lesson aid, the "'Who's Who' in Racial Equality" were all white men, many of them state figures: William Penn, Sam Houston, John C. Calhoun (portrayed as a racial obstructionist), Clarence Darrow, John Collier, and John Brown. Thus, the state's typical racial realism had strong denialist tendencies when it came to the government's culpability. It also portrayed a racially inclusive society in which people of color were pawns and victims, not agents who changed the course of history with their struggle.[80]

Government officials also were known to use cultural media to make direct racial political statements, as Mary McLeod Bethune did when she delivered a strong message of racial realism in 1939. Bethune,

director of Negro affairs in the National Youth Administration, participated in NBC radio's weekly program *America's Town Meeting of the
Air*. Each of the panelists was asked to prepare comments around the
question, "What does American democracy mean to me?" Bethune
took the opportunity to speak on behalf of all US blacks: "Democracy
is for me, and for twelve million black Americans, a goal towards which
our nation is marching. It is a dream and an ideal in whose ultimate
realization we have a deep and abiding faith." She argued that the
"democratic doors of equal opportunity have not been opened wide" to
blacks. Bethune enumerated a litany of black grievances as proof that
the United States did not yet qualify as a democracy—lack of educational opportunities, labor-intensive and low-paying jobs, exclusion
from labor unions, lynchings, and the denial of civil liberties and constitutional rights such as suffrage. Still, as A. Philip Randolph had done
years prior to calm the fears of black communism, Bethune said that
blacks always displayed loyalty whenever "the ideals of American
democracy have been attacked."[81] Here she told the listener of black
participation in US wars since the American Revolution. Bethune
selected her words carefully when she said that blacks had gone to war
not for US democracy but for the *ideals* of US democracy. In other
words, there was no democracy to speak of in the United States, and
blacks fought not to protect what existed but to bring to fruition what
should exist. Her perspective turned on its head the self-congratulatory
script of US democracy in the Office of Education's "Right of Racial
Equality" that cleared the modern state of racial wrongdoing.

Similar to the "'Who's Who' in Racial Equality" lesson aid that
appeared with the "Right of Racial Equality," a theme of Brazil's official cinquentenário commemorations was that abolition largely was the
result of benevolent white leaders. The official denialist story of abolition was one of racial reconciliation that celebrated blacks' contribution to Brazil's formation, especially economically and culturally. The
message was that Brazil had triumphed over its unfortunate slave heritage and emerged united and strong as a country.

A Lei Áurea, the radio play that briefly featured Preta Velha, focused
on the events within the government that led to abolition and made
Princess Isabel the main protagonist. Although the play clarified that
Minister of Justice Ferreira Vianna wrote the speech the princess read
on behalf of Congress announcing the proposal to abolish slavery, it
was Princess Isabel who embodied and personified abolition. A large
image of her face even appeared on the cover of the printed version of

the radio play. It is through Isabel that the state manifested as a Christian, moral, and genuinely humanitarian force that acted with pure intentions as it moved to terminate slavery. In fact, on the occasion of reading the words of the abolition proposal on the Senate floor, Isabel is described as nervous, pausing to take a deep breath and drink water. Once she finished, the crowd exploded in a display of patriotic frenzy, shouting "Vivas" for Isabel and other abolitionists, including Congressman Joaquim Nabuco and the black writer José do Patrocínio. One of the reporters/narrators stated that so many flowers had been thrown on the floor that it was impossible to walk.[82]

A Lei Áurea did contain the Congress's debate about abolition, including the voice of those who wanted to preserve slavery, which Senator Paulino de Souza represented. In fact, Souza's speech covered several pages in the play as he called for patience and predicted grave social and economic consequences that would wreak havoc on the nation. As was commonplace in the nineteenth century, Souza claimed to be anti-abolition, not proslavery. He insisted that he had always considered slavery a flawed and unfortunate institution, but he warned about the dangers of abolishing it, invoking the United States as an example of abolition gone wrong. He accused President Lincoln of being arrogant after his victory in the Civil War and charged him with gratuitously punishing the South. He favored the actions of subsequent president Andrew Johnson, who was conciliatory to the former Confederates at the cost of the freedpeople. However, when Paulino de Souza made these comments from the Senate floor, the Congress received them coldly, and even Souza admitted that his cause was dead on arrival.[83] Abolition plainly was the desired and heroic outcome of the story line, so Souza's opposition to it meant that he was serving as an antagonist in the script, and one who was on the wrong side of history. Yet, as is often the case in Brazil, because he did not articulate racial animus as his motivation, Souza— and by extension the like-minded anti-abolitionists he represented— came across as obstructionist by default.

Lourival Fontes, minister of the propaganda department that commissioned A Lei Áurea, provided context for its message and for that of all the regime's commemorative events when he gave an interview to the newspaper A Noite before the festivities began. Fontes explained that the intention of the cinquentenário programs was to awaken the interest of the public in "the invaluable contribution of the black element" to "aspects of Brazilian life." Music would be a prominent facet of this lesson. Fontes informed A Noite that the propaganda department's

Hora do Brasil would broadcast songs that were considered a part of Brazilian "folklore," "songs influenced by African motifs," and other "genuinely African" musical selections.[84]

Fontes stated that the cinquentenário commemorations were a part of a "clearly nationalist" initiative that aimed "to establish, in a broad and general way, the integration of the black race into the great common project of constructing our nationality." Fontes seemed particularly keen to transmit the message of blacks' influence on Brazil's economic formation, which was one of the commemoration conference's topics as well. He acknowledged that black labor had boosted Brazil's ability to take advantage of "the various resources [that fueled the] national economy." Making Freyre-like statements, Fontes spoke specifically of the sugarcane plantations, where "the largest nuclei of the black population formed," as a site from which the nation had emerged. He said that Brazil had gained from the "cooperation of the servile element" during the monarchy and that this had not only secured Brazil's economic prosperity but also guaranteed "the country's unity."[85] One could also infer from Fontes's comments that the descendants of the enslaved could feel invested in Brazilian progress and prosperity because of their ancestors' sacrifices. In other words, because they helped build it, blacks should feel that the country was theirs too.

Although presented four years before the cinquentenário, it is worth revisiting black communist Édison Carneiro's realist perspective of abolition as a foil to the visions of Fontes and Camargo, especially the latter, who said that his play depicted "the events that marked the end of the black race's suffering in Brazil."[86] While abolition was commemorated with a sense of national pride at the cinquentenário, Carneiro's paper for the first Afro-Brazilian Congress, "Situation of Blacks in Brazil," was a searing report on abolition's impact. As mentioned in chapter 1, Carneiro believed that substituting capitalism for legal slavery worsened blacks' circumstances since it carried "the exploitation of the worker ... to the extreme." At least on the sugar plantations, the enslaved could "always find a slice of meat" and "a bed of sticks," Carneiro argued, whereas under capitalism, blacks and other paid labor merely possessed the right "to die of hunger." He went into graphic detail about postemancipation life for blacks, who were "owners of a fictitious 'liberty,' earning poorly, dressing poorly, eating poorly [and] degrading themselves in unhygienic conditions at a ten-hour a day job." Afro-Brazilians were subjected to racial oppression from the capitalist bosses whose "divide and conquer" strategy led white workers to show blacks "disdain." After abolition, blacks fell into alcoholism and crime in greater numbers. Education did not offer a way out for black youths because schools could be few and far between. Children with schools nearby frequently could not attend because they had to work in order to help support their families financially, even at a very young age. Blacks were stacked in decrepit, cramped, unhealthy housing, where they "suffer[ed] and die[d] without medical care" and passed on their diseases to everyone in the house, with fatal consequences. In rural Brazil, where they were in the majority, blacks lived "in the most desperate, abject poverty," and illiteracy, malaria, smallpox, and hookworm were commonplace. Carneiro concluded that "only a communist society" could end the kind of human exploitation seen in Brazil after abolition.[87]

Carneiro's paper also countered the state's message on cultural unity and integration. Focusing on Bahia, he said that despite constitutionally protected religious freedoms, authorities dishonored black cultural and religious traditions like candomblé by shutting them down, detaining peaceful practitioners, and apprehending their African objects. As some of the originators of samba would recount later, candomblé rituals and samba music often went together, so Carneiro's statement undermined the idea that demarginalization was proof that black culture and people were fully accepted. Overall, "Situation of Blacks in Brazil" advanced a bold action-oriented realism that eroded the denialist nationalism the state formulated simultaneously in the 1930s, including as a salient premise at the cinquentenário.[88]

In the United States, one of the best examples of racial denial in official cultural production was the 1937 WPA film *We Work Again*. The ten-minute film examined the impact of the New Deal's work program on the black community, prioritizing New York and Harlem. It began with a poignant and depressing scene with a manufactured, overly dramatic cinematic quality. As the camera panned across forlorn but well-dressed blacks waiting in a breadline, the narrator stated that, just a few years earlier, "we were a discouraged people." (The "we" is significant, as the voice is free of the black dialect that characterized blacks on film and radio at the time. In fact, the narrator sounded like a typical voice-over for a movie preview.) Similar to the forthcoming "The Negro" episode of *Americans All, Immigrants All,* the introduction stated: "Because we were the first to lose our jobs when Old Man Depression came along, and the last to get them back, we struggled vainly to regain our bearings while depression, fear, and failure stalked the nation. A tenth of the population of the United States, we formed as a race over a sixth of the unemployed."[89]

We Work Again's racial realism was brief and merely served as a point of departure for and a contrast to the film's narrative of Rooseveltian recovery and prosperity. After the dire opening scene, the film's music quickly became cheerfully upbeat as the narrator announced the ways in which the New Deal's work program "changed the haggard, hopeless faces of the breadlines into faces filled with hope and happiness for now we work again!" The same black actors who had stood in the breadline reappeared smiling as they labored in new jobs. One woman had found a career as a nurse, another as a secretary, and men were shown as a bricklayer, an artist, and a musician, among other professions. The remainder of the film focused on the different work programs and projects for which black men and women had obtained employment, in both "unskilled," "skilled," and "white collar" jobs.[90]

One of the key themes of *We Work Again* was that US blacks enjoyed multifarious benefits from the New Deal's works program. For instance, the narrator explained that because Harlem had many residents from Puerto Rico, Central America, and South America, "knowledge of Spanish is valuable to workers, shopkeepers, and others." In the accompanying scene, a black native speaker was teaching Spanish to a group of adults on the WPA's dime. There was also footage of WPA crews tearing down "old tenements and firetraps" to build new, modern living quarters in their place. Nursery schools were established where young children received hot meals and had access to nurses, dieticians, teachers, and cooks, all of whom were now gainfully employed. There was an emphasis on services and resources that targeted women. Black women worked in sewing rooms that made clothes for "needy families." Black women also learned health education, including first aid, and cooking to prepare for paid domestic work or to care for their own families. The narrator invited the viewer to acquire a new skill by observing two women practice how to make a bed properly, "an art which few have mastered." The WPA employed teams to construct a swimming pool, bathhouse, and wading pool in Harlem's Colonial Park, which the narrator described as "particularly valuable to the community" because they were safe alternatives to dangerous swimming holes, the sites of tragic drownings. The children frolicking in the water and on the playground were a multiracial set, and they, along with all the characters that appeared in the short film, were nicely dressed.[91]

Mirroring the strategies we have seen others adopt, several minutes of *We Work Again* demonstrated producers' prioritization of music as a way to advocate black inclusion in US society. In this case, they decided to highlight more than one side of black musical talent. Breaking with the stereotype that blacks and European-derived musical forms did not mix, *We Work Again* first showed a group of blacks singing classical music. A slightly longer clip of Juanita Hall conducting a choir singing a Negro spiritual followed. Before the choir began, the narrator introduced the musical genre: "One of our greatest contributions to the world of music is the spiritual, recognized the world over as a fine example of the folk music of America." The film concluded with a scene from a Negro Unit play, Orson Welles's famous "Voodoo" *Macbeth*.[92]

We Work Again presented the WPA as the consummate action-oriented tool for racial democracy. Certainly the New Deal was a vital lifeline for African Americans during the Depression, and historian Nancy Weiss has identified the works programs as the main motive that led black voters to abandon en masse the Republican Party for the Democratic Party by 1936.[93] Yet, similar to Sterling Brown's work, the writings, activism, and employment situation of many black New Yorkers placed a huge question mark at the end of the film's "mission accomplished" through line. The focus on and assertions about women were particularly revelatory. As it celebrated black women gaining the necessary expertise for jobs in the domestic sector, the *We Work Again* narrator said that these "girls . . . are able to command skilled workers' wages."[94]

Black activists Ella Baker and Marvel Cooke proved that this statement and the glossy portrayal of happily employed African American women in all fields misrepresented the status quo of most black women. In 1935 Baker and Cooke published their renowned investigative exposé, "The Bronx Slave Market," for which they joined black women selling their labor on a New York street corner. They acknowledged the benefits of the New Deal, although their verdict was quite somber when compared to the film: "As inadequate as emergency relief has been, it has proved somewhat of a boon to many of these women, for with its advent, actual starvation is no longer their ever-present slave driver and they have been able to demand twenty-five and even thirty cents an hour as against the old fifteen and twenty cent rate. In an effort to supplement the inadequate relief received, many seek this open market." The report went on to reveal the practices of "unscrupulous" employers who either offered these "unbelievably low rates" for grueling domestic labor, paid less than what was owed, or "too often" refused to pay anything at all.[95]

Federal Writers' Project employee Vivian Morris decided to research the Bronx Slave Market a year after *We Work Again* was released. She found "a dejected gathering of Negro women of various ages and descriptions—youths of seventeen, and elderly women of maybe seventy." The women were insufficiently dressed, some even "partly clothed," for the cold winter weather. Black women were in this position because, as Morris, Baker, and Cooke explained, they did not find the employment agencies helpful for many reasons, most notably their preference for white women.[96] Thus, whereas *We Work Again*'s denial showed black women as New Deal constituents, Baker, Cooke, and Morris showed that in general, they were not. Even those who secured more "legitimate" domestic work were omitted from the New Deal's 1938 Fair Labor Standards Act, which set a minimum wage and protected workplace safety, as the legislation excluded domestic labor. Black realists Brown, Baker, Cooke, and Morris undoubtedly agreed with *We Work Again*'s exaltation of action-oriented racial democracy; they simply wanted to convey it as an unrealized objective, not a fait accompli.

Within both the Brazilian and US states were officials who resisted demarginalization as a form of racial democracy. According to Bryan McCann, "high-cultural sophisticates disdainful of popular tastes" ran the Ministry of Education's radio station.[97] Rádio MES opted for the European musical styles that the white Brazilian elite traditionally enjoyed as opposed to the rhythms that the government promoted at Carnival, which played over the commercially driven Rádio Nacional station. Jerry Dávila shows that MES education reformers shared the predilection for whiteness in Brazilian culture, and they set up the system to culturally whiten Brazil's predominantly black and mixed-race population.[98] In theory, brasilidade was supposed to represent the arrival of Brazil as a modern nation with a unique culture, but there was confusion and debate as to how to define "modern." Whereas many authorities constructed Brazilian culture around the musical ingenuity that emerged from the communities in which blacks predominantly dwelled, others followed the example of the Paulista regionalists who sought to maintain European culture as the modern ideal. A similar episode took place with the US Federal Music Project, when director Nikolai Sokoloff fought off numerous protests from the American Federation of Musicians for his refusal to employ popular artists. Sokoloff's condescending attitude toward popular music such as jazz led him to hire classically trained musicians for Federal Music Project performances during his directorship from 1935 to 1937.[99]

In the United States, obstructionist Martin Dies was highly suspicious of the demarginalization projects of Federal One, especially the Federal

Theatre Project. There were some motives for Dies's radar to detect communist influences in the FTP. For instance, in Theodore Ward's 1938 play *Big White Fog*, the character Lester, a central figure in the drama and son of a Garveyite leader, becomes a communist. In order to identify offenders, Dies compiled a loose list of criteria, namely strong antiracist politics, a prolabor stance, interracial relations, vulgarity, and sexual immorality. In part because, regardless of communist influence, the FTP's Play Bureau was receptive to producing pieces with such content, it became a target of the HCUA. It is also true that a number of these themes appealed to the Left and that leftists occupied many Federal One positions. Artists and entertainers were important members of the Popular Front movement, which contained a vigorous cultural branch that reflected leftist ideologies. As Dayo Gore has shown, black women radicals exemplified the manner in which leftist affiliations and training often prepared activists to obtain work in WPA jobs.[100]

According to Lauren Sklaroff, the HCUA "did not openly object to the existence of the Negro Units . . . but often it made the connection between the presence of African Americans on the project and 'un-American' behavior or theatrical content." We have already seen the consequence of this line of thinking in chapter 2, when the Dies committee interrogated white actress Sallie Saunders about the interracial dating policy among FTP workers. To borrow Saunders's words, in the estimation of the Dies committee, "hobnob[bing] indiscriminately" with blacks was a telltale sign of communism. The spotlight on the FTP intensified after a former WPA employee testified that FTP director Hallie Flanagan was involved in communism, and the HCUA summoned more FTP witnesses. The scrutiny and distrust led the conservative members of Congress to lower all WPA appropriations in 1937, using their objection to the FTP as one of the main justifications. With these cuts, Congress reduced the FTP's funding by 25 percent, shrinking its level of productivity. Many FTP employees were let go, and the black divisions and units were particularly affected. It is no surprise then that from the summer of 1937 on, the Play Bureau was more cautious about the productions it selected, eschewing material with more militant politics, racial and otherwise. In this atmosphere, the FTP began to de-emphasize the economic and social aspects of racial inequality.[101]

Obstructionism in the realm of culture revealed a great deal about the power of anticommunist politicians during the New Deal. They had hoped to target the FTP since 1935 and were largely responsible for the move to decrease its funding in 1937. This fervent cohort was not a powerless, ostracized, or fringe element during the Roosevelt administration. Dies et al. actually forced policy change and had a huge influence on the political ideas and viewpoints allowed to circulate in the United States. They also helped to severely limit black demarginalization through state cultural production. Dies's 1938 investigation of the FTP caused it to be shut down in 1939. In that same year, the only Federal One projects that still existed were run by the states, not the federal government.[102]

For many advocates of official black cultural demarginalization, the resistance of Dies and the MES had at least one dire consequence: the failure to promote employment for black intellectuals and artists. Many realists, such as those in the Federal One black divisions, were fighting for demarginalization with this action-oriented goal in mind. When the US and Brazilian states embraced black artistry as authentic national culture, more black producers found themselves in demand for government or private industry work. In 1939 Alain Locke observed that due to "the Federal Arts Projects and their reasonably democratic inclusion of the Negro artists of various sorts, the growth and geographic spread of Negro art has [sic] been materially enhanced."[103] Clarence Muse, the black director of the FTP's Los Angeles Negro Unit, hired 165 blacks for the play *Run Little Chillun,* most of whom had never been active in the arts. According to Muse, about 40 percent of that group remained in the industry after the play closed.[104]

The numerous testimonies of Afro-Brazilian originators of samba detail their paths toward careers as professional musicians. The memories of one black musician who lived through the demarginalization of samba are worth quoting at length:

> I have been a musician since 1919, but I almost never had work. One day, in 1925, my friend . . . came to my house and advised me that a famous orchestra in the city . . . needed a musician. I went to find the conductor. He asked me what I could play: "guitar, *bandolim, pandeiro,* and the tambourine," I said. Then he asked me: "what am I going to do with you? My orchestra does not have the repertoire that needs to use those instruments. I need a pianist and a violinist." . . . Three years later, I went looking for this same conductor who asked me right away: "do you still want to play for me?" I said, "yes." Then he accepted me. At first I used to wait for the orchestra to play "our music." . . . Some time after, I spent more time playing than waiting my turn, because those dancing wanted samba. After this, I played in an orchestra on the radio: I became known and got to play at the Urca Casino.[105]

In the sambista's story, his initial cultural marginalization manifested as economic marginalization. The fact that he ended up performing in

Rio de Janeiro's most upscale musical venue, the Urca Casino, pointed to the material bonuses that came along with the demarginalization process that the state helped to precipitate. The mainstreaming and commercialization of samba also increased the opportunities for blacks to find work as professional music teachers. Although music instruction between blacks and whites was not a new phenomenon, black testimonies suggest that it occurred with more frequency during this period as samba grew in popularity and more people came into contact with the genre.[106] When MES employees and the HCUA resisted demarginalization, they blocked such financial gains and worked to preserve the kind of economic marginalization the sambista's testimony described at the outset.

The resistance to and obstruction of demarginalization were not the only culprits to curtail black economic empowerment in cultural production; appropriation also played a role. As many historians have written, the Brazilian music scene developed in a way that would privilege white mediators. Radio programs often involved a live audience, and most stations preferred that majority white bands appeared before those audiences. Radio offered some of the best jobs in the music industry, especially the *Programa Casé*, which gave a number of musicians stable and salaried positions. White artists such as Noel Rosa and Carmen Miranda were among the program's regulars. *Programa Casé* did appoint famous black composer and flutist Pixinguinha (Alfredo da Rocha Vianna) as its bandleader in the early 1930s. Pixinguinha, Donga (Ernesto dos Santos)—another revered black samba pioneer—and radio headliner Patrício Teixeira experienced more fame and financial success than most Afro-Brazilian musicians, however. Teixeira was the only black sambista to hold such a high-profile radio position in the 1930s, and dark-skinned blacks in particular found it nearly impossible to gain access to opportunities in radio and film. As Marc Hertzman has written, even Pixinguinha and Donga were "below many of the more celebrated white mediators in material wealth and social prestige."[107] Black musicians survived by selling their compositions (sometimes they would sell the same song to multiple buyers), often to white performers who would claim authorship. Blacks fought for legal protections and proprietary rights as well, but the legal code tended to recognize the rights of white artists at higher rates than black composers.[108]

White cultural mediation also marked the demarginalization process during jazz music's swing era in the United States. Although the state would most embrace jazz as the nation's authentic modern music after the war, its demarginalization was well underway by the 1930s. In fact, the so-called King of Jazz in the 1920s was Paul Whiteman, a classically trained white music entrepreneur who developed "symphonic jazz." As Whiteman explained, symphonic jazz was his way of civilizing what he referred to as the "great American noise [that was] drifting out of the shanties" of black New Orleans. Despite the respectability he purportedly bestowed upon jazz, this racialized image caused it to be aligned with sexual immorality, criminality, and barbarism.[109]

The era of big-band swing began in the mid-1930s, and by the end of the decade, swing comprised about 50 percent of all record sales in the United States. Trailblazers like black bandleaders Duke Ellington, Fletcher Henderson, and Bennie Moten had established the style and sound of swing years before it became a national sensation. Yet the bandleader who would be anointed the King of Swing was white clarinet player Benny Goodman, who bought nearly all of his arrangements from Henderson. Many black jazz artists did have good careers during the swing era. The Ellington band's performance at President Roosevelt's birthday party and some of its shows from New York's white-only Cotton Club were broadcast nationally. Also, in 1938 Benny Goodman was the first to integrate his band, which economically benefited the black musicians who played with him. But none of the black artists matched the commercial success that the King of Swing enjoyed. For instance, Goodman was able to secure a thrice-weekly radio show, *Camel Caravan*, that attracted two million listeners in 1938. Historian Joel Dinerstein has written that the "music industry would never have supported an African American band as it did Goodman's; a black band would not have been let in the front door of some of the nation's most prestigious," and thus high-paying, venues.[110] In the 1940s black musicians like Dizzy Gillespie, Charlie Parker, and Thelonious Monk would create a new style of jazz, bebop, whose complexity did not easily lend itself to appropriation.

When appropriation established a trend in which white artists dominated in the mainstream and the more lucrative performances of black culture, it was a symbolic separation of black bodies from the cultural forms they pioneered. As long as most whites looked upon a black cultural genre as taboo, its mobility was dictated by and limited to the mobility of its black creators. If whites wanted to have contact with that culture, they usually had to have contact with black bodies, which was the case in the early days of samba and jazz. This changed with widespread white mediation, when black entertainment and art were able to infiltrate mainstream and elite private and public spaces in ways that black people typically could not. The preference for white mediators radically minimized blacks' ability to profit proportional to their level of talent, impact, and importance to their cultural industries. Therefore, the two states' decision to administer their initiatives of racial democracy through cultural production fell short for action-oriented realists whose primary goal was large-scale black economic and political empowerment.

CHAPTER 5

The Centrality of Race and Democracy in the US-Brazil Wartime Alliance

During World War II, the Axis nations' impact on Brazilian and US concepts of race and democracy escalated tremendously. Getúlio Vargas and Franklin Roosevelt were rather reticent on fascist racial policy for most of the 1930s, but the war and the news coming from Nazi Germany thrust the topic onto center stage. Both regimes joined in earnest the communities and individuals that had been debating fascism's racial ramifications for years. Thus, while the Soviet Union became a (frequently distrusted) wartime ally and even dissolved the Comintern in 1943, the Axis powers took its place as the dominant external generator of racial political discourse that officials perceived as an existential threat.

The Axis nations and the unique dynamics of the war set new parameters in regard to race that affected diplomatic and foreign relations between many countries. This chapter examines the ways that these new racial political dynamics complicated and shaped the relationship between Brazil and the United States, which was indispensable to both states during the wartime crisis. It outlines how and why racial democracy became a central concern in this alliance, detailing the national security and economic considerations at play, and it provides essential context for the next chapter's analysis of US-Brazil cultural exchanges and collaborations.

In December 1941 the United States entered the Second World War after Japan attacked Pearl Harbor, an event that led the Estado Novo to end its policy of neutrality and to officially break ties with the Axis nations. Tensions rose further with the German assaults on Brazilian merchant marine ships in August 1942 that killed more than seven hundred crew and passengers. Droves of irate Brazilians took to the streets to demand that their government declare war, which would occur just days after the last attack. This move greatly invigorated the Good Neighbor Policy and precipitated the closest relationship ever experienced between Brazil and the United States.[1] Brazil also became by far the most active sovereign Latin American participant in the war, with over 25,000 soldiers in Italy and 450 lost in combat.[2]

Despite its distance from the United States, US authorities typically considered Brazil to be the United States' most important Latin American war ally for many reasons, some being geopolitical in nature. As we saw in this book's introduction, the Brazilian city of Natal is in the farthest eastern region of all the Americas, making it the closest target for the Nazis to invade from the Cape Verde Islands or Dakar.[3] Moreover, Brazil's size as the largest nation in Latin America (with one-third of South America's population), its five thousand miles of mostly undefended coastline, and its shared borders with every South American country save Chile and Ecuador meant that Brazil's vulnerability put the entire Western Hemisphere in danger. One US Office of Strategic Services (OSS) memorandum affirmed that Brazil was "a likely bridgehead for enemy attack on the United States . . . or for invasion of South America." Secretary of the navy Frank Knox also reminded Congress that "modern war, especially [with] the progress made in the air," rendered a German base in Brazil "just as dangerous as a base in Texas."[4] There was so much concern about this scenario in the United States and Britain that President Roosevelt ordered that a plan be drafted to send one hundred thousand troops to Brazil, the so-called operation Pot of Gold, a year and a half before the attack on Pearl Harbor. The Brazilian government was not keen to allow US troops on its soil at that time, and the US military never executed operation Pot of Gold. Nonetheless the United States did set up bases in Brazil by the end of 1941, and Natal, the capital of the state of Rio Grande do Norte, eventually became the site of a key US military base that proved central to victory.[5]

Another issue that drew the attention of the United States to Brazil was the size of the German, Italian, and Japanese communities within the country. US authorities characterized these populations as concentrated, segregated, and/or unassimilated, raising serious loyalty and fifth-column questions among the Allied governments. They considered the Brazilian German and Japanese "colonies" to be "the largest and best organized" in all of South America.[6] FBI director J. Edgar Hoover sent a secret memo declaring that the "western hemisphere's most acute yellow problem centers in Brazil [with] an estimated 250,000 to 300,000 Japanese, as compared to 70,000 in the United States."[7] The US Office of the Coordinator of Inter-American Affairs (OCIAA) reported on the plans to "create a new Germany in Brazil," stating that Brazilians of German descent subscribed to the "Master Race Theory" and that Nazi commercial investments in South America were the most abundant in Brazil.[8] US policymakers were alarmed by the possibility that Brazil's ethnic groups were fostering the "Axis penetration" of the country.

Hermann Rauschning, who appeared in chapter 3, was the source of some of this anxiety. In 1939 the exiled Nazi leader and self-proclaimed former friend of Adolf Hitler disclosed what he asserted were Hitler's high hopes for Brazil. In his book *Hitler Speaks* (also titled *The Voice of Destruction*), Rauschning wrote that Hitler "was specially interested in Brazil" and that in 1933 he personally heard the Führer say, "We shall create a new Germany there."[9] The Germans attempted to reassure the Brazilians that these charges were, to quote Nazi foreign minister Joachim von Ribbentrop, "ludicrous and absurd."[10] However, a Brazilian publisher released Rauschning's book—in which Brazil was labeled "a corrupt mestizo state"—in Portuguese in 1940, and records show that it generated suspicion of Nazi designs within the nation as well. For instance, General Góes Monteiro received an undated anonymous letter from "a patriot" that accused him of being sympathetic to Hitler, "the chief of the most barbarous of all peoples." Quoting Rauschning, the letter writer called upon Monteiro to open his eyes to Hitler's aspirations in Brazil and to defend the nation from Nazi conquest.[11]

Although many scholars discredited Rauschning's book in the 1980s after his death, his account was widely cited as factual in political, academic, and military circles in several nations.[12] President Roosevelt was among the officials to repeat and grant credibility to Rauschning's statements. Thus, the United States found the presence of Nazi sympathizers in Brazil's government and military leadership, including the minister of justice, Francisco Campos, and minister of war, Eurico Dutra, extremely disconcerting, particularly before Brazil formally cut off all ties with the Axis nations in 1942. In light of the concerns that Brazil was in real danger of falling to the Nazis, the United States and other Allied nations concluded that solidarity with Brazil was crucial for the stability and security of the entire region.

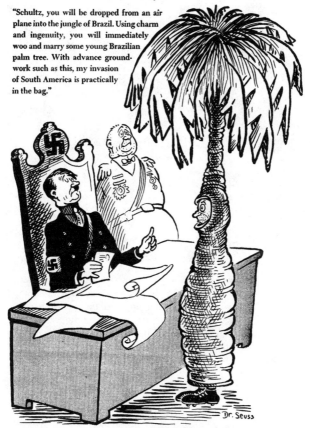

Subversive Activity

"Schultz, you will be dropped from an air plane into the jungle of Brazil. Using charm and ingenuity, you will immediately woo and marry some young Brazilian palm tree. With advance groundwork such as this, my invasion of South America is practically in the bag."

FIGURE 3. "Subversive Activity," a political cartoon by Theodor Seuss Geisel, a.k.a. Dr. Seuss, published in the July 30, 1941, issue of *PM Magazine*. The cartoon both reflected and contributed to the belief that Hitler planned to invade Brazil. Courtesy of Special Collections and Archives, UC San Diego Library.

The United States also was an invaluable Brazilian ally for numerous reasons, many of them economic. From 1935 to 1942 Brazil maintained what historian Gerson Moura coined "pragmatic equidistance" between Germany and the United States. This diplomatic strategy and policy of neutrality allowed Brazil to take advantage of commercial benefits from both governments as they competed for leverage and influence in the country. Before the war, Brazil had made several bilateral trade agreements with Germany, increasing the two nations' economic ties. In the

'Scram! We're busy listening to Sumner Welles!'

FIGURE 4. "Scram! We're busy listening to Sumner Welles!," a
political cartoon by Dr. Seuss published in the January 15, 1942,
issue of *PM Magazine*. The cartoon appeared on the first day of
the Meeting of the Ministers of Foreign Affairs of the American
Republics, held in Rio de Janeiro. It was at this meeting that Brazil
aligned itself with the United States, broke formal diplomatic ties
with the Axis nations, and encouraged other Latin American
nations to follow suit. Courtesy of Special Collections and
Archives, UC San Diego Library.

aftermath of a few diplomatic strains, the British wartime blockade pre-
venting German trade with Brazil, and the latter's eventual declaration
of war, trade between Germany and Brazil fell sharply.[13] The United
States took the opportunity to grant its southern neighbor new trade
and credit concessions.

Brazil was essentially an agrarian and export economy that struggled
during the Depression and continued to have difficulty exporting raw
materials in the early war years, when its foreign trade dropped by
about 40 percent. Vargas promoted industrialization and a nascent
domestic market for Brazilian products like coffee, but the export problem triggered a growing deficit, and from 1938 to 1939 the government
defaulted on its foreign debts. In the first half of the 1940s, the Estado
Novo tackled the export crisis in part by advertising Brazilian coffee to
US audiences as a commodity of the Good Neighbor Policy and an

indispensable beverage of warfare.[14] Yet it was largely the US war industry's insatiable need for strategic materials—especially rubber, "of
which Brazil [was] the most important natural source of supply still
available to the United Nations"—that helped to reverse Brazil's bleak
situation.[15] Furthermore, generous loans propped up Brazil's domestic
development agenda. In fact, 70 percent of all US aid to Latin America
during the war went to Brazil.[16]

The economic and national security priorities that laid the foundation
for the Brazil-US alliance during World War II made it in the best interest
of both states to heed other issues that could strengthen or undermine
their relationship, including its ideological dimensions. These dimensions
were linked to the rhetoric about the values and principles at stake in the
war. For both the United States and Brazil, the war's racial political frameworks produced ideological contradictions that not only had domestic
repercussions but also created unique challenges for their alliance.

By the time Brazil entered the war, Brazilians were aware that the
Allies had chosen *democracy* as the operative word to describe their
mission. Brazilian journals quoted Allied leaders and commentators
praising the very vague notion of democracy as the cause of the day, one
worthy of immense human sacrifice. In his first State of the Union
address after the attack on Pearl Harbor—a speech that Brazilian papers
translated and published in full—President Roosevelt outlined the ideological premises behind proposed US military preparations and actions.
In speaking about the Axis powers, Roosevelt said that "[t]hey know
that victory for us means victory for the institution of democracy—the
ideal of the family, the simple principles of common decency and
humanity." Roosevelt proclaimed antiracism as part and parcel of the
Allies' democratic responsibility as well. Warning listeners that Hitler
relied upon racial and national schisms for his divide-and-conquer tactics, Roosevelt stated that the "United Nations . . . must be particularly
vigilant against racial discrimination in any of its ugly forms."[17]

When Getúlio Vargas chose to align with the United States and the
Allied nations, the Brazilians affirmed the democratic creed as the basis
for the alliance. During a lunch for the US military attaché in Brazil,
Brazil's minister of war, Eurico Dutra, said that the United States and the
Estado Novo were both "loyal to democracy" and that it was this shared
political stance that had sustained Brazil-US solidarity.[18] Thus, the decision to go to war put the Estado Novo in a precarious position as a dictatorship purportedly fighting for democracy. This anomaly placed additional pressure on the government to define the Estado Novo as a

democracy, and one expedient was to utilize the narrative of racial tolerance as a proxy for political democracy. The racial climate of the war
validated this rhetorical maneuvering. The Allied nations characterized
Nazi racial theory as antithetical to democracy, and the Estado Novo
argued that racial tolerance must then signify a democratic society. Thus,
Brazilian racial democracy enabled the Brazil-US alliance to retain some
semblance of ideological coherence. Ironically, it also created problems
for the United States, for allying with Brazil exacerbated the dilemma
that contemporaneous sociologist Gunnar Myrdal famously argued was
the Achilles' heel of US democracy.[19]

For the US government, racism proved to be a huge liability during
the war, and various forces dovetailed to render discursive racial democracy a matter of national security as never before in the twentieth century. Two of these forces were the United States' poor racial reputation
in Brazil and the dissemination of Japanese and German racial propaganda to the Brazilian people. US authorities understood that stories of
the country's racial bigotry fostered distrust among Brazilians and sabotaged US efforts to win hearts and minds in a nation with one of the
world's biggest black and mixed-race populations. In response, the
United States attempted to salvage its racial image, which was in large
part an endeavor to rehabilitate its democratic standing. Thus, whereas
Brazil was compelled to politically democratize its national racial narrative in part because of its alliance with the United States, the United
States was impelled to racialize its notions of democracy to court the
Brazilians, who were deemed necessary for a victorious outcome to
the war.

BRAZILIAN RACIAL PRESTIGE AND DEMOCRACY IN THE AGE OF NAZISM

President Roosevelt's 1941 State of the Union address reflected the
Allies' description of democracy as both the political good against fascist evil and as the antithesis to Nazi racial hatred. Indeed, the Allied
nations showed a newfound respect for societies that seemed to demonstrate racial tolerance. In order to escape its predicament as an authoritarian regime on the side of democracy, the Estado Novo fused the
heightened respect for interracial harmony with the ubiquitous invoca-
tions of democracy into the nationalist concept of racial democracy,
making it a key strand of brasilidade. Thus, the wartime equation of
racism with fascism allowed the Estado Novo to depict itself as a logical

partner of the United States and the Allies, and Vargas would be one of many official voices to exploit this equation.

Despite the reality that wartime conversations about democracy often delegitimized the Estado Novo's authoritarian regime, Getúlio Vargas neither wholly sidestepped nor shied away from the topic. At times Vargas mentioned the contradiction outright and attempted to downplay it, explaining to the Brazilian people that they could rightfully and comfortably see themselves on the side of the Allies. In São Paulo in late 1943, Vargas did not wait long to address the elephant in the room as he inaugurated the Service for Assistance to the Intellectual Worker. Using what he claimed were the words of Brazilian intellectuals, Vargas said, "Brazil, at the side of the Allied nations . . . feels perfectly at ease defending the same cause, because through its traditions, through its organization, through its social life, Brazil is a democratic country. And therefore we [the intellectuals] speak sincerely and do not show any fear in pronouncing the word democracy."[20] Here Vargas used Brazil's most educated class, one that often criticized the Estado Novo, to give an unbiased appearance to his democratic portrayals of the regime.

The dictatorship also enlisted Brazilian intellectuals to do ideological work, exemplified in the monthly magazine of the Department of Press and Propaganda, *Cultura Política* (Political Culture), which has been called the "principal theoretical organ of the Estado Novo." Intellectuals provided many of the magazine's articles, interviews, transcripts of official speeches, news, and other items that covered subjects such as the activities of the government and its leadership, democracy, folklore, history, literature, and race relations.[21] Editor Almir de Andrade wanted *Cultura Política* to "connect the government's political action to Brazilian cultural traditions," which was a characteristic element of the Estado Novo's nationalist venture. Andrade mused over the link between culture and politics in the third issue: "culture represents [the people's] aspirations and necessities of life," but the realization of these desires and needs was dependent on "political order." Thus, "[c]ulture and politics are . . . inextricable [and] all true and healthy politics should be an expression of popular culture, just as all true and fruitful culture should have political meaning. . . ."[22] Vargas applauded such initiatives that relied on the services of intellectuals to marry politics with the realm of art and ideas. In 1943 he congratulated his government for ushering in the first-ever period of "necessary symbiosis between" the intellectual "men of thought" and the political "men of action."[23] Yet, as historian Thiago Nicodemo has argued, artists and intellectuals did not have "privileged institutional space, and their relationship with the State was oftentimes either rarified or troubled" during the Estado Novo.[24]

After Brazil entered the conflict in Europe, *Cultura Política* contributed to the cause—that is, the rhetorical enterprise of positioning the Estado Novo squarely on the team of democracies—often in ways that indirectly drew linkages to racial inclusion. For instance, in January 1943 the magazine printed a recent speech given by Almir de Andrade at the National Institute of Political Science. Liberal democracies had tragically become obsessed with the idea of liberty, Andrade believed, and they failed to recognize that social justice was the true marker of democracy in the modern world. However, he reassured his Brazilian listeners, Vargas had recognized that above all else, democracy must guarantee "the well-being of the people, job security, well-distributed social justice, [and] equality of opportunities." According to Andrade, Brazil's "realist conception of democracy" made the country the world's "example of equilibrium and serenity" during the war and would continue to do so in the future. After all, he emphasized, as the old democracies were "imprisoned by liberal ideology" and totalitarian governments wanted to replace them with violent new regimes, Brazil maintained an alternative democratic model amid the global insecurity.[25]

At this time, Karl Loewenstein, a German Jewish constitutional lawyer and professor exiled in the United States, decided to conduct research in Brazil to determine whether the Estado Novo Constitution was in fact a democratic document. Loewenstein's *Brazil under Vargas* was the first book-length study authored by a non-Brazilian about the Estado Novo's political and constitutional structure as well as its social impact. He firmly believed that Brazilian politics and government necessitated close and systematic examination, being the "key state" of South America and the "most important ally" on the continent. Loewenstein's acknowledgments disclose the degree to which the regime tried to shape his experience in Brazil and his study's outcome. Loewenstein thanked Estado Novo heavyweight leaders such as Minister of Justice and Interior Francisco Campos (also the author of the Constitution) and Minister of Foreign Affairs Oswaldo Aranha. Loewenstein also expressed gratitude to the "many other prominent officials of the federal and state administration" and "members of the opposition" who cooperated and assisted him in his research.[26]

Likely disappointing authorities, Loewenstein did not find the Estado Novo to be what he had earlier termed a "militant democracy" or what they tried to sell him as a "disciplined democracy."[27] No, Loewenstein wrote, the Brazilian state was not a democracy that had merely embraced undemocratic and fascist policies to protect liberalism from a fascist takeover. Brazil, he insisted, was an "authoritarian dictatorship." However, he surely must have frustrated some of the Estado Novo's opposition in his conclusion that Brazil was by no means totalitarian or fascist, which he defined as an oppressive political party that controlled every aspect of private and public life. Loewenstein also pointed out that the state's policies to prevent Axis subversion were in line with the Pan-American Third Meeting of the Ministers of Foreign Affairs at the Rio de Janeiro conference in 1942. He found Brazil to be the most successful Latin American partner in "counteracting foreign subversive infiltration."[28] If Loewenstein did not buy into the notion that Brazil was a new political democratic model, Brazilian officials had at least convinced him not to outright invalidate their claims about social democracy.

After *Brazil under Vargas* was published, the Estado Novo continued to utilize the war as a prism through which it invited others to view its government favorably. Brazil's declaration of war gave the Estado Novo grounds to offer a nationalist vision of the country as a military force and as a uniquely harmonious nation that could guide the world from chaos to calm. *Cultura Política* picked up on this theme to commemorate the one-year anniversary of Brazil's entrance into the war. In this special issue, Brazil was described as a country that "never declared war"—but did respond to acts of violence initiated by other nations—and whose people had always "evolved in peace."[29] Characterizing Brazil as a special beacon of "functional and realist democracy" (this time the words of Vargas, not Almir de Andrade), *Cultura Política* informed its readers that their nation embodied the "social peace of the future" and would "capture the attention of the world's scholars." The Estado Novo would also provide the "premises of the postwar world" recovering from the onslaught of totalitarianism.[30] Although these particular articles did not mention race, there are parallels between Brazil's peace loving, social democracy narrative and its racial story line in terms of their statements about Brazilian exceptionalism.

Brazilian lieutenant colonel Newton O'Reilly's article "Race of Mestizos" was a *Cultura Política* piece that explicitly introduced race into the scenario of Brazil as international trendsetter, making the case that the war granted the chance to prove it. Quoting sociologist Vicente Licínio Cardoso, the epigraph set the tone for the article: "[As a] race of mestizos . . . we Brazilians will perhaps have to complete a grand mission in the world, which is to make obvious the fallacy of the theory of pure races and the mistaken fantasy that cold climates are the most beneficial to human development." Only disagreeing with the word "perhaps," O'Reilly elaborated upon Cardoso's sentiment. The article romanticized the mixture of Portuguese, indigenous, and African blood and customs that gave birth to the modern Brazilian. These groups were praised for contributing, respectively, intelligence, a strong independent spirit, and servility to "Brazilian nationality," all guided by the spiritual morality of the Jesuits. For O'Reilly, brave and selfless acts of Brazilians aboard the merchant ships attacked by Germans evinced the quality and character of this mixed-race nation, despite its relative inexperience in warfare. He cited these cases and Brazil's unified, resolute decision to declare war in response as proof of the "fallacy of the theory of pure races."[31]

Castro Costa, a journalist and politician from the state of Goiás, directly interlinked the democratic and racial components of brasilidade in the pages of *Cultura Política,* describing the "fundamental characteristic" of democracy in the Estado Novo as "equality for all before the law" to rid the world of all "racial and religious taboos."[32] There was a Nazi allusion here; Brazilian racial democracy clearly was being held in opposition to Third Reich fascism. Thus, while *Cultura Política* issues anchored brasilidade to the notion of Brazil as a rare, successful, egalitarian, and mixed-race social democracy, many of its contributors highlighted racial tolerance in a way that harnessed the world's anxiety about Nazi policies.

The Estado Novo's newfound rhetorical prioritization of Nazism as public enemy number one led to attacks on Hitler's racist ideologies and the advancement of a slightly revised brand of Brazilian racial democracy as propaganda. In 1942, during the "Week of the Child," Minister of Health and Education Gustavo Capanema articulated the racial creeds that underpinned brasilidade, using language that was contingent upon World War II:

> Brazil, ladies and gentlemen, does not base its culture on racial prejudice. We do not base our nationality . . . affirming that one race is worth more than the others, that one race should dominate the others, that one race has the right to bring down and annihilate the others. . . . Brazil does not base its civilization and its culture on this terrible social philosophy that gives human beings, by their color or appearance, the right to consider themselves above all others, to judge that they have the right to liquidate, remove, or reduce them to nothing. Brazil bases its civilization on the principle of equality and not on a prejudice of equality. (Applause)[33]

The vision of Brazil that Capanema presented in his speech was neither original nor a product of the war. However, the Nazi backdrop that he set to this familiar narrative allowed him to grandstand about Brazilian racial beliefs with a degree of hubris unavailable to previous generations of patriotic politicians.

Wartime Pan-Americanism, which emphasized the defense of and the Good Neighbor alliance between the American Republics, added yet another twist and a broader feel to the official ideology of Brazilian racial democracy. Brazil's minister of foreign affairs, Oswaldo Aranha, was one of the country's preeminent and most prolific spokespersons for Pan-Americanism. At the end of 1940, Aranha spoke at a conference at the invitation of the DIP, which later published the speech as a booklet. The war loomed large in Aranha's talk on the Americas, as he warned the Brazilian public that "the responsibilities of the American peoples have never been so large, since their destinies were never as threatened as they are in these times." According to Aranha, these responsibilities and destinies of the Americas were caught up in "Good Neighbor practices" and their common racial history. Borrowing from Mexican scholar José Vasconcelos, Aranha characterized the "fusion of numerous ethnic elements" of the American peoples as a novel "cosmic race." Aranha described the cosmic race as the new races and nations that were born exclusively in the Americas. This cosmic race was "the motive by which the Americas repudiated any and every system aiming" to imbue the concept of civilization with a racial ideal. The Americas could not accept such a closed, racialized definition of civilization that would "negat[e] their own essence." After all, upon independence the American peoples "brought liberty and equality to slave [and] enemy races" and instituted "religious tolerance" because the "conscience" of the Americas "never accepted the category of master and slave" that Old Europe had implemented.[34] In other words, racial democracy was a Pan-American phenomenon.

A revisionist history at best, Aranha's address fulfilled the Good Neighbor duty of unifying the past, present, and future fates of the American Republics and identifying the war as a great menace to the hemisphere, using race in part to do so. Nevertheless, *Cultura Política* and other official voices show that despite Aranha's lecture, Brazil attempted to appear not as just another Pan-American racial democracy but rather as a standout case. Aranha's words located Brazil and its racial democracy in the context of the New World and its potential, even while the nation tried to advance itself as the region's racial vanguard.

The Brazilian reputation for racial harmony that the state vigorously promoted led to an explosion of interest in the country in the 1940s, and many US and Brazilian scholars rushed to study the phenomenon, often making comparisons to the United States. The *Cultura Política* proposition that the world would look to Brazil as a leading exemplar of "equilibrium and serenity" would prove prophetic, not in the Estado Novo's political organization but rather in Brazil's famed peaceful coexistence among races. During and after the war, eminent social scientists fascinated with Brazilian race relations flocked to the country, producing a slew of studies that tackled race from various angles.[35] US scholars in particular found Brazil to be such a rich research site that they wore out their welcome with some Brazilian counterparts. In 1941 a leading racial scholar in Brazil, Mário de Andrade, complained to the celebrated Brazilian artist of black subjects Cândido Portinari that his own work was "extremely hindered by these North Americans who show up every week and are very nice and all, but deep down they are really irritating and give some bad lectures that . . . we are obliged to tolerate."[36] In fact, Brazil drew such attention that the newly formed United Nations Educational, Scientific and Cultural Organization (UNESCO) commissioned postwar research on racial questions in Brazil, which ironically resulted in data revealing racial discrimination in the country.[37]

As World War II entered its final phase, Getúlio Vargas saw the inevitability of his dictatorship's end and the coming of redemocratization, and he turned to Brazilian racial democracy to help quell the accusations that his regime had been totalitarian. Vargas highlighted the racist aspects of Nazism and asserted, in a 1944 speech reprinted by the DIP, that Brazilians only had reason to perceive themselves "in a dignified position" for fighting a would-be global "slave regime based on political discrimination and racial hatred."[38] During Brazilian redemocratization in 1945, Vargas revisited the subject in his highly anticipated first press conference in years. At the press conference, he specifically condemned those who labeled the Estado Novo totalitarian because it was not a representative government. According to Vargas, these critics misled the public, in part because "extreme racial limits" existed in totalitarian nations, and Vargas asked: "Where are these characteristics in our constitution?"[39] With this rhetorical question—alluded to in leading foreign newspapers such as the *New York Times*[40]—Vargas classified totalitarianism as racism and democracy as racial tolerance. Vargas had faith that his defense of the Estado Novo was convincing, and it certainly did resonate because of the contemporaneous link made between race and democracy, one that his regime had advanced for years. Thus, as his government had done all along, he used a "racial inclusiveness" definition of democracy to deflect attention from definitions emphasizing more open political processes.

It is hard to overestimate the significance of Vargas's press conference during redemocratization. In it and the long companion statement he distributed to the press—which addressed five topics, including the Estado Novo's "supposed totalitarian tendencies"—Vargas attempted to control the legacy of his dictatorship and the way in which he and the Estado Novo would be remembered. Vargas claimed that the dictatorship had come about out of necessity and not a power play, and he reminded the people that members of the Brazilian fascist movement, the integralistas, had attempted to overthrow his government in 1938. The failed coup proved that the fifth column and Axis threats in Brazil had been real, Vargas said, and that the Estado Novo had successfully fended it off. However, as the Brazilian journal *Diário de Notícias* editorialized, communism and the 1935 leftist uprisings had been the regime's excuse for shutting down Congress, canceling elections, and throwing out the 1934 Constitution, not integralism or Nazism.[41]

Vargas's rewriting of history, his use of integralism and fascism as justification for the dictatorship, and his equation of totalitarianism with racism appropriately drew to a close the regime's racial political strategy during the war. The Vargas regime had morally elevated the Estado Novo by painting the government as a defender against racism, Nazis, and fascism alongside the so-called democracies. Sometimes directly and other times indirectly linking Estado Novo democracy with ideals of racial harmony, the government articulated a special wartime version of racial democracy that rationalized its authoritarianism as well as its place among the Allies. In the process, the Estado Novo contributed to the manner in which political democracy and racial inclusion became interconnected concepts in new ways.

US RACISM PLAYS OUT IN BRAZIL

In 1943 Alberto Rondon—who worked for the OCIAA Radio Office in Hollywood and entertained Latin American journalists—warned his superiors about a worrying trend he had observed.[42] In his "confidential and frank chat[s]" with these Latin Americans, Rondon noted that they "persistently" questioned "the true attitude of this country toward the colored population." Rondon continued: "They seem to be quite disturbed as to whether any prejudices against colored people are apt to include eventually the Indian population of Latin America. Evidently the facts are exaggerated and they are under the impression that US democracy does not equally apply to all races." The memo was forwarded to Francis Jamieson, head of the OCIAA's Department of Information at the time, whose office replied that the Press Division had already "processed many stories on the colored people of the United States, their participation in the war, war production, cultural activities, etc., for distribution to Latin America."[43]

This anecdote reflects how official concerns about the United States' racial reputation in Latin America moved policymakers to cultivate an image of racial democracy and multiracial national identity. The suspicions that Latin Americans expressed were not just born of this moment. From the US-Mexican War in the 1840s to the publication of demeaning political cartoons, Latin Americans had long dealt with the impact of US racist attitudes toward the region.[44] When they appeared in Brazil during World War II, US state actors classified these suspicions as extremely troublesome for at least three reasons: Brazil's racial makeup as the largest black population of the Americas, Brazil's strategic importance during the war, and institutional memory within US agencies about the United States' racist reputation in Brazil. Indeed, US civilian and military officials had profiled race in Brazil for decades, providing authorities with a knowledge base about Brazilian racial customs and attitudes, and detailing Brazilian perspectives on those in the United States. This state institutional memory guided authorities through the charged racial milieu of the Second World War and helped render discursive racial democracy an urgent and necessary weapon of warfare.

Brazilian immigration debates often illuminated the complexity of racial thought in the country, showing how US practices informed its laws and that Brazilians took being the foil to US racial policy seriously. US military intelligence and embassy documents in the 1920s and 1930s agreed that racial discrimination generally did not exist in Brazil, although "exceptions" were seen with such issues as who should be let into the country. As Jeffrey Lesser has detailed, Brazil's 1934 constituent assembly clashed over Japanese immigration. Those in favor prioritized the perceived economic benefits, whereas those opposed fretted about what they believed to be the Japanese's negative impact on the Brazilian race. The assembly decided to follow the United States' 1924 immigration law, and the constitution designated quotas based on national origin that restricted Japanese immigration.[45]

US diplomatic and military personnel had been following these attitudes for years. Homer Brett, the American consul in the state of Bahia, for instance, reported in 1924 that there was strong sentiment in the state for white immigration only.[46] To his memo about the impact of US racial exclusion on Brazil's immigration policy, Brett attached "The Intrusive Japanese," an article by Nestor Duarte that had been printed in the journal *Diário da Bahia*. It began by situating Brazil's willingness to accept Japanese immigrants in order to establish itself as a moral superior to the racist United States, a position that Duarte lamented sarcastically:

> With the strong and egoistic gesture of the United States closing its doors to the race of Nippon, now we Brazilians have the admirable opportunity of demonstrating our sentimental . . . urbanity by opening our tolerating arms to the yellow immigrant. . . . The United States may be, patriotically, an indelicate nation, but not we. We profoundly love the international reputation that rates us as a friendly, polished, and good-natured country. And that this conception may not be disputed we will allow Japan the rudeness of overloading our shoulders with the numerous excess of her prolific population.

Citing "nationalism" and "ethnic integrity," Duarte insisted that Brazilians "cannot be tolerant" merely for the sake of "diplomatic courtesy." He reminded the reader that Brazil was still in need of "extirpating [the] last stains of the horrible and degenerate racial mixture" and contended that the inclusion of the Japanese—deemed unassimilable and "most ugly" by Western standards—only added insult to injury.[47]

Duarte considered feebleminded those who conjured racial immigration policy in the United States as a reason to support Japanese immigration to Brazil. The US vice-consul in Vitória, capital of the state of Espírito Santo, provided an example of this mentality in 1929. The vice-consul reported on an article published on the front page of the "state official morning daily," *Diário de Manhã*. The article found that discrimination against the Japanese had "no reason to exist" in Brazil. Such prejudice, it stated, "could only have been the fruit of a condemnable imitation, because 'Yankee' laws have closed the ports of the United States to the current of immigration from Japan." While such laws made sense in the United States, where there was "a raging struggle of races," the writer felt that Brazil's process of "intelligent melting" rendered it illogical "to attempt the prohibition practiced by North America."[48]

In 1925 the US embassy in Rio de Janeiro sent a memo to notify the State Department that Brazil's Congressional Finance and Agricultural Committees had backed barring black immigration to the country by comparing Brazil to the United States. The two committees juxtaposed Brazil's "favorable treatment and gradual assimilation of the Black race" to the "atmosphere of hatred and isolation which is supposed to surround their racial prototypes in North America." Yet the committees determined that it would be unwise for Brazil to "attempt to absorb further installments of Negroes from abroad." An enclosed copy of *Parecer*, a publication of the Brazilian Congress (Federal Chamber of Deputies), went into greater detail. *Parecer* elaborated on Brazil's tradition of meritocracy without distinction of color and argued that the country had resolved its racial dilemma with much more "humanity" than the United States. The Brazilian Congress was self-congratulatory, praising the country's supposed lack of segregation and antipathy between the races for allowing the "dilution" and eventual "disappearance" of the black race. The Brazilian government pointed to its own tolerance of racial mixture as more effectual in solving the racial "problem"; in its view, the US stance on segregation only cemented the regrettable existence of blacks, while Brazil's progressive and more sensible whitening approach promised to eradicate blackness altogether. Clearly, with this rationale, black immigration would only serve to extend, disrupt, or, worse, reverse the race's erasure. The committees, however, did favor Japanese immigration, which, according to the dispatch, countered the general consensus among Brazilians and was far from the norm among government officials.[49]

Together these dispatches forwarded to the State Department indicated that US diplomats understood how US race relations played a prominent role in the battles waged over race and immigration in Brazil. US authorities were aware that the nationalist desire to act as a racially harmonious antithesis to its discriminatory North American neighbor was strong in Brazil and likely affected its policies. US Foreign Service and military personnel also had documented the idiosyncrasies of this tendency that would pertain to US wartime anxieties fifteen to twenty years later: the whitening ideal was popular among the Brazilian elite, which, despite all the talk of racial tolerance, would not make the presence of Nazi sympathizers in the government strange or surprising.

Racial exclusion in the United States, the myth of Brazilian racial inclusion, and immigration debates before World War II set a foundation that affected the way US officials understood the wartime racial landscape, and in some cases, their Foreign Service experiences could also be a factor. In 1924 the chargé d'affaires at the US embassy in Tokyo contributed to the analysis on Japanese immigration to Brazil, noting that Brazil was the preferred Latin American destination for the Japanese. He wrote that Japanese immigrants seemed to adapt well in Brazil because of agricultural conditions and because "[r]acial antipathy [there was] said to be practically non-existent." As the temporary diplomatic head in Japan observing the immigration issue, he may have read the reports from the US embassy and consulates in Brazil, including the Brett/Duarte memo, copies of which had been forwarded to the embassy in Tokyo. By the late 1930s, this very chargé d'affaires, Jefferson Caffery, would be the US ambassador to Brazil, serving in this post until nearly the end of the war.[50] At a time when the United States had the most to fear in terms of its racial reputation in Brazil, and when Japanese and German racial propaganda critiquing the United States was rampant, its ambassador grasped the profundity and longevity of the problem.

The Military and Naval Intelligence Divisions also had a long history of studying Brazilian racial attitudes and reactions to the United States, and there were parallels between their reports before and after the war. In 1923 Major F. L. Whitley sent a memo from Brazil to the War Department in which he opined that "Brazil is almost free from color prejudice" and that US racism undercut the nation's goodwill in Brazil.[51] In 1943 a naval intelligence observer stationed in Recife reported, "'race,' in the accepted sense of the word, does not exist here." He cited a lack of both hostility between racialized groups and clearly demarcated racial lines, which, he concluded, made Brazil "in many ways more of a 'melting pot' than the United States."[52] The two reports focused on differences in practice, conveying explicitly or implicitly that Brazilians would not respect those found in the United States. Since military organizations were at the table when domestic and international "information" and "psychological warfare" campaigns were conceived in the United States, these racial narratives would help guide US wartime propaganda to Brazil.

In its research capacity, the OSS—the precursor to the Central Intelligence Agency (CIA)—gathered tactical information for the military and alerted policymakers about the injury that racist attitudes could exact on US wartime objectives in Brazil. In 1942 the OSS Research Bureau's Latin American Division analyzed a speech by Brazilian colonel Estillac Leal that had been featured in the state-controlled daily journal, *A Manhã*. In an attempt to generate national opposition against the Axis powers, Leal argued that the Germans would be thrilled to conquer Brazil for its natural resources and predicted that the outcome of this scenario would be the enslavement of the Brazilian people. Leal condemned Nazi racism in what the OSS called "violent terms": "[W]hat can we expect from Nazism, we who have in our veins the blood of the Portuguese, negroes and indians *[sic]*?"[53] An opinion piece by Gilberto Freyre translated in a naval intelligence report echoed the sentiment, criticizing priests who were Axis sympathizers. Freyre wrote, "a people like ourselves, must be on the alert, for our whole organization lies on the mixing" as well as the rights of all races, not just whites.[54] (As we saw in chapter 4, Freyre's racial perspectives reflected that of the federal government, but not the Pernambucan state regime, which detained him for publishing this article.)[55]

The United States wanted to fan the flames of these anti-Axis appeals among Brazilians and to avoid the expression of similar concerns about the United States. Enter the United States' vast Latin American propaganda machine. The OSS, Military and Naval Intelligence Divisions, and State Department were key participants in sending propaganda to Latin America during the Second World War. The principal wartime agency responsible for propaganda in the region, the OCIAA, was under the authority of the State Department and exchanged information with the OSS Research Bureau's Latin American Division. The OCIAA also met frequently with Military Intelligence and War and Navy Department representatives.[56] War Department records show that the Military Intelligence Division furnished the OCIAA with information, intelligence reports, analyses of enemy propaganda, and suggestions for propaganda and counterpropaganda.[57] OCIAA head Nelson Rockefeller was a more than willing participant in this collaboration. After Pearl Harbor, he told his staff that the OCIAA was in the "first line of defense" because of the other American Republics' importance in "defending [their] flank" and supplying the United States with resources that would become "materials of war." As his biographer Cary Reich has written, Nelson Rockefeller "seized every opportunity to mobilize his agency in support of US military objectives."[58] These interagency connections were incredibly significant, as they married state institutional memory to World War II machinations, which projected antiracist ideals as an essential piece of the United States' offensive and defensive information campaign in Brazil.

When Axis and even Nazi propaganda made every effort to exploit US racism in order to rally and recruit supporters in Latin America, authorities from these various official organs grew nervous. The OCIAA was charged with undermining the Axis assault with its own propaganda, creating what the military referred to as "a weapon of war."[59] A 1943 issue of the OCIAA's secret bulletin *Hemisphere Weekly*, which compiled information from various state organizations, confirmed that US race relations had become a debilitating handicap to its Good Neighbor war priorities. Under the subtitle "Destroying the Influence of the United States and the Allies," the bulletin reported that the United States' "[v]ulnerable points, particularly those likely to impress Latin Americans," included Japanese testimonies that the United States "discriminate[s] against and exploit[s] negroes *[sic]*, Japanese [and] workers on the Brazilian rubber plantations. Race disorders like those in Detroit and Philadelphia are grist to this mill."[60] Another event, the lynching of a black oil-mill worker, resulted in the Japanese deployment of explicit democratic rhetoric to advance its racial messaging in Latin America: "Democracy . . . may be an ideal and noble system of life, but democracy as practiced by the Anglo Americans is stained with the bloody guilt of racial persecution and exploitation."[61]

The Japanese—often drawing upon the US black press's coverage of the African American freedom struggle—broadcast stories internationally to show that the United States was hostile to people of color and could not be trusted by Latin Americans. Indications that black leaders in the United States were critical of the government were especially desirable material for the Japanese. On the heels of Pearl Harbor, NAACP head Walter White warned that the "dark-skinned citizens" of Latin America would not cooperate with a racist United States. White also worried about the fact that black Brazilians visiting the United States would suffer segregation firsthand.[62] The OCIAA's *Daily Bulletin* published an example of the Japanese capitalizing on such reproaches in 1944, stating that Tokyo transmitted a report to Latin America that an unnamed "Negro leader, head of 5,500,000-member association," had characterized the wartime labor of US blacks as a form of enslavement. Japan also broadcast to Latin America that its premier had declared the "elimination of racial discrimination" as Japan's "war aim," an overt attempt to frame the war as one for racial equality. In this paradigm, it was the United States, not Germany, that was the poster child for extreme racism, with Japan serving as the champion of racial justice.[63]

That Japan placed itself and the United States on opposing ends of its spectrum of racial policy is not surprising; that the Nazis also called out US racism in their propaganda to Brazil is, at the very least, ironic. A

1944 issue of the OCIAA bulletin announced that Nazis "emphasized [their] race superiority in their appeals to certain upper classes who wished to believe in racial supremacy" in Brazil but "emphasized their own fantastic interpretations of our treatment of Negroes to influence certain Negroid groups in Brazil."[64] As British intelligence reported, the Axis countries also spread stories that an Allied victory would introduce racial segregation into Brazil "similar to that operating in the Southern States of the U.S.A."[65] These accusations, which paralleled Brazilian racial critiques of the United States before the war and Japan's condemnation of US democracy during it, undermined the democratic claims upon which the United States rhetorically based its war efforts.

The Axis powers found it in their best interest to highlight racism in order to deter multiracial societies like Brazil from supporting the United States, while the OCIAA and other US agencies struggled to maintain moral superiority, even over the Nazis. The institutional memory of the country's racial reputation in Brazil over the years made the nation's vulnerability on this point clear. Furthermore, OSS records stating that 22 percent of Brazilians had "negro [sic] blood," and "14% (or over 5 million)" were said to be "pure negro [sic]" stressed how crucial the situation was in what one *Congressional Record* article labeled "the largest Negro nation."[66] In its response to this situation, the United States and its many agencies disseminated propaganda of racial democracy as a measure of national security and wartime defense in order to counter Axis racial psychological warfare.

While the United States' racial injustices became a serious issue for its wartime exigencies in Brazil, Estado Novo authorities discovered a combination of opportunities and challenges presented by the war. The focus on democracy made the dictatorship's partnership with the United States and the Allied nations paradoxical, to say the least. However, the spotlight on race gave the Brazilians an out, as they manipulated the link between racism and Nazism and fascism to rationalize their membership among the Allies. As a result, Brazilian wartime racial democracy was a case of racial denial enabling democratic denial, and this was reflected in its propaganda to the United States. For both nations, articulations of racial democracy reinforced their wartime relationship and its ideological, financial, and militaristic implications.

CHAPTER 6

A Partnership in Cultural Production

The Brazil-US Racial Democracy Exchange

Brazilian and US state cultural production generated two-way channels of propaganda that advanced both countries' racial democracy agendas. Their exchange was asymmetrical, since Brazil did not have the resources to inundate the United States with propaganda to the same extent as the United States did with Brazil. Unfortunately, the primary sources are similarly lopsided.[1] However, the fact that Estado Novo censors were sent to the United States to help oversee US propaganda about and to Brazil gave the Brazilians a measure of control in the propaganda swap. This collaboration also recovers the racial bias in Brazilian cultural policy. The US-Brazil wartime alliance was shaped by geopolitical factors (Japan and Germany remained huge concerns), anxieties about internal "Axis populations," military engagement, and financial incentives, making this relationship critical to each government. Thus, even though neither country delivered messages of racial democracy exclusively to the other, their relationship became a major overall driving force in their cultural propaganda.

Operating under national security imperatives, these states' wartime propaganda utilized racial discourse and representations to court sympathy from the other side. Policymakers also deployed propaganda to overcome the manner in which the war uniquely challenged the states' democratic status, in part claiming to be antiracist and embracing black culture in new ways. The strategy to capture hearts and minds in the other nation was largely a form of denial: the United States glossed over its escalating racial tensions in its attempt to dissuade Brazilians from sympathizing with the Axis powers, while Brazil showcased its nominal racial utopia in a democratic light to ideologically align itself with the United States.

Black cultural demarginalization, white cultural mediators, and state projections of racial democracy were interconnected during the Second World War. As we have seen, black culture had already begun to move toward the mainstream in Brazil and the United States over the previous two decades, a movement marked by white artists and intellectuals adopting black cultural expressions. This chapter also examines high-profile white mediators of black culture such as US artists Benny Goodman and Orson Welles and Brazilians Vinícius de Moraes and Carmen Miranda, who was born in Portugal, before and during the war. The focus on white mediators in this chapter is not to suggest the irrelevance of black artists but rather to highlight the two states' racial partiality in these cultural projects.

The Brazilian and US reliance on primarily white artists to demarginalize elements of black culture in itself articulated and represented official racial democracy. First, consistent with the message of racial democracy, whites who embraced the black subculture of their society could be perceived as an example of a friendly and harmonious interracial milieu. After all, if black culture was accepted, wouldn't blacks be as well? However, white cultural mediators as agents of racial democracy encapsulated the shortcomings of the doctrine—namely, the failure of those in power to pursue action-oriented realism. The demarginalization of black culture in official propaganda did not translate into the economic, social, or political demarginalization of most blacks, nor did it require black corporeal presence in certain social or cultural circles. As was the case in the 1930s, black culture performed by black bodies often remained peripheral to official national culture. Finally, these mediators indicated that US and Brazilian authorities looked to the white cultural, artistic, and intellectual elite—many scholars of blacks and their art—to help build political consensus. They also were employed to create nationalist and Pan-American fervor for each country's war effort and, in Brazil, to valorize the dictatorship. In both nations the state-hired intelligentsia ordinarily voiced the more progressive official perspectives on racial democracy, which repeatedly put intellectuals at loggerheads with more powerful authorities.

This chapter shows that many state projects made explicit statements about the nature of race relations and clearly meant to engage the discourse of democratic racial inclusion so prevalent during the war. Others advanced rhetorical or visual imagery that drew a picture of a multiracial society (even if frequently minimized and whitened). Regardless of the method employed, with few exceptions messages of racial democracy in the form of cultural propaganda exposed the doctrine's significant limitations and were fraught with exclusionary viewpoints.

THE OFFICE OF THE COORDINATOR OF INTER-AMERICAN AFFAIRS AND RAYFORD LOGAN

In direct response to Axis activity in Latin America and undergirded by the Good Neighbor Policy, the US State Department formed the Division of Cultural Relations in 1938—the nation's first state entity established to oversee cultural diplomacy as a branch of foreign policy. Two years later, Roosevelt created an agency responsible for the US cultural, economic, and media agenda in Latin America, which became the Office of the Coordinator of Inter-American Affairs. Similar to the Division of Cultural Relations, the OCIAA was founded out of a concern for Axis exploits in Latin America. It was the United States' first propaganda agency established specifically to counter Axis influence.[2]

Nelson Rockefeller, head of the OCIAA, hoped to counter the pervasive economic and media activities of Axis nations in Latin America with commercial, cultural, and informational measures. The future governor of New York and vice president of the United States had a passion for Latin America and had traveled south frequently for business and to collect art. In 1940 Rockefeller's business ventures in Venezuela opened his eyes to the dire impact the war in Europe was having on Latin American economies, and he became greatly concerned about Nazi economic leverage in the entire region. Along with his colleague Beardsley Ruml, he drafted a memo that suggested the government work together with the business sector to develop a comprehensive investment, trade, diplomatic, cultural, educational, and scientific plan in Latin America to eclipse that of the Germans. This memo influenced the creation of the OCIAA and Rockefeller's appointment to the unpaid coordinator position.

Preceding the Office of War Information and other wartime agencies, the OCIAA launched a propaganda campaign to oppose the Axis powers' media pursuits in Latin America. Although required to clear its activities with the State Department, the OCIAA maintained its mandate in the region throughout the war, despite initial skepticism by various authorities and takeover attempts by subsequent wartime agencies.[3]

FIGURE 5. A display board sponsored by the OCIAA local committee in Natal, Rio Grande do Norte, Brazil. Such displays highlighted US efforts in the war and are examples of the OCIAA's work on the ground in Brazil. Courtesy of the National Archives and Records Administration, College Park, MD.

Most OCIAA authorities and collaborators embraced the fact that its mission largely was to carry out US propaganda, plain and simple. The military, for one, designated the OCIAA as the agency that conducted its "plan for propaganda . . . based on the requirements of military strategy" in the Latin American countries.[4] In fact, the military's Psychological Warfare Branch offered "propaganda and counter-propaganda" suggestions to the OCIAA.[5] According to the military's own definition of *propaganda,* the OCIAA was charged with the "dissemination of ideas, information, gossip, or the like, often by secret or clandestine means, for the purpose of helping [the United States' cause] or of damaging the enemy's cause" in Latin America.[6] Therefore, by requiring that cultural relations be a function of the OCIAA, the government framed the state's Pan-American cultural work as propaganda. Since it had been against propaganda, the State Department's Division of Cultural Relations was at first uncomfortable with the openly propagandistic position of the OCIAA, yet many State Department leaders and officers began to accept, advocate for, and justify propaganda in Latin America. The US ambassador to Brazil even agreed, calling for a short-lived cultural program that served wartime propaganda exigencies. After all, as Rockefeller said, "intellectual imperialism, the imperialism of ideas, was . . . just as serious a threat to the security and defense of the hemisphere as the possibility of military invasion."[7]

The OCIAA's treatment of race in its propaganda developed out of necessity but was also the result of pressure that US blacks exerted. Publisher Claude Barnett, founder of the Associated Negro Press, lobbied Rockefeller to include black life in OCIAA cultural and media projects. Chandler Owen, former coeditor with A. Philip Randolph of the black journal the *Messenger,* called for the creation of an OCIAA "Negro Division." Owen argued that US blacks were "'the recognized leaders of all Negroes in the hemisphere' and played an important role in the 'maintenance of morale among the large Negro population of Brazil—the biggest of our Good Neighbors.'" Eventually Rockefeller accepted Mary McLeod Bethune and the National Council of Negro Women's proposition that an African American be added to the OCIAA advisory committee.[8]

Although Bethune provided the name and résumé of a woman, Pearl Vincent Morton, for the job, it appears as though the OCIAA never seriously considered asking her to join its advisory committee, focusing instead on male candidates. Howard University professor Rayford Logan was a leading contender because of his knowledge of the Caribbean. Logan's Howard colleague E. Franklin Frazier was also considered because—as Alain Locke argued, signaling Brazil's importance—Frazier had just conducted research in Brazil and "had such recent information about Brazilian conditions [that] his point of view might be more valuable [than Logan's] at the present time." Upon this suggestion, Mary Winslow, the OCIAA adviser on women's organizations who vetted the finalists for Rockefeller, interviewed Frazier but felt that Logan was the better option, citing the support he had with the blacks she had consulted at Howard and elsewhere.[9]

Logan accepted the unpaid appointment to the advisory committee with the belief that the OCIAA should give "adequate and equitable consideration of all phases of the Negro problem" and tackle racism holistically, as a hemispheric, Pan-American problem. Reflecting many of the concerns blacks at Howard University had discussed with Mary Winslow, Logan pushed in part for research on Afro-Latin American history as well as cultural and educational exchanges among blacks in the hemisphere.[10] Logan's major project proposal was a fifteen-month study of black history in Latin America, and he was also asked to participate in the Inter-American Conference on Negro Studies spearheaded by the private American Council of Learned Societies (ACLS) that was to occur in Port-au-Prince, Haiti, in 1942.[11]

This ill-fated conference—overseen by the OCIAA, State Department, and ACLS in a Joint Committee on Cultural Relations—exemplified how state-sponsored Pan-American cultural projects located cultural work within the sphere of national defense and included race as a part of such security missions. The conference's primary purpose was to strengthen Pan-American solidarity through US, Latin American, and Caribbean scholars of black studies in the Americas. In the process, the joint committee stated, the conference would be "an excellent vehicle to counteract Nazi propaganda attacking the United States in connection with alleged mistreatment of negroes [sic] [and] an antidote to the Nazi glorification of the superiority of the 'pure races.'"[12] State Department committee member Richard Pattee, who had translated Arthur Ramos's seminal *The Negro in Brazil* into English in 1939, opined that the conference would also deflect accusations that the group ignored issues affecting US blacks.

If the Joint Committee on Cultural Relations hoped that the Inter-American Conference on Negro Studies would avert criticism that the committee neglected matters of importance to blacks, it encountered protest for excluding and marginalizing black scholars. The committee, especially the ACLS, refused to approve the ideas that black scholars advanced or to allow many of them to participate in the conference or similar events.[13] The Inter-American Conference on Negro Studies never took place, due in part to the outbreak of war and escalating Brazil-Axis tensions, which presumably would have made travel difficult for the Brazilian intellectuals who were slated to attend (Gilberto Freyre, Mário de Andrade, and Arthur Ramos).[14]

Rayford Logan was disappointed by a lack of support for his projects and angered over the way the joint committee sidelined him, but he remained undeterred in his advocacy for Pan-American racial democracy. The OCIAA whittled down his fifteen-month Latin American research trip to five months, and the State Department and ACLS trimmed off another three. In the end, Logan agreed to study the "Negro Contribution to Hemispheric Solidarity, with Special Reference to Cuba, the Dominican Republic, and Haiti." In his diary, Logan wrote that in light of the reduced research time, he had chosen to exclude Brazil because "more study had been made of [the] Negro in Brazil than in any other country." Logan foretold the findings of the study when he laid out his vision of racial democracy to Nelson Rockefeller directly, strategically utilizing Rockefeller's own words as foundation. Rockefeller had justified the OCIAA's economic mission in part by arguing that democracy in Latin America could not be achieved so long as the masses remained impoverished. Logan explained to Rockefeller that such a statement had racial implications, since the majority of blacks in Latin America were among the poor. Logan carried this economically based version of racial democracy to another level in his postresearch report.[15]

In the study he submitted to the OCIAA, Logan sought solutions for the poverty that the majority of black Latin Americans experienced. Logan transformed the idea of racial democracy that he had discussed with Rockefeller into a detailed, action-oriented plan that he called a Western Hemisphere or Good Neighbor New Deal. Logan concluded that long-term support to the region was required. He also argued that the United States should give loans and grants to the poorer Latin American countries to fund projects that could pull people out of poverty, like investments in education and low-income housing. Logan also contended that North Americans and wealthier countries in the hemisphere should pay more for goods from the economically vulnerable nations so that laborers might earn a living wage. Although the OCIAA never responded to his report, through his realist analysis about blacks and hemispheric solidarity, Logan delivered a powerful argument that race, economic development, and democracy were connected.[16] Logan's official presence on the OCIAA advisory committee gave a degree of importance to his insertion of race into Rockefeller's economic definition of democracy.

Logan's retooling of Rockefeller's notion of economic democracy made clear that the economic and social aid programs that government agencies like the OCIAA executed had racial ramifications, intentionally or not. Yet the economic component of racial democracy was not the focus of most government officials during the war. When they addressed race, most authorities projected the culturally specific angle of racial democracy that Alain Locke advanced.[17] The result was state cultural production that made more symbolic and non-action-oriented gestures to include blacks in democracy and society.

NATIONAL IDENTITY EXPORTED: BRAZIL AND THE UNITED STATES EXCHANGE IMAGERY OF RACIAL DEMOCRACY

The OCIAA could not afford to ignore the onslaught of racial propaganda from Axis nations throughout Latin America and especially in

Brazil, since the United States had much damage control to undertake there. In Brazil the United States fought not only the exposure of its own racial tensions but also the stories that the United States sought to "Brazilianize" Jim Crow.[18] OCIAA work in Brazil should in no way be seen as a mere imposition of US policy and the hegemonic "Americanization" of Brazilian culture, as has been argued in the past.[19] On the contrary, Brazilian state authorities were so actively involved in what the OCIAA produced and disseminated for Brazilian consumption that these materials constituted Brazilian domestic propaganda as well.

In 1943 the OCIAA's Coordination Committee in Brazil described its relationship with Brazil's Department of Press and Propaganda, which in part oversaw tourism and the state's radio programming, and also censored theater, cinema, commercial radio, the press, and social as well as political literature. The committee wrote that the DIP had "cooperated fully in our publicity effort in Brazil."[20] Scholars Gisela Cramer and Ursula Prutsch have written that the Brazilian government obtained "a certain level of control" over US cultural and media work in Brazil by cooperating with the OCIAA. Brazilian censors exercised power over the OCIAA's local coordination branches in Brazil, and they also enjoyed significant control over the OCIAA's Brazilian operations in the United States. The OCIAA actually hired Estado Novo censors to work in the United States in order to "monitor all [US] radio contents destined for retransmission" in Brazil. With DIP members on the OCIAA's team, the dictatorship allowed the OCIAA access to Brazil's state-controlled broadcasting system.[21] The Brazilian government and the OCIAA even partnered to develop the office's programming.[22]

In March 1942 the OCIAA's Brazilian Division reported that five Brazilians, all DIP officials or people selected by the DIP, were heading to the United States to help produce the OCIAA's daily news and commentary broadcasts on the Estado Novo's nightly *Hora do Brasil* radio program.[23] *Time* magazine stated that the five Brazilians arrived with their families in tow, temporarily relocating to the United States to perform a rather odd duty: "In international broadcasts, the receiving country seldom helps to prepare the programs it receives, but [the Brazilians] reached Manhattan for just that purpose."[24] That these broadcasts were to be carried on the Estado Novo's radio program—which all radio stations in the country were obliged to either transmit or go off the air—makes this an extraordinary partnership. These five-minute OCIAA-DIP broadcasts, as well as their subsequent transcription and publication in the Brazilian press, also with the DIP's help, were "forceful and interesting reports on the United States" that especially applauded the performance of US troops in the war.[25] Soon thereafter, the US DIP team also broadcast fifteen-minute weekly commentaries from New York to eight major stations in Brazil.[26]

Júlio Barata—director of DIP's Radio Division, future minister of labor, former member of a Brazilian fascist organization, and head of the New York team—had to check and clear every program before the Brazilian government would allow the United States to rebroadcast over Brazilian airwaves. Barata resided in the United States until 1944, remaining engaged in these radio activities and lecturing on Brazil to audiences at twenty-six conferences held at US universities and chambers of commerce.[27] The other members of the group were journalist and playwright Raymundo Magalhães, who was an assistant to DIP head Lourival Fontes; Orígenes Lessa, novelist and magazine director; Pompeu de Souza, journalist and radio commentator; and Francisco Assis Figueiredo, director of the DIP's Division of Tourism and DIP assistant director in charge of US relations.[28] The US government spent $31,000 a year on the US-based DIP employee salaries.[29] In addition, DIP's director of distribution, Alfredo Pessoa, not only had direct contact with Nelson Rockefeller but also spent at least a year and a half working for the OCIAA in the United States as a Brazilian consultant. These experiences informed his articles and daily broadcasts to Brazil.[30]

Estado Novo authorities in the DIP and other sectors of the state worked closely with the OCIAA on various projects that complemented the radio serials, and the Brazilians even solicited US propaganda. The OCIAA Brazilian Division's 1943 annual report lists a host of Brazilian state and private organization collaborators, including the Ministry of Education and Public Health (a leading organ of national cultural management), the Ministry of War, the Brazilian Press Association (controlled by the DIP), and, of course, the DIP itself.[31] The results of these relationships were impressive: another annual report reveals that "thousands of feature articles and tens of thousands of photographs" were sent to some twelve hundred newspapers and magazines throughout Brazil, and US articles and photographs appeared "with gratifying frequency on the front pages of the leading Rio and São Paulo newspapers as well as papers in the interior."[32] Brazilian police also reached out to US authorities in their midst. In February 1942 the São Paulo police force contacted the US military attaché to request that "counter-activity be initiated to neutralize" Japanese radio propaganda in Brazil.[33] In other words, the São Paulo police asked the United States to propagandize Brazilians.

With the DIP's mandate to clear all radio programming to Brazil, its representatives would have approved and possibly collaborated on the OCIAA's radio scripts that emphasized Nazi racism against mixed-race (i.e., racially "inferior") people. The weekly half-hour *Estamos em guerra* (We are at war), which CBS broadcast from New York to Latin America, was one program that performed this task. The show, a weekly US news report "presented in dramatic form," touched upon the theme of Nazi racism in some of its wartime story lines.[34] Referring to the Allied forces as "the democracies" throughout, one 1942 episode dramatized Franklin Roosevelt's Four Freedoms. In the scene that portrayed the freedom from want, the narrator described the setting as Poland, Czechoslovakia, France, or "all lands occupied by the Nazis." A police whistle blows as a Nazi commands others to apprehend a suspect, asking what it was he had stolen. The suspect himself answers that it was "a piece of bread and a little cheese . . . for my family." The Nazi retorts: "Aren't you satisfied with the generous ration that the Fuehrer provides you?" "Yes, sir," the man politely replies, "but it's not enough for all of us . . . and they are dying of hunger." The Nazi's callous reaction should have caught the attention of Brazil's nonwhite listeners: "And that is how all of you should die . . . *people of inferior race*s. . . . Only the Aryan race has the right to life." The Nazi ordered that the man be held in prison before joining the group facing the firing squad the following morning.[35] As the narrator preached in another *Estamos em guerra* episode, human life meant nothing to Nazis, "and much less the existence of races that they consider inferior."[36]

Anxious to remove the United States' racist label and pin it on the Nazis, the OCIAA often fashioned *Estamos em guerra* into a poorly disguised lecture series that juxtaposed the proclaimed racial doctrines on both sides. One episode produced in 1943 exemplified this feature of US wartime propaganda. During the episode, the narrator explained the Nazi motto "Blood and Soil": "Blut und Boden . . . means that the superior race—made up by them according to what they themselves proclaim—is united by blood ties: Only one blood, only one homeland. The racial madness of the Nazis contradicts a concept of the United Nations: Blood is a symbol of common sacrifice, the good of all races without distinction between them . . . . The United Nations do not have, like the totalitarians, contempt for human life."[37]

The OCIAA also used cultural policy to counter Axis racial propaganda by publishing historical comic books in Portuguese and Spanish for distribution throughout Brazil and the rest of Latin America. One showed an ominous Nazi-enslaved world where Catholics were persecuted (a common theme in US materials to Latin America)[38] and all the rights the Allies stood for, such as the freedom of speech and the right to live, were violently denied. The comic juxtaposed this depressing scene with a happily harmonious Allied society. As the narrator for the peaceful world, Roosevelt and thus the Allied nations are the champions for the values he articulates, including the people's desire to have a society in which "equal opportunity for all" is the reality. To indicate that this "all" was truly multiracial, two men—one white and one brown or black—are shown working side by side. The bottom of the page validates this portrayal with a quote from US undersecretary of state Sumner Welles, confirming, "Our victory should bring with it liberty for all people. It will have to end discrimination of race, creed, or color." These words are accompanied by an image of men from various racial, class, and professional backgrounds with their arms around one another.[39]

On the page following these representations of racial democracy, a middle-class Latin American man reassures his wife (a stand-in for the reader) that with an Allied victory, "there will be a better world for us all." The depiction of the better world illustrates people of both genders and all races standing together, smiling over a thriving metropolis and cornucopia. The caption reads, "Racial inequality will end." Using gross stereotypes, the same comic book also portrayed the Japanese leadership's perception of the attack on Pearl Harbor: "We should attack democracy, now or never, if we want to dominate the Asiatic continent."[40] Here the OCIAA contended that Japan's air strike against the United States threatened genuine democracy, a democracy that promised a more racially egalitarian society.

In this comic book, tellingly titled *Our Future—Free Men or Slaves,* the OCIAA advanced a comprehensive statement about US racial democratic ideals that aided important wartime propaganda missions in Brazil. In general, *Our Future* tackled Axis accusations in Latin America about US racism as well as the United States' long-standing poor racial reputation with visual and verbal messages about a country unequivocally dedicated to racial equality for men and women of all classes. Indeed, although the messenger was described as the Allied countries, the quotes from Roosevelt and Welles specified that racial inclusion was a US principle. In particular, the comic history contradicted the rumor that the United States would implement Jim Crow in Brazil. It also suggested that the United States—not Japan, as Japan had claimed—would be the world's leader in racial equality, and it constructed Japan as the

FIGURE 6. President Roosevelt appears alongside language and images of racial democracy in the OCIAA comic history, *Nuestro futuro—¿Hombres libres o esclavos?* (Our future—Free men or slaves?). Courtesy of the Rockefeller Archive Center.

FIGURE 7. In this paternalistic message, the OCIAA promises a cosmopolitan cornucopia in which racial equality thrives. From the OCIAA comic history, *Nuestro futuro—¿Hombres libres o esclavos?* (Our future—Free men or slaves?). Courtesy of the Rockefeller Archive Center.

enemy of all that was democratic, including the racial democracy that the United States supposedly represented. This argument flipped on its head the racial narrative that the Japanese government had disseminated throughout Latin America. In addition, Brazilians could identify with the multiracial, multiclass Allied society that the comic's illustrations presented, which fulfilled the Good Neighbor objective of encouraging southern neighbors to relate to the United States. Finally, the comic did not open the Pandora's box of contemporary practices of racial discrimination, focusing instead on the familiar OCIAA theme of Nazi persecution of Catholics as a warning to this very Catholic region. The OCIAA avoided the issue of racism in the United States, conveniently sidestepping the United States' own racial record. After all, the racial utopia that the comic laid out portrayed a future, post–World War II scenario under Allied leadership and depicted the ideals for which the United States claimed to fight, not its current reality. The comic's racial democracy was a futuristic fantasy distinct from standard denial in that it did not rebut the existence of racism in the United States per se. *Our Future* mainly served to dissuade multiracial peoples like Brazilians from sympathizing with the Axis powers.

Dissuasion tended to be quite paternalistic, and this comic history is no exception. The voice of authority that quotes Roosevelt and Welles is the middle-class husband, who is explaining the stakes to his confused and fearful wife. The husband easily convinces the wife not only that the Allied nations must win the war but also that they must support the Allies and the prosperous, peaceful, racial democracy they will bring to fruition. The woman exclaims, "Oh God! What will become of us if we do not conquer this heroic new world?" The husband concurs, insisting that failure is not an option.[41] Through the husband, the US government successfully persuades the wife, or Latin America, to follow its lead.[42] Moreover, a huge benefit of the comic book format is that even without the dialogue, the illustrations tell the fundamental moral of the story: it is clear in the pictures who the "good guys" and the "bad guys" are. The comic histories conveyed the OCIAA's messages with plain language for those with limited reading proficiency and pictures for those with little or no literacy.

Film was another cultural medium that the US government used to propagate its message of racial democracy to audiences illiterate and literate alike.[43] A prime example is the OCIAA's short film on Pearl Harbor hero Doris "Dorie" Miller, the black mess attendant on the USS *West Virginia* who, after moving injured men to safety, successfully operated

FIGURE 8. In the two images at the foot of the page, the OCIAA maligns Japanese officials and portrays the strike on Pearl Harbor as a plan to "attack democracy." From the OCIAA comic history, *Nuestro futuro—¿Hombres libres o esclavos?* (Our future— Free men or slaves?). Courtesy of the Rockefeller Archive Center.

an antiaircraft machine gun against Japanese fighter planes even though he had not been trained to use it.[44] Miller was the first African American to win the Navy Cross Medal, and officials believed that his story "should be effective in showing that we do have a democracy and that the colored people have a vital stake in winning the war, since they too are making sacrifices."[45] Kenneth Macgowan, director of production of OCIAA films, sold the film idea to the State Department by promising it would "counteract the prevalence of the feeling in the other American republics that the negro [sic] did not have any opportunities in the United States."[46]

US authorities knew that many Latin Americans, especially Brazilians, believed that racist restrictions on US blacks might foreshadow their own oppression by the North Americans. Thus, in addition to the Dorie Miller film, Nelson Rockefeller revealed to a concerned Rayford Logan that the OCIAA's newsreel section had prepared countless stories about enlisted black men and that a script "dealing with blacks and democracy" was being seriously considered. These nontheatrical films and newsreels were intended to ease Latin American fears that the United States opposed racial democracy. They also answered Logan's appeal that US films refrain from "portray(ing) Negro Americans in certain stereotypes."[47] Logan's request dovetailed with domestic pressures exerted by the NAACP's antistereotype Hollywood campaign and the black press's constant denunciation of racism to create more favorable representations of black people in film.[48]

An important aspect of the consciously racial images the OCIAA's Motion Picture Division mounted was the attempt to tiptoe around or positively present black and Japanese American segregation in the United States. John Dreier, a top State Department official who had helped to establish the OCIAA's first field committee, in Rio de Janeiro, advised the OCIAA that its newsreels referencing units of "colored troops" inadvertently highlighted US racial segregation, which "certainly [did] not help achieve [the government's] objective" of countering "enemy propaganda regarding discrimination against negroes [sic]." He cautioned OCIAA producers that Jim Crow was "not practiced in most of the countries to which this material is sent," implying it would generate objections. Dreier was pleased to see a subsequent newsreel that referred to black troops merely as US Army soldiers, "without obviously calling attention to their color," "indicat[ing] that people of both races are fighting in the United States forces" while avoiding the embarrassing fact that they were segregated.[49] State cultural propagandists also worked to undercut the "capital [the Axis garnered] out of the so-called 'Concentration Camps' [of Japanese] in the United States." Here a request was made to distribute to Latin America the OWI film *Japanese Relocation,* which the OCIAA praised. This documentary short supposedly demonstrated the humane treatment of the Japanese Americans segregated and imprisoned in incarceration camps.[50]

In addition to cultural media, US black culture itself was part of the artistic material being transmitted to Brazil and other Latin American countries as a sign of racial democracy in the United States. During World War II, whites often performed US black culture in the state's cultural projects, although this did not necessarily translate into an attempt to hide the art forms' racial origins. The OCIAA partly financed and organized the sixty-three-member, all-male, likely all-white[51] Yale Glee Club's hugely successful summer tour to Brazil (Rio de Janeiro and São Paulo), Uruguay, Argentina, Chile, Peru, and Panama.[52] During the tour, the glee club acquainted its southern neighbors with its particular style of choral singing, impressed them with its interpretations of songs by local composers (including Brazilian Heitor Villa-Lobos), and introduced them to US folk music.

Showcasing US folk music was one of the top goals and achievements of the Yale Glee Club's tour, and notably, the group prepared more Negro spirituals (eight) than any other genre of US folk music. In his report of the tour, Glee Club director Marshall Bartholomew emphasized the importance of the folk performances: "I was told many times that this was the first opportunity that South American audiences had ever had to become acquainted with our traditional folk music. Many of them were not aware that we had any." Renowned Brazilian music critic Andrade Muricy reflected this sentiment in his review of the group's shows in Rio de Janeiro. Muricy was delighted that there was much more to US culture than what emanated from its film and music industries, which, to his chagrin, the Brazilian youth imitated. According to Bartholomew, among the most popular numbers were "the negro *[sic]* spirituals, which in many cases had to be repeated" due to audience calls for an encore. Reports in the Brazilian press reflected Bartholomew's description, demonstrating that the spirituals were enthusiastically received and, significantly, that Brazilians knew the white choir was singing black music. Andrade Muricy included the three "admirable Negro spirituals" in his glowing article about the glee club.[53] Echoing Muricy's observation about the richness of US culture, respected folklorist Luís da Câmara Cascudo cited the "incomparable" spiritual "There Is a Balm in Gilead" as part of the repertoire that received "applause," "extras," "encores," and "shouts."[54]

Well before the famous State Department tours of the Cold War era, jazz music was another US black musical genre that reinforced the government's cultural propaganda to Brazil and the rest of Latin America during the Second World War. Although black bandleaders and star performers may have been showcased to some degree, government records suggest that white celebrity musicians were highlighted in state-produced jazz programming in Latin America. For example, in 1944 the OCIAA was authorized to produce twenty fifteen-minute programs in Portuguese and Spanish titled *Concert of Popular Music*. The shows remade the successful *Concert in Jazz* radio program in order to satisfy Latin America's big appetite for US popular music. The programs, spotlighting "modern" music played in venues such as Carnegie Hall, were to maintain the jazz flavor of the original series. The OCIAA Radio Division wanted to feature musicians the likes of the white "symphonic jazz group" the New Friends of Rhythm and white bandleader Benny Goodman.[55]

Minstrel shows appeared in at least one episode of the radio program *Music in American Life* that was broadcast to Brazil. The same episode that played songs by the white New Orleans bandleader Larry Clinton (whose jazz orchestra appeared to be all white in scenes from the 1940 Warner Bros. film *Dipsy Doodler*) included songs by that city's minstrel performers. In Portuguese the announcer explained to the Brazilian audience what they were listening to and provided some history: "We now hear a number by the Minstrels, who are comics disguised as blacks that sing and clown around. . . . We can say that the Minstrels are part of the United States [and] for almost a century they were very popular in these bands."[56] Although minstrelsy transmitted through the radio is a rather extreme representation of whites "reproducing" black culture, it characterized the broader tendency to rely on white entertainers to usher in what was considered to be black music to a Brazilian audience.

"[M]usic which is sent to the other American Republics should include examples of the Negro music in the United States." OCIAA adviser Mary Winslow wrote these words in a memo to Nelson Rockefeller to relay the suggestions of black Howard University professors, including Rayford Logan, whom she met with shortly after the OCIAA's inception. Rockefeller and Winslow sought the black intellectuals' perspectives on inter-American affairs; in response the intellectuals raised the importance of "introducing . . . the cultural contributions of the Negro in the United States to the people of the other American Republics."[57] The Howard group must not have intended that white mediators largely would be the Pan-American agents to disseminate US black music to Latin America, especially when those mediators were in black-face.[58] Ironically, as the OCIAA heeded recommendations that US black culture be shared with hemispheric neighbors, creating an official space for black music as national art and entertainment in the process, it side-lined the very black innovators behind that music.

Yet another component of US cultural propaganda to Brazil was the endeavor to illuminate the fallacies of Axis racist doctrine. This took various forms, including the printing and distribution throughout Brazil of the pamphlet *Italy and the Theory of the Master Race,* which exploited Brazil's Catholic sensibilities to deter its people from sympathizing with Axis ideologies. The project's authorization paraphrased its content: "The Theory of the Master Race is a theory completely exploded not only by science but by . . . the Catholic Church."[59] Similarly, the OCIAA distributed short films such as *Does Nature Prefer Blondes?*—which OCIAA records labeled a "propaganda project" that "discredit[ed] the Nazi theory of racial superiority"—throughout Latin America.[60] The function of these materials for fulfilling US objectives was at least threefold. First, they served as a form of dissuasion, seeking to convince potential Nazi adherents (especially those of German descent) to disavow Third Reich racial teachings. Second, they provided ammunition, validation, and encouragement to those who already shunned Nazism. Finally, they seemed to prove that the United States was truly opposed to racism.

Brazilian authorities both solicited and worked on US propaganda to their country, causing Estado Novo agencies to act as junior partners in the construction and dispersal of propaganda that characterized the United States as a racial democracy. In exchange, the DIP expressed the Brazilian government's desire to have "more publicity" in the United States and thus correct the lopsided nature of the US-Brazil propaganda exchange. In particular, it wanted "arrangements for retransmission of Brazilian radio programs to the United States," causing the OCIAA group in Brazil to approve a fifteen-minute broadcast from Rio de Janeiro to air on NBC in the United States in 1943. The DIP's radio division already had received permission for the rebroadcast of five fifteen-minute music programs per month on US commercial radio.[61] Therefore, although the United States had more access to Brazil than vice versa, Brazil's requests were at times granted by US agencies. This was also the case when the US government sent Hollywood's most acclaimed young filmmaker to Rio de Janeiro to film a Good Neighbor documentary.

After spending a couple of months developing his idea for a film adaptation of real, lived experiences, twenty-six-year-old Orson Welles finally settled on a four-part movie titled *It's All True* by July 1941. "The Story of Jazz" would be based on Louis Armstrong's life; "The Captain's Chair" would be about the life of a prospector in Canada; "Bonito, the Bull" would follow the friendship of a Mexican boy and a bull raised to fight in the ring; and "Love Story" would be about the romance of an Italian-American couple. But before Pearl Harbor, Assis Figueiredo, DIP's assistant director in charge of US relations, expressed the department's desire that Welles create a documentary of Rio de Janeiro's Carnival. The OCIAA agreed and asked Welles to fly to Brazil in 1942 as an official cultural goodwill ambassador.[62] Welles's role as US representative acquired new import on the eve of his arrival, when the post–Pearl Harbor meeting of the ministers of foreign affairs of the American republics in Rio de Janeiro closed. At this meeting, Brazil led most other Latin American countries to formally break diplomatic ties with Germany, Japan, and Italy. Thus, Orson Welles landed in Brazil to help tend to a relationship that was increasingly fundamental to both nations as they navigated an escalating war. Considering the filmmaker's penchant for black culture and artistry, including as a former Federal Theatre Project director, it is not surprising that Welles both represented and struck the pressure points of US and Brazilian doctrines of racial democracy.[63]

Welles decided to revamp *It's All True*, keeping the jazz and Bonito storylines but adding Carnival and the true story of four raft fishermen, *jangadeiros*, from Brazil's Northeast. The jangadeiros had spent sixty-one days at sea traveling to Rio de Janeiro in order to secure social benefits from President Vargas for exploited and impoverished fishermen. At the time, Welles was under contract with RKO Radio Pictures, whose board members included Nelson Rockefeller and OCIAA Motion Picture Division head John "Jock" Whitney. The film was technically an RKO and OCIAA coproduction, although RKO essentially oversaw the project. The producers paid for Welles's living and travel expenses while in Brazil, but he agreed to work pro bono.[64]

The DIP's request that Orson Welles make a Carnival documentary was a sign that the Estado Novo was ready to sell the huge jamboree's music, Afro-Brazilian–derived samba, to the world as a national treasure—almost. The significance of this step cannot be denied, for merely two decades earlier, authorities generally shunned samba. In using Carnival as the proverbial carrot to attract foreign tourism and to introduce the United States to its South American neighbor, the Estado Novo was making a strong, and novel, statement. The DIP's Division of Tourism was charged not only with drawing foreign dollars to Brazil but also with shaping the country's image. Thus, the work and constant presence in the state-censored media of Orson Welles—recently voted best actor and director in a Rio de Janeiro poll—can be seen as a definitive official proclamation that Rio's Carnival was a prime representation of national culture.[65]

Samba's racial history did not mean, however, that the Estado Novo intended for Welles to film Carnival as a black and mestizo phenomenon. Brazil's own Carnival movies up to that point had minimal interracial and cross-class interaction. They also wouldn't show Rio's grittier urban landscape for another decade, and they generally relegated black actors to the background or to roles as comic relief. Welles diverged from this tendency. In the words of Pery Ribeiro, who appeared in the film as a child, Welles "show[ed] the real Brazil as it truly was." Black Brazilian actor and *It's All True* star Grande Otelo added that the film showed "the entire community through that mixture of races [Welles] saw in Brazil." Otelo said that in Welles's film he had the rare opportunity to transcend the subordinate black characters to which he had been limited. With the guidance of Grande Otelo and Ribeiro's father, the musician Herivelto Martins, Welles's portrayal of samba and Carnival was equally against the grain. The Brazilian movie industry portrayed samba as "a white cultural product" before and well after Welles's arrival.[66] In other words, the state embraced what Catherine Benamou dichotomizes as the "modern, 'legitimate' (i.e., big-band and 'whiter')" samba styles of the exclusive casinos and eschewed the "traditional, 'illegitimate' (i.e., 'blacker' and improvisational)" forms of samba performance and Carnival celebrations. Even though Welles also shot scenes from the upscale, white "samba for sale and for hire," his interest in working-class "samba to hide" was far greater than what the state preferred.[67]

An exchange of letters in 1941 between the Brazilian Ministry of War's secretary-general and the minister of education offers valuable insight into the racial mind-set that dictated the government's response to Welles's project. In these letters, Secretary-General Valentim Benício da Silva bemoaned a musical performance in which a *mulata* personified Brazil. Notably, Silva preceded his complaint to Minister Capanema with an elaborate salute to the "blacks in the formation of our nationality," singling out the Mãe Preta and black soldiers for praise. Yet he insisted, "to make the black person or the *mulato* the national type; to choose that as the model of our race exhibited as the Brazilian standard to foreigners . . . and even to send it abroad [are] unacceptable." Capanema, the great orator of racial equality whose words appeared in the previous chapter, concurred with Silva in his response. In fact, Capanema told him to write to the DIP, which signals an understanding that Silva's complaint would register with and correspond to the policy of the Estado Novo agency responsible for Brazil's internal and external profile.[68]

This correspondence helps explain Orson Welles's experience working with the DIP, which seemed keen to hide certain racial and social elements of samba and Carnival from the filmmaker. Welles's team reported that the DIP was not forthcoming with the information he requested regarding samba and Carnival, offering mainly "a small brochure of dull facts." When Welles and his team solicited the events schedule, the DIP provided a program of festivities that was "invariably inaccurate," "always incomplete," and "heavily edited." The crew believed it was being "misled" by Brazilian officials.[69]

Welles eventually sought his own informants to get a better idea about Carnival and the roots of samba in ways that attracted much resistance. His Brazilian advisors, researchers, and film collaborators led him to the favelas and their large black and mestizo, poor and working-class populations. Welles understood that this was not the origin story of samba that many in the government wanted him to tell: his team reported that there were "authorities who maintain that Samba is principally a product" of Rio's (predominantly white) commercial music industry. In fact, in light of the crew's description of its myriad difficulties getting help from the DIP, which wanted control over the group's activities, it is telling that one of the DIP's rare fulfilled promises was its staging of the elite Municipal Theater Ball. Welles had less luck when the DIP said it could easily arrange for him to film the noticeably blacker street Carnival party from the air but reneged on its pledge to supply an aircraft to do so.[70] Alex Viany, who worked for the DIP, said that the Brazilian government was unhappy that Welles was filming blacks.[71] Elizabeth Amster (Wilson), one of the film's crewmembers, believed that "the Vargas government began to recognize the fact that this was not going to be a film that would bring tourists to Brazil." Welles himself later described the surveillance and intimidation that he suffered, recalling a night when he and his crew, shooting in a favela, were surrounded and attacked with "a siege of beer bottles . . . stones, bricks, and I hate to think what else."[72]

The fact that many US authorities involved with the film also were displeased with Welles's focus on black culture and the favelas influenced Estado Novo officials. *It's All True*'s RKO manager in Rio, Lynn

Shores, told certain DIP authorities that Welles was center-staging blacks and mestizos in a way that would be a problem in both countries. He wrote to the DIP's director of distribution, Alfredo Pessoa (who had worked and would work again for the OCIAA as a Brazilian specialist), attesting that the Brazilian government would not approve of Welles's "continued exploitation of the negro [sic] and the low class element around Rio." Shores specifically cited Welles's filming in various favelas and the Teatro República (qualified as "the Teatro where blacks celebrate carnival"), all of which he felt was "in very bad taste." Shores asked to meet with Pessoa before sending film negatives to be developed, and the DIP subsequently appears to have kept some of the film in its possession for a while. Right after receiving Shores's letter, Pessoa called Welles's collaborator, Richard Wilson, to his office to discuss the many protests waged over the favela scenes.[73]

Exacerbating the suspicion Welles generated among certain Brazilian authorities was the fact that the police began to label Jacaré—the leader of the four fishermen who would tragically drown re-creating their journey for the film—as communist due to his longtime agitation for social justice. According to journalist and Welles-commissioned researcher Edmar Morel, Welles's association with Jacaré led to rumors that Welles too was communist. The claim only gained traction as Welles highlighted the socioeconomic oppression that the jangadeiro community suffered in the documentary.[74] Elizabeth Wilson observed that "the blaze of publicity that followed [Welles] wherever he went in Brazil was in one way to call the presidential bluff [and] to remind [Vargas] of his promises" to Jacaré and the jangadeiros.[75]

RKO eventually suspended and jettisoned the production of *It's All True*. Although a change in studio management and leadership, financial concerns, and a general hostility toward Welles likely caused the film's demise, the project's racial dynamics did contribute.[76] Using more overtly racist language than he had with Alfredo Pessoa, Lynn Shores frequently derided the "niggers" and "dirty and disreputable nigger neighborhoods" that occupied so much camera time in the documentary to his RKO colleagues. Shores understood that the Brazilian government took exception to Welles's chosen "Negro and low class" principals. Another RKO employee brooded over how the US South would respond to the film, especially its interracial "intermingling" that was prohibited by Hollywood's Production Code.[77] There was also dismay that the advanced cinematic technology Welles used, Technicolor, visually enhanced the color discrepancy between the darker-skinned and lighter-skinned Brazilians dancing with one another. For these reasons, an RKO executive suggested that only two of Welles's many film reels would be usable.[78] For its part, the OCIAA seemed to fall on both sides of the debate. On the one hand, the OCIAA Brazilian Coordinating Committee reported favorably on the public's response to Welles and his role as US goodwill ambassador: his visit went down as one of the office's most successful cultural projects in Brazil. Nelson Rockefeller even invoked *It's All True* as evidence of the OCIAA's success in combating negative stereotypes about blacks in a letter to the office's advocate and conscience on the matter, Rayford Logan. On the other hand, when word got to the office about Welles's racial inclinations, a memo was sent to RKO advising that references to miscegenation be avoided and that scenes including conspicuous appearances of mulattos or mestizos be cut.[79]

The OCIAA's dual position on the documentary's racial angle uncovers, to use Daryle Williams's term, the culture wars that occurred within Brazilian government agencies and the press over the appropriate cultural representations of national identity. Some journalists in the DIP-censored press made their disgust and discomfort with Welles's dark-skinned subjects and their neighborhoods clear, deriding how Carnival would appear "very dark on the screen," with "cinema sequences in which only black people figure, as though Rio were another Harlem." "Instead of showing . . . our possibilities," Welles went to the hills to film "no good half-breeds [and] filthy huts of the favelas." Yet some Brazilians joined those in the OCIAA who looked positively upon Welles's racial realism. In an unofficial capacity were participants like Grande Otelo and Herivelto Martins who insisted on a realistic portrayal of the Carnival they knew, the one enjoyed by the black and mestizo working class. The film also enjoyed semiofficial support from film critic Vinícius de Moraes, who would become a famous poet, diplomat, songwriter, singer, and the playwright who penned *Black Orpheus*, adapted as the 1959 Oscar-winning film. Moraes, the self-proclaimed "blackest white man in Brazil," was pleased with Welles's portrayal of Brazil. Moraes eventually became good friends with Welles and showered him with praise in his column in *A Manhã*, the daily newspaper created by the Estado Novo in 1941 to support its agenda and spread its principal ideas. Moraes felt that Welles was producing "the most impressive propaganda yet created in favor of our national values."[80]

As the *A Manhã* film critic, Vinícius de Moraes held an important, if at times contentious, role as the dictatorship's voice on the movie industry, and thus, his take on *It's All True* can be considered a semiofficial promotion of Welles's Carnival racialization. Moraes, who also wrote about Welles's work with US blacks, declared Welles a "master of our carnival [and] its mannerisms, rhythms, [and] instruments." He called Welles a "great Brazilian" because he was "beginning to know Brazil, or at least an important side of the soul of Brazil," and he opined that the filmmaker's "vision is at times raw, but he never sins through injustice." DIP employee Alex Viany agreed with Moraes that Welles accurately grasped Carnival and samba. As a Welles-commissioned researcher, Viany had helped Welles to understand samba as a black phenomenon from the favelas. In his research essay, Viany described the "democracy" that occurred when blacks came down from the hills to the city and culturally transformed "the white man."[81] Thus, not everyone affiliated with the Estado Novo wanted to whitewash samba and Carnival for foreign and domestic consumption, although such perspectives tended to wield little power in the government.

Orson Welles created a great dilemma for Brazilian officials who wanted to promote tourism in Brazil and mold the contours of the nation's identity. The Brazil to appear in *It's All True* was overwhelmingly poor and greatly exceeded the limitations for the black population that Brazilian authorities established for Hollywood movies in Brazil. Furthermore, in both "Carnaval" and "Jangadeiros," Welles glorified black protagonists, characterizing them as authentic Brazilian heroes in a way that had been reserved for whites in Brazilian cinema.[82] However, Welles, freshly adorned with an Oscar for *Citizen Kane,* was perhaps the most prestigious, publicity-generating, and tourism-promoting international white mediator the DIP could have solicited. Welles was, after all, a US goodwill ambassador, and he did often enjoy treatment as such, made evident by photographs of him hobnobbing with Estado Novo authorities like Oswaldo Aranha and by his participation in Getúlio Vargas's birthday commemorations. Yet many, if not most, Brazilian state actors frowned upon Welles's racial realism and failure to prioritize white mediators in the film. Although it was RKO that pulled the plug on *It's All True,* the studio justified its decision in part by an understanding that the dictatorship was generally displeased with the film's racial imagery.[83]

Although he exoticized and stereotyped his Afro-Brazilian protagonists in statements about his experience in Brazil, Welles's realism was considerably more racially inclusive and honest in spotlighting the economic injustices and despair that most black Brazilians confronted than customary Estado Novo renditions of racial democracy.[84] The national and international exposure of Vargas's inadequate populist policies, revealed in Rio's favelas and Fortaleza's jangadeiro fishing community, undermined Estado Novo tourism and propaganda initiatives. Thus, although the DIP instigated its production, *It's All True* was not DIP-like propaganda. Welles's depiction of Brazil subverted the controlled, racially demarcated democracy that the Estado Novo hoped he would deliver, one that would acknowledge Afro-Brazilian culture with little or no exposure of Afro-Brazilians.

The Estado Novo's role in the *It's All True* saga offers a glimpse into the Brazilian dictatorship's direct intervention in US filmmaking ventures; OCIAA reports of the discussions between Hollywood studios and DIP censors, particularly about race, provide another. In these reports and correspondences, the reaction of Brazilian audiences and censors to Hollywood movies was gauged, and lists were generated on what to avoid in future films. The list—whose provenance was almost certainly Israel Souto, DIP motion picture and theater director—included amusing tidbits, such as the demand that films "[n]ever say anything derogatory about coffee." It also pointed to the Brazilian government's discomfort with and sensitivity to race. In films about Brazil, "[r]ace should not be referred to—especially 'mulatto' or negro *[sic]*, and [they] should not be cast in roles of inferiority, such as criminals, traitors, drunkards, etc."[85] An officer in Rio de Janeiro also wrote that "[n]owadays [Brazil's] Department of Press and Propaganda refuses to authorize films showing many black people, afraid that the United States may get the wrong impression that the blacks predominate over the white."[86] The DIP even seemed to quantify what constituted too many blacks. One 1941 OCIAA report on conversations held at Warner Bros. Studios made in-the-know assertions with respect to DIP censorship codes. The report brought to light the policy that "not more than twenty percent of people appearing in the scenes [of Brazil] should be colored."[87]

The US movie studios cooperated with such Estado Novo racial wishes and allowed the US government to intervene in their filmmaking in hopes that their movies would be shown in Brazil and would garner profit as well as goodwill. (Two well-known examples of such cooperation are the Disney Good Neighbor films in which the OCIAA and Rockefeller were involved—*Saludos Amigos* and *The Three Caballeros*. In both films, Aurora Miranda, Carmen's sister, starred in whitewashed scenes that erased blacks from samba and Carnival, even though the latter movie was set in Bahia, the epicenter of Afro-Brazilian culture.)[88] Souto had used the Nazis as leverage to strong-arm Hollywood studios into respecting Brazilian requests. He warned US authorities that "representatives of German productions [had] cooperated with him in [the] best possible manner . . . at all times attending to any request he might have to make, thus creating a most favorable atmosphere for themselves."[89] For the movie studios, Souto's statement was virtually an ultimatum, as the inaccessibility of the European market and the exigencies of the Good Neighbor Policy during the war made it desirable to please the DIP. To some degree, the DIP therefore managed to turn the most influential entertainment machine in the world, Hollywood, into a source of Estado Novo propaganda, racial and otherwise.

The DIP's close working relationship with the OCIAA boosted its mission to steer Hollywood and to ensure the latter's adoption of white mediators to introduce US audiences to Afro-Brazilian culture. The director of the OCIAA's Motion Picture Division, Jock Whitney, prompted and facilitated the censorship of Hollywood's Latin American portrayals by forming the Motion Picture Society for the Americas (MPSA) in March 1941. The MPSA was an autonomous "nonprofit, privately controlled California corporation" that "worked in close cooperation with" the OCIAA's Motion Picture Division and the State Department. In the words of film historian Alfred Richard Jr., this collaboration was largely why "a voluntary censorship over Hollywood-made films which contained Hispanic [i.e., Latino] themes was so quickly and effectively established." Committees were set up in the major studios to review "Latino content." The OCIAA also urged the industry's Production Code Administration to hire a Latin Americanist to supervise the studios' efforts. As part of the goal was to break down stereotypes and foster goodwill and solidarity between the United States and the other American countries, many of the films of this period (i.e., *Brazil*) "destroyed assumed racial barriers," although they certainly constructed others. Reflecting this trend, Brazil's Hollywood makeover began with a character of "a significant amount of black blood" who fit into "primitive or [urban] low class Brazilian stereotypes" and emerged, frankly, as Carmen Miranda. Miranda's career trajectory skyrocketed alongside these new censorship activities.[90]

Carmen Miranda, the (Portuguese-born) "Brazilian Bombshell," became the highest paid actress in the world, the cinematic and theatrical incarnation of the Good Neighbor Policy, and the most recognizable white cultural mediator of Afro-Brazilian culture.[91] Miranda's success was not merely because Hollywood and US and Brazilian authorities worked to create Latin American portrayals more palatable to the region's elite; she was, after all, extremely popular and well received by the US public. Nonetheless, Hollywood's newfound Latin American focus helped to create and broaden space for Miranda on-screen, in part by feeding the largely state-induced Latin American craze that had been growing in the United States since the 1930s and was in full swing by 1941. Professor Richard Behrendt stated it succinctly in a 1941 *Washington Post* book review when he noted that "[i]nterest in things Latin American is *en vogue* today."[92] *Good Neighbor* was an expression that often accompanied the media's coverage of Carmen Miranda, like the gushing review that ran in the *New York Times* of her musical numbers in the 1941 film, *That Night in Rio*: "As good neighborly gestures go, we put most store by Miss Miranda's."[93] As biographer Ruy Castro wrote, Miranda herself said she didn't mind being "used as 'political ammunition' for the professionals of the Good Neighbor Policy. She knew what she was doing, she considered it a just cause, and she only wanted the films to be better."[94]

From her fruit-embellished turbans, inspired by Afro-Brazilian *baianas* balancing items on their heads to transport, to many of her song lyrics, Carmen Miranda epitomized the centrality of black culture, generally presented by whites, in wartime Good Neighbor propaganda. Miranda was exposed to Afro-Brazilian culture growing up, and as a performer in Brazil she collaborated with blacks. Miranda revealed her awareness of the cultural and racial roots she appropriated in many ways. The lyrics to many of her songs—such as "O Nego no samba" ("The Black Man in Samba"), which mocked whites' efforts to dance "black folks' samba"—constituted one piece of evidence. Miranda also made statements about the Afro-Brazilian inspiration for her costumes, which many Brazilians told her she could not wear because they were "Negroes'" clothes. The movie studios often obliged Miranda to perform a smorgasbord of rumbas and other non-Brazilian musical genres, making her an exoticized "generic *latina*" in her films. However, it would be a mistake to think that the blackness of the Brazilian culture she embodied was similarly hidden from her US fans.[95]

A March 1941 *New York Times* article titled "The Samba Down in Rio" demonstrates how Miranda's fame led to an attempt to understand authentic samba and Brazilian culture more broadly. It began: "With Carmen Miranda as sponsor, a new dance rhythm boasting the Brazilian name 'samba' has entered the echoing halls of Tin Pan Alley. . . . In its unmodified form, samba is a mixture of African voodoo rhythm, pagan ceremonial dancing and spontaneous Negro singing."

The musical performances of soprano Elsie Houston, who likely considered herself white in Brazil but who was perceived as an amorphously nonwhite Brazilian in the United States, were also equated with voodoo, and much more so. From the late 1930s until her suicide in 1943, Houston's many stage performances throughout the United States evoked ceremonies of macumba ("voodoo," as per the US public), the Afro-Brazilian religion. The fact that many people in the United States associated Brazilian culture with voodoo—a catchall for exotic black spiritualism—makes it clear that at least a contingent of US moviegoers understood that Carmen Miranda was a light-skinned version of something black. The *Times* article made this distinction; if samba "unmodified" was "African voodoo," "that which Miranda sings" was samba "[i]n its refined version."[96] Other white artists further painted Brazil as a black nation and centered black Brazilian subjects. The Brazilian and US governments sponsored many of these artists, including US photographer Genevieve Naylor, Brazilian painter Cândido Portinari, and Brazilian dancer and choreographer Eros Volusia.[97] The reliance on white cultural mediators to serve as official transmitters of Brazilian racial nationalism did not mean that the US audience was completely unaware of the black origins of Brazilian culture.

The Estado Novo also attempted to influence its North American neighbors by disseminating English-language literature throughout the United States that articulated Brazilian racial democracy. Some of these texts showcased that at least one set of national narratives for foreigners positioned blacks as important historical contributors to Brazilian society. Explaining the role of enslaved blacks in the early colonial economy, the DIP book *Facts and Information about Brazil,* published in 1942, stated: "Without the African slave . . . the cultivation of sugar cane would not have been possible, and without the cultivation of sugar it would not have been possible to set the definite bases of Brazilian civilization." *Facts and Information* also contended that the sociocultural traits of blacks were critical in national formation, since "more easily than the Indians, [they] mixed deeply with national life, lending many of their characteristics and even affecting the form of the catholic [sic] religion, the common way of speaking and the habits and customs."[98] Another DIP book published in the same year, *Brazil in America,* credited the "African element" for providing "qualities of robustness and of imagination to the [Brazilian] population that was being formed."[99] The DIP described the enslaved Africans who came to Brazil as arriving "with a certain grade of education," particularly those from northern Africa who lived in "Arabian and Christian civilization." These Africans knew the "rudimental technic of land work and mining, which was very useful for the exploration of" Brazilian mines.[100]

The Estado Novo promoted the cliché of Brazil as a racist-free, inter-racial nirvana in its propaganda to the United States (and wherever else these texts may have been distributed) during the war. *Brazil in America* noted that Brazil's "political, administrative, and economic [development] could not have been carried out without the powerful contribution of strong, adventurous races," praising the indigenous, Portuguese, and African "blood." The book also told of the "racial trilogy [of military leaders] composed of a white man, a negro *[sic]* and an Indian" that bravely led "magnificent" Brazilian soldiers against the Dutch in colonial times.[101] The DIP's *Facts and Information,* clearly meant for a US audience with its profuse references to the United States, informed readers that "[n]ever has there existed a 'black line' in Brazil." In fact, virtually since Brazil was discovered, the Portuguese, Africans, and indigenous "intermixed and intermarried" since "[n]either the Portuguese nor the Brazilians had any qualms about mixing with any race."[102] As we have seen, the racial mixture narrative has tended to be white and Portuguese-centric, crediting the "open-mindedness" of the Iberian Europeans to engage socially, culturally, and sexually with darker-skinned peoples, rather than vice versa.

Estado Novo propaganda to the United States during the Second World War shows that the Brazilian elite had not dispensed with the idea of actually whitening the Brazilian populace, as some have argued.[103] The texts may have described Afro-Brazilians as key historical actors whose cultural and spiritual gifts and physical labor had been essential to Brazil's national formation, but blacks evidently were vanishing after leaving their mark. *Facts and Information* cited historians who quoted the number of enslaved Africans brought to Brazil at about six million, which caused Brazil's black percentage to peak at 50 percent of the overall population by 1840. The slave trade's prohibition was said to have decreased the black populace precipitously, so that by 1922 the Brazilian census showed blacks to have dropped from 50 percent to 10 percent of the national population. The book made sure to point out that 10 percent was "equivalent to [the black population] of the United States." In 1922 racially mixed and "half-caste" Brazilians were calculated as 50 percent and the indigenous as 5 percent; whites had risen to 35 percent.[104]

If the reader didn't catch the overall racial trajectory the census numbers ostensibly projected, the DIP books spelled it out quite painstakingly:

> The influx of the Europeans from the Mediterranean or the Nordic countries has [contributed] and still is contributing to alter the primitive composition of the Brazilian population. The original Africans are tending to disappear more rapidly in the south than in the north of Brazil. The general tendency in Brazil is toward Aryanism. The importation of African negroes *[sic]* ceased a hundred years ago and, therefore, the race, which, as in the United States, forms the poor part of the population, is gradually dying out. The general color of the masses of the Brazilian population tends toward white-brown like Europeans of the Mediterranean. Thus it is not hard for the observer to still find the influence of the three races which make up the present Brazilians. However, the one which always predominated, because it represented the superior cultural element, was the Portuguese. By its moral and material civilization, *Brazil is as much a European or occidental country as, for example, the United States or the Argentine Republic.*

Brazil in America concurred; after expressing admiration for "all the races of the earth [that] contributed to this American homogeneity which is Brazil," it assured the US public that "the differentiations [between the races], little by little, desappear *[sic]* into the civilized Western man."[105]

In the Ministry of Foreign Affairs' tome *Brazil, 1943: Resources and Possibilities,* the objective to whiten Brazil was reflected in its explanation of state policy. Even though its section about immigration quoted Vargas expressing the desire to bring to Brazil only those Europeans who would be loyal to the country and its values, it was clear that Europeans were targeted. Vargas emphasized that Brazilians did not want "morally undesirable elements" flooding the country. He also labeled "immoral" those Europeans who would bring foreign ideologies and "false creed[s]" to Brazilian soil.[106] However, for Vargas, morality was also a Western patent. *Facts and Information*'s statement that the moral fiber of Brazil was "European or occidental"—the "superior cultural element" of all the races that made up the Brazilian people—provided a key for North Americans to decipher the racial subtext of the Estado Novo's standards of moral desirability. Moral immigrants in the Brazilian tradition were European—selectively so, but European nonetheless. Brazil's official English-language propaganda disclosed the fact that the whitening ideals so prominent in the Brazilian elite's hopes for the nation earlier in the century continued even during the Second World War.[107]

The Estado Novo's whitening of national culture for foreign consumption was also evident in these English-language texts. In fact, the

"Music" section of *Facts and Information* did not even mention the word *samba*. Instead, it stated that for "a long time the Brazilian music reflected the Italian and French influence." The book spoke of Carlos Gomes's "great national opera, The Guarany" that, despite the indigenous themes of the novel it was based on, "was of clear Italian technic." This short paragraph concluded with a sentence that acknowledged the ways in which "numerous composers have perfected, with success, interesting popular rhythms where African negro [sic] and Indian traditions have been blended."[108]

Brazil in America devoted more space to Brazilian cultural development and music in particular, and it also underscored Gomes's operas, including *O escravo* (The slave). Samba was at least mentioned in passing, along with maxixe, and both were credited with holding the potential to "increase national character" musically. *Lundus,* described as "certain negro [sic] dances," and other folk musical genres were depicted as "typically Brazilian manifestations." However, the recognition for nationalizing African-derived and folkloric rhythms in Brazil went to white artists of "erudite" music that incorporated them into more classical compositions. Among those named were Heitor Villa-Lobos, Francisco Mignone, Alexandre Levy, and Alberto Nepomuceno, the latter two hailed as the first two "pioneer[s] of our national music."[109] Nowhere does the US reader learn about the well-known Afro-Brazilians who constituted the generation of samba inventors, such as Pixinguinha (who was to appear in Welles's *It's All True*), Donga, and João da Baiana. Further, the organization of the book made it abundantly clear that the cultural production of predominantly black communities was not legitimate: it hardly was acknowledged in the formal section on Brazilian culture, which touched upon literature, painting, music, and indigenous art. Instead, the DIP presented this popular culture under the "Hills and Suburbs" (i.e., favelas and poor and working-class peripheries) subtitle. It stated: "[The hills are] known as the birth places of popular inspiration for dances and music. There the old Afro-Brazilian culture produces the enchanting marches, the sambas, and the songs . . . which form the picturesque and musical life of the carioca (Rio de Janeiro) Carnival. There likewise take place the old 'macumbas' and some acts of religious witchcraft. The hills of Rio de Janeiro, celebrated by traditions of popular life, of music, of dancing and art, are the Favella [sic]. . . ."[110]

The DIP not only largely confined Afro-Brazilian culture to the hills but used terms like "old" and "nostalgia" to describe it, situating blacks' historical and numerical importance as safely in the past. This strategy of nationalizing blackness by honoring blacks' bygone roles in Brazilian society offered Brazilians a convenient way to broadcast their relative racial harmony, portrayed as democracy, to the United States without compromising the Estado Novo's attempt to establish racial parity with their Good Neighbor wartime ally. Despite their blacker origins, the Brazilians had become, in the DIP's words, "as European or occidental" as the United States because of the lack of prejudice among the Portuguese who brilliantly mixed with people of color and, in doing so, made them white(r). Because "mestizo nationalism," as Hermano Vianna has called it, carried the assumption that Brazilian miscegenation went hand in hand with interracial goodwill (both keystones— particularly the latter—of Brazilian social democracy in the war years),[111] the Brazilians could simultaneously claim white racial affinity with the North Americans and secure themselves as democratic partners of the Allies.

Without compromising this construction of US-Brazilian racial similarity, the Vargas regime's most convincing self-promotion as an action-oriented, racially democratic state was expressed in the explanation of its Two-Thirds Law in the book, *Brazil, 1943*. This law, first passed in 1930 and strengthened in 1939, required that Brazilian nationals make up at least two-thirds of most businesses' workforce. It mandated that at least two-thirds of companies' total salaries go to their Brazilian labor force as well, and Brazilians were not to earn a lower salary than any foreigner for the same work. Despite protections against gender discrimination in Brazilian labor legislation (the 1943 Consolidation of Labor Laws used the phrase "without distinction to sex" in six circumstances),[112] the Two-Thirds Law did not contain any language about race and did not prohibit racial bias in the workplace. Nonetheless, to its English-speaking foreign audience, the Two-Thirds Law was labeled as Brazil's greatest feat of racial democracy since abolition. *Brazil, 1943* highlighted the law's "loftier purpose of the social incorporation of the lower classes of the proletariat, principally coloured people systematically excluded by numerous foreign companies exploiting public utility services." The book concluded: "It may therefore be declared without exaggeration that the remote episode of the emancipation of the slaves was thus fully consummated [with this law] and to all good Brazilians of the negro [sic] race was now assured an ascent to higher levels of existence through dignified labor."[113] The Two-Thirds Law certainly did benefit black Brazilians in cities like São Paulo and enabled them to better compete with immigrant workers. However, the state created another myth when it presented the law—which explicitly exempted the agricultural sector—as a panacea for racial discrimination and economic inequality that "assured" a better standard of living for blacks.[114]

The Brazilian Ministry of Foreign Affairs' claim that the Two-Thirds Law secured opportunities of upward economic mobility for its black population was a noteworthy statement of racial democracy. The claims resonated with the prevailing US nationalist narrative, that of the self-made man who could achieve economic success if he (the figure was masculine) subscribed to the right work ethic. This allowed the regime to make democratic assertions and to help rationalize its alliance with the United States. It also managed to keep the focus on Brazil's racial reputation, which the government relied upon to highlight what was considered the nation's flattering, more democratic side.

It was a tricky proposition for the Brazilian and US states to ingratiate themselves with each other's public during a war that connected democracy and racial inclusion. Despite the benefits of circulating racially inclusive propaganda, the Estado Novo was aware of the strong anti-black racism and laws that existed in the United States. Meanwhile, US policymakers were conscious of Brazil's huge black and mixed-race population and of whitening's appeal among the Brazilian elite and authorities. US and Brazilian cultural production navigated this scenario as each state's propaganda addressed their foreign audience's various racial perspectives even while they reflected their own nation's racial biases. Both states also availed themselves of samba, jazz, and other black-identified artistic expressions that proved popular and could draw respect for and interest in their national cultures.

In the US-Brazil cultural propaganda swap, the United States sought to curtail the distrust that US racism generated within segments of the Brazilian population and to dissuade sympathy for the Axis powers. US propaganda to Brazil showed US race relations and treatment of people of color in a positive light and featured black culture, but the prominence of white mediators did not compromise the nation's image as a predominantly white nation. Brazil promoted its unique culture to the United States and adhered to its message of racial denial, portraying itself as free of racism and, therefore, a democracy. White mediators made it possible to do this without undermining the desire to appear as a nation in the process of whitening. Black people as desirable national contributors either were frozen in the past or watched as white mediators appropriated their artistic traditions.[115] Thus, in neither regime did influential state agents find the doctrine of racial democracy to be incompatible with values of racial preference.[116] However, US and Brazilian antiracist activists did not accept this official stance; they attempted to transform wartime racial democracy into an action-oriented tool for greater equality.

CHAPTER 7

Wartime Racial Democracy at Home

Domestic Pressures and In-House Propaganda

The internal battles that World War II precipitated within Brazil and the United States demonstrated the boomerang effect of war, as social, political, and economic repercussions of the conflict abroad came back into both nations. Domestic Brazilian and US activists against racism were no different: they capitalized on the Allied-Axis moral binary and the democratic mission that had rhetorically justified the war to demand equal rights. In the United States, where the growing civil rights movement gave black leaders more leverage with policymakers, realist efforts were more immediately successful than in Brazil, where state initiatives of racial democracy took several years and the involvement of foreign personalities to come to fruition. Despite these gains, both states made action-oriented progress toward racial equality secondary to the objectives of national security and dissuasion that drove these concessions.

In the United States, the milieu for wartime racial democracy was one of a nation undergoing tremendous change. Massive defense industry production and the deployment of millions of US denizens to the war zone caused an immense demand for labor. The impact on the black community was manifold, the most visible occurrence being the second wave of the Great Migration, when two million blacks moved from the rural South to the industrial North and West and another million migrated to cities within the South itself to take advantage of work opportunities. For many US blacks, exchanging the difficult life of the rural South for urban living turned out to be an experience with oppressions of a different sort. For instance, a housing shortage led to race riots and other forms of interracial violence in cities like Detroit as whites struggled to keep the lines of segregation firmly intact. Blacks looking to benefit from the labor demands still found many jobs off-limits, and when they successfully won the right to integrate areas of employment that traditionally had excluded them, white workers often went on "hate strikes" to protest.[1]

This chapter in part analyzes how US black activists fought for equality by channeling the war and formulating their own wartime discourse of racial democracy in ways that directly led to the implementation of antiracist policy. Two of these efforts were the March on Washington Movement (MOWM) and the Committee on the Participation of Negroes in the National Defense Program (CPNNDP), headed by A. Philip Randolph and Rayford Logan, respectively. The pressure that blacks in the MOWM exerted prompted Roosevelt to sign Executive Order 8802 in June 1941, which established the Fair Employment Practices Committee (FEPC) in order to end racial discrimination in defense industry jobs.[2] The FEPC had real impact on the economic circumstances of blacks, who were able to gain new access to certain jobs. Yet this chapter's study of the executive order's language and the FEPC's limitations shows that the committee operated not on the state's power of enforcement but on the symbolic influence of racial democracy.

It should be noted that the fears US authorities harbored about a strong black–Japanese alliance facilitated the concessions that US blacks earned during the war. As a 1942 Military Intelligence Division report title indicates, officials believed that "Japanese Racial Agitation among American Negroes" was great cause for concern. The report claimed in part that the Japanese recruited operatives in the black community for their subversive agenda, and it blamed black unrest on Japanese racial provocation as a strategy to win the war.[3] Roosevelt's executive order incarcerating over one hundred thousand Japanese Americans in internment camps revealed the extent to which the government marked this community—and by extension, those perceived to be their political allies—as a public enemy. Indeed, as we will see with the FEPC and Mexican Americans, the state's displays of racial democracy were not evenly applicable to all nonwhites. The security considerations in regard to blacks that instigated the creation of the FEPC conflicted with foreign policy and defense objectives in ways that excluded, at first, those of Mexican descent.

In Brazil in 1941, the firmly entrenched Estado Novo had so effectively repressed the opposition from the Left and the Right that it demonstrated no real signs of decline and faced no full-fledged formidable challenges. That would change the following year when the Brazilian public demanded retribution for German attacks on its ships in August, and the Brazilian government declared war against Germany and Italy later that month. The declaration of war intensified the pressure placed on the dictatorship to explain its lack of liberal democracy not only to the Allied skeptics abroad but also to those at home. Brazil's entrance into the war signaled the end of the first, "most fascist phase" of the Estado Novo, as Vargas purged many perceived Axis sympathizers from the government. Those included in the purge were high-profile people such as DIP head Lourival Fontes,[4] Rio de Janeiro chief of police Filinto Müller, and minister of justice and Estado Novo Constitution author Francisco Campos. (Notably, General Góes Monteiro and Minister of War Eurico Dutra, who would be elected president in 1945, remained.) The end of the dictatorship was imminent, and virtually all government officials knew and prepared for that reality, including Getúlio Vargas. Emboldened voices that the Estado Novo had forcibly silenced from 1937 to 1941, such as the labor movement, reemerged.

The restoration of liberalism created more opportunities for antiracists to act as well, and blacks launched newspapers and a slew of associations. Historian Edilza Sotero has shown that whether or not they engaged in party politics, black Brazilians mobilized and strategized to shape the political scene after the end of the Estado Novo.[5]

During the war and the gradual collapse of the Estado Novo, supporters of the dictatorship, including Vargas himself, became increasingly defensive on the question of democracy. As they did when addressing foreigners, authorities harnessed race to offset pro-democracy critics of the regime in Brazil. Perhaps the most poignant example of this was Vargas's 1945 press conference in which he linked racism and totalitarianism in order to dodge the charges that his dictatorship was authoritarian.[6] Chapter 5 demonstrated how such statements relied upon the discursive work that state actors had already performed, applying the war's racial and democratic tropes to construct this oppositional binary between Brazil/the Estado Novo and Germany/the Third Reich. This chapter examines how these themes unfolded on Brazilian soil and composed elements of the regime's domestic message of racial democracy during the war. This chapter also shows that while many in the Brazilian government used Nazi racism to elevate Brazil's democratic image, realists both outside and inside the politically liberalizing state evoked the wartime enemy to argue that the nation was not a racial democracy.

Black Brazilian activists and their allies were among the most insistent voices to link democracy, antiracism, and Nazism in a way that challenged the state, even insisting that racial justice be codified in the post–Estado Novo constitution. The use of Nazism to fight racism in Brazil both helped and hurt blacks in the struggle. On the one hand, Nazism provided powerful rhetorical justification for their cause, but on the other, it gave material to those who would call them reverse racists.[7] The latter was indicative of the responses that blacks such as Abdias do Nascimento and José Correia Leite elicited from authorities who articulated racial democracy as a form of dissuasion or denial. Such attitudes also were reflected in what could have been a great victory for Afro-Brazilian realists, the antidiscriminatory Afonso Arinos Law of 1951, which was a variation of a proposal that blacks formulated in 1945.

THE FORCES OF RACIAL DEMOCRACY ON THE HOME FRONT: BRAZIL

The Estado Novo did not unravel magically once Brazil entered the war on the side of the Allies and embraced rhetorical democracy. Domestic players who refused to accept the Vargas regime's redefinition of democracy in lieu of liberalism were opportunists who pressured the dictatorship. One of the first major events to push Brazil toward siding with the Allies and democratic ideals occurred shortly after the German attacks on Brazilian ships in 1942. Among the groups agitating for Brazil's entrance into the war were university and high-school students led by the União Nacional de Estudantes (National Union of Students, or UNE), who expressed their pro-Allied, anti-Axis stance with a protest march in the capital city Rio de Janeiro on July 4, 1942, US Independence Day. The students were supported by important Estado Novo authorities like the dictatorship's most unabashed US advocate, Minister of Foreign Affairs Oswaldo Aranha, who was lauded during the march as the "champion of democracy." Although Rio's Nazi-sympathizer chief of police, Filinto Müller, threatened to block the march, it went ahead peaceably. A few days later, Vargas fired Müller and others in the anti-Axis fury that enveloped the nation. Encouraged by the march's success, other student mobilizations followed.[8]

The July 4, 1942, student protest march helped move the country toward democracy without being critical of the Estado Novo (to the contrary, the students presented Vargas in a favorable light). However, a few high-profile events that followed denounced outright the dictatorship in their calls for liberalism and redemocratization. One of the most significant of these was the famous publication of the *Manifesto dos Mineiros* in late October 1943, after Brazil had declared war. The manifesto—with ninety-two signatories of the liberal elite hailing from the state of Minas Gerais—not only harshly attacked fascism but also pointed out the hypocrisy of the Estado Novo's war against a system of government that was similar to its own: "If we fight against fascism, on the side of the United Nations, so that liberty and democracy be restored to all people, certainly we do not ask too much agitating to secure the same rights and guarantees that they characterize for ourselves."[9] The manifesto, which considered unfulfilled the promises of Vargas's Revolution of 1930, rebuked mere nominal liberalism and envisioned a postwar society that actualized a "democracy [in which] all Brazilians can live a dignified life in liberty, respected and admired by our brothers in America and the entire world."[10] The Mineiros enacted the first major sign of what John French has called "the growing revanchism of the elites defeated in 1937" when they were stripped of political power by a regime that many of them had supported in 1930.[11]

The month following the *Manifesto dos Mineiros* produced an even more extreme outcry against the Estado Novo. In November 1943, Hélio Mota, president of the University of São Paulo Law School's Centro Acadêmico XI de Agosto, shouted during a dance celebrating the Americas, "Death to Getúlio! Long live democracy!" Mota was arrested the next day, and students mobilized to free him, resulting in one protest march in which the police fired on the crowd, killing two and injuring twenty-five. The tragedy did not stop Paulista law students; in April 1944 they launched the short-lived clandestine newspaper *Resistência,* which stated: "We want a democratic Brazil that can stand shoulder to shoulder with the other nations that make up the democratic coalition, one that can present itself without opprobrium in the postwar world. *Resistência* will fight for an effective democracy in Brazil."[12] The title of the student newspaper reflects this broader movement of resistance against the dictatorship that on some level had always existed but was heavily and violently repressed; the movement finally gained a great degree of momentum by relying on Brazil's involvement in the war (for which they had campaigned) to make the case for democracy.

Pushed in part by the First Congress of Brazilian Writers' January call for direct suffrage, the Vargas regime amended the Estado Novo Constitution in February 1945 with the Additional Act, which established a ninety-day deadline to set a date for elections and sparked the formation of numerous political parties that held aloft the banner of democracy. Even the names that some of the major parties selected indicated each one's general obsession with advancing its own plan for democracy. The first party to declare a presidential candidate for the elections that would take place on December 2, 1945, was the relatively liberal National Democratic Union, followed by the leftist Socialist Democratic Union and the more conservative Democratic Social Party. The latter nominated the eventual presidential winner, ex–minister of war Eurico Dutra. Just as in the 1930s, the integralists on the right also made democratic assertions at the time, if not as blatantly as the others did with their names. In 1945 the Integralista Party of Popular Representation defined the so-called ethical state they intended to install with the simple line, "[the] ethical State is the democratic State par excellence."[13]

Enjoying a brief period of legality that began in May 1945, the communists continued their tradition of self-labeling as a democratic movement and vied for black support, relying upon racialized characterizations of democracy to help do so. Since at least 1943, illegal communist cells had begun to spring up around Brazil. Most either maintained the "National Union" motto that had emerged since 1938, fully praising the Estado Novo as an unequivocal member of the war's democratic forces, or supported the war *and* fought against the dictatorship.[14] By 1945 their agitation for the Estado Novo's end was largely in place: the PCB organized a number of mobilizations, including strikes and rallies, and established the Unifying Workers' Movement (MUT), a "Communist-dominated labor confederation."[15] The MUT's April 1945 manifesto is a perfect example of the democratic and racial rhetoric that constituted its message. Exalting the benefits of unity among workers of all classes, the manifesto identified unification as permitting "the efficient and correct fight . . . for Democracy [and against] Nazi-fascism [and] all oppression and intolerance." The manifesto later stated that the MUT's fight for democracy brought together "men and women of all colors and beliefs . . . to conquer the right to live with dignity."[16]

Ironically, the MUT's proclamations did not necessarily equate to a belief that racism, outside the extremes of Nazism, was a major issue of concern for communists. After the late 1920s to mid-1930s radical Third Period of the Comintern—which Stalin dissolved in 1943—many communists had ceased to give even lip service to racism as a unique, if related, problem of class oppression. As we will see, black Brazilian activists during redemocratization were often at loggerheads with those who espoused or sympathized with communist ideology. Black leader Abdias do Nascimento has written that communists tried to infiltrate and derail, sometimes successfully, black-identified mobilizations that emerged during the mid-1940s.[17] Despite the antiracist politics of black communists like Édison Carneiro and Claudino José da Silva, Brazilian communism was much less radical on racial questions during postwar redemocratization than it was in the first half of the 1930s, when communists similarly discussed infiltrating the Brazilian Black Front and called for black self-determination.[18]

The development of these and other forces of redemocratization that commenced with Brazil's declaration of war in 1942 prompted a response from Vargas and his supporters that attempted to address the merging international and internal challenges the Estado Novo faced. For instance, the Vargas regime, which had been trying to build an active political base for the inevitable postwar elections since 1942, both encouraged and feared the reinvigoration of labor. As part of a party-less dictatorship (the Estado Novo did not represent a political party—all political parties were outlawed), Vargas's minister of labor, Marcondes Filho, spearheaded efforts to "preempt the left" and court labor support for Vargas. Although Vargas had always been described as a man of the people, it was during this second phase of the Estado Novo that he reframed himself as an ultrapopulist with rhetoric and policies that claimed to privilege and also hoped to forge a political alliance with the working class, which constituted so-called *trabalhismo* (laborism).[19]

As Vargas attempted to recruit future electoral support from would-be voters and stand out from potential competitors, his regime employed a few basic tactics, such as answering domestic calls for democracy with an increased utilization of the word itself. In addition, Vargas began to call the Estado Novo—also the name of Portugal's authoritarian regime under António Salazar—the Estado Nacional (National State), creating a more positive, democratic-friendly image. Vargas also finally released communist leader Luís Carlos Prestes, imprisoned for nine years, as a way to court the communists. However, instead of joining Vargas's Partido Trabalhista Brasileiro (Brazilian Workers' Party, or PTB), the communists formed the aforementioned MUT.[20] Perhaps in the continued effort to attract leftist-leaning voters, in mid-September 1945 the PTB passed a program containing one clause that was similar to the tepid racial language used by the MUT. The twenty-fourth clause of the program approved the "[d]evelopment of the spirit of solidarity between all citizens, without prejudice of color, class, origin, or religion."[21]

Black Brazilians were a force in the redemocratization movement, challenging the Estado Novo's politicized language of social democracy in an attempt to ensure that racial realism was integral to the new political structure. For many black Brazilians, the lukewarm, nonspecific rhetoric of racial inclusion that the major parties preferred, which was not much different from the language in the 1934 Constitution, did not suffice. These women and men—who managed to remain organized in cultural, religious, social, and recreational groups during the Estado Novo—resurfaced as political agents and exerted pressure on the collapsing regime in what one scholar has termed the "Black Rebirth."[22] Although Afro-Brazilian activists were by no means in agreement over means and objectives, ideals of race and democracy were central to the various rhetorical strategies they employed to tackle the ills that the black community experienced. In these efforts, black Brazilians made great strides, even if their role was not always acknowledged and if the legislation they helped bring about failed to materialize as the protector of black rights for which they had fought.

The following discussion of black Brazilian realism during the period of redemocratization focuses on a small selection of the most influential black associations, players, and projects that emerged in the period of redemocratization. Of all the black leaders at the time, Abdias do Nascimento arguably had the most impact on national politics due to his relationship with the PTB and other parties in the federal district of Rio de Janeiro at a time when many Afro-Brazilian activists eschewed party politics. Furthermore, Nascimento assumed leadership positions in an array of activities, including journalism, cultural movements—as a founder of Rio's Black Experimental Theater group (Teatro Experimental do Negro, or TEN)—and candidacy for political office.[23] That said, his perspective should not be taken as a universal black position in the least, especially when, by his own admission, he often disagreed with other black activists. In addition to the organizations and activities associated with Nascimento in Rio, we will concentrate on those connected to José Correia Leite in São Paulo. This section also examines the antidiscrimination legislation that had roots in the first post–Estado Novo election cycle. Even though the law was not enacted until 1951, it was certainly a legacy of this earlier period.

As soon as the Estado Novo's tight grip on social and political agitation loosened, renowned journalist and organizer José Correia Leite joined forces with other former collaborators from the Brazilian Black Front, the Black Socialist Front, the Clube Negro de Cultura Social

(Black Club for Social Culture), and the defunct black newspaper *O Clarim d'Alvorada* to fight for black rights. Hoping to "recuperate the work lost since 1938" and "resume what was halted during the Estado Novo," Leite, Fernando Góes, and Raul Joviano do Amaral launched the Associação do Negro Brasileiro (Association of Black Brazilians, or ANB) and its accompanying newspaper, *Alvorada*—a restoration of *O Clarim d'Alvorada*. This multidimensional organization offered cultural, sports, artistic, and social assistance services and activities similar to that of the bygone Frente Negra. Leite would say that the ANB operated in the spirit of other black organizations that had begun taking shape in São Paulo in the 1940s. Notable among them was the Associação José do Patrocínio, which formed in 1941 and advocated for black domestic workers. Before the "Black Rebirth" was in full swing, the Associação José do Patrocínio attempted to get Vargas's support for its protests against employers that placed advertisements for light-skinned or white women only.[24]

Although it steered clear of party politics, the São Paulo–based ANB was not apolitical. As the nation was preparing for its post–Estado Novo political future, the ANB produced the *Manifesto in Defense of Democracy,* which criticized Vargas and implored blacks to hark back to the "democratic and antiracist Republic called Palmares," an exemplar of black resistance to racial prejudice. The juxtaposition of "democratic" and "antiracist," especially as descriptors for the Palmares Maroon society, was a not-so-subtle assertion that the terms forged a natural partnership. Even more significant for understanding the ANB's vision of racial democracy was the manifesto's call for the criminalization of racial discrimination, becoming one of the earliest articulations of this action-oriented idea.[25]

Early issues of *Alvorada* took advantage of the war and Allied propaganda to campaign for racial justice. Journalist Manoel Antonio dos Santos employed this strategy in an August 1945 article, setting the stage for his protest with a characterization of how the world's interconnectedness had pulled "horrified and apprehensive" Brazilians into the events of "Old Europe." He wrote: "Apprehensive, we say, because [Old Europe] is a race that, becoming attached to a fictitious superiority, wants to subjugate and destroy other races that don't have in their epidermal coloring or in their red blood cells the Aryan characteristics" of the so-called supreme race. Santos shrewdly aligned such racist attitudes with the wartime enemy, explicitly labeling them un-Brazilian. "Thank God [that] this atrocious and calamitous persecution" was taking place in lands so far away, he said, expressing certainty that it was a virtual impossibility that such a problem would reach Brazilian shores, since the country's "laws are magnanimous, our people summarily welcoming and tolerant."[26]

Particularly in the context of this introduction, Manoel Antonio dos Santos's subsequent condemnation of the discrimination that he and other black Brazilians faced on their own soil tethered the perpetrators to Brazil's Nazi enemy. He decried the fact that well-dressed blacks whose grandparents had "helped to construct [this land] with work, tears, and sacrifices" were denied entrance to certain named entertainment venues. Santos concluded that such places were run by Aryan managers who wanted to "transport . . . ideas and regimes" to Brazil that had already demoralized other nations. Black Brazilians, however, were "not diminished by the ignorance of half a dozen individuals intoxicated by the whiteness of their own skin." Blacks instead "took pity on ignorance [and] vanity," since, he assured readers, "as the Brazilians that we are, equal before the law, we energetically protest and demand the abolition of such prohibitions, because it not only lacks consideration for Brazilians in their own country, but it is a flagrant disregard for the laws of the land, an insult to our democratic institutions, and a condescension to our authorities."[27]

Santos's denunciation offers a prime example of the ways that black activists in Brazil engaged the war to make claims about their rights and to shame those who would deny them. Santos structured his argument so that racial prejudice was a threat to national identity, countered the country's traditions, and maintained the Nazi mentality that had just been defeated after great sacrifice. Brazilian racists were traitors to the nation and opened the door to the very phenomenon that Brazilians had fought and died to destroy. If Brazil's brave troops had helped annihilate the Nazi threat abroad, internal racists kept its spirit alive and "transport[ed]" it into Brazil. By refusing to accept racists' "intoxicat[ion] by the whiteness of their own skin," black racial realists were homeland warriors, carrying out the war's battle domestically against those who sought to Nazify the "welcoming and tolerant" Brazilian disposition. Here Santos also relied upon a common black tactic—one that glorified the Brazilian racial utopia myth in order to hold the nation up to its own standards.[28] By consciously linking this to the war, Santos harnessed the Estado Novo's nationalist wartime propaganda that had graced Brazil with unprecedented prestige and helped the dictatorship join the Allied nations ideologically. The final sentence of the article, which invoked Brazil's democratic institutions, was his way of merging antiracism and democracy, consistent with the ANB's earlier *Manifesto in Defense of Democracy.*

Ironically, the same anti-Nazi sentiment that black antiracist agitators engaged to bolster racial realism was also utilized to condemn them. Accusing black organizations that maintained strong racial politics of practicing reverse racism was nothing new in Brazil; Nazism was merely fodder and heightened patriotic justification for this mind-set. José Correia Leite later recounted the ways that many Brazilians used wartime racial rhetoric to denounce black leaders. Leite related a meeting with black poet and activist Fernando Góes in which the latter complained about being called racist—a term, Leite pointed out, that "was in vogue" after the war. Leite explained: "Hitler's war was a racist war, a question of racial superiority. Blacks never formed a racist movement, with the idea of being superior to anyone . . . [but] this word 'racism,' after the war, came to reinforce that somewhat irritating situation: Every time a black man wanted to talk about his problems, he was called racist. Today this doesn't happen anymore . . . [at least] not in the gratuitous sense like they were doing in the beginning, right after the end of the war."[29] Abdias do Nascimento also remembered how World War II flavored opinions about his Black Experimental Theater, as some critics referred to elements of its first production in 1945 as racist and fascist, despite what Nascimento called its "progressive world politics." The charges stuck with TEN; even in 1957 one critic responded to Nascimento's play *Sortilégio* by labeling TEN's members "racists" and "Nazis."[30] Therefore, the deployment of anti-Nazism was a double-edged sword for black racial realists, for the disagreement among Brazilians about what did or did not qualify as racism (i.e., who and what did or did not follow in the Nazi tradition) presented multiple obstacles for them.

The journal *Diário Trabalhista*'s column "Problems and Aspirations of Black Brazilians" showcased blacks' use of journalism to relay and explain racism from the perspective of those who experienced it. The journal itself also demonstrates how the ruling elite attempted to rally blacks in its favor, which in 1946 meant drawing support for the winner of the December 1945 presidential election. Indeed, *Diário Trabalhista* "aimed, in reality, to guarantee popular [i.e., working class] backing for Dutra's government, with whom it had connections." Among these connections was one of the paper's four owners, Mauro Renault Leite, who was Dutra's son-in-law.[31] Although Abdias do Nascimento was not at the time a loyalist of the president's party, he was a reporter and theater critic for *Diário Trabalhista* and editor of "Problems and Aspirations of Black Brazilians."[32] In light of the paper's objectives, it is clear that the owners largely intended "Problems" to attract black-identified Brazilian readership to the journal's broader progovernment message. However, Nascimento and his collaborators commandeered this goal; by highlighting black grievances and Brazilian racism, they made it clear that action-oriented racial realism was required to earn Afro-Brazilian political support.

In addition to publishing analyses that the black intelligentsia articulated, "Problems" included assessments made by working-class blacks, proving that the use of overtly democratic language to advance racial realism transcended class. A 1946 issue published the opinion of Aladir Custódio, black elevator operator, poet, and eventual leader of the black folklore movement. Custódio identified and bemoaned the color line that often barred blacks and *mestiços* from certain diplomatic and military careers, a common grievance. Although Custódio was against race-based political parties as a means of overcoming such barriers (they would undermine Brazil's tolerant tradition, he believed), he praised black associations that removed the cultural and social disconnect (and thus, misunderstanding) between blacks and whites. Custódio felt that this would eventually help to eradicate racism and dismantle the racial barriers constructed by the state and others that blocked the progress of "a nation on the long trek toward democracy." Domestic worker Arinda Serafim also criticized government policy toward majority black communities as undemocratic. Referring to the removal of families, mostly black, from the favela Jacarezinho as part of postabolition urban renewal, she sounded an important modern-day message for the government: it was "necessary for democracy to become a reality in the hills, too."[33]

Nascimento worked with other black Brazilians to insert racial realist objectives into the redemocratization process. For instance, in September 1945 Nascimento and Isaltino Veiga dos Santos founded the Convenção Política do Negro Brasileiro (Political Convention of Black Brazilians), which soon became the Convenção Nacional do Negro Brasileiro (National Convention of Black Brazilians). The convention managed to receive expressions of support from Social Democratic Party candidate and soon-to-be president General Eurico Dutra and from many other political parties. Although he respected certain politicians, at the time Nascimento felt no loyalty to any one party, believing they all "were the same in their essential fraud against black people." Still, in the post–Estado Novo period, he fished for a political organization that would create space for him and a racial realist platform. Nascimento, who would be elected to Congress in 1983, attempted to establish such political space by running for elected office with various parties during this period but failed to find one that would allow him to do so.[34] The majority of politicians expressed denial and often pointed to anecdotes that supposedly proved the racial paradise narrative, which exasperated Nascimento.

The party with which Nascimento enjoyed the most success was the Vargas-established PTB, for which he, his longtime collaborator Sebastião Rodrigues Alves, and others spearheaded a Diretório Negro (Black Affairs Department) in the capital city. The PTB's program reflected the demands of the National Convention of Black Brazilians, which historian Edilza Sotero attributes to the presence of convention leaders such as Nascimento in the Diretório. Among other points, Article 24 of the PTB's program singled out the need to end color discrimination, especially in the armed forces and the diplomatic corps, as well as the government's responsibility to provide quality education and health care for blacks. The PTB's Diretório hoped to get a black person elected to champion the interests of the black population, and it nominated Nascimento as its candidate for representative. This hope for elected office was short-lived; the party pulled Nascimento from the ticket, citing his integralist past. As Elisa Larkin Nascimento has written, "the idea of a black group with autonomy inside a political party was entirely new and [the Diretório] was not able to move forward effectively for lack of support within the party." Nascimento also confronted difficulties running for city council as a candidate with the more conservative Social Democratic Party (or PSD, the party of President Dutra), which opted to transfer his candidacy to the level of federal Congress. Because he was unknown and had no prior experience in office, the probability that Nascimento could compete at the federal level was extremely low.[35] Nascimento's efforts in electoral politics exposed the problems that black racial realists faced when they used the traditional route to gain political power in order to push forward their agenda.

In another explicitly political maneuver, Abdias do Nascimento, Rodrigues Alves, and Aguinaldo Camargo in Rio de Janeiro took a similar step to their ANB contemporaries in São Paulo: they center-staged the word *democracy* in their struggle. Around the same time that Leite and the Paulista Association of Black Brazilians launched their *Manifesto in Defense of Democracy,* leaders of the Carioca TEN formed the Comitê Democrático Afro-Brasileiro (Afro-Brazilian Democratic Committee), an organization open to blacks and nonblacks alike. Whites in the organization were mainly associated with and met in the headquarters of the UNE, an entity with strong ties to the PCB, that had opened its headquarters to the committee's meetings and activities.[36] In the beginning, the black and nonblack members of the Afro-Brazilian Democratic Committee worked together in the shared mission to secure amnesty for Estado Novo political prisoners, but the UNE was unwilling to participate in political campaigns for racial realism, "raising the specter of 'reverse racism' and division of the working class."[37] Similar to what the PTB did shortly thereafter, the UNE also insisted that Nascimento publicly confess and denounce his integralist past. Nascimento refused to succumb to what he would describe as "leftist whitemail," so the UNE majority expelled not only Nascimento but also Alves and Camargo.[38]

Black Brazilians did have some friends in Congress who represented their concerns in political arenas. This was especially the case with Senator Hamilton Nogueira of the União Democrática Nacional (National Democratic Union, or UDN), who would be coined "senator of the blacks." Nogueira was elected senator of the Federal District to the National Constituent Assembly, the body charged with drafting and passing the nation's new constitution in 1946. By the time of the assembly, Nogueira had already attended the National Convention of Brazilian Blacks that the TEN had organized in São Paulo in 1945.[39] The convention, with its hundreds of black participants, drafted a "Manifesto to the Brazilian Nation" that emphasized black autonomy and self-determination, and especially demanded that "color and race prejudice be prohibited by law, as crimes against the State," thus mirroring the manifesto of the ANB. The convention forwarded its official declaration to all the political parties, prompting written responses, mostly of support, from the major parties and their presidential candidates. PTB congressman Manoel Benício Fontenelle decided to take up the manifesto's call, authoring an amendment that guaranteed equal legal rights for people of all races and presenting it to the Constituent Assembly.[40]

Excluded from the Constituent Assembly, the leaders of the National Convention of Brazilian Blacks evidently asked Senator Nogueira to push for anti–racial discrimination language in the Constitution, and he became the figurehead of the cause and the most outspoken proponent of Fontenelle's amendment. Likely having picked up ideas from the Black Convention, Nogueira gave a lengthy speech at the Constituent Assembly to justify the need for the antidiscriminatory legislation that resembled a historical and social scientific lecture on the fallacy of theories about racial purity and superiority.[41] Nogueira examined intellectuals of racial thought, such as Arthur de Gobineau, Franz Boas, and of course his Brazilian colleague Gilberto Freyre. He employed literary, political, and other examples of gifted men (always men) of color whose brilliance and talent derailed any assumption of their inferiority. He also discussed historical events that shed light on these issues, such as wars, and logically, Nogueira tapped into the emotion and the rhetoric of the war just won.

Paralleling Manoel Antonio dos Santos in his *Alvorada* article of the previous year, Hamilton Nogueira capitalized on lingering World War II sentiments to make the case for racial realist democracy at the Constituent Assembly on behalf of blacks. Early in his talk, Nogueira expressed his intention to broach the topic of racism and followed with the obvious question: "Does the issue of racism exist in Brazil?" Nogueira answered his own query, declaring that racism existed not only "in relation to our black brothers [but also] in relation to our Israelite brothers." He would later say that his focus would be on the former problem, but he continued to link antiblack racism to anti-Semitism and therefore to the war. Nogueira quoted part of de Gobineau's diatribe against blacks, which labeled them animalistic and unintelligent, as well as instinctively and intrinsically violent. Beginning with the First World War and moving to the most recent conflict, Nogueira debunked these conclusions. In this segment of his speech, he energized the assembly with reflections of World War II, particularly the homicidal acts of de Gobineau's exalted whites and the role that blacks played in the Allies' self-described fight for democracy: "[I]n this last drama . . . from which side sprang spontaneous massacre if not from the same so-called superior race? And on which side were blacks, of the Belgian Congo, of the English colonies, of America, of Brazil—on what side were these men? They were spilling their blood for the victory of liberty, for the implantation of true Democracy! (*Applause*) This is the response of the so-called inferior race, the so-called race of animals."[42]

In this part of his speech before the assembly, Nogueira invoked the war not only to disprove racist eugenic theory but also to render blacks globally as agents of democracy. With words that reverberated with Brazil's wartime discourse, Nogueira gave credit to black Brazilians for supporting the country's ability to align with the Allies. According to Nogueira, by disproving Nazi racial philosophies and by sacrificing their lives alongside other Allied forces to ward off international fascism, Brazil's black soldiers helped make it possible for the nation to call itself a democracy. Here black Brazilians were not only agents of democracy but were also Brazilian democracy personified, which marked discrimination against them as antidemocratic.

Nogueira made other explicitly democratic realist appeals as well, arguing that Brazil's hour of redemocratization was a prime time to instill the nation's emergent legal landscape with racial protections. Nogueira told the assembly that in "this moment of our country's history . . . we seek to implant not a nominal democracy, but one with a humanist foundation, in which all the rights of men should be respected . . . permanently, in our Constitution [and that these rights be enjoyed by] men of all conditions and of all races." During the speech, Nogueira had already made it clear that such rights did not exist in Brazil, highlighting the state's "restriction of entry by blacks into the Military, Naval and Air Force Academies, and especially in diplomatic careers." Although he was thankful that Brazil's racial discrimination was not as extreme as that of its infamous northern neighbor the United States, he felt that Brazil still needed to take advantage of the chance to draft a new constitution that officially rejected racist theory, purged racial discrimination, and honored the black veterans who fought in the war.[43]

During the Constituent Assembly's debate of the antidiscrimination clause, Gilberto Freyre, Nogueira's UDN colleague and state of Pernambuco assembly representative, used similar language to voice his opinion about it. As the ANB's *Alvorada* journal reported, Freyre described Nogueira's campaign as an attempt to ensure that the new constitution "consecrate, among its democratic principles, equal opportunity for all born-Brazilians, regardless of race or of color," especially in diplomatic service. Freyre added that there should be no room for color prejudice in Brazil, for the country must be the "masters of democracy" on this issue, avoiding the US model, which, despite all its democratic accolades, exhibited the "worst of the least democratic and least Christian" of qualities.[44] By printing this short excerpt on the front page of the *Alvorada*, the ANB both spotlighted the parts of the debate that validated political discourse of racial realism and allowed Freyre's words to be a proxy of sorts for their own perspective, thus asserting a voice in the assembly that they had not been granted formally.

The Constituent Assembly rejected the antidiscrimination clause and the racial realism it represented because of a "lack of concrete examples" that racism in Brazil was an issue requiring such legal action—a display of classic denial. Not even PCB member Claudino José da Silva, the only black member in the entire assembly, voted in favor of the clause. Evidently the PCB, which had sent a letter from Luís Carlos Prestes to the National Convention of Black Brazilians fully supporting their manifesto, was behind Silva's vote.[45] In fact, two months after Nogueira's pitch for the clause, Silva made a racial realist entreaty himself during the assembly's 13 de maio celebration of abolition. Silva said that the "National Constituent Assembly could very well insert into our Magna Carta a democratic provision . . . assuring to all, whites or blacks, the broadest possible participation in national life." Perhaps Silva, who later claimed that he personally favored the antidiscrimination clause but had followed the party's directive to oppose it, was attempting to make amends with his appeal.[46] At the very least, he helped keep alive the argument that the racial qualities of democracy should be unequivocally stated in Brazil's new constitution.

In addition to bypassing the antidiscrimination clause, for the most part the Constituent Assembly also rejected the conviction upon which it and Claudino José da Silva's proposal were based: that language specifically addressing values of racial inclusion should be inserted in the new democratic charter. The assembly deemed sufficient the 1946 Constitution's declaration that "[a]ll are equal before the law." The constitution did contain racial wording that clearly stamped the racial lessons of World War II into its fabric, but only in Article 141, which carried guarantees for the freedom of expression, with limitations. Among the restrictions was a provision that affected published materials: "Propaganda of war . . . or of race or class prejudices will not be tolerated." Interestingly, Article 113 of the pre–Estado Novo Constitution of 1934 did more in this sense, actually articulating equal protections based on race: "All are equal before the law. There will be no privileges, nor distinctions" due to "race," among other things. The 1946 Constitution resembled that of 1934 in its mention of philosophical, religious, and political plurality, but it relegated race to the antipropaganda provision only. In fact, Article 157 of the 1946 Constitution mandated equal pay for equal work regardless of sex, age, nationality, or marital status, but it did not include race.[47] Contrary to the example set in 1934 and the worldview of racial realists, the 1946 Constitution ignored the fact that safeguarding society against racist propaganda alone would be futile without other protections in place. After all, propaganda is only dangerous when it incites people to act. The Constitution ratified in 1946 was a document that reflected a rhetorical, non-action-oriented form of racial democracy—one that denied the problem of racial bias and proscribed the language of racism as opposed to racist actions.

The "concrete example" accepted as proof that racial prejudice was a problem in Brazil would come years after the Constitution was approved, and it would be followed by a law that was hailed by many as the most significant legislation for racial realism to be enacted in the country since abolition. A year after the National Convention of Black Brazilians saw the antidiscrimination clause die at the Constituent Assembly, a scandal erupted when Irene Diggs, a black anthropologist from the United States, was not permitted to stay at Rio de Janeiro's swanky Hotel Serrador. Three years later, in 1950, renowned US black dancer/choreographer Katherine Dunham was denied entry into the room she had reserved at São Paulo's upscale Esplanada Hotel. In both instances, the women and black Brazilian activists, particularly TEN members, cried racial discrimination publicly and loudly. This was especially true in the Dunham case, making its exposure of Brazilian prejudice and racial segregation a national embarrassment that sparked the push to revisit antiracism legislation. The author of the bill, UDN congressman Afonso Arinos de Melo Franco, argued in Congress that the Dunham situation was evidence that racism in Brazil was significant enough to require legislative action. An article in the black journal *Redenção* noted that Congressman Gilberto Freyre, who voted in favor of the bill, also mentioned Dunham when speaking about it to Congress. At the end of many speeches and debates, the Brazilian Congress passed the Afonso Arinos Law in 1951, which outlawed specific instances of racial or color discrimination in public services, education, and employment. The law transformed these discriminatory acts into misdemeanors.[48]

If the Afonso Arinos Law (a legacy of Afro-Brazilian struggles during redemocratization in the 1940s) was an expression of racial realism rarely advanced by Brazilian national politicians, their debates and the final product itself show how the law actually extended long-held denialist and dissuasion tendencies. As Congress debated Arinos's bill, mentalities surfaced that demonstrated a real difficulty for a Congress without a single black representative to accept racism as an endemic Brazilian problem. Even though Arinos cited discrimination suffered by his black chauffeur and Dunham as events that both inspired and justified his bill, and despite his insistence that racism was a widespread reality in Brazil, Arinos indicted non-Brazilians living in the country as the key perpetrators. (His chauffeur had, after all, been subjected to racism at the hands of immigrants in Rio de Janeiro.) Years later, when he discussed the bill, Arinos reiterated his position that "the agents of [racial] injustice are almost always *gringos* who are ignorant of our traditions and insensitive to our old customs of racial fraternity."[49] Gilberto Freyre took a similar position in Congress during its debates of the bill, submitting that it was "not surprising that [the Dunham incident] occurred in São Paulo, because commercialism, mercantilism, business, the dollar ("dollarism"), immediacy, all the 'isms' inseparable from the vigorous and triumphant civilization in industrial America operate in São Paulo and with a vengeance."[50] In other words, in their eagerness to mimic US economic success, Paulistas had unfortunately imbibed one of the North Americans' greatest sins, one that was antithetical to Brazilian customs: racism. Although the supporters of the Afonso Arinos Law at least acknowledged the practice of racial discrimination in Brazil, they labeled it a foreign import and failed to recognize or admit that it was native to their country. In this sense, the celebrated Afonso Arinos Law was ironically an expression of denial; it maintained Brazil's racism-free myth even as it proscribed actions that proved racism's existence.

UDN congressman Plínio Barreto also circulated language of racial inclusion in support of the Arinos bill and denounced racial barriers in a manner that focused on dissuading the blacks that would resist it. Action-oriented steps to counter racism were necessary, Barreto argued, in order to avoid disintegrating into a nation ripe with race wars, à la the United States. He referred to the Dunham case and bemoaned the fact that "certain civil careers" banned blacks and "the Navy and the Air Force create[d] unjustifiable difficulties for blacks seeking to enter." Barreto felt that such policies provided such an "example of hateful discrimination [that] we should not be surprised when commercial establishments prevent blacks from entering their doors." This, Barreto concluded, was as sure a way as any to set Brazil on the United States' "terrible" course of racial conflict. As George Reid Andrews has written, the fear of black antiracist mobilization—which was (and is) associated with so-called US-style confrontational identity politics and interracial relations—propped this line of thinking.[51] Indeed, the racial tensions that concerned Barreto materialized only when blacks proactively responded to and organized against the discriminatory practices that he condemned. Thus, while many Brazilians were suspicious of blacks who struggled against racism, their fight for racial equality was also perceived as a potential mode by which interracial violence could be introduced to Brazil.

Other congressional champions of the law, including Arinos and Freyre, blatantly expressed their disdain for black racial politics and organizations. After the Katherine Dunham affair, Freyre labeled the

"Brazilian Negro caricatured as North American" as profoundly troublesome. With a nod to the PCB's racial rhetoric, if also a misunderstanding of it, Freyre believed that political parties, particularly the Communist Party, promoted black consciousness for purely political ends and encouraged an opposition to racism that was itself racist. Arinos, upon the passing of his law, articulated a similar viewpoint: "During the parliamentary debates of my bill, I sought to show the pernicious side of [black organizations and associations], the spirit of which the bill opposed with its concern to establish more positive foundations for the integration of the black element in Brazilian social life." The "insistence" on forming black organizations was "a manifestation of black racism," he argued.[52] Therefore, the lawmakers' racial inclusivity was part and parcel of a strategy to dissuade blacks from creating groups that rallied around issues of prejudice and fostered racial solidarity, which they and others characterized as un-Brazilian, US qualities. Black activists were aware of these objectives, causing many to conclude that the law set out to "cool off" blacks who were galvanized in the struggle against color prejudice and other social ills.[53]

If many black Brazilians looked upon the Afonso Arinos law cynically, the reactions of other Afro-Brazilians must have given hope to congressional dissuaders that the new legislation satisfied black democratic aspirations. Many blacks saw much promise in the law, labeling it the "new *13 de maio*." One journal reported that the legislation was "well received" among blacks, quoting an Afro-Brazilian man as saying that "the blacks of Brazil are exultant. This law is a democratic step and will ensure a place in the sun for those of my race." Some blacks who lauded the Afonso Arinos Law reflected the attitudes of Congress; they blamed foreigners for "creat[ing] the segregation of blacks" in Brazil. The law, they believed, would prevent foreigners from shutting out blacks from economic opportunities and reserving them exclusively for relatives or fellow countrymen and -women. Another group of Afro-Brazilians that scholars Bastide and Fernandes identified in their study believed that blacks "should take advantage of" the law, which they considered to be a product of black activists' efforts "made on democratic terrain." However, the group was also skeptical and knew that many of the legislation's congressional supporters hoped it would enervate black mobilization for greater social and political rights.[54]

Some negative black opinions about the Afonso Arinos Law were due to the belief that the legislation was simply a way for Brazil to save face after the "scandal" involving Katherine Dunham and was "not made to resolve the problems of the black Brazilian." One black interviewee said that the "situation continues and will continue the same. That is, we will continue seeing and suffering, simultaneously, the consequences of color discrimination (racial discrimination does not exist). . . . If we [threaten to invoke this law] we will be punished . . . as communists."[55] Whether they identified discrimination as race- or color-based, many black Brazilians did not agree with those in their community who perceived the law as a true action-oriented antidote to the prejudice darker-skinned Brazilians confronted. Instead, they saw the legislation as, at best, a way to protect the rights of foreign black tourists, or, at worst, a tactic of racial dissuasion that would incapacitate antiracist activism that could engender true results.

The Afonso Arinos Law's naysayers were eventually validated, as the legislation proved not to be an action-oriented tool to combat racial discrimination in the way its supporters claimed. The law remained in effect until 1988, when it was supplanted by the Lei Caó, and despite the fact that many violations of the law were apparently presented to the police in its thirty-seven years of existence, only three cases went to trial, resulting in two convictions. In 1980 Afonso Arinos expressed his disappointment in the law's effectiveness: "I would like it very much, and I really hope that someday there may be a judgment under the law, that a bar or restaurant [which had discriminated] might be closed, that a public official who had committed this crime might be fired. But nothing has ever gone that far."[56] If Arinos wondered why that was, the answer was likely that the law was too specific and circumscribed in what constituted an act of discrimination, that the misdemeanor penalties were too light, and that it mandated evidence of discriminatory intent, which is virtually impossible to obtain. Unlike the Afonso Arinos Law, however, the National Convention of Brazilian Blacks' *Manifesto,* upon which Fontenelle based the 1946 antidiscrimination clause, did not limit offenses to any particular list and instead made more general demands that prejudice in "private businesses[,] civilian associations and public and private institutions, be prohibited by criminal law." The convention also wanted racial and color prejudice to be defined as a crime greater than a misdemeanor. Arinos was opposed to more rigorous legislation, and even when the verdict was in about his law's inadequacy, he voted against the bill that fortified its penalties in the new Lei Caó, using the familiar argument that they would foment "racial antagonism."[57]

Brazil's involvement in World War II was a huge boost to the redemocratization process that occurred in the first half of the 1940s. Calls for representative democracy came from the Left, Right, and Center, and the connection between race and democracy so prevalent during the war was an important part of these demands. Here black activists were leaders, attempting to ensure that action-oriented racial realism was integral to the legal foundation that was being reconstructed. State actors did eventually respond with gestures toward racially inclusive democracy, but the result favored dissuasion and denial, not action-oriented realism. Those who alleged that black activism would eventually lead to US-like race riots framed their dissuasion as a pro-security tactic that maintained "the peace." However, preserving the peace, as they saw it, also kept Brazilians who were subjected to racial prejudice from experiencing an action-oriented democracy that collapsed racial hierarchy and reversed its grave economic, social, and political side effects.

THE FORCES OF RACIAL DEMOCRACY ON THE HOME FRONT: THE UNITED STATES

Similar to the Afonso Arinos Law, the US Fair Employment Practices Committee, which set out to address racial discrimination in defense industry jobs, was another state intervention that did not completely warrant its reputation as an action-oriented victory. The FEPC was the result of blacks' refusal to be denied the economic opportunities found in the booming defense industry. The struggle that ensued between blacks and the government, the language that blacks used to demand state intervention, and the wording of the executive order that established the FEPC all provide a fascinating look at the boomerang effect of the war's rhetorical racial democracy. Analysis of the FEPC also complicates the "who" of the state's racially inclusive wartime democracy. A one-size-fits-all model of racial inclusion did not exist, as the case with Mexican Americans demonstrates. Because the FEPC's implementation was, at least in part, related to the concerns of anticommunist authorities, it is worth revisiting the issue that was so important to the development of discursive racial democracy in the United States during the 1930s. We will quickly assess the state of official anticommunism during the war as well as the general domestic racial political milieu from which the committee emerged.

During the Nazi-Soviet Pact from 1939 to 1941, federal, state, and local authorities had ramped up their anticommunist activities as even liberal critics of red-baiting, like Roosevelt, came to perceive the communists' newfound opposition to war as a threat to national security. The Russian nonaggression agreement with the Nazis marked the end of the first Popular Front era and forced communist loyalists to make a drastic U-turn from staunch antifascism to an antiwar crusade. Communist opposition to national war preparations was especially worrisome for Roosevelt and other authorities as their influence in the labor movement led to concerns about strikes and labor stoppages, especially in the defense industry, at a crucial moment. Subsequently, communists like CPUSA general secretary Earl Browder received harsh sentencing for any infraction. Congress also passed the Alien Registration Act that gave the Justice Department tremendous powers to broadly define sedition in order to deport immigrants. After the Germans breached their pact and invaded Russia in 1941, the Russians joined the Allied forces and anticommunism ebbed as the CPUSA became one of the strongest voices in favor of the war and the defense industry, religiously backing labor's "No Strike Pledge." Earl Browder was even released early from jail. Still, the reliable anticommunist sectors of the state—notably J. Edgar Hoover, whose FBI ballooned in size and jurisdiction, the military, and Martin Dies, whose House Committee of Un-American Activities kept strong and relentless during the war—remained undeterred from labeling domestic communism an issue of national defense.[58]

Just like the first Popular Front period, the communists' renewed wartime Popular Front strategy produced widespread democratic rhetoric and a less radical stance on racial issues, as we saw in Brazil. Ben Davis—the first black communist elected to office in the United States, replacing Adam Clayton Powell Jr. as New York City councilman in 1943—represented in many ways the party's official perspective on race during the war. Communist commitment to the war effort led some black activists to accuse Davis and the party of abandoning its racial platform. Several black leaders reacted negatively to Davis's criticism of A. Philip Randolph's March on Washington Movement, which the former said wrongly tackled the government and unions instead of Hitler.[59] Davis did speak out against racism and encouraged the CPUSA to follow suit, but the party moderated its militant racial edge during the war. At least one prominent black journalist, Horace Cayton, bemoaned the communists' relative desertion of issues critical to blacks, insisting that the country "need[ed] radicals to lead the way."[60]

Regardless of the party and Moscow's conciliatory tone, steadfast anticommunists continued to suspect that racial rights activists were subversive and communist inspired. Martin Dies remained wary of anti-racist organizations and responded with racial denial and dissuasion, using his committee to advance the notion that US democracy was an ideal example of interracial coexistence. Those who spoke openly against racism, such as Mary McLeod Bethune and E. Franklin Frazier, were accused of being communists. In 1942 J. Edgar Hoover stated that the communists were "still loudly championing the cause of civil rights at the slightest provocation." The FBI must have been involved in the meetings between "secret agents of the Federal Government" and leaders of the Randolph-led Brotherhood of Sleeping Car Porters to discuss communism. Indeed, these meetings likely shaped Secretary of War Stimson's conclusion on this issue, since the War Department worked closely with Hoover on domestic countersubversive activities. Secretary Stimson, who was "confident of the superiority of the white race," compromised with Randolph, who he believed was genuinely attempting to ward off a communist monopoly of the racial justice movement.[61] We have seen that realist congressman Hamilton Fish Jr., Dies's predecessor, was also motivated to stunt the growth of communism in the black community. Anticommunist congressman Fish agreed to sponsor an amendment that Rayford Logan drafted to the Military Appropriations Bill of 1941. The amendment to ban racial discrimination in military personnel hiring and training passed, although it proved to be rather ineffective.[62]

Similar to the Afro-Brazilian activists, US black leaders and journalists capitalized on anti-Nazi sentiment during the war by placing racism under the rubric of what they called "Hitlerism," effectively equating racial discrimination with the anti-US, undemocratic enemy. Black activists agilely moved between supporting the president and criticizing him; emphasizing black loyalty and patriotism and issuing warnings of low morale and skepticism among blacks; preaching US greatness and bemoaning US injustice and hypocrisy. Despite the discord and tension between different organizations and personalities, almost without exception they all seemed to rally in their fight for justice around the wartime mantra of democracy, as each defined it. In doing so, these various agents promoted an action-oriented realist vision of racial democracy, rejecting lip service and demanding concrete steps that benefited the black community. This was the case with the March on Washington Movement as well as the Committee for the Participation of Negroes in the National Defense Program. In its response to such organizations, the government, like blacks, walked a fine line, making concessions that moved toward action-oriented racial democracy while simultaneously impeding it with racial dissuasion.

In its November 1940 election issue, the NAACP's *Crisis* magazine weighed in on the debate about Franklin Roosevelt's impact on the black community with criticism, but also with the following praise: "[The] most important contribution of the Roosevelt Administration to the age-old color line problem in America has been its doctrine that Negroes are a part of the country as a whole."[63] The NAACP's assessment of Roosevelt reflected the varied opinions of blacks nationally, as several complained about New Deal shortcomings while others credited the Works Progress Administration with employing a great number of blacks and celebrated the modest increase in government diversity.[64] However, as the conflict in Europe spread and the United States mobilized for war before Pearl Harbor, blacks became increasingly concerned that the wartime economic boom would leave them behind, especially as the WPA ground to a halt.

To fight for the inclusion of US blacks in all levels of the armed forces and defense industry, the *Pittsburgh Courier* launched the CPNNDP in 1939 with the participation of black sororities and fraternities, the Association for the Study of Negro Life and History, and others. Led by Rayford Logan, the Howard University professor who would also serve on the OCIAA's advisory committee, the CPNNDP took a two-pronged approach to secure blacks' place in the mobilizations for war. The committee established military and civilian goals to ensure that blacks were well represented as army officers, military doctors and nurses, flying cadets, and aviation mechanics. It also campaigned for blacks to have access to defense-industry training and jobs. The CPNNDP disapproved of segregation but found it acceptable if it translated into black officers leading the segregated units.[65]

Rayford Logan, who also believed blacks should fashion a "course of action" for the postwar world, argued the committee's case by attempting to convince different branches of government and society at large that action-oriented racial democracy was part and parcel of the broader war effort.[66] Logan used racial inclusion in the military as a paradigm for US democracy as he testified before the Senate Committee on Appropriations to argue in part that African American units gain combat status. The United States should, Logan contended, "go forward in the direction of a fuller participation by all of the American people in all of the rights and obligations of Americans, and especially at a time when we are holding out against totalitarian ideologies the moral force of the principles of American democracy."[67]

After issuing similar remarks to the House Committee on Military Affairs, Logan introduced Charles Houston, special counsel for the NAACP and representative of the *Pittsburgh Courier,* who foreshadowed the racial anxieties that US Pan-American policymakers would express imminently. Houston skillfully linked his comments to those of Frank Knox, secretary of the navy, who had testified before Logan. Secretary Knox had spoken of time he had spent in South America, returning to the United States "convinced that the only safety for us was in hemispheric defense." (It was during this hearing that Knox made the statement cited earlier in this book that "a base in Mexico is just as dangerous as a base in Texas or in Brazil.") Piggybacking on Knox's testimony, Houston reminded the committee that "the Negro minority is the colored majority in the Western Hemisphere." When the United States needed to call upon this "colored majority" of the American Republics for aid, which Houston suggested was inevitable, he wondered whether or not they would cooperate "unless there [was] a different [racial] situation created" in the United States. With these circumstances, Houston contended, the United States should "fight for the type of democracy which (would) be safe for whites and Negroes and all elements of citizens."[68]

In his writings, Logan similarly examined the United States in the context of the entire Western Hemisphere, placing racial injustice, especially in the United States, at the epicenter of the region's "crisis of democracy." Logan, known for his frequent use of the term "half-democracy" in reference to the United States, wrote: "The real and unmistakable crisis of democracy as I see it lies in the failure to recognize the fact that there never has been a democracy here." Democracy never developed in the Americas, Logan explained, because of the exploitation of indigenous populations and the "forced migration of some ten millions of Africans." Although he cited the United States as having the worst democratic infractions in the region, Logan did single out racism in Brazil, Venezuela, Haiti, Cuba, and other American republics. Particularly in the United States, blacks remained "the acid test" of what he called "functional democracy"—that is, "a system of government and a way of life that definitely promote the opportunity for every one to develop and utilize to the best good of all whatever abilities he may possess or acquire."[69] For Logan, democracy that excluded entire

254 | Chapter 7

groups of people because of race was not and could not be democracy at all. Furthermore, his definition of "functional democracy" indicated his emphasis on the work that democracy was supposed to do, ensuring economic, social, and political justice for all.

Logan pushed for the implementation of a functional, or action-oriented, racial democracy, and he eventually got Congressman Fish to sponsor his clause in the final conscription act. The amendment was verbatim what Logan had written and presented during his House hearing: "In the selection and training of men under this act, and in the interpretation and execution of the provisions of this act, there shall be no discrimination against any person on account of race or color."[70] However, Walter White, who wanted outright desegregation in the military, wrote that the Logan-Fish amendment had been invalidated by another condition of the draft act. The section he referred to permitted army and navy heads, already proven to be hostile to racial equality in the military, to deny the admittance of anyone they found to be unacceptable. With such ambiguity, White and other black leaders like A. Philip Randolph sought clarification from the president himself.[71]

Just as they had used their testimonies in front of the House Committee of Un-American Activities in the 1930s to argue for the eradication of racial injustice, Randolph and White met with Roosevelt to secure what they deemed democracy in the military—the end of segregated troops. Boosted by a looming election and Roosevelt's desire for the black vote, Randolph, White, and the National Urban League's T. Arnold Hill were granted a meeting with the president, the assistant secretary of war, and the secretary of the navy in September. Not only did Roosevelt and the military leaders reject integration, but the White House reported their decision to the press as if Randolph et al. had accepted it. Even worse, just after the failed conference with the president and military heads, the Senate shelved the antilynching bill for which the NAACP and others had fought tirelessly for years. Disappointed blacks—including Randolph, White, and Hill—protested, warning the president that "at a time of National peril" it was dangerous that he "should surrender so completely to enemies of democracy who would destroy national unity by advocating segregation."[72]

Likely the most high-profile proponents of the argument that action-driven racial democracy was required for national unity was A. Philip Randolph and what became known as the March on Washington Movement. After several failed attempts to meet again with Roosevelt, Randolph made an appeal in late January 1941 for ten thousand blacks to march on Washington, DC, and rally in front of the Lincoln Memorial. Randolph's call, published in the *Pittsburgh Courier,* stated that the demand of the march would be "jobs in National Defense and placement as soldiers and officers of all ranks we are qualified for, in the armed forces." Randolph promised black readers that no one could accuse march participants of undermining national unity, since the movement would be fighting for "the right to play our part in advancing the cause of national defense and national unity." Besides, he assessed, "there can be no true national unity where one-tenth of the population are denied their basic rights as American citizens."[73]

At first, few believed that ten thousand blacks would mobilize around Randolph's call, but within a few months the black press and leadership began estimating that one hundred thousand would come out in support of the movement that most involved referred to as "democratic." The March on Washington Committee (as it was first called) was joined by local committees around the country and gained backing from most black leaders. It began to receive nonstop coverage and endorsements from the black press as well.[74] In its support of the march, the black press pushed for Logan-like, functional racial democracy with direct, to-the-point language. One article described the march as a "Crusade for Democracy," while march slogans included "Let Negroes Serve Democracy Now," "Total Democracy Includes Us," "Democracy Here Is Our First Line of Defense," "Total Democracy for Total Defense," and "Make Democracy Work, Give Us Jobs."[75]

As these slogans demonstrate, black would-be marchers on Washington characterized democracy as racially universal, endowed with the classic rights and duties of citizenship which they insisted must materialize, above all else, in the economic realm. Exemplified by the slogan "Let Negroes Serve Democracy Now," the MOWM highlighted the duties aspect of racial democracy for many blacks, for as Randolph proclaimed, the movement wanted the black community to be held equally accountable for the defensive expectations of US citizens. The racial undertones of "Democracy Here Is Our First Line of Defense" and "Total Democracy for Total Defense" further engaged the MOWM's military theme, insinuating that national security rested on systemic racial democracy in national defense industries and the armed services. The double entendre conveyed in "Make Democracy Work, Give Us Jobs," rendered "work" as both a verb and a noun in order to emphasize the economic dimensions inherent in the MOWM's democratic aspirations. According to marchers, racial democracy was meant to have real, tangible effects on the black community; it should provide that *work*, the noun, be accessible to blacks, and it should also *work* to ensure job security for those across the racial spectrum.

Just days before the march was to take place, Franklin Roosevelt finally signed Executive Order (EO) 8802, banning discrimination in defense industry employment. The MOWM remained strong and vigilant to ensure its implementation. Roosevelt's order created the Fair Employment Practices Committee, the body charged with investigating discrimination complaints in national defense hiring practices.[76] Randolph called off the protest march, to the delight of the president and some black leaders who feared the turnout would disappoint, but his MOWM continued to mobilize blacks. A case in point was the June 1942 MOWM rally at New York City's Madison Square Garden, which echoed Logan's assertion that blacks served as the litmus test for US democracy: "Winning Democracy for the Negro Is Winning the War for Democracy," declared the rally's motto. Twenty-five thousand attendees listened and cheered speakers elaborating on the theme, one explaining that "we want to be a part of this democracy. We don't want to be like a label on a bottle—all around it, but not in it." Adam Clayton Powell Jr. deflected accusations of black disloyalty by stating that blacks were just "demanding a full share of this democracy." The *Pittsburgh Courier* reported on its front page that the event was an exercise in "defin[ing] 'Real Democracy.'" Movement leader Randolph led the chorus of democratic appeals, later clarifying that the MOWM was part and parcel of a broader demand for "equality in politics, education, labor unions, business—racial, economic, and social."[77] But Randolph's position that democracy equaled material racial equality proved to be too radical for the government.

Mary McLeod Bethune, the best known of the MOWM women leaders, also relied upon the discourse of democracy to outline the objectives of the movement, and she consciously gendered the black struggle in national defense. In 1940 Bethune—the National Youth Administration's director of Negro affairs, the president of the National Council of Negro Women, and the so-called "First Lady of Negro America"— wrote an open letter to Roosevelt about the role of black women in national defense. She stated that blacks had been "fighting for a more equitable share of those opportunities which are fundamental to every American citizen who would enjoy the economic and family security which a true democracy guarantees." Black women wanted to be recognized as full US citizens who "have a right and a solemn duty to serve their nation," Bethune affirmed. Among the black community, she continued, were extremely capable, loyal women anxious to execute "the types of service so necessary in a program of national defense." Black women would sacrifice greatly to demonstrate their yearning for "a more realistic American democracy as envisioned by those not blinded by racial prejudices."[78] Bethune's gender-specific rhetoric provided an alternative to some of the male-focused slogans that would grace the movement's literature, such as "Mobilize Now! Manhood, Courage, Guts, Determination" and "Justice-Democracy-Freedom and Manhood Rights."[79] Bethune's voice in the battle for racial democracy before, during, and after the MOWM helped forge a space for black women to be perceived as benefactors and agents of both national security and a true democratic society.

If appeals to the government to enact policies like the antilynching bill remained unanswered, the administration's reaction to the MOWM revealed that the dissuasion of black dissent could motivate a rare, specifically antiracist initiative. As Randolph wrote in his original call for the march, the government had offered "polite assurances that Negroes will be given a fair deal," but he lamented, "it all ends there. Nothing is being done to stop discriminations." Even government officials who fought for black rights were sabotaged by those "full of race hatred," Randolph added.[80] As the MOWM gained steam, Roosevelt remained silent on the policy changes it petitioned, despite the administration's verbal adherence to ideals of racially inclusive democracy since the mid-1930s. The president, the first lady, and New York mayor Fiorello La Guardia had made several efforts short of the executive order to appease the MOWM's leadership, but the group refused to cancel the march.[81] The MOWM's grassroots popularity and the leadership's uncompromising stance finally forced FDR's hand to issue EO 8802 and establish the FEPC. Randolph's insistence that the MOWM be a black-only movement in an attempt to keep out communists also encouraged military leaders to collaborate with him in hopes of dissuading blacks from joining the Communist Party.[82]

Roosevelt constructed the FEPC with an eye toward safeguarding national security. The EO 8802 preamble began with the statement that it was US policy "to encourage full participation in the national defense program by all citizens . . . regardless of race, creed, color, or national origin, in the firm belief that the [US] democratic way of life . . . can be defended successfully only with the help and support of all groups within its borders." Defense industry discrimination also compromised "national unity," another prerequisite for war preparation and prosecution.[83] As Rayford Logan observed, Hitler had broken the 1939 Nazi-Soviet Pact with the invasion of the Soviet Union just two days before Roosevelt signed EO 8802; thus, defense production was elevated as an ever more urgent national priority.[84] Even in this pre–Pearl Harbor context, the executive order's rhetoric articulated racial inclusion as a nationalist, democratic principle that protected the nation from foreign threat—not necessarily as a worthy goal in itself.

The fight to win the FEPC produced some positive results: statistics for war industry employment and training increased for blacks.[85] Although the FEPC must have made a difference here, we also know that the war's high labor demands and the deployment of skilled white male labor in the millions opened doors for many groups, including women, normally excluded from certain industries. Once the United States declared war, improvements in employment and training prospects for women and people of color were inevitable. Thus, the gains made by many groups during the war were a combination of factors, the FEPC being just one of them.

Despite these benefits, the FEPC could not live up to the MOWM leaders' expectations as an action-oriented tool to help in the fight for racial democracy, for the committee lacked the power of enforcement. The committee's inability to act against and remedy defense industry racism was illustrated when US foreign policymakers urged the FEPC not to pursue reports of discrimination against Mexicans and Mexican Americans in the Southwest. As in Brazil, stories of US racism garnered much press in Mexico, especially when suffered by people of Mexican descent, striking an embarrassing blow to Good Neighbor imperatives. State Department official Laurence Duggan called for private hearings, but as the FEPC clarified, companies practicing racial discrimination were coerced into changing their policies only by the prospect of a "public hearing in which the practices of the industries would be exposed."[86] Outside of public humiliation, the FEPC was basically powerless, for the EO 8802 permitted the committee only to investigate and hold hearings on defense industry employment practices and recommend measures of enforcement to the government.[87] Even when Randolph et al. drove Roosevelt to draft the stronger Executive Order 9346 in 1943, creating a more autonomous FEPC and expanding its jurisdiction, other cases proved that there was no statutory structure and not much will in the government to compel obstinate companies that outright refused to modify racist policy.[88]

The public hearings function of the FEPC was a compromise between Randolph's demand for action-oriented racial democracy and the state's rhetoric-focused preference. The FEPC presented a unique form of dissuasion that set out to influence both blacks and the defense establishment: blacks were dissuaded from marching on Washington, DC, and there was an attempt to dissuade defense industry employers from discriminating. Nonetheless, many state officials held black leaders and the FEPC responsible for a series of 1943 race riots that involved mainly blacks, whites, and Mexican Americans, the most serious occurring in Detroit. Mississippi congressman John Rankin argued that the committee's "crazy policies" that tried to "mix the races in all kinds of employment," as well as black leaders who urged their community to be "'militant' in the struggle for racial equality," were to blame.[89] The FEPC continued on course regardless, and it even gained State Department support. Secretary of State Cordell Hull finally allowed discrimination hearings against the employers of Mexican and Mexican Americans in hopes that the US government would "appear . . . to implement practically and effectively the Good Neighbor Policy."[90] Yet the FEPC still did not possess the capability to actualize policy; it was ultimately the company's decision whether or not to reverse racist practices, which seemed to rest upon the public's reaction to racism in the national defense industry. Like many blacks, Mexican Americans would be among those disappointed in the FEPC's limitations. In particular, they felt that the committee should have made greater strides to provide the necessary training for more Mexican Americans to enter into skilled professions.[91]

When the war's themes of race and democracy boomeranged back into the United States and Brazil, age-old domestic dilemmas took on added weight as both governments feared disunity and unrest during the time they most needed solidarity and stability. The FEPC and the Afonso Arinos Law were seen as important steps that both states took toward promoting the wartime ideals of racial democracy. It is evident from the official language in and surrounding these initiatives, however, that the blacks who fought for their implementation found government partners who were largely concerned with protecting the national image, strengthening national defense, and/or discouraging protest. This does not mean that no benefit came to blacks as a result of these initiatives or that it is uncommon for those engaged in policymaking from within and outside the state to come to the table with different goals and objectives. The point here is that it does matter when a racial policy is enacted with motives other than improving the economic, social, or political circumstances of blacks or of any group. In many instances, looking to such policies as proof or models of social progress, which is often the case, can be misleading. The danger is not just that such practices create a false narrative of the past and of a nation's historical trajectory toward equality but that those beliefs also inform subsequent social, political, and economic priorities. As a result, a society may nurture a flawed sense of security that it has overcome certain injustices even when it has not. Thus, for action-oriented realists, a major policy achievement often means not that a victory is won, but that the work continues.

Conclusion

In this book, I have argued that from 1930 to 1945, the Brazilian and US states were compelled to adopt racially inclusive nationalisms. As a part of this process, the racial meanings of democracy were reworked and emphasized in new ways, becoming rhetorically bound to ideals of inclusion. Communism, fascism, and World War II were the international security pressures that most propelled this shift, and black activism helped to make certain that these global phenomena had compelling domestic implications. I have also analyzed the historic partnership that the United States and Brazil forged during the war, one in which interconnected ideals of race and democracy gained significance. Furthermore, policymakers helped to sustain and strengthen the Brazil-US wartime alliance by collaborating on racial democracy–themed cultural propaganda. Black culture, its demarginalization, and white cultural mediators played an important role in the propaganda exchange between Brazil and the United States as well as in the evolving racial political narratives within each nation. The final chapter focused on the Afonso Arinos Law, the Fair Employment Practices Committee, and the battles blacks waged to see their promises fulfilled. The shortcomings of these state antiracist remedies reveal the challenges black activists confronted when trying to institute their model of racial democracy. Certainly one of the hallmarks of black activism in both countries has been the attempt to replace discursive and symbolic forms of racial democracy with action-oriented realism.

The picture of racial democracy that emerges from this study is one of a doctrine that was—and is—contingent upon place and time. When official statements or cultural materials have praised racial inclusion as a covenant of democracy, the historical, national, social, political, and economic context must be assessed to interpret the message fully. What a Brazilian politician said about racial democracy in 1944, on the verge of redemocratization, would have a different meaning when pronounced by a Brazilian politician in 2018, even if the statements were verbatim. This book also shows that the idea of racial democracy—considered to be a proprietary nationalist doctrine of Brazil and other Latin American societies, constructed in contrast to US racial nationalism—was already in ascendancy in the United States during the 1930s.

From 1930 to 1945, the distinctive qualities of official Brazilian racial democracy were the overwhelming domination of denial, largely predicated upon a reputation of interracial harmony, and efforts to legitimate and democratize Vargas's authoritarianism. As a result of its strong denialist culture, Brazil claimed that its racial democracy was already realized. The state projection of racial democracy in the United States was distinguished by the more prevalent race-based anticommunist rhetoric, sensitivity to a reputation for violent racial antagonism, relatively stable liberal democracy, and a stronger presence of realism. That said, one of the commonalities between these state articulations of racial democracy was the prominence of denial, although it was greater in Brazil. In large part because of this denial, I have argued that official racial democracy was inherently restricted in its ability to redress racial inequalities in either country.

This period, which I contend was the most critical for the emergence of rhetorical racial democracy in both nations, established significant patterns that carried into the Cold War. In fact, processes that have been associated with the Cold War had precedents in and continuities with the earlier era. For instance, policymakers' reliance on denial in order to manage perceived security threats during the Roosevelt and Vargas regimes created a serious problem for US and Brazilian realists: their portrayal of society undermined the narrative that most authorities claimed was essential for national defense. The racial realist perspective, therefore, was declared a menace to the nation. Ironically, as these states became open to racially inclusive political beliefs, they simultaneously delegitimized the point of view necessary to bring those ideals to fruition.

These dynamics persisted during the Cold War age of decolonization, when the so-called red scare came back with a vengeance in Brazil and the United States.[1] In Brazil the fear of communism was used to install another dictatorship. The military dictatorship (1964–85) was more durable than the Estado Novo, partly because it did not rely on the public persona of just one man. As Dulce Pandolfi has suggested, Brazil's military dictatorship was a legacy of the manner that Vargas utilized notions of democracy to justify the absence of representative government.[2] To legitimate and rationalize its existence, the military dictatorship created what was called the Doctrine of National Security and Development. The Doctrine of National Security identified the purpose of the dictatorship as the need to protect the nation from communism and other threats that it deemed harmful to economic development and to the regime's other aims.[3] The dictatorship evoked such perils to invalidate any movement, claim, or grievance perceived to weaken the regime. Racial realism was clearly one such threat, as it emphasized the inadequacies of the government and Brazilian capitalism, eroded the power of denialist racial democracy to strengthen Brazil's image, and revealed cracks in national unity.

The military dictatorship's response to black activism exposed the tension between the competing doctrines of national security and action-oriented racial realism. The Estado Novo's anticommunist, defense-based self-vindication was a precursor to this reaction. For their part, blacks in the postwar era took advantage of and contributed to the rights-laden, humanitarian democratic discourse that circulated the globe after World War II. Afro-Brazilians formed new black associations and demanded full citizenship rights. Here blacks continued their pattern of insisting that racial questions be prioritized when Brazilians were revisiting and reconsidering the merit and function of democracy, just as they had during the hopeful moments following the Revolution of 1930 and redemocratization in the 1940s. Denialists, still relishing Brazil's international racial repute after the fall of Nazism, criticized black Brazilians' action-oriented efforts to empower and liberate their communities as reverse racism and un-Brazilian. They accused black activists of foolishly importing their assertive racial consciousness from a place where it was relevant, the United States, to Brazil, a country where it was not.[4]

Once the military dictatorship firmly set the National Security Doctrine in place, the government perceived black activists' actions and rhetoric as increasingly dangerous. The so-called favela communities, with their large black populations, were often the sites of clashes between action-oriented realists and the authorities that constantly targeted the favelas for removal. Since at least the 1940s and 1950s, authorities feared that these "ignorant and manipulable" residents were prone to communism, and authorities believed these areas to be hotbeds of immorality and social deviance. Worse yet, these communities reflected poorly on the government as conspicuous and irrefutable visual evidence that the nation's political and economic systems were failing.[5] Thus, when the military dictatorship came into power, it ramped up the government's favela reduction and policing campaign. Benedita da Silva, who would become Brazil's first black female senator, began as a leader in her Chapéu Mangueira neighborhood association, and she experienced the unwanted police attention firsthand. She wrote that the government "unleashed a massive wave of repression against us," accusing community organizers of communist involvement even though she insisted that the PCB's influence was minimal. She later recalled: "The repression touched every part of our lives. We didn't have the same visibility as the intellectuals or middle class activists who went abroad into exile. We were exiled in our own country. We weren't allowed to sing our religious hymns or celebrate our festivals. . . . We couldn't keep minutes of our meetings because it was considered subversive to demand better living conditions like electricity, plumbing or paved roads." Facing possible imprisonment, torture, or death, many activists who worked to improve the conditions of and services for their communities went into hiding.[6]

Silva's story relates to the experiences of many action-oriented realists who confronted the dictatorship's racialized National Security Doctrine. While black community activists were "exile[d] in their own country," some of the nation's high-profile black leaders started to leave Brazil in 1968.[7] Authorities branded black activists, especially those who showed solidarity with African independence movements, as "black racist groups" and communists. Blacks as well as white intellectuals who addressed racism and countered the dictatorship's official denialist account of racial mixture were charged with racial "disaggregation," which presumably splintered Brazil's legendary and covetable racial cohesion. At certain points, the secret police outlawed race-based activism and suppressed realist dialogue. In 1969 the state was behind the effort to push into premature retirement three prominent, racially liberal white faculty members at the University of São Paulo, Brazil's most prestigious academic institution.[8] The secret police investigated black artists who destabilized the military regime's denial with their "bold blackness," artistic preferences, or realist messaging, such as the Brazilian soul music performers who consumed James Brown and the

US black power soundtrack.[9] The dictatorship took a hard line on the adherence to the narrative of miscegenation and racial harmony, and the realists who resisted—especially during the most repressive "years of lead" (1968–74)—often risked life and limb to do so.[10] Thus, for at least the second time in the twentieth century, a security milieu propped up by a repressive denial that was intolerant to blacks' quest for action-oriented racial democracy directly followed a period of political liberalization. This became a vicious cycle that plagued the Afro-Brazilian struggle during the twentieth century.

In the United States, the government's attempt to stave off the global spread of communism both benefited and hampered the postwar black freedom struggle. Chapter 1 dispels the popular belief that the communists' international racial campaign, which drew attention to US racism in order to discredit its liberal democracy, began during the Cold War. Still, the response of state and public obstructionists to postwar civil rights activists in the age of television provided communists with more effective free advertising than the Scottsboro case ever did. Indeed, the scenes of peaceful black protesters being attacked by angry white mobs, police dogs, and hoses strong enough to throw bodies to the ground shocked and outraged the world. The protests undercut the believability of denial; the entire world would have been firmly unconvinced by any suggestion that racism was not a problem in the United States. The international reaction to the violent repression of civil rights activists helped push Presidents Truman, Eisenhower, Kennedy, and Johnson to take concrete steps, such as passing civil rights legislation and sending out the National Guard to ensure the safety of children integrating schools. In other words, in the context of the Cold War, the mobilization of racial realists pressured the US government to defend its system of democracy to the world with action-oriented dissuasion. It hoped in part to dissuade those in newly or imminently independent African and Asian nations from aligning with the Soviets rather than with the US government, particularly because some of these countries were rich in raw materials essential for nuclear weapons. As part of the international dissuasion strategy, US policymakers borrowed another tactic from the earlier period, a strategy that also has been considered a postwar phenomenon: the use of cultural demarginalization to control the nation's racial democratic image across the globe. US policymakers also intended to dissuade civil rights activists from continuing their movement, as it exposed the depths and ugliness of US racial antagonism and inequality.[11]

The US-Soviet Union rivalry may have facilitated certain civil rights gains, but US realists also encountered the Cold War doctrine of containment, which, as Nikhil Singh has shown, stunted international antiracist aspirations. The policy prioritized the objective to contain communism to the Soviet Union and, as its main architect George Kennan articulated, to maintain the United States' disproportionate possession of global wealth. Singh argues that the "[w]artime conversations about the rights of racial minorities and colonial subjects, and their relationships to the projections of American national power, were in this context subordinated to a generalized anticommunism." With the emphasis on protecting US political and economic liberalism and confining communism, containment not only sidelined antiracist struggles but also discouraged them as potential destabilizers that could harm US interests. Therefore, although containment typically has been characterized as foreign policy, it also had strong repercussions for the domestic front, particularly in terms of race.[12] Like the Doctrine of National Security in Brazil, containment also reined in the spread and efficacy of action-oriented realism.

Domestically, containment may have been most evident in the ramping up of state-sponsored red-baiting and the blow to the struggle for economic justice. During the Cold War, US leftists faced an uphill battle fighting for racial equality, as McCarthyism took Martin Dies's anticommunist activities to new extremes. Senator Joseph McCarthy alleged the widespread infiltration of Soviet spies in the government, Hollywood, and universities, blacklisting the accused and creating a climate of intense paranoia and distrust that peaked in the United States during the 1950s. If Brazil had the power of a dictatorship to suppress communism, the United States had McCarthyism—which often cost people their reputation, social standing, and jobs—as an effective tool to subdue domestic leftist politics. In this environment, language of economic justice was tagged as Marxist doctrine and connected to the existential threat of nuclear war. The government even abandoned the New Deal's project of full employment and economic rights.[13] Those who fought to restructure the US (and indeed the global) economic system and who challenged racial inequalities under capitalism were perceived as threats to national security. Some blacks were self-proclaimed communists and leftists, including Claudia Jones, Vicki Garvin, and Paul Robeson; others, such as Martin Luther King Jr., were not. Like their Brazilian counterparts, many of these action-oriented black realists found themselves living abroad during the suffocating US Cold War years. Vicki Garvin chose to live several years in Nigeria, Ghana, and China, and Trinida-dian-born Claudia Jones was deported.[14]

To borrow the words of Benedita da Silva, activist and artist Paul Robeson, who made a living performing around the world, became an exile in his own country after the government withdrew his passport. It was revoked after Robeson made a public declaration at the 1949 Paris Peace Conference that was misconstrued, and he was labeled as a trai-tor who incited blacks to support the Soviet Union. As a result, Robeson and other black leaders were called to testify before the House Un-American Committee (the former HCUA, now HUAC) that Martin Dies had originally created in 1938. Black hero Jackie Robinson, the first African American to play in Major League Baseball, agreed to be the voice of dissuasion and took Robeson to task. HUAC hoped that Robinson's testimony would convince blacks to shun communism.[15] The decision to depict Robeson as black enemy of the state took a huge toll on his career and economic well-being, which had an adverse effect on his financial contributions to the civil rights movement. In general, the aggressive red-baiting hurt black realists profoundly, as contain-ment encouraged the mentality popularized by Dies and others in the 1930s that antiracist organizing and communism went hand in hand.

As we have seen, many of the Brazilian and US states' Cold War strategies had roots in the 1930s or the World War II era. Brazil's Doc-trine of National Security and the US policy of containment—which both had strong racial elements and consequences for the realist viewpoint—had ties to official anticommunist tactics of the 1930s. The analysis of these policies provides a fuller picture of the barriers to racial justice, particularly in societies that confuse discursive inclusivity with material and quantifiable equality. The parallels to the earlier period and the ways that Cold War policies continued to thwart action-oriented realists point to a distinct twentieth-century trend: the coexistence of widespread antiracist ideals with enduring racial inequity.

Although state-articulated racial democracy did not tend to be action-oriented and instead served purposes other than equality, the values it represented did matter. On their own, the values did not bring about substantial and tangible change, but the willingness of realist activists to confront opposition and even violence for the causes of eco-nomic and social justice have made a big impact. The shift toward inclusive nationalisms that occurred between 1930 and 1945 made activists' calls for equality resonate, and it allowed them to present their cases within a nationalist and patriotic framework, even if denialists repudiated that vision. Others have rejected the politics of nationalist respectability to forge a new path, knowing they would face a great deal of resistance but willing to be the pioneers for the next generations. Either way, one thing is for certain: the legacy of inclusive nationalism has less to do with what the state implements than with what the people make of it.

Notes

A NOTE ON TERMINOLOGY

1. Despite the historical existence of US biracial terms like *mestizo* and *mulatto,* the United States famously has functioned under the "one-drop rule," which renders black those people with African ancestry regardless of pheno-type.

2. Alberto, *Terms of Inclusion,* 22.

3. Hanchard, "Identity, Meaning, and the African-American."

4. Alberto, *Terms of Inclusion,* 22.

5. Souza, "Ações Afirmativas, cotas para negros nos concursos públicos fed-erais e os desafios para sua efetividade" (paper presented at the Latin American Studies Association Annual Conference, San Juan, Puerto Rico, May 30, 2015). Santos voiced his criticism of the term in an informal conversation after Souza's conference presentation and in an email correspondence with the author, dated January 13, 2019. Santos also explores the question of black identity in "Who Is Black in Brazil?"

INTRODUCTION

1. Chapter 5 provides a more thorough discussion of these claims.

2. Office of the Coordinator of Inter-American Affairs, *Brazil: Introduction to a Neighbor.*

3. I borrow the idea of unsteady racial progress from Klinkner and Smith, *Unsteady March.*

4. In Brazil this is based on the 1940 census, which unfortunately did not have a separate category for the indigenous. Brazil did not conduct a census in 1930, and the 1920 census did not include any questions about race or color. In terms of the black populations in both nations, it is worth noting that Brazil received an

estimated five million enslaved Africans, whereas the United States received about four hundred thousand. See Camargo, "Mensuração racial e campo estatístico"; Oliveira, "Pardos, mestiços ou caboclos"; and Silva and Barbosa, "População e estatísticas vitais," 50. Racial statistics from the US Census of 1930 can be found in the following official report: https://www2.census.gov/library/publications/decennial/1930/population-volume-2/16440598v2ch03.pdf. Estimates of the transatlantic slave trade can be found at www.slavevoyages.org.

5. Boris Fausto has written that during the 1930s, capitalism's promise of equal opportunity and abundance "entered a black hole from which it seemed helpless to emerge" and both capitalism and liberal democracies "seemed to be things of the past." See Fausto, *Concise History of Brazil*, 203. C.B. Macpherson stated that up to a certain point during the cold war, "liberal-democracy and capitalism [had always gone] together." Macpherson, *Real World of Democracy*, 4.

6. See Motta, *Em guarda contra o perigo vermelho*, 179–84.

7. See Brinkley, *Voices of Protest*; Warren, *Radio Priest*; and Schrecker, *Many Are the Crimes*, 12–15.

8. Andrews, *Blacks and Whites in São Paulo*, 144–45; Hine, Hine, and Harrold, *African American Odyssey*, vol. 2.

9. Painter, *Creating Black Americans*, 216–17; McDuffie, *Sojourning for Freedom*, 61. US communist activism was not limited to the northern region. For instance, see Kelley, *Hammer and Hoe*.

10. Leite, *Frente Negra Brasileira*, 75–76.

11. Domingues, "'O recinto sagrado.'"

12. See Macpherson, *Real World*, 12–34. Macpherson used the term "nonliberal democracy" to refer to communist states and to the post–World War II governments that were emerging in newly independent African and Asian nations.

13. Macpherson, 2–11.

14. Crick, *Democracy*, 3, 5.

15. For their discussions about the possibility of disconnecting liberalism and democracy, see Macpherson, *Real World*, 12–45; Chantal Mouffe, *Democratic Paradox*, 2–6, 18–19; and Laclau, *On Populist Reason*, 166–68. Macpherson is quoted on pp. 36–37. For more on Macpherson's position on Nazism and fascism, see Dahlquist, "The Young Macpherson."

16. Macpherson, *Real World*, 36–37. Mouffe, "Feminism, Citizenship and Radical Democratic Politics"; Davis, *Women, Race and Class*; Mills, *Racial Contract*; Pateman, *Sexual Contract*; and Hanchard, *Spectre of Race*. Macpherson argues that revolutions can generate unique ephemeral circumstances that make it acceptable to tolerate undemocratic regimes, even dictatorships, as nonliberal democracies if they are a temporary first step toward the fulfillment of the moral objectives partially laid out above.

17. McCann, *Brazilian-American Alliance*, 259–90.

18. Unabashed racism was much more mainstream in the US South than in São Paulo or Rio Grande do Sul.

19. Pincus and Novak, "Political History." Pincus and Novak state that "subjects and citizens themselves turn to the state precisely because its coercive

power can aid in implementing particular social and ideological visions[.]" These "coercive powers and capabilities of law and statecraft" are actions that go beyond rhetoric.

20. Nascimento, "Myth of Racial Democracy," 380. Black communist Édison Carneiro would make a similar accusation. See Silva de Lima, "Comunismo contra o racismo," 210.

21. Young, "Linguistic Turn, Materialism and Race," 336.

22. Gary Gerstle uses the term "racial nationalism" instead. For Gerstle, racial nationalists understand the nation "in ethnoracial terms, as a people held together by common blood and skin color and by an inherited fitness for self-government." I deploy "racial nationalism" as a descriptor for generic race-based nationalist ideas. Gerstle, *American Crucible*, 4.

23. Horsman, *Race and Manifest Destiny*, 2.

24. Gerstle, *American Crucible*, 6–7, 14–43.

25. See Jacobson, *Whiteness of a Different Color*. For more on Social Darwinism in the United States, see Degler, *In Search of Human Nature*.

26. Rodrigues, *As raças humanas e a responsabilidade penal no Brasil*; Rodrigues, *O animismo fetichista dos negros bahianos*.

27. Stepan, *Hour of Eugenics*, 135. See also Schwarcz, *Spectacle of the Races*.

28. See Skidmore, *Black into White*; Domingues, *Uma história não contada*; Santos, "Historical Roots of 'Whitening'"; Hofbauer, *Uma história de branqueamento*; and Borges, "Recognition of Afro-Brazilian Symbols," 62.

29. Weinstein, *Color of Modernity*, 87–92.

30. Decreto n° 528, Capítulo 1, Art. 1°. See http://www2.camara.leg.br /legin/fed/decret/1824–1899/decreto-528-28-junho-1890-506935-publicacao-original-1-pe.html (accessed December 2018).

31. Andrews, *Blacks and Whites*, 136–44; Meade and Pirio, "Afro-American 'Eldorado'"; Gomes and Fagundes, "'Idiossincrasias cromáticas'"; and Alberto, *Terms of Inclusion*, 42–44. Gomes and Fagundes also discuss the international labor force that helped build the Madeira-Mamoré railroad in the Amazon forest. Over twenty-one thousand foreign workers arrived between 1907 and 1912, most coming from the West Indies, especially Barbados. See Gomes and Fagundes, "'Idiossincrasias cromáticas,'" 206–8.

32. See Skidmore, *Black into White*, 130. See also Oliveira, *O Brasil dos imigrantes*. For more on immigration and national identity, see Lesser, *Negotiating National Identity*.

33. See Ngai, *Impossible Subjects*, 21–90. Natalia Molina also discusses the ways in which Mexicans were legally white but socially and culturally marked as "other." See Molina, *How Race Is Made*, 2.

34. Holt, foreword to *Race and Nation*, x.

35. Seigel, *Uneven Encounters*, 9, 190; Ferrara, "A imprensa negra paulista," 201; and Butler, *Freedoms Given*, 90–91.

36. Alberto, *Terms of Inclusion*, 69–71, 139; Zuburan, "Narrativas étnico-raciais e de gênero na campanha ao monumento da 'Mãe Preta'"; Seigel, *Uneven Encounters*, 213–17, 221. Seigel shows that some Afro-Brazilians did seek to

distance modern blacks from the premodern, submissive stereotype of the Mãe
Preta. Okezi Otovo also analyzes the Mãe Preta as a perceived "threat" to the
public health of elite whites in Bahia. See Otovo, *Progressive Mothers*, 39–43.

37. The Centro Cívico Palmares was not alone. Black men and women
founded at least 248 organizations in São Paulo, Porto Alegre, and Pelotas
alone between abolition and 1937. See Domingues, "Movimento Negro
Brasileiro."

38. Butler, *Freedoms Given*, 67–128; Fernandes, *A integração do negro*, vol.
2, 1–95; and Gomes, *Negros e política*, 30–47.

39. Gallicchio, *African American Encounter*, 6–29.

40. There are many excellent studies on this movement. Two classics include
Lewis, *When Harlem Was in Vogue*, and Wall, *Women of Harlem Renaissance*.
Scholarship that examines the cultural renaissance outside of Harlem includes
Baldwin and Makalani, *Escape from New York*, and Edwards, *Practice of
Diaspora*.

41. James, *Garvey, Garveyism, and Antinomies*, 179–80. Garveyism was
not limited to northern and urban locales like Harlem and Chicago. See, for
instance, Rolinson, *Grassroots Garveyism*.

42. Seigel, *Uneven Encounters*, 9, 180–82, 192–205, 222–34; Butler,
Freedoms Given, 108, 110; and Pereira, "'O mundo negro,'" 113–14.

43. Alberto, *Terms of Inclusion*, 64–66.

44. For an analysis of the cannibalist theme in Brazilian modernism, see
Boaventura, *A vanguarda antropofágica*; and Andrade, *Manifesto antropófagos e outros textos*.

45. See Borges, "Recognition of Afro-Brazilian Symbols," 59.

46. See Hertzman, *Making Samba*, 49–50, 97. For more on the *cronistas*, or
writers and journalists, see Chazkel, "Beyond Law and Order."

47. Domingues, "'Este samba selvagem'"; and Seigel, *Uneven Encounters*,
69, 200–201. The Brazilian black press did not universally dislike the Charleston, but most of the black press looked upon it negatively and associated the
Charleston with things like degeneracy. Some considered it modern art and/or
the "apotheosis of the Afro-Diasporic culture in the transatlantic world." See
Domingues, 196.

48. See Vianna, *Mystery of Samba*, 1–9; Seigel, *Uneven Encounters*, 123–35;
and Hertzman, *Making Samba*, 107–13.

49. Barlow, *Voice Over*, 20. See also Chauncey, *Gay New York*, 246–47; and
Lewis, *When Harlem Was in Vogue*.

50. Kallen, *Culture and Democracy*; Ngai, *Impossible Subjects*, 231.

51. Marc Hertzman shows that contrary to long-held beliefs, samba was not
formally illegal. See Hertzman, *Making Samba*, 31–65.

52. Querino, *O colono preto*; Querino, *Costumes africanos no Brasil*;
Alberto, *Terms of Inclusion*, 113–16. Arthur Ramos edited and wrote the preface to *Costumes africanos*—a collection of Querino's work—in 1938. Ramos
praised Querino and credited him with being the "only voice" during a pro-
longed period that challenged Rodrigues with a counternarrative about blacks'
positive contribution to Brazilian society. Ramos, preface and notes in *Costumes africanos*, 5.

53. US deputy commissioner general, Brazilian Centennial Exposition, letter to Theodore Mare, May 27, 1922, file folder, Application (Non Portuguese), L-R, 112.032, record group 43, Administrative Correspondence, 1922–1923, 112.022–112.064 Administration, box 5, National Archives and Records Administration (hereafter NARA).

54. For more on State Department–sponsored jazz tours, see Von Eschen, *Satchmo Blows Up the World;* and Davenport, *Jazz Diplomacy.*

55. Savage, *Broadcasting Freedom,* 103. *Freedom's People* aired in 1941 and 1942. As Savage argues, this and similar productions marked the beginning of the government's shift away from the "nationalist strategy of exclusion [that] characterized the period" and toward one of ideological inclusion (45).

56. See Cohen, *Making a New Deal;* and Higham, *Strangers in the Land.* Matthew Frye Jacobson also provides a great historical analysis of white immigrant racial categorization in *Whiteness of a Different Color.*

57. In 1938 the US Office of Education produced the radio broadcast *Americans All, Immigrants All* to encourage tolerance and inclusiveness. The need for national unity for the war effort was among the primary instigations for the show, which demonstrated the contribution groups such as immigrants and African Americans had made to US life and society. See Savage, *Broadcasting Freedom,* 21–62.

58. Ngai, *Impossible Subjects,* 231.

59. Gerstle, *American Crucible,* 8–9. Civic nationalism is very similar to my racial democracy, but its definition of US democracy is much more specific than I offer, since I am dealing with movements and actors that claimed democracy but not necessarily egalitarian ideals. In other words, I focus not on the egalitarian virtues of US democracy, as civic nationalism does, but on the racial pluralist values of those who invoked and interpreted democracy in myriad ways. This explains why Gerstle and I slightly diverge on what is and is not racist (my racially exclusive) nationalism, as the discussion of Martin Dies in chapter 2 will demonstrate. Gerstle borrowed the term "civic nationalism" from Michael Ignatieff, who discusses the distinction between civic and ethnic nationalisms in *Blood and Belonging,* 5–9.

60. See Gerstle, *American Crucible,* 128–267; and Stuckey, *Defining Americans,* 200.

61. See Andrews, *Blacks and Whites,* 151. See also de Almeida, da Silva, and Gonçalves, *Presos políticos e perseguidos estrangeiros.*

62. See Borges, "Recognition of Afro-Brazilian Symbols"; and Alberto, *Terms of Inclusion,* 7–11. Lilia Moritz Schwarcz also examines the ways that the indigenous occupied a central role in nationalist symbolism after Brazil became an independent monarchy in 1822. When they appeared, blacks were portrayed as being loyal "submissive objects." See Schwarcz, "Mestizo and Tropical Country." See also von Martius and Rodrigues, "Como se deve escrever a história do Brasil"; and Guimarães, "Nação e civilização nos trópicos."

63. See Domingues, "O mito da democracia racial e a mestiçagem no Brasil"; and Alberto, *Terms of Inclusion,* 114.

64. Freyre, *Masters and the Slaves,* xxx.

65. Freyre, 46.

66. Freyre, 71.

67. Freyre.

68. Vianna, *Mystery of Samba,* 53.

69. See Guimarães, "Democracia racial," www.fflch.usp.br/sociologia/asag /Democracia%20racial.pdf, accessed November 4, 2009. This article was first published in English as "Racial Democracy" in Souza and Sinder, *Imagining Brazil.*

70. Freyre, *Casa-grande e senzala,* x–xi. All translations are mine unless otherwise noted.

71. See Pallares-Burke, *Gilberto Freyre,* 263–411. Freyre singled out Franklin H. Giddings, but Pallares-Burke discusses other intellectuals who left their mark on Freyre, and she shows that he did not take to Boasian thought quickly.

72. Borges, "Brazilian Social Thought," 148; Mesquita, "O projeto regionalista de Gilberto Freyre e o Estado Novo," 118–19; Seigel, *Uneven Encounters,* 221; Weinstein, "Racializing Regional Difference," 238; Weinstein, *Color of Modernity,* 13–14; Costa, conclusion to *Brazilian Empire;* Alberto, *Terms of Inclusion,* 21; Guimarães, *Classes,* 137–68.

73. In addition to the studies mentioned above, other scholars who also challenge Freyre-centrism and the myth paradigm are Hertzman, *Making Samba;* Sheriff, *Dreaming Equality;* Guimarães, *Classes;* Maio, "Tempo controverso"; Dávila, *Hotel Trópico;* and McCann, *Hello, Hello Brazil.*

74. See Bastide and Fernandes, *Brancos e negros em São Paulo;* and Fernandes, *Negro in Brazilian Society.* There are innumerable studies in multiple disciplines that have illuminated various issues related to racial inequality, discrimination, and exploitation in Brazil. I refer the reader to the bibliography, where many are cited, but a few of the most recent English-language books are Alves, *Anti-Black City;* Caldwell, *Health Equity in Brazil;* Hordge-Freeman, *Color of Love;* Larkins, *Spectacular Favela;* Mitchell, *Constellations of Inequality;* Mitchell-Walthour, *Politics of Blackness;* Otovo, *Progressive Mothers;* Perry, *Black Women against the Land Grab;* Smith, *Afro-Paradise;* Paschel, *Becoming Black Political Subjects;* and Williams, *Sex Tourism in Bahia.*

75. Schneider, "Iberismo e luso-tropicalismo na obra de Gilberto Freyre"; Guimarães, "Democracia racial," 4–6; Guimarães, *Classes,* 151–54; Pandolfi, introduction to *Repensando o Estado Novo,* 11. During and after its hostilities, Freyre and others explicitly connected this discussion of Brazilian racial exceptionalism to World War II. See Castelo, "Uma incursão no lusotropicalismo de Gilberto Freyre," 267; and Guimarães, *Classes,* 142–51.

CHAPTER 1

1. "Scottsboro Boys Shall Not Die," in *Songs of the People,* 44; and "Hino do Brasileiro pobre," in Vianna, *Pão, Terra e Liberdade,* 553–54.

2. See Dudziak, *Cold War Civil Rights.*

3. A brief discussion of Comintern's international Scottsboro campaign can be found in Weiss, *Framing a Radical African Atlantic,* 392–96.

4. Gilmore, *Defying Dixie,* 7.

5. Makalani, *In the Cause of Freedom*, 4. The still canonical work on black Caribbean radicals in the United States is James, *Holding Aloft the Banner*. See also Adi, *Pan-Africanism and Communism*.

6. Chadarevian, "Raça, classe e revolução no Partido Comunista Brasileiro," 257. Chadarevian writes that although the PCB had problematized the status quo of the indigenous, the party neither included Afro-Brazilians in this discussion nor identified racism as a national problem until the early 1930s. It should be noted that this book does revise Chadarevian's periodization. Chadarevian contends that the PCB largely ignored the racial question until 1934. However, at least part of the PCB had already begun to circulate its antiracist policy, including self-determination, by 1932.

7. Aruã Silva de Lima recently has written what is, to my knowledge, the first lengthy study on this topic for the period in question. See Silva de Lima, "Comunismo contra o racismo." See also Anita Leocádia Prestes, "A conferência dos Partidos Comunistas da América do Sul e do Caribe (Moscou, Outubro/1934) e os Levantes de Novembro de 1935 no Brasil." Prestes is the daughter of PCB communist leaders Luís Carlos Prestes and Olga Benário Prestes, whom the Nazis killed five years after she gave birth to Anita in a concentration camp. Anita was given to her Brazilian grandmother when she was fourteen months old.

8. Chadarevian, "Raça, classe e revolução no Partido Comunista Brasileiro," 256.

9. See José Correia Leite's memoir, . . . *E disse*, 139–40. Leite says that black communists Luiz Lobato and Solano Trindade did not believe that a "racial nature" accounted for the difficulties and injustices Afro-descendants confronted. Instead, Leite recalls, they felt it was a result of "a class problem, an economic problem." Leite also attended socialist and communist meetings in the 1930s where the same class analysis was applied in debates about the plight of Afro-Brazilians. See Lima, "Comunismo contra o racismo," 110.

10. Chadarevian argues that Carneiro's essay can be considered "the first Marxist analysis of the black issue in Brazil." Chadarevian, "Raça, classe e revolução no Partido Comunista Brasileiro," 265.

11. Lima, "Comunismo contra o racismo," 12–13.

12. See Makalani, *In the Cause of Freedom*, 152–53; Weiss, *Framing a Radical African Atlantic*, 120; Gilmore, *Defying Dixie*, 101–2.

13. For another Brazilian example of international race-based communist solidarity, see Graham, "A virada antirracista do Partido Comunista do Brasil," 363–70.

14. Wilson Record assesses the complicated way in which the party in the United States and its black members dealt with black organizations, sometimes reaching out to them even while denouncing them rhetorically. See Record, *Negro and the Communist Party*.

15. Rebelo, *Jornal "A classe operária,"* 31–32.

16. The "second emancipation" refers to blacks liberating themselves from the land and rural labor in order to seek a new life in the urban, industrial north. Grossman, *Land of Hope*, 19.

17. Vladimir Lenin's first theses on the subject in 1920 stated: "*Only the urban and industrial proletariat,* led by the Communist Party, can liberate the working masses." Lenin, "Preliminary Draft Theses," 152.

18. "Al Comite Provisional del Socorro Rojo del Brasil," instructions from the Executive Committee of the International Red Aid to the Socorro Vermelho do Brasil, April 28, 1931, p. 2, document 1250, Coleção Internacional Comunista, CEDEM (CIC/CEDEM); and "Relatório à I.C. apresentado pela delegação brasileira por ocasião do IV Congresso da I.S.V.," p. 4, 1928, CIC/CEDEM.

19. The October 26, 1928, resolution was reproduced in *The Communist Position on the Negro Question: Self-Determination for the Black Belt* (New York: Workers Library Publishers), 58, Solomon and Kaufman Research Files on African Americans and Communism, file: Communist Party, 1931–1933, box 1, Tamiment Library and Robert F. Wagner Labor Archives, New York University (hereafter SKF/Tam). The latter document has no date, but based upon the articles it cites, it must have been published in, or shortly after, 1932.

20. See Gilmore, *Defying Dixie,* 47; Robinson, *Black Marxism,* 221–22; Turner, chaps. 5–7 in *Caribbean Crusaders,* 123–224.

21. Negro Department of the Central Committee of the Communist Party of the USA, "Outline for the Discussion of the Negro Question" (undated), file: Communist Party, 1929–1931, box 1, SKF/Tam.

22. South American Bureau of the Communist International, "Tesis del Bureau Sudamericano Sobre la Situación del Brasil y las Tareas del Partido Comunista" (undated), 20, CIC/CEDEM. The document does not have a date, but the finding aid suggests it may have been published in 1931.

23. Makalani, *In the Cause of Freedom,* 16.

24. Weiss, *Framing a Radical African Atlantic,* 120–22. With the input of "Coloured" ANC and CP of South Africa leader James La Guma, the Comintern did adopt a Native or Black Republic resolution for South Africa in 1927. See Adi, *Pan-Africanism and Communism,* 53–59.

25. The ABB had, at most, eight thousand members at its peak. Its international agenda was "liberating Africa, ending colonialism and racial oppression, and contributing to the cause of freedom everywhere," according to Makalani, *In the Cause of Freedom,* 45. Its domestic platform included black enfranchisement in the South, equal rights for blacks, armed defense against lynching, and the end of legalized segregation. See Kelley, *Race Rebels,* 106.

26. Makalani, *In the Cause of Freedom,* 5, 84, 99–101, 114, 120, 122; Gilmore, *Defying Dixie,* 41.

27. See Adi, *Pan-Africanism and Communism,* 22–29; and Makalani, *In the Cause of Freedom,* 90–97.

28. Makalani, 90–97, 248.

29. Makalani, 90–97.

30. The UNIA had at least seven hundred branches in thirty-eight states. For a good study of Garveyism, see James, *Garvey, Garveyism, and Antinomies;* and Taylor, *Veiled Garvey.*

31. Hall/Haywood, *Black Communist in the Freedom Struggle,* 110; Makalani, *In the Cause of Freedom,* 48.

32. Makalani, 67, 96. Garvey's newfound conservatism seems to have been connected to the Department of Justice's accusations of sedition and refusal to allow him to enter the United States for several months.

33. Kelley, *Race Rebels*, 107; Makalani, *In the Cause of Freedom*, 96.

34. See Naison, *Communists in Harlem*, 80.

35. Kelley, *Race Rebels*, 107; Robinson, *Black Marxism*, 223–24; Makalani, *In the Cause of Freedom*, 67, 120–31.

36. Good explanations of the self-determination policy (which was known by other monikers as well, including the Black Belt thesis) can be found in the CPUSA Negro Department's "Outline for the Discussion of the Negro Question," in Haywood, *Black Bolshevik*, 218–43; and in Adi, *Pan-Africanism and Communism*, 59–66, 70–72.

37. Gore, *Radicalism at the Crossroads*, 21–32; Kelley, *Race Rebels*, 114; Adi, *Pan-Africanism and Communism*, 78; and McDuffie, *Sojourning for Freedom*, 44, 50.

38. Degras, *Communist International*, vol. 2, 519. Excerpts are from the "Programme of the Communist International adopted at its Sixth Congress" (September 1, 1928). The Comintern continued to express concern over the impact of Garveyism in later years, as evidenced by its October 26, 1930, ECCI Political Secretariat resolution on the Negro question in the United States. See Degras, vol. 3, 132–34.

39. Negro Department of the Central Committee of the Communist Party of the USA, "Outline for the Discussion of the Negro Question" (undated), 4, 7–8, file: Communist Party, 1929–1931, box 1, SKF/Tam.

40. See Kelley, *Race Rebels*, 106. Briggs's quote is also cited in Kelley, 106. For Briggs's evolving ideas about the location of the "colored autonomous state," see Hall/Haywood, *Black Communist in the Freedom Struggle*, 105–6. Briggs first published an article on the subject in 1917.

41. Holger Weiss points out that the self-determination policy was reassessed in 1930 and that the communists opted to lighten their stance, ceasing to *demand* a "Negro Soviet Republic" but continuing to assert the right of self-determination for blacks if they so chose. He also states that the language in the 1928 resolution that anoints US black communists as the leaders of the African Diaspora was excluded in 1930. See Weiss, *Framing a Radical African Atlantic*, 120–22.

42. Degras, *Communist International*, vol. 2, 556–57.

43. International Trade Union Committee of Negro Workers of the RILU, "A Trade Union Program of Action for Negro Workers," in Foner and Shapiro, *American Communism and Black Americans*, 13.

44. James S. Allen, "The American Negro" (New York: International Pamphlets, 1932), 19–20, folder: Communist Party, 1931–1933, box 1, SKF/Tam.

45. McDuffie, *Sojourning for Freedom*, 29–30, 40–42, 59; Turner, *Caribbean Crusaders*, 164–67. The Huiswoud quote is in Turner, *Caribbean Crusaders*, 167.

46. Degras, *Communist International*, vol. 3, 134 (italics in the original). This excerpt is from the ECCI Political Secretariat's 1930 Resolution on the Negro Question.

47. Harry Haywood, "The Road to Negro Liberation: Report to the Eighth Convention of the Communist Party of the USA" (New York: Workers Library Publishers, 1934), 5, 9, 11, folder: Communist Party, 1933–1936, box 1, SKF/ Tam.

48. McNeil, *Groundwork,* 107.

49. McDuffie, *Sojourning for Freedom,* 59–60. The other two factors were travel to the Soviet Union and the Great Depression. Dayo Gore also notes that the Scottsboro case pulled many blacks into the CPUSA and specifically cites Claudia Jones and Audley Moore. See Gore, *Radicalism at the Crossroads,* 21, 29.

50. League of the Struggle for Negro Rights, *Equality Land and Freedom,* 12–13.

51. Haywood, *Road to Negro Liberation,* 62.

52. McDuffie, *Sojourning for Freedom,* 83. McDuffie also points out that black women communists often did not find it contradictory to work with "traditional black protest groups," even if they disagreed with much of their social and political thought (59).

53. See Haywood, *Black Bolshevik,* 439–40. For a broad discussion of the LSNR, see Record, *Negro and the Communist Party,* 77–83.

54. See Caballero, *Latin America and the Comintern,* 88.

55. Quoted in Record, *Negro and the Communist Party,* 58.

56. See Kelley, *Race Rebels,* 104–8, 121–58; Makalani, *In the Cause of Freedom,* 96; and Adi, *Pan-Africanism and Communism.*

57. Haywood, *Black Bolshevik,* 124–25; and Makalani, *In the Cause of Freedom,* 96–97.

58. Andreucci, "Idéias malditas," in *Cultura amordaçada,* 144. For a discussion of Comintern's so-called "discovery" of Latin America, see Pinheiro, *Estratégias da ilusão,* 147–96.

59. See Pinheiro and Hall, *A classe operária no Brasil,* 309–13; Caballero, *Latin America and the Comintern,* 158.

60. Caballero, 54–58.

61. See Jules Humbert-Droz, letter to Jenny Humbert-Droz, from the ship *Andes,* May 2, 1929, in Pinheiro and Hall, *A classe operária no Brasil,* 310. This compilation of original documents was translated into Portuguese. The translation from Portuguese into English is mine.

62. Sección Sudamericana de la Internacional Comunista, *El movimiento revolucionário Latino Americano* (Buenos Aires: La Correspondencia Sudamericana, 1929), 271, 302. According to published facts about this meeting, Brazil had the second highest number of delegates, with four, second only to host Argentina, which was documented as having eight. See Caballero, *Latin America and the Comintern,* 54–58.

63. Lima, "Comunismo contra o racismo," 124–31. Under Guralsky's leadership, Comintern's Latin American Secretariat would become the South American Bureau.

64. Lima, 126.

65. Jules Humbert-Droz, letter to Jenny Humbert-Droz, from the ship *Andes,* May 2, 1929, in Pinheiro and Hall, *A classe operária no Brasil,* 309–13.

66. Sección Sudamericana de la Internacional Comunista, *El movimiento revolucionário Latino Americano,* 271, 302.

67. Lima, "Comunismo contra o racismo," 118–31.

68. Lima, 111.

69. Octávio Brandão, letter to "Camaradas do B.P.," dated October 21, 1931, p. 2, document 270; questionnaire from Octávio Brandão to "Camaradas," dated October 23, 1931, document 266, CIC/CEDEM; and Carneiro, "Situação do negro no Brasil," 240 (italics in questionnaire mine). For more on Brandão's reflections on his and the PCB's evolution on the racial question, see Lima, "Comunismo contra o racismo," 217–27.

70. Quoted in Chadarevian, "Raça, classe e revolução no Partido Comunista Brasileiro," 261–63.

71. Gomes, *Negros e política,* 56, 48.

72. See Domingues, "'O caminho da verdadeira emancipação,'" 159.

73. Arlindo Veiga dos Santos's explanation of this idea is in Fernandes, *A integração do negro na sociedade de classes,* 41.

74. Butler, *Freedoms Given,* 48, 59–66, 115–28.

75. This figure comes from Chadarevian, "Raça, classe e revolução no Partido Comunista Brasileiro," 263.

76. Chadarevian, 257.

77. For instance, see Butler, *Freedoms Given,* 120.

78. Those affiliated with the movement later discussed the FNB's work against many such cases. For instance, see Lucrécio in *Frente Negra Brasileira,* 56; and Nascimento, *Memórias do exílio,* 28.

79. "Os negros são expulsos dos rinks burgueses," *A Classe operária,* December 15, 1931, 2, Fundo Astrojildo Pereira, CEDEM (FAP/CEDEM).

80. The pamphlet must be referring to the battalions of the Legião Negra, or the Black Legion, which blacks organized themselves to participate in the Constitutionalist War. The Black Legion was in part an expression of racial pride and a desire to prove blacks' valor and make claims to equal citizenship. Legionnaires were also drawn to the Legion for the material benefits it offered. See Domingues, "Os 'pérolas negras'"; Weinstein, *The Color of Modernity,* 133–46.

81. O Partido Comunista do Brasil (Região Rio de Janeiro), "A Todos os Trabalhadores Negros e ao Proletariado em Geral!," Panfletos Apreendidos, Delegacia Especial de Segurança Política e Social (DESPS), 1933–44, Arquivo Público do Estado do Rio de Janeiro (hereafter APERJ); Comitê Regional do Rio de Janeiro do Socorro Vermelho do Brasil, "Trabalhadores Negros!," 1934, document 1263, FAP/CEDEM. The former document does not have a date, but information provided in the text indicates that it was published in 1932 or 1933, most likely the latter.

82. O Partido Comunista do Brasil (Região Rio de Janeiro), "A Todos os Trabalhadores Negros e ao Proletariado em Geral!"; Panfleto n° 863, "Manifesto Programma do Partido Communista do Brasil ao Povo Trabalhador," no date, pp. 2–4, DESPS, 1933–44, APERJ (this pamphlet was likely published in the early 1930s); and Comitê Regional do Rio de Janeiro do Socorro Vermelho do Brasil, "Trabalhadores Negros!" Brazilian Trotskyites took the PCB to task

for this self-determination line, calling the PCB racist separatists. See Dulles, *Anarchists and Communists*, 473–74.

83. Letter from the Secretariado da América do Sul e Central do Comitê Executivo do Internacional Comunista to the Comitê Central do Partido Comunista do Brasil (likely January 1933), p. 4, document 279, FAP/CEDEM; letter stamped April 11, 1935, p. 4, document 288, FAP/CEDEM.

84. Hugh Gibson, ambassador to Brazil, memo to secretary of state, Rio de Janeiro, October 22, 1934, file folder 4102B Brazil, 1925–1936, box 201, Record Group 263, NARA.

85. *Tese do Bureau Sul-Americano da Internacional Juvenil Comunista à Federação da Juventude Comunista do Brasil*, 1931, p. 48; and Resoluções Adoptadas pelo 5° Plenum do Partido Comunista do Brasil (Séc. Brás. da Internacional Comunista) (Rio de Janeiro: Editorial "Soviet," 1932), 49, Livros Apreendidos, Polícia Política, 1933–1983, APERJ.

86. "Os negros são expulsos dos rinks burgueses"; Comitê Regional do Rio de Janeiro do Socorro Vermelho do Brasil, "Trabalhadores Negros!"

87. "Carta do Secretariado da América do Sul e do Centro [sic] ao C. C. do P. C. B." (April 29, 1933), p. 6, document 281, FAP/CEDEM.

88. Vargas did, in fact, hold secret-ballot elections in 1933 for a constituent assembly that elected him to a four-year term and drew up a constitution in 1934 that was, as indicated, more politically liberal and socially responsible. However, Vargas would cancel the scheduled 1938 elections, dismantle Congress, and begin his eight-year Estado Novo dictatorship in 1937.

89. Holt, Adler, and Holland, *Theses, Resolutions and Manifestos*, 7, 41.

90. Holt, Adler, and Holland, 7, 12–14, 41–42. Herbert Aptheker also notes the Marxists' self-perceived struggle for democracy in "Marxism, Democracy, and Science," in Aptheker, *Marxism and Democracy*, 18.

91. Engels's and Marx's perspectives on democracy evolved over time, shifting from praise to denunciation, but Lenin married these two outlooks. Lenin simultaneously attacked capitalist democracy as fraudulent and relied on the communist definition of "true democracy." Here, Lenin followed Engels's belief that true "democracy nowadays is communism[,] that social equality of rights is implicit in democracy." Engels also wrote, "Democracy has as its necessary consequence the political rule of the proletariat, and the political rule of the proletariat is the first condition for all communist measures." Lenin conceived democratic structures in the proletarian dictatorship in the form of soviets, local councils elected by the working class. Quotes in Levin, *Marx, Engels and Liberal Democracy*, 16–17, 19–20.

92. Panfleto n° 330, "Por um 13 de maio de protesto contra a falsa libertação dos negros no Brasil!," by O Comitê Regional do D. Federal do Partido Comunista do Brasil (Seção Internacional Comunista), no date, Panfletos Apreendidos, DESPS, 1933–1944, APERJ; and Panfleto n° 372, "Trabalhadores! Escravos," by the Secção R. da I.C. (A Cellula E. 15 do P.C.B.), no date, Panfletos Apreendidos, Delegacia Especial de Segurança Política e Social (DESPS), 1933–1944, APERJ.

93. Panfleto n° 330, "Por um 13 de maio de protesto contra a falsa libertação dos negros no Brasil!," by O Comitê Regional do D. Federal do Partido Comu-

nista do Brasil (Seção Internacional Comunista), no date, Panfletos Apreendidos, DESPS, 1933–1944, APERJ; and Panfleto n° 904, "A Todos os Trabalhadores Negros e ao Proletariado em Geral!"

94. Panfleto n° 904, "A Todos os Trabalhadores Negros e ao Proletariado em Geral!" For more on Palmares, see Gomes, *Palmares*.

95. Panfleto n° 372, "Trabalhadores! Escravos," by the Secção R. da I.C. (A Cellula E. 15 do P.C.B.), no date, Panfletos Apreendidos, Delegacia Especial de Segurança Política e Social (DESPS), 1933–1944, APERJ; and Panfleto n° 330, "Por um 13 de Maio de protesto contra a falsa libertação dos negros no Brasil!," by O Comitê Regional do D. Federal do Partido Comunista do Brasil (Seção Internacional Comunista), no date, Panfletos Apreendidos, DESPS, 1933–1944, APERJ; and Panfleto n° 904, "A Todos os Trabalhadores Negros e ao Proletariado em Geral!"; Carneiro, "Situação do negro no Brasil," 237.

96. *Communist International,* vol. 3, 126–27.

97. Testimony of Ralph de Sola, November 31, 1938, *Investigation of Un-American Propaganda Activities in the United States,* Hearings before a Special Committee on Un-American Activities, House of Representatives, 75th Cong., Third Sess. on H. Res. 282, vol. 3 (Washington, DC: US Government Printing Office, 1939), 2397, 2412–13. De Sola was a former member of the CPUSA and had written natural history articles and cartoons for the *New Pioneer* for two and a half years. He testified that although the *New Pioneer* did not state so outright, it was a communist product and the Young Communist League was responsible for its publication.

98. Negro Department of the Central Committee of the Communist Party of the USA, "Outline for the Discussion of the Negro Question" (undated), p. 1, file: Communist Party, 1929–1931, box 1, SKF/Tam.

99. Negro Department of the Central Committee of the Communist Party of the USA, "Outline for the Discussion of the Negro Question," 1–2.

100. Communist International, *Theses, Resolutions and Manifestos,* 13, 330–31.

101. Quoted in Haywood, *Black Bolshevik,* 336.

102. Haywood, "Theoretical Defenders of White Chauvinism in the Labor Movement," in *Communist Position on the Negro Question,* 50. The booklet notes that this article also appeared in the *Communist* magazine in June 1931.

103. See, for instance, CPUSA General Secretary Earl Browder's piece, "Theoretical Defenders of White Chauvinism in the Labor Movement," in *Communist Position on the Negro Question,* 3–18. This piece, which had also been a speech, was meant to reflect the CPUSA Central Committee's views on this question.

104. Negro Department of the Central Committee of the Communist Party of the USA, "Outline for the Discussion of the Negro Question," p. 5, folder: Communist Party, 1931–1933, box 1, SKF/Tam (underlining in the original).

105. Negro Department of the Central Committee of the Communist Party of the USA, "Outline for the Discussion of the Negro Question," p. 11.

106. James S. Allen, "The American Negro" (New York: International Pamphlets, 1932), 29–30, folder: Communist Party, 1931–1933, box 1, SKF/Tam; and Bush, *End of White World Supremacy*, 226.

107. Solomon, *Cry Was Unity*, 113.

108. Lima, "Comunismo contra o racismo," 209–10.

109. Panfleto n° 863, "Manifesto Programma do Partido Communista do Brasil ao Povo Trabalhador," no date, p. 4, DESPS, 1933–44, APERJ. This pamphlet was likely published in the early 1930s.

110. On March 25, 1931, nine black teenagers were arrested for fighting with a group of white teenagers on a train and were taken to a jail in Scottsboro, Alabama. Upon their arrest, the young black men were also charged falsely (as one of the alleged victims later confessed) with raping two white women who were discovered on the train with them. All of the Scottsboro Nine were convicted of rape, and eight of them were sentenced to death. Two US Supreme Court decisions reversed the convictions, but seven retrials all resulted in guilty verdicts. It was not until 1950 that the final Scottsboro Boy, by then a man, was released from jail. See Goodman, *Stories of Scottsboro*.

111. Bastide and Fernandes, *Brancos e Negros em São Paulo*, 226; and Lima, "Comunismo contra o racismo," 110. Bastide writes that after 1914–18, blacks began to have consciousness about their lot and gave credit in part to the "socialist and communist parties that actively did propaganda among the proletariat of color, particularly on the occasion of the case of Scottsboro" (my translation).

112. Panfleto n° 446, "Abaixo a Justiça Burguesa de Classe!," by the C.C. [likely "Comitê Central"] do Socorro Vermelho Internacional, no date, Panfletos Apreendidos, Delegacia Especial de Segurança Política e Social (DESPS), 1933–1944, APERJ.

113. Hugh Gibson, ambassador to Brazil, to secretary of state, Rio de Janeiro, August 22, 1933, Brazil file, file folder 4102B Brazil, 1925–1936, box 201, Record Group 263, Murphy Collection, NARA (embassy's translation). The embassy translated the name of the group as International Red Relief, but it was, in fact, the International Red Aid (Socorro Vermelho Internacional). The Russian acronym for this organization was MOPR, and its affiliate in the United States was the ILD.

114. "Brazilian Toilers Express Solidarity with American Workers," *Daily Worker*, December 2, 1935, 4102B Brazil, 1925–1936, box 201, RG 263, Murphy Collection, NARA. The *Daily Worker* did not say whether the original letter was written in English or if this was a translation.

115. Panfleto n° 904, "A Todos os Trabalhadores Negros e ao Proletariado em Geral!"

116. Panfleto n° 330, "Por um 13 de Maio de protesto contra a falsa libertação dos negros no Brasil!," by O Comitê Regional do D. Federal do Partido Comunista do Brasil (Seção Internacional Comunista), no date, Panfletos Apreendidos, DESPS, 1933–1944, APERJ.

117. "Ford Calls for Release of Santos," *Daily Worker*, March 3, 1936, Brazil file, file folder 4102B Brazil, 1931–1943, box 201, Record Group 263, Murphy Collection, NARA. An earlier article advertised the meeting: "Ford Will Address Meeting to Protest Terror in Brazil," *Daily Worker*, March 1,

1936, Brazil file, file folder 4101B Brazil, 1931–1943, box 201, Record Group 263, Murphy Collection, NARA.

118. "U.S. Probe of Barron Death Asked," April 4, 1936, Brazil file, file folder 4101B Brazil, 1925–1936, box 201, Record Group 263, Murphy Collection, NARA.

119. "Ford Will Address Meeting to Protest Terror in Brazil," *Daily Worker,* March 1, 1936, Brazil file, file folder 4101B Brazil, 1931–1943, box 201, Record Group 263, Murphy Collection, NARA; "Ford Calls for Release of Santos," *Daily Worker,* March 3, 1936, Brazil file, file folder 4102B Brazil, 1931–1943, box 201, Record Group 263, Murphy Collection, NARA.

120. *Luís Carlos Prestes,* 12.

121. *Luís Carlos Prestes,* 18, 33; and Fausto, *Concise History of Brazil,* 185.

122. Quoted in McKenzie, "Soviet Union," 214. Original quote from Schuman, *Soviet Politics,* 273.

123. See Karepovs and Neto, "Os Trotskistas Brasileiros," 116; and Degras, preface to *Communist International,* vol. 3, vii.

124. Communist International, *VII Congress of the Communist International,* 145.

125. The South American and Caribbean delegates were actually in Moscow for Comintern's Seventh Congress, originally scheduled for 1934. However, the Seventh Congress was postponed until the following year, so the Third Conference of South American and Caribbean Communist Parties occurred at the last minute to take advantage of their presence in Moscow. See Prestes, "A conferência dos Partidos Comunistas da América do Sul e do Caribe," 132–53.

126. Quoted in Prestes, 7.

127. See Nascimento and Nascimento, *Africans in Brazil,* 19, 30.

128. "Struggles of the Communist Parties of South and Caribbean America: The Results of the Third Conference of the Communist Parties of South and Caribbean America" (source: *Communist International,* New York, no. 10, May 20, 1935, 564–76), general file, file folder 4102B general, 1937–1939, box 210, Record Group 263, Murphy Collection, NARA. The government's records copied the *Communist International*'s false report that the meeting had occurred in Uruguay, not Moscow. For an analysis of why Comintern may have lied about this, see Caballero, *Latin America and the Comintern,* 58–59.

129. Although the ANL became quite militant and did not support the Vargas regime until 1938, the revolt's prescribed government, the Governo Nacional Popular Revolucionário (National Revolutionary Popular Government), was still in line with Popular Front tactics, as the call for power to the Popular Front replaced the old "power to the Soviets" slogan. See Prestes, "A conferência dos Partidos Comunistas da América do Sul e do Caribe," 132–53; and Fausto, *Concise History of Brazil,* 198–236.

130. See Prestes, "A Conferência dos Partidos Comunistas da América do Sul e do Caribe," 132–53.

131. "Hino do Brasileiro pobre" (lyrics by Agildo Barata), in Vianna, *Pão, Terra e Liberdade,* 553–54.

132. Prestes had already been appointed the ANL's honorary president while in exile abroad, with Hercolino Cascardo as the titular head, but this was the first

time he confirmed his alliance with the movement. Prestes dated his letter from Barcelona, although he had secretly been back in Brazil since April 1935. Prestes, "A conferência dos Partidos Comunistas da América do Sul e do Caribe," 132–53.

133. "Carta de Luís Carlos Prestes à Aliança Nacional Libertadora" (addressed to Hercolino Cascardo, Barcelona, April 25, 1935), in Vianna, *Pão, terra e liberdade*, 285–89. See Prestes, "A Conferência dos Partidos Comunistas da América do Sul e do Caribe."

134. Luís Carlos Prestes, "Manifesto da Aliança Nacional Libertadora" (July 5, 1935), in Bonavides and Amaral, *Textos políticos da história do Brasil*, 108. Anita Leocádia Prestes discusses the Comintern's influence on this manifesto that her father signed. See Prestes.

135. Quoted in Domingues, "'Constantemente derrubo lágrimas,'" 153. See also Nascimento and Nascimento, *Africans in Brazil*, 19, 30.

136. Panfleto nº 501, Panfletos, Delegacia Especial de Segurança Política e Social (DESPS), 1933–1944, APERJ; and Levine, *Vargas Regime*, 75.

137. See Levine, 73.

138. Carol H. Foster, American consul general, São Paulo, to R. M. Scotten, chargé d'affaires ad interim, American embassy, Rio de Janeiro, March 10, 1939, general file, file folder 4102B general, 1937–1939, box 210, Record Group 263, Murphy Collection, NARA.

139. "International Congress of American Democracies," Strictly Confidential report (no other information provided), April 1, 1939, general file, file folder 4102B general, 1937–1939, box 210, Record Group 263, Murphy Collection, NARA.

140. Testimony of Ralph De Sola, November 21, 1938, *Investigation of Un-American Propaganda Activities in the United States*, Hearings before a Special Committee on Un-American Activities, House of Representatives, 75th Cong., 1st Sess. on H.R. Res. 282, vol. 3 (Washington, DC: US Government Printing Office, 1939), 2408, 2413.

141. Naison, *Communists in Harlem*; and Kelley, *Hammer and Hoe*.

142. *Communist Election Platform, 1938*, 6, 9–13.

CHAPTER 2

1. Although the Estado Novo always referred to these revolts, anticommunism was a staple of Vargas's rule from the beginning. See Silva, *Onda vermelha*. For a good analysis of the ways in which Vargas used the 1935 coup to defend the Estado Novo dictatorship, see Motta, *Em guarda*.

2. Other targeted groups included Jews, vagrants, delinquents, gypsies, and the Japanese. See Carneiro, "O Estado Novo, o Dops e a ideologia da segurança nacional," 335; and Fausto, *Concise History of Brazil*, 209.

3. Schrecker, *Many Are the Crimes*, 15.

4. Schrecker, 64–67.

5. For an example of the effects of red-baiting on black organizations, see Ellen Schrecker's discussion of the NAACP in *Many Are the Crimes*, 393–94.

6. See Suely Robles Reis de Queroz's introductory remarks on the cover of Motta, *Em guarda*; and Vianna, introduction to *Pão, terra e liberdade*, 15–20.

7. The term *militant democracy* was coined by Karl Loewenstein in 1937 and is still used by constitutional lawyers and political scientists today. Loewenstein worried about the fascist takeover in many European countries. He believed that "[d]emocracy and democratic tolerance [had] been used for their own destruction," as fascist movements had first garnered power through normal party/parliamentary politics in order to eventually abolish liberal democratic processes altogether and install fascist regimes (Loewenstein, "Militant Democracy and Fundamental Rights, 1," 423). Loewenstein argued that democracy must become militant as it had in some countries to prevent fascist takeover. Obviously the Vargas regime highlighted communism and not fascism as the justification for militant democracy. Loewenstein later published the first manuscript-length analysis of the political, constitutional, and legal situation in Brazil under the Estado Novo, which is discussed in chapter 5. See Loewenstein, "Militant Democracy and Fundamental Rights, 1" and "Militant Democracy and Fundamental Rights, 2."

8. For instance, the Birmingham City Commission and other Alabaman organizations exhibited obstruction in their appeals to the HCUA to investigate the Southern Conference for Human Welfare, which worked to end legalized Jim Crow and supported antilynching legislation. See "South Denounces Action Taken at Big Conference," *Pittsburgh Courier*, December 10, 1938; and "Birmingham Urges Dies to Probe Southern Human Welfare Confab," *Atlanta Daily World*, November 30, 1938, sec. J.

9. The Dies committee became a permanent committee in 1945.

10. Fish, *Memoir*, 41. Congress allotted $25,000 for the committee's investigation. See "House Red Hearings Open Here Tuesday," *New York Times*, July 10, 1930.

11. "Fish Urges Inquiry on Reds' Activities," *New York Times*, April 18, 1930. Fish informed the House that Acting Attorney General Charles Hughes Jr. had expressed to him in a written statement that the Department of Justice had "not in recent years had any function to perform respecting activities of Communists."

12. Fish, "Menace of Communism," 55.

13. Fish, 60–61 (italics mine).

14. "Reds Are Accused of Inciting Races," *Washington Post*, June 11, 1930. Fish quotes Hoover here. Hoover also had been repressing black militancy for several years. See Kornweibel, *Seeing Red*.

15. "Question of Negro Pushes to Fore in Probe of Radicals: Congressional Committee Told Communists Have Made Little Headway, but Have Fertile Soil in Racial Discrimination," *New York Amsterdam News*, July 23, 1930.

16. Hamilton Fish Jr. (chairman), Carl G. Bachmann, Edward E. Eslick, and Robert S. Hall, *Investigation of Communist Propaganda: Report,* pursuant to H. Res. 220, 71st Cong., 3rd Sess., House Report no. 2290, January 17, 1931, 32.

17. "Amtorg Called Link in Financing Reds," *New York Times*, July 20, 1930.

18. See "Amtorg Called Link in Financing Reds," *New York Times*, July 20, 1930. See also George Schuyler, "Views and Reviews," *Pittsburgh Courier*, February 7, 1931. Schuyler gave great credit to the communists and Foster based

upon this testimony, opining: "Whatever one thinks of William Z. Foster and the American Communist Party, it must be admitted that they are sound on the race question. . . . As a consequence, while I question some of their tactics, I have more respect for them than any group in the United States."

19. "Question of Negro Pushes to Fore in Probe of Radicals: Congressional Committee Told Communists Have Made Little Headway, but Have Fertile Soil in Racial Discrimination," *New York Amsterdam News*, July 23, 1930.

20. "Amtorg Called Link in Financing Reds," *New York Times*, July 20, 1930; and "Negro Communist Gains Are Reported," *Washington Post*, November 16, 1930. According to the *New York Times*, Randolph testified that he thought there were only about fifty blacks who were actual members of the CPUSA in New York.

21. "Lynchings Food for Soviets," *Chicago Defender*, October 4, 1930.

22. "The Week," *Chicago Defender*, October 11, 1930, national edition.

23. "Investigating Reds," *Pittsburgh Courier*, July 26, 1930. Twenty thousand was a huge underestimate and likely came from the testimony of a Mr. Leary, who estimated that number of CPUSA members in New York alone. See "Amtorg Called Link in Financing Reds," *New York Times*, July 20, 1930.

24. Cyril Briggs, "Lynch Terror Haunts Congressional Probers," *Pittsburgh Courier*, August 2, 1930.

25. Fish was an open isolationist and FDR critic, and he did not favor US participation in the war in Europe. Reflecting his sensitivity to the disgrace of being marked a Nazi sympathizer, his memoir, published right after his death, contained a long chapter on his work "in support of the Jews," in which he detailed his Zionist bill and efforts. Fish also drafted bills to mount a monument to black soldiers, to create a Negro division in the army, to open all branches of the service to blacks, and to mandate a presidential designation of two blacks per year to West Point, and in 1940 he sponsored an amendment that banned racial discrimination in the training and selection of military personnel. (See chapter 7.) See Fish, *Memoir*, and "Fish Promises Aid in Congress Fight," *New York Amsterdam News*, May 7, 1938.

26. Fish, *Memoir*, 26–31.

27. Fish, 33, 36.

28. Jeannette Carter, "News from the Nation's Capital," *Chicago Defender*, March 13, 1937, national edition; and Marvel Cooke, "Fish Promises Aid in Congress Fight," *New York Amsterdam News*, May 7, 1938. In both reports, Fish was speaking before black audiences, the first at the men's day program at Asbury M.E. Church, and the second at a mass meeting at St. Mark's Church in Harlem.

29. See Gerstle, *American Crucible*, 130, 158–59.

30. Chairman Martin Dies, testimony of John C. Metcalfe, November 19, 1938, *Investigation of Un-American Propaganda Activities in the United States*, Hearings before a Special Committee on Un-American Activities, House of Representatives, 75th Cong., 3rd Sess. on H.R. Res. 282, vol. 3 (Washington, DC: US Government Printing Office, 1939): 2339.

31. Quoted in Gellermann, *Martin Dies*, 245–46. Dies made the statement on the House floor.

32. "Mr. Dies Speaks Wisely," *Pittsburgh Courier*, December 17, 1938.

33. Quoted in Gellermann, *Martin Dies,* 185.

34. Testimony of William Z. Foster, national chairman of the Communist Party of the United States, September 29, 1939, *Investigation of Un-American Propaganda Activities in the United States*, Hearings before a Special Committee on Un-American Activities, House of Representatives, 76th Cong., 1st Sess. on H.R. Res. 282, vol. 9 (Washington, DC: US Government Printing Office, 1939): 5352–55; 5410–12.

35. Testimony of William Z. Foster, 5359–60.

36. Adam Lapin, "Reports of Interracial Parties Shock Probers of Un-American Activities," *Chicago Defender,* September 3, 1938, 4; and quoted in Gellermann, *Martin Dies,* 74–76.

37. Gore, *Radicalism at the Crossroads,* 32–34. Gore shows that black women radicals considered this issue a hindrance to the recruitment of black women into the party.

38. James W. Ford and James S. Allen, *The Negroes in a Soviet America* (New York: Workers Library Publishers, 1935). Excerpts from this pamphlet became HCUA exhibit no. 102 and can be found in *Investigation of Un-American Propaganda Activities in the United States*, Hearings before a Special Committee on Un-American Activities, House of Representatives, 76th Cong., 1st Sess. on H.R. Res. 282, Appendix-Part I (Washington, DC: US Government Printing Office, 1940), 749–50.

39. Dies, *Trojan Horse in America,* 118, 121.

40. Dies, 119–20. Dies explained that similar practices occurred during training trips to Russia, after which blacks reassured others that Soviet racial democracy was a reality.

41. See Gellermann, *Martin Dies,* 245–46.

42. Gellermann, 118–19 (italics mine).

43. Gellermann, 118–20, 129.

44. It is clear in the records of the HCUA's hearings that the Klan was discussed to some degree, but the committee for the most part ignored the white supremacist organization.

45. Cliff Mackay, "The Globe Trotter," *Atlanta Daily World*, May 28, 1939, and November 12, 1939; P. L. Prattis, "The Horizon," *Pittsburgh Courier*, May 13, 1939; "Dies Committee," *New York Amsterdam News*, December 2, 1939.

46. "Mr. Dies Reports," *Pittsburgh Courier*, January 13, 1940; "Congress Asked to Curb Dies for Failure to Probe Mobs," *Los Angeles Sentinel*, January 4, 1940; and "Dies' Failure to Probe Klan May Stop Funds," *Chicago Defender,* January 6, 1940.

47. "Denounce Dies Committee as Race Baiter," *Chicago Defender*, November 4, 1939.

48. "Mr. Dies and True Un-Americanism," *Chicago Defender*, October 14, 1939.

49. Adam Lapin, "Reports of Interracial Parties Shock Probers of Un-American Activities," *Chicago Defender*, September 3, 1938.

50. "Mr. Dies and True Un-Americanism," *Chicago Defender,* October 14, 1939.

51. Dies, *Trojan Horse in America*, 122–23.

52. Dies, 118–21.

53. President Roosevelt was not a fan of the Dies committee. Although not opposed to inquiries about Nazis and fascists, Roosevelt abhorred the Dies committee's red-baiting of organizations like the American League for Peace and Democracy and tactics such as the committee's public release of 563 names of government employees affiliated with "communist" organizations. Roosevelt also accused Dies of using the HCUA to influence elections. "Dies, Attacked by Roosevelt, Sticks to Guns," *Chicago Daily Tribune*, October 28, 1939. For Dies's account of his tensions with Roosevelt over the HCUA during the late 1930s, see *Martin Dies' Story*, 139–46.

54. Quoted in Gellermann, *Martin Dies*, 245. Dies spoke these words from the House floor in 1942.

55. Quoted in Gellermann, 181.

56. Quoted in Gellermann, 175.

57. Fish, *Memoir*, 41–42.

58. "Red Spy Hunted Here as Link of Amtorg to Espionage Groups," *New York Times*, July 31, 1930.

59. George Gallup, "The Gallup Poll," *Washington Post*, November 1, 1939; "Dies Inquiry Found Favored by Voters," *New York Times*, December 15, 1939; George Gallup, "Dies Committee's Work Wins Increasing Public Support," *Los Angeles Times*, December 4, 1940. When Congress debated the continuation of the committee in January 1940, those in favor of the extension (which was granted) cited the Gallup Poll and said that 75 percent of the public wanted the committee's work to continue. See Gellermann, *Martin Dies*, 188.

60. On this point, I differ from Gary Gerstle, who, for obvious reasons, places Dies firmly in his category of racial, or racist, nationalism. See Gerstle, *American Crucible*, 157–64.

61. See Motta, *Em guarda*, 6–8. Motta shows that the exception was in 1927 with a brief and effective congressional move to demobilize the PCB, experiencing some success with its Bloco Operário, or Worker's Bloc party.

62. Motta, 8–9.

63. Motta, 183.

64. Both PCB and Comintern leadership seem to have contributed to the idea and plans for the insurrections, although the decision to begin the first revolt in Natal was made by the army militants on the ground. See Motta, 186–87; Pinheiro, *Estratégias da ilusão*, 288–97; Levine, *Vargas Regime*.

65. Levine, *Father of the Poor*, 46–52; Levine, *Vargas Regime*, 123. The fabricated communist plot was the so-called Cohen Plan, ostensibly authored by a Jewish communist. Captain Olímpio Mourão Filho actually wrote the document that laid out violent plans for a fake communist insurrection.

66. Motta, *Em guarda*, 182–83, 202. The first meeting took place on December 7, 1935, just days after the rebellion was suppressed.

67. See *Dicionário Histórico-Biográfico Brasileiro Pós-1930*, CD-ROM (Rio de Janeiro: Centro de Pesquisa e Documentação de História Contemporânea do Brasil, Fundação Getulio Vargas, 2000), s.v. "Francisco Campos."

68. For the way in which the Brazilian state approached propaganda and ideological sanitation as a national security issue, see Carneiro, "O Estado Novo," 327–40.

69. *Polícia política preventiva: Serviço de inquéritos políticos sociais* (Rio de Janeiro: Brasil: Departamento Federal de Segurança Pública, 1939), 9, Biblioteca Nacional (hereafter BN).

70. See Brasil, Departamento Nacional de Propaganda, 20 *Anos de tragédia experiência*, 3–4, BN.

71. *20 Anos de tragédia Experiência*, 3, 7.

72. Chap. 7 in *O Brasil é Bom* (n.p.: Departamento Nacional de Propaganda/Agência Nacional, 1938). Motta assesses the ways in which Brazilian anticommunism attacked the symbol of the "Soviet paradise" with imagery and rhetoric of communism as slavery, inherently violent, and evil, among other things. See Motta, *Em guarda.*

73. Vargas, *Ordem e democracia*, 8, BN. The speech was given on September 7, 1936, and such speeches likely were broadcast over the radio.

74. Vargas, *Dever do estado e defesa do regime*, 5–6, BN.

75. Motta, *Em guarda*, 37–40.

76. See Lauerhass, *Getúlio Vargas*, 136–37. For a summary of this interview published in a newspaper at the time, see "Ecos e novidades: Ideal democrático," *A Noite*, January 19, 1938, 2.

77. Departamento Nacional de Propaganda, *Exposição Nacional do Estado Novo* (n.p.: Departamento Nacional de Propaganda, 1939), 7.

78. *O Brasil é bom.*

79. *Exposição nacional do Estado Novo*, 7, 82. Scholars like Robert Levine have pointed out that much of this legislation to protect workers looked great on paper but that the Estado Novo lacked the administrative infrastructure to enforce it. See Levine, *Father of the Poor.*

80. Chap. 25 in *O Brasil é bom.*

81. *Exposição nacional do Estado Novo*, 7.

82. Chap. 7 in *O Brasil é bom.*

83. Chap. 25 in *O Brasil é bom.*

84. Vargas, *Palavras aos Brasileiros*, 11. This exact passage was also quoted on a poster that indicated Vargas had given the speech on January 1, 1936.

85. See Carneiro, *Livros proibidos, idéias malditas*, 47–48. See also Andreucci, "Idéias malditas,"in *Cultura amordaçada*, 31–32.

86. See Andreucci and de Oliveira, *Cultura amordaçada*, 102.

87. See Oliveira, "A música, o DEOPS e o ideal revolucionário," 71. The excerpt is quoted from the song "Abre as asas sobre . . ." (ellipsis theirs).

88. "Hino do brasileiro pobre," lyrics by Agildo Barata, in Vianna, *Pão, terra e liberdade*, 553–54; see also Andreucci and Oliveira, *Cultura amordaçada*, 82.

89. See Carneiro, "O Estado Novo," 330.

90. According to José Correia Leite's recollection, Santos did not secure "anything positive" from the meeting, creating deep disappointment among the leadership. He claims that this episode contributed to Santos's expulsion from the organization. See Leite, . . . *E disse*, 105.

91. See Domingues, "'Constantemente derrubo lágrimas,'" 250–51. Domingues published two different versions of this article with the same title. Both are referenced in this book.

92. Statement by Isaltino Veiga dos Santos to the M. M. Juiz Comissário Dr. Alexandre Delfino de Amorim Lima, December 6, 1935, fl. 24, inquirição de presos políticos (interrogation of political prisoners), São Paulo, prontuário (police file) no. 2018, Isaltino Veiga dos Santos, Delegacia Estadual de Ordem Política e Social (DEOPS), São Paulo, Arquivo do Estado de São Paulo (hereafter DEOPS/SP, AESP). Historian Petrônio Domingues states that it is unclear exactly why Isaltino dos Santos left the Black Front. See Domingues, "'Constantemente derrubo lágrimas," 150, 164; and Domingues, "O 'messias' negro?," 527–28.

93. The *Frente Popular pela Liberdade* manifesto denounced social problems, the persecution of labor and unions, and the fascist tendencies within the government. See Domingues, "'Constantemente derrubo lágrimas,'" 153.

94. Report authored by Luis Tavares da Cunha, Delegado de Ordem Política, May 8, 1936, prontuário no. 2018, fl. 14, Isaltino Veiga dos Santos, DEOPS/SP, AESP.

95. Memo by Luis Tavares da Cunha, Delegado de Ordem Política, to Egas Botelho, Superintendente de Ordem Política e Social, February 11, 1936, fl. 65, prontuário no. 2018, Isaltino Veiga dos Santos, DEOPS/SP, AESP (italics mine). In the letter cited below, Santos's brother Arlindo wrote that he never heard of the federation and believed it existed only on paper.

96. The date and purpose of Santos's detention can be found in a few reports. One of them is Report to Superintendente Botelho from the Delegado de Ordem Política, January 25, 1936, prontuário no. 2018, fl. 14, Isaltino Veiga dos Santos, DEOPS/SP, AESP.

97. Domingues, "'Constantemente derrubo lágrimas,'" 152.

98. Memo from Luis Tavares da Cunha, delegado de Ordem Política, to Egas Botelho, Superintendente de Ordem Política e Social, February 11, 1936, fl. 65, prontuário no. 2018, Isaltino Veiga dos Santos, DEOPS/SP, AESP (italics mine). There is a note on the memo indicating that it was forwarded that same day to the federal Department of Political and Social Order (political police).

99. Memo (no name, no date), fl. 37, prontuário no. 2018, Isaltino Veiga dos Santos, DEOPS/SP, AESP. For a list of people that the DEOPS claimed were members of the organization, see n. 13 in Domingues, "'Constantemente derrubo lágrimas,'" 166.

100. Isaltino Veiga dos Santos to Exmo. Snr. Dr. Egas Botelho, MD, Superintendente da Ordem Política e Social, São Paulo, from the Maria Zélia Political Prison, January 26, 1936, prontuário no. 2018, Isaltino Veiga dos Santos, fls. 53–56, DEOPS/SP, AESP.

101. Isaltino Veiga dos Santos to Exmo. Snr. Dr. Egas Botelho, MD, Superintendente da Ordem Política e Social, São Paulo, from the Maria Zélia Political Prison, May 15, 1936, prontuário no. 2018, Isaltino Veiga dos Santos, fls. 46–48, DEOPS/SP, AESP.

102. Isaltino Veiga dos Santos to Ilmo. Snr. Dr. Carlos de Carvalho Amarante, MD, Diretor do Presídio político da Capital, from the Maria Zélia Polit-

ical Prison, January 12, 1936, prontuário no. 2018, Isaltino Veiga dos Santos, fls. 40–44, DEOPS/SP, AESP. Caiuby's position is stated in Domingues, "'Constantemente derrubo lágrimas,'" 248.

103. Isaltino Veiga dos Santos to Ilmo. Snr. Dr. Armando Franco Soares Caiuby, from the Maria Zélia Political Prison, January 29, 1936, prontuário no. 2018, Isaltino Veiga dos Santos, fls. 57–62, DEOPS/SP, AESP.

104. Letter from Armando Franco Soares Caiuby to Egas Botelho, Superintendente da Ordem Política e Social, São Paulo, January 31, 1936, prontuário no. 2018, Isaltino Veiga dos Santos, fls. 45A–45D, DEOPS/SP, AESP.

105. Letter from Arlindo Veiga dos Santos to Dr. Egas Botelho, MD, Superintendente da Ordem Política e Social, São Paulo, June 20, 1936, prontuário no. 2018, Isaltino Veiga dos Santos, fls. 49–52, DEOPS/SP, AESP (capital letters are his).

106. Letter from Armando Franco Soares Caiuby to Egas Botelho, Superintendente da Ordem Política e Social, São Paulo, January 31, 1936, prontuário no. 2018, Isaltino Veiga dos Santos, fls. 45A–45D, DEOPS/SP, AESP.

107. Alberto, *Terms of Inclusion*, 133, 136; Butler, *Freedoms Given*, 118, 123. These ideological disagreements led to six major quarrels and resulted in four splinter black organizations. Also, former FNB leader Francisco Lucrécio stated that "blacks did not come to understand what *patrianovismo* was," and Leite had a similar impression. Lucrécio, quoted in Domingues, "O 'messias' negro?," 527 (translation mine). See Leite's testimony in Ribeiro and Barbosa, *Frente Negra Brasileira*, 68. However, Regina Pahim Pinto wrote that Santos was not the only FNB leader to articulate political ideals in line with *patrianovismo* in the FNB's newspaper. See Pinto, "O movimento negro em São Paulo," 129.

108. Letter from Armando Franco Soares Caiuby to Egas Botelho, Superintendente da Ordem Política e Social, São Paulo, January 31, 1936, prontuário no. 2018, Isaltino Veiga dos Santos, fls. 45A–45D, DEOPS/SP, AESP; and Domingues, "O 'messias' negro?," 521–26.

109. Butler, *Freedoms Given*, 18–23; Leal, *Coronelismo, enxada e voto;* and Owensby, *Intimate Ironies.*

110. Letter from Arlindo Veiga dos Santos to Dr. Egas Botelho, MD, Superintendente da Ordem Política e Social, São Paulo, June 20, 1936, prontuário no. 2018, Isaltino Veiga dos Santos, fls. 49–52, DEOPS/SP, AESP; letter from Armando Franco Soares Caiuby to Egas Botelho, Superintendente da Ordem Política e Social, São Paulo, January 31, 1936, prontuário no. 2018, Isaltino Veiga dos Santos, fls. 45A–45D, DEOPS/SP, AESP; and Isaltino Veiga dos Santos to Ilmo. Snr. Dr. Armando Franco Soares Caiuby, from the Maria Zélia Political Prison, January 29, 1936, prontuário no. 2018, Isaltino Veiga dos Santos, fls. 57–62, DEOPS/SP, AESP.

111. See Domingues, "'Constantemente derrubo lágrimas,'" 226, 232–33, 246–48, 251. Whether or not Isaltino truly subscribed to leftist viewpoints is a mystery, but Domingues suggests that job opportunities could be a plausible explanation for his political shift. He also cites José Correia Leite's opinion that Isaltino's leftism was due to "opportunis[m]," but Domingues reminds us that as a rival of the Santos brothers, Leite was biased.

112. Isaltino Veiga dos Santos to Ilmo. Snr. Dr. Armando Franco Soares Caiuby, from the Maria Zélia Political Prison, January 29, 1936, prontuário no. 2018, Isaltino Veiga dos Santos, fls. 73–74, DEOPS/SP, AESP; Arlindo Veiga dos Santos to Dr. Egas Botelho, MD, Superintendente da Ordem Política e Social, São Paulo, June 20, 1936, prontuário no. 2018, Isaltino Veiga dos Santos, fls. 49–52, DEOPS/SP, AESP.

113. Arlindo Veiga dos Santos to Dr. Egas Botelho, MD, Superintendente da Ordem Política e Social, São Paulo, June 20, 1936, prontuário no. 2018, Isaltino Veiga dos Santos, fls. 49–52, DEOPS/SP, AESP (underline his).

114. Letter from Filena Veiga dos Santos to Arthur Leite de Barros, MD, Secretário da Segurança Pública, February 1936 (no day given), prontuário no. 2018, Isaltino Veiga dos Santos, fl. 66, DEOPS/SP, AESP.

115. Isaltino Veiga dos Santos to Exmo. Snr. Dr. Egas Botelho, MD, Superintendente da Ordem Política e Social, São Paulo, from the Maria Zélia Political Prison, May 13, 1936, prontuário no. 2018, Isaltino Veiga dos Santos, fls. 57–62, DEOPS/SP, AESP; and letter from Isaltino Veiga dos Santos to Ilmo. Snr. Dr. Carlos de Carvalho Amarante, MD, director of the Political Prison of the Capital São Paulo, from the Maria Zélia Political Prison, January 12, 1936, prontuário no. 2018, Isaltino Veiga dos Santos, fls. 40–44, DEOPS/SP, AESP.

116. See Levine, *Father of the Poor?*; and Dávila, *Diploma of Whiteness*.

CHAPTER 3

1. Macpherson, *Real World*, 2.
2. O'Shaughnessy, *Selling Hitler*, 41.
3. This chapter focuses on black reactions to Nazism, although there was a strong response to the Spanish Civil War and especially the Abyssinian War between Ethiopia and Italy as well. See Bekerie, "African Americans and Italo-Ethiopian War"; Kelly, *Race Rebels*, 123–58; Domingues, "'O caminho da verdadeira emancipação'"; and Alberto, *Terms of Inclusion*, 140–41.
4. Gilmore, *Defying Dixie*, 158, 160.
5. *Speeches of Adolf Hitler*, 784–85, 790.
6. *Speeches of Adolf Hitler*, 1557–58. Hitler's constitutional approach succeeded in part because of his strategy to exclude Communist and Social Democratic Party members from participating in the votes that eventually installed the Nazi dictatorship. For an explanation of the events leading up to the dictatorship, see Bendersky, *Concise History of Nazi Germany*, 82–96.
7. *Speeches of Adolf Hitler*, 456–58.
8. Bendersky, *Concise History of Nazi Germany*, 32–33, 99–100, 129.
9. O'Shaughnessy, *Selling Hitler*, 41, 156–59, 224.
10. *Speeches of Adolf Hitler*, 1557–58. For a summary of the events surrounding the annexations, see Bendersky, 155–62.
11. See Rauschning, *Hitler Speaks*, 70.
12. See Rauschning, 70. Since at least the 1980s, scholars have rigorously debated Rauschning's credibility in this book. Chapter 6 discusses this debate in more detail.
13. *Speeches of Adolf Hitler*, 783–84.

14. *Speeches of Adolf Hitler,* 783, 1638–39.

15. Gilmore, *Defying Dixie,* 194–95.

16. Whitman, *Hitler's American Model,* 5, 9–13, 32–34, 136.

17. Whitman, 53, 121–23. For a study of the links between US eugenicists and Nazism, see Kühl, *Nazi Connection.*

18. See Dietrich, *Nazismo Tropical?,* 17. The Nazi Party had branches in eighty-three countries.

19. Griffin, *Nature of Fascism,* 150.

20. Klein, *Our Brazil Will Awake!,* 21–22, 27; *Dicionário Histórico-Biográfico Brasileiro,* s.v. "Gustavo Barroso."

21. Cavalari, *Integralismo,* 41–52. See also *Dicionário Histórico-Biográfico Brasileiro,* s.v. "Integralismo."

22. See Bertonha, "Entre Mussolini e Plínio Salgado: O Fascismo Italiano, o Integralismo, e o problema dos descendentes italianos no Brasil," 87, 101; and Levine, *Vargas Regime,* 88. Bertonha points out that the Italians came to consider the AIB an important organization that was in the best position to spread fascism in Brazil. It was upon this decision that the consistent transfer of funds took place.

23. Dietrich, *Nazismo Tropical?,* 113–14. Other analyses of the relationship between the AIB and the Nazis in Brazil include Cruz, "O Integralismo," 32–50; and Gertz, *O fascismo no sul do Brasil.*

24. See Graham, "A virada antirracista do Partido Comunista do Brasil, a Frente Negra Brasileira, e a Ação Integralista Brasileira na década de 1930," 353–76.

25. Cruz, "O Integralismo," 80–99, 247, 260. "A verdadeira síntese social" (a true social synthesis) are Gustavo Barroso's words, quoted in Cruz, 248.

26. Cruz, 80–99, 260.

27. Maio, *Nem Rotschild nem Trotsky,* 105–6, 108–9, 113–19. See Levine, *Vargas Regime,* 88.

28. Maio, *Nem Rotschild nem Trotsky,* 105–6, 108–9, 113–19.

29. Cruz, "O Integralismo," 174–79. Salgado seems to have been more flexible about Japanese inclusion in Brazilian homogenization, at least by 1965, when he included them in his list of immigrant communities that "mixed their blood" with Brazil's European-African-indigenous racial foundation. See Cruz, "O Integralismo," 254.

30. See Oliveira, "A evolução dos estudos sobre o integralismo," 119–20. Leandro Silva Teles translated Hunsche's dissertation from German under the title "O integralismo brasileiro: História do movimento fascista no Brasil." Decades later, in the 1970s, a slew of AIB studies emerged that were obsessed with the issue of European mimesis. Scholars like Hélgio Trindade argued that integralism was largely a copy of European fascism (see Trindade, *Integralismo*), whereas academics like Gilberto Vasconcellos strongly disagreed (see Vasconcellos, *A ideologia curupira*). Oliveira offers a great summary of the evolution of scholarship about integralism, as does Edgar Bruno Franke Serratto in "Estudos sobre o Integralismo e seus momentos."

31. Letter from Antonio Gallotti to Vienot, August 30, 1937, p. 2, document 1937_08_003.PDF, Fundo Plínio Salgado, Arquivo Público e Histórico de Rio Claro.

32. All quotes in Cruz, "O Integralismo," 248–50.

33. As Weinstein argues, these comparisons usually were made without the Constitutionalist leadership resorting to "explicitly racist terms." See Weinstein, *Color of Modernity*, 88. The Constitutionalists demanded that Vargas's provisional government, which ruled in the years following his successful 1930 revolution, return to constitutional law and hold elections after having suspended the 1891 Constitution. Federal forces quelled the three-month war on October 2, 1932, after which Vargas finally scheduled an election for the constituent assembly that drew up the 1934 Constitution.

34. Ação Integralista Brasileira, *Manual da Integralista: Fascisculo I*, 2nd ed., DESPS, Folheto 10, APERJ (the manual does not have a date, but within it is the entire text of the Manifesto of October 1932, which is the source of this quote); *A Doutrina Integralista*, 12, DESPS, Folheto 280, APERJ.

35. Cruz, "O Integralismo," 247–52.

36. Quoted in Klein, *Our Brazil Will Awake!*, 18.

37. Quoted in Klein, 23, 24.

38. *A Doutrina Integralista*, DESPS, Folheto 280, APERJ. Beginning on page 8 is the *Departamento de Doutrina*'s "Cartilha do Integralismo Brasileiro," dated from São Paulo, March 8, 1933.

39. *A Doutrina Integralista*, 8, 9, 14, DESPS, Folheto 280, APERJ.

40. Braga, "O candidato do povo," *Anauê!*, July 1937, Localização EL—R178, no. 17, Fundo Edgard Leuenroth, Centro de Pesquisa e Documentação Social, Instituto de Filosofia e Ciências Humanas, Arquivo Edgard Leuenroth (AEL), Universidade Estadual de Campinas (Unicamp).

41. Plínio Salgado, "Estado totalitário e estado integral," *A Ofensiva*, no. 326, Pasta Ano 1936, Fundo Plínio Salgado, Arquivo Público e Histórico de Rio Claro.

42. All quotes in Horne, *Color of Fascism*, vii, xi, xv, xviii, xxi–xxiv, 55, 71, 85.

43. All quotes in Horne, vii, xi, xv, xviii, xxi–xxiv, 55.

44. Horne's conclusion echoes historian Allyson Hobbs's research about the push and pull factors that historically caused blacks to opt for racial "exile." See Hobbs, *Chosen Exile*.

45. Horne, *Color of Fascism*, 17–30.

46. Dennis, *Coming American Fascism*, 197–99.

47. Although *The Dynamics of War and Revolution* just missed making the bookstalls in the 1930s, its 1940 publishing date and length almost certainly meant that Dennis began writing it in the previous decade. As Dennis was regularly called upon as a keynote speaker and the voice of US fascism in debates, many of the points he raised in this book must have reflected those of his speaking engagements in the 1930s as well.

48. Dennis, *Dynamics of War*, xix–xxii.

49. Dennis, xix–xx.

50. Lawrence Dennis, "Political Anti-Semitism in a Fascist America Is Unthinkable, Says Advocate of Strong Ruler," *Emanu-El-Jewish Journal* (October 26, 1934), in Published Articles, folder 27, Lawrence Dennis Papers, Hoover

Institution, Stanford University. Part of this article is quoted in Horne, *Color of Fascism*, 64–65.

51. Dennis, *Coming American Fascism*, 109–10.

52. Horne, *Color of Fascism*, 71, 75.

53. Quoted in Horne, 67, 91.

54. Quoted in Horne, 90.

55. Sigrid Schultz, "Remember Fate of Indians, Nazis Tell Roosevelt," *Chicago Daily Tribune*, October 28, 1938.

56. In 1932 an FNB delegation met with Vargas and successfully requested that he desegregate São Paulo's Civil Guard. See Alberto, *Terms of Inclusion*, 131.

57. Whitman, *Hitler's American Model*, 6–7. Whitman also discusses the fact that Roosevelt "received distinctly favorable treatment in the Nazi press until at least 1936 or 1937."

58. Leite, . . . *E disse*, 94; Domingues, "O 'messias' negro?": 526–28.

59. See Kössling, "Os afro-descendentes," 22.

60. "13 de maio," *Anauê!* 16 (June 1937): 25, Localização EL—R178, no. 16, Fundo Edgard Leuenroth, Centro de Pesquisa e Documentação Social, Instituto de Filosofia e Ciências Humanas, AEL, Unicamp.

61. See Sentinelo, "O lugar das 'raças,'" 151.

62. Arlindo Veiga dos Santos, "Fogo Neles," *A Voz da Raça*, January 6, 1934.

63. See Leite's testimony in Ribeiro and Barbosa, *Frente Negra Brasileira*, 75–76.

64. Santos, "Fogo Neles."

65. Quoted in Domingues, "O 'messias' negro?," 526–29.

66. Alberto, *Terms of Inclusion*, 133–34.

67. "Vai-vai," *A Voz da Raça*, February 3, 1934.

68. See the summary of Romão's 2004 recorded interview in Alberti and Pereira, *Histórias do movimento Negro no Brasil*, 105.

69. Nascimento, *Memórias do exílio*, 29–30.

70. See Ribeiro and Barbosa, *Frente Negra Brasileira*, 72–73.

71. Jaqueline Tondato Sentinelo mentions the presence of blacks in photos published in the social pages of *A Ofensiva*. Sentinelo, "O lugar das 'raças,'" 151. Photographs in São Paulo's State Archives and in Plínio Salgado's papers in the Rio Claro, São Paulo, archives also contain photographs of black integralists.

72. Nascimento, *Memórias do exílio*, 29–30.

73. See Leite's testimony in Ribeiro and Barbosa, *Frente Negra Brasileira*, 68; and Butler, *Freedoms Given*, 118.

74. J. A. Rogers, "Rogers Lauds Pres. Roosevelt for His Forceful Speeches: Praises President for Taking Rap at Dictatorships," *Pittsburgh Courier*, January 16, 1937; Franklin D. Roosevelt, "Annual Message to Congress," January 6, 1937, available online at Gerhard Peters and John T. Woolley, *American Presidency Project*, https://www.presidency.ucsb.edu/documents/annual-message-congress-1.

75. J.A. Rogers, "Rogers Lauds Pres. Roosevelt for His Forceful Speech: Praises President for Taking Rap at Dictatorships," *Pittsburgh Courier,* January 16, 1937.

76. Asukile, "Joel Augustus Rogers," 325–29.

77. "U.S. Woos Negro Troops As Another World War Looms," *New York Amsterdam News,* October 1, 1938; Franklin D. Roosevelt, "Letter to Adolf Hitler Seeking Peace," September 27, 1938, available online at Gerhard Peters and John T. Woolley, *The American Presidency Project,* https://www.presidency.ucsb.edu/documents/letter-adolf-hitler-seeking-peace.

78. "U.S. Woos Negro Troops As Another World War Looms," *New York Amsterdam News,* October 1, 1938.

79. "U.S. Woos Negro Troops as Another World War Looms."

80. See Wintz and Finkelman, *Encyclopedia of the Harlem Renaissance,* vol. 2, *K–Y,* 773. The late 1930s was when the *Afro-American* reached its highest circulation.

81. Ralph Matthews, "Watching the Big Parade: Is Democracy a Failure?" *Baltimore Afro-American,* February 11, 1939.

82. "Home Style Nazism," *New York Amsterdam News,* May 13, 1939, 10.

83. Adam C. Powell Jr., "Soap Box," *New York Amsterdam News,* December 3, 1938.

84. Powell, "Soap Box."

85. Harlem Civic Association, "This Week's Guest Editor Says: Open Letter to President Roosevelt," *New York Amsterdam News,* April 16, 1938.

CHAPTER 4

1. Sklaroff, *Black Culture and New Deal,* 1–3.

2. See Skidmore, *Politics in Brazil,* 33–35; and Weinstein, *Color of Modernity.*

3. Leuchtenberg, *Franklin D. Roosevelt,* xv, 333–35.

4. See Sklaroff, *Black Culture and New Deal.*

5. See Hertzman, *Making Samba,* 31–65, 195–98.

6. See Williams, *Culture Wars in Brazil;* and Sklaroff, *Black Culture and New Deal.* Sklaroff borrows the term "cultural self-determination" from Grace Hale, quoting a 2006 lecture. See Sklaroff, 6.

7. See Sklaroff, 81–121; and Stewart, *Long Past Slavery,* 13–14.

8. Stewart, 120–31.

9. McCann, *Hello, Hello Brazil,* 59–60; Hertzman, *Making Samba,* 131, 195–98.

10. Marc Hertzman and Hermano Vianna also use the term "white cultural mediators" and analyze their role in the world of samba. See Hertzman, *Making Samba,* 116–17; and Vianna, *Mystery of Samba,* 15.

11. See Sklaroff, *Black Culture and New Deal;* Stewart, *Long Past Slavery,* 120–31.

12. Velloso, "Os intelectuais e a política cultural," 149–51 (translation mine). Velloso borrows the term "official business" from Sérgio Miceli.

13. Bryan McCann assesses these financial stresses and the appeals of the officials who led state cultural and censorship bodies. See McCann, *Hello, Hello Brazil*, 8, 20–21, 26–34, 65–70.

14. Carneiro, "O Estado Novo," 334–37.

15. "Apontamentos para a mensagem do Sr. Presidente da República," no date, p. 25, Gustavo Capanema Papers, Code GC f 1935.05.00, rolo 19, fotograma 8[3], CPDOC/FGV. Although the document has no date, we can at least pinpoint the year, as it states the notes are for "a Mensagem de 1935," or an address to be given in 1935. Gustavo Capanema drafted the decree that Vargas signed in October 1937 creating the MES's National Security Division (Secção de Segurança Nacional). See Decreto N° 2.036—de 11 de Outubro de 1937, Gustavo Capanema Papers, code GC i 1935.12.00, rolo 68, fotogramas 2[2] and 3[1].

16. See Carneiro, "O Estado Novo," 335.

17. Flanagan, *Arena*, 44.

18. Kalfatovic, *New Deal Fine Arts*, xi, lxiv.

19. Van Rijn, *Roosevelt's Blues*, 80.

20. See Sklaroff, *Black Culture and New Deal*, 9.

21. Buhite and Levy, *FDR's Fireside Chats*, ix–xx; McCann, *Hello, Hello Brazil*, 26–28. The *Hora do Brasil* program began in 1934.

22. McCann, *Hello, Hello Brazil*, 23–24.

23. McCann, 23, 31; Jambeiro et al., *Tempos de Vargas*, 49.

24. Jambeiro et al., *Tempos de Vargas*, 63, 66.

25. Quotes in McCann, *Hello, Hello Brazil*, 19, 31.

26. Jambeiro et al., *Tempos de Vargas*, 44, 65.

27. Cabral, "Getúlio Vargas e a música popular brasileira," 39.

28. Savage, *Broadcasting Freedom*, 12–13; Barlow, *Voice Over*, 26–27; and Hilliard and Hall, *Radio Broadcasting*, 20.

29. Loviglio, *Radio's Intimate Public*, 6.

30. Buhite and Levy, *FDR's Fireside Chats*, xiv.

31. Brown, *Manipulating the Ether*, 21.

32. Savage, *Broadcasting Freedom*, 13, 288.

33. McCann, *Hello, Hello Brazil*, 29.

34. Savage, *Broadcasting Freedom*, 43. Savage wrote that "the evolution of each new mass medium has been marked by virulent racial stereotyping, requiring African Americans to protest each new form in kind."

35. Savage, *Broadcasting Freedom*, 10–12; Barlow, *Voice Over*, 41–44; and Ely, *The Adventures of Amos 'n' Andy*.

36. Barlow, 2–9, 33–41.

37. Sklaroff, *Black Culture and New Deal*, 6.

38. Savage, *Broadcasting Freedom*, 14.

39. Barlow, *Voice Over*, 79–80; Sklaroff, *Black Culture and New Deal*, 17–18.

40. Stewart, *Long Past Slavery*, 128–29.

41. Sklaroff, *Black Culture and New Deal*, 32–35, 45–46, 49.

42. Sklaroff, 7, 49; and Stewart, *Long Past Slavery*, 13–14.

43. Barlow, *Voice Over*, 32.

44. Stewart, *Long Past Slavery*, 121.

45. Sklaroff, *Black Culture and New Deal*, 3–4.
46. Savage, *Broadcasting Freedom*, 21–22, 25; and Selig, "Celebrating Cultural Diversity."
47. Savage, *Broadcasting Freedom*, 21–24, 36–42.
48. Sklaroff, *Black Culture and New Deal*, 34, 59.
49. Peretti, *Jazz in American Culture*, 74–75; and Stewart, *Long Past Slavery*, 15–16.
50. Cabral, "Getúlio Vargas e a música popular Brasileira," 37; McCann, *Hello, Hello Brazil*, 47–48.
51. Jambeiro et al., *Tempos de Vargas*, 39; and Cabral, "Getúlio Vargas e a música popular Brasileira," 37.
52. Carneiro, "O Estado Novo," 334–36; and McCann, *Hello, Hello Brazil*, 52–67.
53. McCann, 58–60.
54. Quoted in McCann, 47.
55. Pereira, *Cor, profissão e mobilidade*, 218–19, 222–23, 232.
56. Hertzman, *Making Samba*, 59–60.
57. Hermano Vianna emphasizes the connections between black *sambistas* and elite whites in the mainstreaming of samba in the country. See Vianna, *Mystery of Samba*.
58. Hertzman, *Making Samba*, 97, 125, 131–35.
59. Pereira, *Cor, profissão e mobilidade*, 217.
60. Hertzman, *Making Samba*, 127–32.
61. Quoted in Hertzman, 134–35. Hertzman's translation of Paulo da Portela's decrees.
62. Mesquita, "O projeto regionalista de Gilberto Freyre," 129–242. The 1936 democratic reference is from Freyre's *Sobrados e mucambos (The Mansions and the Shanties)*, and Freyre's 1937 quote is from a talk he gave in Lisbon at a conference about Lusophone miscegenation. The MES published the latter.
63. Mesquita, "O projeto regionalista de Gilberto Freyre," 110–28; and Domingues, "'Constantemente derrubo lágrimas,'" 223.
64. Lourival Fontes spoke about many of the different components of the celebrations to reporters. See *A Noite*, March 31, 1938, 1–2.
65. See Cunha, "Sua alma em sua palma," 257.
66. Cunha, 257–71. Similar themes about relegating blacks to the past are examined in Romo, *Brazil's Living Museum*.
67. Camargo, *A Lei Áurea*, 11–15.
68. Evaristo de Moraes, "Antes dos colonos europeus foram os pretos que engrandeceram São Paulo," *O Diário da Noite*, March 26, 1938.
69. Weinstein, *Color of Modernity*. As Weinstein shows, this portrayal of the bandeirantes was a whitewashed and largely revisionist history. Historically, bandeirantes were European and indigenous mixed-raced men who were infamous for kidnapping and selling the indigenous as slaves. Weinstein, 36–46.
70. Evaristo de Moraes, "Antes dos colonos europeus foram os pretos que engrandeceram São Paulo," *O Diário da Noite*, March 26, 1938.
71. Tidwell and Tracy, *After Winter*, 9–10.
72. Quoted in McDonogh, *Florida Negro*, ix.

73. Tidwell and Tracy, *After Winter*, 9–10.

74. Quoted in Ferris, "Sterling Brown 1901–1989," in *Storied South*, 104–10.

75. Weisberger, *WPA Guide to America*, 135–36.

76. Tidwell and Tracy, *After Winter*, 9–10.

77. Calhoun and Calhoun, *Let Freedom Ring!*, v. Commissioner of Education Studebaker authored the foreword.

78. Calhoun and Calhoun, 348–49.

79. Calhoun and Calhoun, 357–68.

80. Calhoun and Calhoun, 372.

81. Mary McLeod Bethune, "What Does American Democracy Mean to Me?," *America's Town Meeting of the Air*, NBC radio, November 23, 1939.

82. Camargo, *A Lei Áurea*, 16–18.

83. Camargo, 27–32.

84. *A Noite*, March 31, 1938, 1–2.

85. *A Noite*, March 31, 1938, 1–2.

86. "As comemorações do cincoentenário [sic] da abolição," *A Noite*, March 25, 1938, 1.

87. Carneiro, "Situação do negro no Brasil," 237–40.

88. Carneiro, 237–40. Candomblé often fell under the category of *feitiçaria*, which was outlawed in Brazil's 1890 Penal Code. For sambista testimonies about the connection between candomblé and early samba, see Fenerick, "Nem do morro, nem da cidade," 91–95.

89. Works Progress Administration, *We Work Again*, 1937.

90. Works Progress Administration, *We Work Again*.

91. Works Progress Administration, *We Work Again*.

92. Works Progress Administration, *We Work Again*.

93. Weiss, *Farewell to Party of Lincoln*.

94. Works Progress Administration, *We Work Again*.

95. Ella Baker and Marvel Cooke, "The Bronx Slave Market," *Crisis*, November 1935, 330.

96. Vivian Morris, "Bronx Slave Market," interview of Minnie Marshall, 1938, US Work Projects Administration, Federal Writers' Project Manuscript Division, Library of Congress, https://www.loc.gov/item/wpalh001468/; Baker and Cooke, "The Bronx Slave Market," 340; Harris, "Marvel Cooke."

97. Bryan McCann, *Hello, Hello Brazil*, 21.

98. Jerry Dávila, *Diploma of Whiteness*, 1–20.

99. Bindas, *Swing, That Modern Sound*, 11–12; Sklaroff, *Black Culture and New Deal*. This seems to have changed after Sokoloff's tenure, as a 1939 Negro Arts Committee Federal Arts Council report listed the FMP as having one of the highest black employment rates in all the Federal One programs. See Stewart, *Long Past Slavery*, 122.

100. Gore, *Radicalism at the Crossroads*, 25–26; Kelley, *Race Rebels*, 103–22; and Denning, *Cultural Front*, 77–83.

101. Sklaroff, *Black Culture and New Deal*, 61–64; Stewart, *Long Past Slavery*, 127–29.

102. Denning, *Cultural Front*, 45.

103. Sklaroff, *Black Culture and New Deal*, 1–14; and Locke, "Negro's Contribution," 528.

104. Sklaroff, *Black Culture and New Deal*, 48–49.

105. Pereira, *Cor, profissão e mobilidade*, 230–31.

106. One black musician remembered, "day by day we felt the music gaining prestige, principally with the appearance of white singers and instrumentalists, some even from good families." Pereira, *Cor, profissão e mobilidade*, 230–31.

107. Hertzman, *Making Samba*, 118, 129; McCann, *Hello, Hello Brazil*, 49–50, 57, 109.

108. See Hertzman, *Making Samba*, 116–45, 169–71; McCann, *Hello, Hello Brazil*, 58–59.

109. Dinerstein, *Swinging the Machine*, 50–52.

110. Dinerstein, 141; Caponi-Tabery, *Jump for Joy*, 9–10.

CHAPTER 5

1. See Fausto, *Concise History of Brazil*, 227–28. The German attacks on Brazilian ships were in large part a response to the Estado Novo dictatorship's breaking of diplomatic and economic ties with the Axis nations after Pearl Harbor, a break that was officially declared at the second meeting of the American Republic Foreign Affairs Ministers in Rio de Janeiro in January 1942.

2. See Levine, *Father of the Poor?*, 69–70. Mexico—the other Latin American country to declare war on the Axis powers—sent about three hundred volunteers to fight in the Philippines.

3. For a good analysis of the geopolitical significance of Cape Verde during the war and German and Allied military strategies regarding the archipelago, see Gomes, "Cabo Verde e a Segunda Guerra Mundial."

4. Secret Memorandum (no date or other information), pp. 2–3, folder P.G. 6, Coordination of Brazilian Psychological Warfare, Field Station Files, Wash-PLNG, Group-AD-3–4, box 8, Record Group 226, NARA; and "Ministry of Information (British) Overseas Planning Committee, Plan of Propaganda for Brazil, Appreciation," Secret Paper 157 (n.d.), p. 1, folder 64273–64275, box 777, Office of Strategic Services, 64–262–64, 339, Record Group 226, NARA. For Secretary Knox's testimony before Congress, see Senate Committee on Appropriations, House Committee on Military Affairs, *Compulsory Military Training and Service: Hearings before the Committee on Military Affairs*, 76th Cong., 3rd Sess., August 14, 1940, 578–79.

5. "Ministry of Information (British) Overseas Planning Committee, Plan of Propaganda for Brazil, Appreciation," Secret Paper 157 (no date), folder 64273–64275, box 777, Office of Strategic Services 64–262–64, 339, Record Group 226, NARA. In his memoirs, Cordell Hull says that "(w)ithout the air bases Brazil permitted us to construct on her territory victory either in Europe or in Asia could not have come so soon." Quoted in McCann, *Brazilian American Alliance*, 213. McCann also addresses Pot of Gold in "Brazil and World War II." Operation Pot of Gold is discussed briefly in Friedman, *Nazis and Good Neighbors*, 2. Boris Fausto has written that the United States lacked official permission to set up the bases in 1941; see *Brazil: A Concise History*, 228.

6. "Ministry of Information (British) Overseas Planning Committee, Plan of Propaganda for Brazil, Appreciation," Secret Paper 157 (n.d.), p. 1, folder 64273–64275, box 777, Office of Strategic Services 64–262–64, 339, Record Group 226, NARA. The Italians were deemed the most assimilated of the three immigrant groups.

7. "Japanese in Brazil," confidential memorandum from J. Edgar Hoover to William J. Donovan, March 19, 1942, folder 13768–13793, box 63, Office of Strategic Services 13759–13834, Record Group 226, NARA.

8. "OIAA (Office of the Coordinator of Inter-American Affairs) Study, First Phase—Part I. Axis Penetration of South America," box 11, folder 84, Report Drafts, 1944, Nelson A. Rockefeller Personal Papers, Washington, DC, files, Series O, Record Group 4, Family Collection, Rockefeller Archive Center (hereafter RAC).

9. Hermann Rauschning, *Hitler Speaks* 69. *The Voice of Destruction* was the title of the US version.

10. See Hilton, *Hitler's Secret War,* 21. Von Ribbentrop told all German diplomats in South America to refute Roosevelt's statements on the topic.

11. Undated anonymous letter to Góes Monteiro, Fundo Góes Monteiro, Série 4, Subsérie 2, Notação SA 669, Arquivo Nacional, Rio de Janeiro. The letter references the book's statement that Brazil was "governed and inhabited by corrupt mestizos [*mestiços corrompidos*]." The book was published in Brazil as *O Hitler me disse* in 1940 and was reissued in 1943.

12. In the 1980s, Wolfgang Hänel argued in a conference paper that Rauschning's work was fiction, contending that he had met with Hitler on only a handful of occasions, not over one hundred times, as Rauschning claimed. Among other things, Hänel also said that French and New York-based writers and publishers had commissioned the book. Other scholars, such as David Redles and Martin Broszat, are skeptical of Hänel and the other naysayers. Redles defends the cautious use of the book. See Redles, *Hitler's Millennial Reich,* 191–98. For an English-language summary of Hänel's findings, see Weber, "Swiss Historian Exposes Memoir."

13. Moura, *Autonomia na dependência;* Moura, *Relações exteriores do Brasil;* and Fausto, *Concise History of Brazil,* 226–27. Problems arose between Brazil and Germany on the eve of war for several reasons, including President Vargas's naming of ex-ambassador to the United States and Pan-Americanist Oswaldo Aranha as minister of foreign affairs; the fascist *integralista* movement's attempted coup at the presidential palace, which resulted in a crackdown on Nazi-friendly groups; the arrest of a Nazi agent in the South of Brazil; and the subsequent yet temporary ousting of the German ambassador.

14. Skidmore, *Politics in Brazil,* 42–43; Tota, *Seduction of Brazil,* 67–69; and Hilton, *Hitler's Secret War,* 20–27.

15. "Ministry of Information (British) Overseas Planning Committee, Plan of Propaganda for Brazil, Appreciation," Secret Paper 157 (n.d.), folder 64273–64275, box 777, Office of Strategic Services 64–262–64, 339, Record Group 226, NARA. Other Brazilian war materials resources included manganese, tungsten, iron ore, and industrial diamonds.

16. "Ministry of Information (British) Overseas Planning Committee, Plan of Propaganda for Brazil, Appreciation," Secret Paper 157 (n.d.), pp. 3 and 7, folder 64273–64275, box 777, Office of Strategic Services 64, 262–64, 339, Record Group 226, NARA; and Levine, *Father*, 65–66, 71.

17. "As forças armadas americanas estarão presentes em todos os oceanos," *Jornal do Brasil*, January 7, 1942, 7. For the full text of Roosevelt's address in English, see https://www.presidency.ucsb.edu/documents/state-the-union-address-1 (accessed July 2017).

18. "Fiéis à democracia e aos compromissos assumidos com a sua própria história," *Jornal do Brasil*, April 11, 1943, 6.

19. See Myrdal, *American Dilemma*.

20. Getúlio Vargas, "Assistência ao trabalhador intelectual" (speech given to inaugurate the Serviço de Assistência ao trabalhador intelectual, or the Agency of Assistance to the Intellectual Worker, at the DEIP de São Paulo, December 21, 1943), in Vargas, *A nova política do Brasil X*, 207.

21. See Lauerhass, *Getúlio Vargas*, 141–42. The magazine ran from 1941 to 1945.

22. Oliveira, "O pensamento de Almir de Andrade," in Oliveira, Velloso, and Gomes, *Estado Novo*, 31; Almir de Andrade, "Política e Cultura," in *Cultura Política*, vol. 1, no. 3 (April 1941), 4–8.

23. Quoted in Oliveira, "O pensamento de Almir de Andrade," in Oliveira, Velloso, and Gomes, *Estado Novo*, 34.

24. Nicodemo, "State-Sponsored Avant-Garde," 132.

25. Almir de Andrade, "As diretrizes da nova política do Brasil," *Cultura Política* 3, no. 23 (January 1943): 12, 17, FGV/CPDOC.

26. Loewenstein, *Brazil under Vargas*, vii–viii, xi.

27. As chapter 4 has shown, Karl Loewenstein lays out his famous notion of "militant democracy" in "Militant Democracy and Fundamental Rights, 1" and "Militant Democracy and Fundamental Rights, 2."

28. Loewenstein, *Brazil under Vargas*, 136–39, 371–73.

29. Silvio Peixoto, "A coerência histórica de uma atitude política," *Cultura Política* 3, no. 31, edição extraordinária (August 1943): 52, 60.

30. Djacir Meneses, "Contribuição brasileira para a paz no mundo de amanhã," *Cultura Política* 3, no. 31, edição extraordinária (August 1943): 339, 340.

31. Newton O'Reilly, "Raça de Mestiços," *Cultura Política* 3, no. 28 (June 1943): 83–88.

32. Castro Costa, "Conceito de democracia no Estado Nacional," *Cultura Política* 3, no. 32 (September 1943): 25–26.

33. Draft of speech dated October 13, 1942, G.1942.10.13, rolo 7, fotograma 690, Records of Gustavo Capanema, FGV/CPDOC.

34. Aranha and Soares, *A Revolução e a America*, 9, 17–20, 23–26.

35. See Williams, *Culture Wars*, 221. Some of these scholars include anthropologists Ruth Landes and Melville Herskovits, black sociologist E. Franklin Frasier, and Austrian American historian Frank Tannenbaum.

36. See Fabris, *Portinari amico mio*, 93. In a footnote, Fabris writes that two US scholars had presented at São Paulo conferences around the time of

Andrade's letter, including Melville Herskovits, who spoke at a conference on blacks in the New World.

37. See Costa, *Brazilian Empire*, 238. For more on these studies, see Maio, "UNESCO and the Study of Race Relations in Brazil."

38. Getúlio Vargas, *Discursos* (Rio de Janeiro: DIP, 1944), 19, Biblioteca Nacional. This speech was given at an Associação Brasileira de Imprensa (Associated Brazilian Press) luncheon on April 15, 1944.

39. "A 'entrevista' distribuída," *Diário de Notícias*, March 3, 1945, 4. Vargas's original phrase was "extremos limites de raça."

40. "Vargas Is Evasive on Running Again," *New York Times*, March 3, 1945, 8.

41. "As declarações do sr. Getúlio Vargas," *Diário de Notícias*, March 3, 1945, 4.

42. Many books and articles refer to the office as the OIAA, which is anachronistic for this period as its name changed to the Office of Inter-American Affairs only in 1945.

43. Memorandum from Alberto Rondon to Gerald Smith, May 12, 1943 (stamped); memorandum from Gerald Smith to Frank Jamieson, May 14, 1943; and memorandum from John Robey to Gerald Smith, June 4, 1943, file folder Negroes, box 411, General Records, Central Files, Information, Science and Education, Race, OCIAA, Record Group 229, NARA. The records hold not Rondon's original memo but a typed transcription of it that contains a few spelling errors. I have corrected the errors here.

44. See Johnson, *Latin America in Caricature*.

45. Lesser, *Negotiating National Identity*, 116–28.

46. Homer Brett, American consul, Bahia, Brazil, to the Department of State, September 4, 1924, p. 1 (National Archives Microfilm Publication 1910–1929 Lands), Record Group 59, NARA.

47. Homer Brett, American consul, Bahia, Brazil, to the secretary of state, October 21, 1924 (National Archives Microfilm Publication 1910–1929 Lands), Record Group 59, NARA. The translation was provided along with the original article. Nestor Duarte's *Diário da Bahia* article "O Japonez Intruso" appeared in the October 18, 1924, issue.

48. R. J. Clarke, American consul, Vitória, Espírito Santo, to the Department of State, May 29, 1929 (National Archives Microfilm Publication 1910–1929 Lands), Record Group 59, NARA.

49. Edward V. Morgan, Rio de Janeiro, to the secretary of state, August 13, 1925 (National Archives Microfilm Publication 1910–1929 Lands), Record Group 59, NARA.

50. Jefferson Caffery, chargé d'affaires, s.i., to the secretary of state, October 1924 (National Archives Microfilm Publication 1910–1929 Lands), Record Group 59, NARA. Caffery's memorandum was also sent to the US embassy in Brazil. Caffery would not have read the Clarke memo from Espírito Santo, as he was acting as US envoy to Colombia by 1929. Caffery was ambassador to Brazil from 1937 to 1944. See the website of the US Department of State's Office of the Historian: http://history.state.gov/departmenthistory/people/caffery-jefferson (accessed September 9, 2009).

51. Major R. L. Whitley, military attaché, Brazil, memo no. 218 to the War Department, January 12, 1923, file folder 2656-K-1 to K-5, 2656-KK-1, 2656-L-1 to L-5, and 2656-LL-1, Military Intelligence Division Correspondence, 1917–1941, box 1611, Records of the WFGS, Record Group 165, NARA. Whitley was reporting on the Brazilian outcry over a US nurse heading a nurse-training program in Brazil, who evidently refused to allow black and mixed-race women to enter the program.

52. Confidential intelligence report from US Naval observer in Recife, Brazil, to the Navy Department, June 14, 1943, folder 40,065–40,075, box 453, Office of Strategic Services 39977–40142, Record Group 226, NARA.

53. "Democratic Trends in Brazil," Office of Strategic Services confidential memo, December 5, 1942, folder 25,456–25,465, box 233, Office of Strategic Services 25,440–25,547, Record Group 226, NARA.

54. Confidential intelligence report of the Navy Department, from H. A. Richey, US naval observer in Recife, Brazil, to the Navy Department, July 18, 1942, folder 21250–21272, box 155, Office of Strategic Services 21,222–21,387, Record Group 226, NARA (translation theirs).

55. See Mesquita, "O projeto regionalista de Gilberto Freyre," 122.

56. After the formation of the coordinator of information (COI) in 1941 under Colonel William J. Donovan, representatives of the OCIAA, COI, and military intelligence met weekly. When the Office of War Information (OWI) was created in 1942, it headed a Committee on War Information Policy, with representatives of the secretaries of state, war, and navy, the Joint Psychological Warfare Committee, and the OCIAA. The OWI was responsible for domestic and overseas propaganda outside Latin America. See Carl Spaeth, assistant coordinator of the OCIAA, to Nelson A. Rockefeller, coordinator of inter-American affairs, September 1941 (no exact date), Family Collection, Record Group 4, Nelson A. Rockefeller, Personal, Series O, Washington, DC, files, box 5, folder 37, William Donovan, 1941–1946, Rockefeller Archive Center (RAC); and Office of Inter-American Affairs, Rowland, *History of the Office of the Coordinator of Inter-American Affairs*, 200, 204.

57. "Report of Propaganda Branch," November 30, 1943, to March 1, 1945, pp. 1–4, folder PW Planning October–December 1943, box 12, PW Planning: January to December 1943, Record Group 218, NARA.

58. Reich, *Life of Nelson A. Rockefeller*, 228–29.

59. This statement is common throughout military records during this period. For one example, see memorandum for the chief of staff from Sherman Miles, brigadier general, US Army, subject: coordination of intelligence, public relations, and morale, August 29, 1941, folder: chronological files—1920s, 1930s through 1940, chronological files: World War I to March 1943, box 3, Record Group 218 (Joint Chiefs of Staff Historical Office, Dr. Edward P. Lilly [Papers] on Psychological Warfare), NARA.

60. "Japan Vis-à-vis Latin America: A Brief" (OCIAA confidential brief, "Content Directive"), January 1945, p. 20, folder 20, box 3, Nelson Rockefeller Personal Papers, Washington, DC, files, Record Group 4, Series O, Family Collection, RAC.

61. Quoted in Foley, *Quest for Equality*, 27–28.

62. Foley, 26. White hoped to parlay negative opinions that Latin Americans held about race in the United States into the attainment of more rights for US blacks (Foley, 27).

63. "Propaganda Analysis, Daily Bulletin: Enemy Broadcasts to Latin America," January 24, 1944, folder 8, reactions to report by Sen. Hugh Butler, 1943–44, box 10, Nelson Rockefeller Personal Papers, Washington, DC, files, Record Group 4, Series O, Family Collection, RAC. Citation is from the OCIAA bulletin report.

64. Memo from Dwight Jennings to Nelson Rockefeller, November 14, 1944, forwarding a draft of the OCIAA report that in large part studied "Axis Penetration in South America," folder 49, Dwight D. Jennings, 1944–1946, box 6, Nelson Rockefeller Personal Papers, Washington, DC, files, Family Collection, Record Group 4, Series O, RAC.

65. "Ministry of Information (British) Overseas Planning Committee, Plan of Propaganda for Brazil, Appreciation," Secret Paper 157 (n.d.), p. 10, folder 64273–64275, box 777, Office of Strategic Services 64–262–64, 339, Record Group 226, NARA.

66. "Ministry of Information (British) Overseas Planning Committee, Plan of Propaganda for Brazil, Appreciation," Secret Paper 157 (n.d.), p. 1, folder 64273–64275, Box 777, Office of Strategic Services 64–262–64, 339, Record Group 226, NARA. "Brazil: The Largest Negro Nation" was an article written by Charles Gauld that presented Brazil as a racial utopia.

CHAPTER 6

1. Both Daryle Williams and Tania Regina de Luca have written that the majority of the records for Brazil's most important propaganda agency, the Department of Press and Propaganda, have "disappeared." Williams suggests that neglect and institutional decay were to blame. Luca also discusses how some of DIP's international propaganda can be recovered in US archives. See Williams, *Culture Wars*, 16–19, 83; and Luca, "A produção do Departamento de Imprensa e Propaganda," 272–73.

2. Ninkovich, *Diplomacy of Ideas*, 27–28, 35–37. Only when cultural relations with Latin America were presented as an emergency related to national interests did Congress fund the division.

3. See Reich, *Life of Nelson A. Rockefeller*, 170–88, 233–35; and *History of the Office of the Coordinator of Inter-American Affairs*, 181–220.

4. "The Shortwave Radio Situation," report from R. E. Danielson, Major, GSC, to Colonel Solbert, December 11, 1941, folder Chronological Jan–Mar 1942, Chronological Files World War I to March 1943, box 3, Record Group 218, NARA.

5. "Report on Propaganda Branch (30 November 1943 to 1 March 1945)," folder PW Planning: January to December 1943, file Propaganda Warfare Planning Oct–Dec 1943, box 12, Record Group 218, NARA.

6. Edward P. Lilly's notes taken from a mimeographed copy of the "Joint Dictionary of Military Terms for Army-Navy Use," May 28, 1946, folder Definitions, OCIAA to Directives, box 5, Record Group 218, NARA.

7. Quoted in Ninkovich, *Diplomacy of Ideas*, 36–40.

8. Memo from Mary Winslow to Nelson Rockefeller, July 8, 1941, General Records, Central Files, Information, Science and Education, Race, file folder Negroes, box 411, Records of the Office of Inter-American Affairs, Record Group 229, NARA; and memo from Mary Winslow to Nelson Rockefeller, July 24, 1941, file folder Negroes, General Records, Central Files, Information, Science and Education, Race, box 411, Records of the Office of Inter-American Affairs, Record Group 229, NARA. For the Owen quote, see Foley, *Quest for Equality*, 28.

9. Memo from Mary Winslow to Nelson Rockefeller, July 8, 1941, General Records, Central Files, Information, Science and Education, Race, file folder Negroes, box 411, Records of the Office of Inter-American Affairs, Record Group 229, NARA; and memo from Mary Winslow to Nelson Rockefeller, July 24, 1941, file folder Negroes, General Records, Central Files, Information, Science and Education, Race, box 411, Records of the Office of Inter-American Affairs, Record Group 229, NARA. A brief biography of Winslow can be found at https://hollisarchives.lib.harvard.edu/repositories/8/resources/5752 (accessed February 21, 2019).

10. Memo from Mary Winslow to Nelson Rockefeller, May 14, 1941, General Records, Central Files, Information, Science and Education, Race, file folder Negroes, box 411, Record Group 229, NARA. Rayford Logan wrote that the position was unpaid in his diary entry that described the meeting with Winslow. Logan diary entry, August 5, 1941, folder 5 (1941), box 3 (Family Papers and Diary and Related Materials), Rayford W. Logan Papers, Manuscript Division, Library of Congress. Barnett advised Rockefeller that blacks were dissatisfied with the manner in which the State Department isolated Latin Americans from US blacks. See Plummer, *Rising Wind*, 100–101.

11. See Janken, *Rayford W. Logan*, 136–38. Janken lists Cuba as the chosen site for the conference, but it was Haiti that was eventually decided upon. See letter from Waldo Leland to John M. Clark, March 21, 1942, file folder Inter-American Conference on Negro Studies OEMcr 64, General Records, Central Files, Information, Science and Education, Race, box 411, Records of the Office of Inter-American Affairs, Record Group 229, NARA.

12. Donald Goodchild to Kenneth Holland, May 1, 1943, file folder Negroes, General Records, Central Files, Information, Science and Education, Race, box 411, Records of the Office of Inter-American Affairs, Record Group 229, NARA.

13. See Janken, *Rayford W. Logan*, 138–43. W. E. B. DuBois was among the black intellectuals who complained about being excluded from the conference and from ACLS-directed projects in general. Although Logan was confident that Rockefeller was genuinely racially liberal and in his corner (Rockefeller made an appeal to the ACLS to include DuBois in the conference), Logan, DuBois, and other black scholars felt that leading white academics of African Diasporic studies, like Melville Herskovits, stifled the inclusion of black intellectuals. Evidently, Herskovits and the ACLS's Committee on Negro Studies felt that black intellectuals were not adequately scientific in their research methodologies. For a breakdown of the way the OCIAA-ACLS-State Department

Joint Committee on Cultural Relations operated, see Ninkovich, *Diplomacy of Ideas*, 38.

14. Waldo Leland to John M. Clark, March 21, 1942, file folder Inter-American Conference on Negro Studies OEMcr 64, General Records, Central Files, Information, Science and Education, Race, box 411, Records of the Office of Inter-American Affairs, Record Group 229, NARA. The joint committee rescheduled the time and location of the conference a few times before giving up on it. The year after the conference's cancellation, the ACLS appealed to the OCIAA for funding for an inter-American journal of Negro studies to be titled *Afro-America*. I have not seen evidence that this project came to fruition either. See letter from Donald Goodchild to Kenneth Holland, May 1, 1943, file folder Negroes, General Records, Central Files, Information, Science and Education, Race, box 411, Records of the Office of Inter-American Affairs, Record Group 229, NARA.

15. See Rayford Logan diary entry, October 30, 1941, folder 5 (1941), box 3 (Family Papers and Diary and Related Materials), Rayford W. Logan Papers, Manuscript Division, Library of Congress; Janken, *Rayford W. Logan*, 138–41. Both Janken and the diary entry detail Logan's conversation with Rockefeller.

16. See Janken, *Rayford W. Logan*.

17. Alain Locke delivered a series of lectures in Haiti on the theme "Contribution of the Negro to the Culture of the Americas," in which "special emphasis was given to the Negro in the United States." The lectures were hosted by the Haitian Ministry of Education, and the trip was at least in part paid for by the OCIAA, which also published Locke's lectures as the book *Le rôle du nègre dans la culture des Amériques*. The OCIAA's hope was that "the publication of the lectures would help dispel some of the misconceptions prevalent in Haiti about the American Negro." In the lectures, Locke consistently interlinked his discussion of black culture with ideas about race and democracy. In addition to the lectures, Locke called upon the OCIAA to fund the exchange of black students and educators in the Americas, translations of US black literature into Spanish and Portuguese, and a traveling black art exhibit, to name a few ideas. See Project Authorization PHA-30, from Joseph Montllor to Nelson Rockefeller, June 15, 1943, file folder Race, General Records, Central Files, Information, Science and Education, Country Files, Haiti, Honduras, box 428, Records of the Office of Inter-American Affairs, Record Group 229, NARA; Alain LeRoy Locke, *Le rôle du nègre dans la culture des Amériques* (Port-au-Prince: Impr. de l'Etat, 1943), file folder Race, General Records, Central Files, Information, Science and Education, Country Files, Haiti, Honduras, box 428, Records of the Office of Inter-American Affairs, Record Group 229, NARA; memo from Alain Locke to Mary Winslow, June 30, 1941, file folder Negroes, General Records, Central Files, Information, Science and Education, Race, box 411, Records of the Office of Inter-American Affairs, Record Group 229, NARA; and letter from Alain Locke to Kenneth Holland, January 28, 1943, file folder Negroes, General Records, Central Files, Information, Science and Education, Race, box 411, Records of the Office of Inter-American Affairs, Record Group 229, NARA.

18. "Ministry of Information (British) Overseas Planning Committee, Plan of Propaganda for Brazil, Appreciation," Secret Paper 157 (n.d.), p. 10, folder:

64273–64275, box 777, Office of Strategic Services 64,262–64,339, Record Group 226, NARA.

19. Using another acronym common for the organization, Robert Levine has written that the OCIAA was disparagingly referred to as the "DIP-OIAA" by left-leaning Brazilians who saw this period as one of unrestrained US cultural imperialism. See Levine, *Brazilian Photographs of Genevieve Naylor*, 24.

20. Office of the Coordination Committee for Brazil Project Authorization (Special Project no. 61), Rio de Janeiro, January 28, 1943, Records of the Department of Information, Regional Division, Coordination Committee for Brazil, General Records (E-99), 03.1, file folder 03.1 (c), Projects Summary, box 1271, Record Group 229, NARA.

21. Cramer and Prutsch, "Nelson A. Rockefeller's Office," 804.

22. Antônio Pedro Tota has described the DIP's rebroadcasting of OCIAA newscasts over Brazilian airwaves as being a major factor in the Americanization of Brazilian culture during World War II. See his *O Imperialismo Sedutor: A Americanização do Brasil na época da Segunda Guerra* (São Paulo: Companhia das Letras, 2000). The book was revised and published in English as *The Seduction of Brazil*.

23. Memorandum from the Brazilian Division to the coordinator, attn: Mr. Robbins, Rio de Janeiro, March 19, 1942, Records of the Department of Information, Regional Division, Coordination Committee for Brazil, General Records (E-99), 03.1, file folder 03.1 (f), Project Review (Brazilian Division), box 1273, Record Group 229, NARA; and Assuntos a Serem Tratados (no other information), Records of the Department of Information, Regional Division, Coordination Committee for Brazil, General Records (E-99), 03.1, file folder 03.1 (f), Project Review (Brazilian Division), box 1273, Record Group 229, NARA.

24. "Help from Brazil," *Time*, March 30, 1942.

25. "Report of the Activities of the Radio Division," from Don Francisco to Berent Friele, June 18, 1942, Records of the Department of Information, Regional Division, Coordination Committee for Brazil, General Records (E-99), 03.1, file folder 03.1 (c), Projects Summary, box 1271, Record Group 229, NARA; and "Assuntos a Serem Tratados" (no other information), Records of the Department of Information, Regional Division, Coordination Committee for Brazil, General Records (E-99), 03.1, file folder 03.1 (f), Project Review (Brazilian Division), box 1273, Record Group 229, NARA. The OCIAA's focus on US troops in its reports to Brazil is in Oliveira, "O Intelectual do DIP," in *Constelação Capanema: Intelectuais e políticas*, 38. The report about printing the radio commentaries in the Brazilian press is documented in Project Review of the Office of the Brazilian Division, Rio de Janeiro, April 18, 1942, Records of the Department of Information, Regional Division, Coordination Committee for Brazil, General Records (E-99), 03.1, file folder 03.1 (f), Project Review (Brazilian Division), box 1273, Record Group 229, NARA.

26. "Report of the Activities of the Radio Division," from Don Francisco to Berent Friele, June 18, 1942, Records of the Department of Information, Regional Division, Coordination Committee for Brazil, General Records (E-99), 03.1, file folder 03.1 (c), Projects Summary, box 1271, Record Group 229,

NARA; and Project Review of the Office of the Brazilian Division, Rio de Janeiro, May 2, 1942, Records of the Department of Information, Regional Division, Coordination Committee for Brazil, General Records (E-99), 03.1, file folder 03.1 (f), Project Review (Brazilian Division), box 1273, Record Group 229, NARA.

27. Memo from Don Francisco to Nelson Rockefeller, March 5, 1943, folder 4, box 1, Family Collection, Record Group 4, Nelson A. Rockefeller Personal Papers, Series O, Washington, DC, files, RAC. The fascist organization was the Ação Social Brasileira. For Barata's biographical information, see *Dicionário Histórico-Biográfico Brasileiro*, s.v. "Barata, Júlio."

28. "Report on Hospitality, Months of February, March, and April, 1942," submitted by Melanie W. Gordon Barber and Mrs. William A. Barber, folder 3, box 1, Family Collection, Record Group 4, Nelson A. Rockefeller Personal Papers, Series O, Washington, DC, files, RAC; and "Assuntos a Serem Tratados" (no other information), Records of the Department of Information, Regional Division, Coordination Committee for Brazil, General Records (E-99), 03.1, file folder 03.1 (f), Project Review (Brazilian Division), box 1273, Record Group 229, NARA. The name that frequently appeared as "Assis de Figueiredo" must have been Francisco de Paula Assis Figueiredo, who became director of DIP's division of tourism after he suggested the creation of a federal tourism agency. See Filho, "O Turismo na Era Vargas e o Departamento de Imprensa e Propaganda—DIP," 105–7; Amaral, "Getúlio Vargas—O criador de ilusões."

29. Confidential Fund Projects (no date), folder 32, Confidential Projects, 1941–1942, box 4, Family Collection, Record Group 4, Nelson A. Rockefeller Personal Papers, Series O, Washington, DC, files, RAC.

30. The OCIAA records refer to Pessoa as "Diretor da Divisão de Divulgação." He would also hold positions as "Brazilian Consultant" to Francis Jamieson, head of the OCIAA's information program, and then as the "Director of the Brazilian Information Bureau in New York." It is unclear which agency Pessoa's new position was with. Letter from Alfredo Pessoa to Nelson A. Rockefeller, June 16, 1943, Family Collection, Record Group 4, Nelson A. Rockefeller Personal Papers, Series O, Washington, DC, Files, box 1, folder 5, RAC; letter from Alfredo Pessoa to Francis A. Jamieson, December 4, 1945; and letter from Nelson A. Rockefeller to Alfredo Pessoa, January 2, 1946, Family Collection, Record Group 4, Nelson A. Rockefeller Personal Papers, Series O, Washington, DC, files, box 1, folder 8, RAC.

31. "Annual Report of the Activities of the Office of the Coordinator of Inter-American Affairs in Brazil, during the calendar year 1943, March 2, 1944," p. 3, Records of the Department of Information, Regional Division, Coordination Committee for Brazil, General Records (E-99), 03.1–02.4, folder Annual Report of Activities (Brazil), box 1259, Record Group 229, NARA.

32. Coordinator of Inter-American Affairs Annual Report, 1945, p. 11, file folder Annual Report of Activities (Brazil), Records of the Department of Information, Regional Division, Coordination Committee for Brazil, General Records (E-99), 01.3–02.4, box 1259, Record Group 229, NARA.

33. "Summary of Subversion Information Received during the Week Ending February 7, 1942, Report no. 49," folder Latin America, Subversive—Facists

[sic] Activities (South America), MID "Regional File," 1922–44, Latin America Subversive, box 2357, Record Group 165, NARA.

34. Report of the Activities of the Radio Division Coordinator of Inter-American Affairs, May 20, 1942, file folder 03.1(c) Projects Summary, Records of the Department of Information, Regional Division, Coordination Committee for Brazil, General Records (E-99), 03.1, box 1271, Record Group 229, NARA.

35. *Estamos em Guerra*, August 16, 1942, pp. 16–17, file folder RA-1238, Scripts Estames en [sic] Guerra, Portuguese (1), General Records, Central Files, Information, Radio, Programs, box 247, Record Group 229, NARA.

36. *Estamos em Guerra*, series 11, numero 10, July 25, 1942, p. 20, file folder RA-1238 Scripts Estames en [sic] Guerra, Portuguese (1), General Records, Central Files, Information, Radio, Programs, box 247, Record Group 229, NARA.

37. *Estamos em Guerra*, June 20, 1943, p. 16, file folder RA-1238 Scripts Estames en [sic] Guerra, Portuguese (7), General Records, Central Files, Information, Radio, Programs, box 247, Record Group 229, NARA.

38. Some issues of the OCIAA's pictorial war magazine in Latin America, *Em guarda* (*En guardia* to the Spanish-speaking countries), included photos of bombed-out Catholic churches in Germany, presumably destroyed by the Nazis. Furthermore, the OCIAA's pamphlet *A Guerra Nazista contra a Igreja Católica* (The Nazi War against the Catholic Church) was hailed as both "favorably received" and as possibly "one of the most powerful individual weapons . . . made available" to the OCIAA's Committee in Brazil. See Project Authorization, Special Project no. 63, February 4, 1943, Records of the Department of Information, Regional Division, Coordination Committee for Brazil, General Records (E-99), 03.1, file folder 03.1 (b), Special Projects, box 1271, Record Group 229, NARA; and "Annual Report of the Activities of the Office of the Coordinator of Inter-American Affairs in Brazil, during the calendar year 1943, March 2, 1944," p. 20, Records of the Department of Information, Regional Division, Coordination Committee for Brazil, General Records (E-99), 03.1–02.4, folder Annual Report of Activities (Brazil), box 1259, Record Group 229, NARA.

39. *Nuestro futuro—¿Hombres libres o esclavos?*, p. 41, folder 122, box 17, Series O, Record Group 4, Nelson A. Rockefeller Personal Papers, RAC. Although I found only a Spanish-language copy of this particular issue, it is almost certain that a Portuguese translation existed and was distributed to Brazil. Each of these comic histories was published in Portuguese for Brazilian distribution, and the archive contained other comic issues in both Portuguese and Spanish. In the other comic histories I found, Spanish-language issues differed from their Portuguese-language counterparts only in material that was specific to certain Latin American countries, not for such broad, general messaging as found in this issue.

40. *Nuestro futuro—¿Hombres libres o esclavos?*, 42, 33.

41. *Nuestro futuro—¿Hombres libres o esclavos?*, 42.

42. This tendency to represent Latin America as female has a long history. See, for instance, Johnson, *Latin America*, 74–116. Catherine L. Benamou also discusses the feminization of Latin America in Good Neighbor musicals in *It's All True*, 200–202.

43. Pennee Bender, "Policies and Productions of the Motion Picture Division of the Office of the Coordinator of Inter-American Affairs," 3 (paper presented at the symposium Imagining Latin America: United States Film Policy and Its Impacts during World War II, New York University, April 24, 1993). Bender points out that the OCIAA Motion Picture Division in part influenced the feature films produced by the big studios as well as the newsreels shown in Latin America, and also that the division produced, sponsored, or distributed 466 nontheatrical documentaries, such as the one laid out here. The OCIAA distributed over 300 of these nontheatrical films to Latin America, which were seen by three million people a month. See Bender, "Policies and Productions," 3–4.

44. This short film is not to be confused with the Hollywood movie *Crash Dive* (1943), which was also inspired by Miller. See Doherty, *Projections of War*, 212–13. Cuba Gooding Jr. also played Miller in Touchstone Pictures' 2001 film *Pearl Harbor*.

45. Richard Rogan, executive assistant to director, Motion Picture Division, to [name illegible] [date illegible], file folder Racial, General Records, Central Files, Information, Motion Pictures, Plans-Policy-Procedure, Films, box 214, Record Group 229, NARA. Despite the fact that Miller was eventually hailed as a wartime hero, Thomas Doherty has pointed out that at first "the white press and the Navy were less than forthcoming with the news of his action (demonstrating an early) reluctance of wartime America to salute its black patriots." See Doherty, *Projections of War*, 212.

46. Memorandum of conversation between Kenneth Macgowan and John Begg, February 14, 1942, file folder Racial, General Records, Central Files, Information, Motion Pictures, Plans-Policy-Procedure, Films, box 214, Record Group 229, NARA.

47. Rayford Logan to Nelson Rockefeller, July 11, 1942, file folder Racial, General Records, Central Files, Information, Motion Pictures, Plans-Policy-Procedure, Films, box 214, Record Group 229, NARA; and Nelson Rockefeller to Rayford Logan, August 14, 1942, file folder Racial, General Records, Central Files, Information, Motion Pictures, Plans-Policy-Procedure, Films, box 214, Record Group 229, NARA.

48. See Washburn, *Question of Sedition;* and Doherty, *Projections of War*, 212. One of the best-known films to emerge during this time was the War Department's *The Negro Soldier*, which was shown in movie theaters across the country, except for most of the South. Black critics praised the film enthusiastically. See Doherty, *Projections of War*, 213–15.

49. Memo from John Dreier to Harry Frantz, October 6, 1942, file folder Negroes, box 411, General Records, Central Files, Information, Science, Education, Race, Record Group 229, NARA.

50. Memo from Jack Leighter to Francis Alstock and Walter Wanger, October 16, 1942, file folder Propaganda Films, box 214, General Records, Central Files, Information, Motion Pictures, Plans-Policy-Procedure, Films, Record Group 229, NARA. A memo in response from Karl Macdonald of the Motion Picture Division stated that the OCIAA had screened it. Macdonald referred to it as "a very good reel for our program." See memo from Karl Macdonald to Jack Leighter, October 30, 1942, file folder Propaganda Films, box 214, General

Records, Central Files, Information, Motion Pictures, Plans-Policy-Procedure, Films, Record Group 229, NARA.

51. In a telephone conversation with Yale Glee Club business manager Sean Maher on September 27, 2010, I was told that the picture of the 1941 Glee Club did not seem to include any people of color. He pointed out the possibility that some members who traveled to South America might not have been present when the photograph was taken, but he believed it was unlikely that there would have been students of color in the group. Yale was still an all-male university in 1941.

52. Report of the Yale Glee Club South American concert tour, June 20 to August 11, 1941, by Marshall Bartholomew, director, September 15, 1941, box 12, folder 92, Trips—South America, 1942, Family Collection, Record Group 4, Nelson A. Rockefeller Personal Papers, Series O, Washington, DC, files, RAC. Information about the OCIAA's subsidizing the trip is in a memorandum from Arthur Jones and Dudley Easby Jr. to John Lockwood and Berent Friele, subject: Field Projects in Brazil, Argentina, and Uruguay, July 10, 1941, Records of the Department of Information, Regional Division, Coordination Committee for Brazil, General Records (E-99), 03.1, file folder 03.1 (c), Projects Summary, box 1271, Record Group 229, NARA. The tour was characterized as a grand success in many government documents and in some Brazilian journals.

53. Report of the Yale Glee Club South American concert tour, June 20 to August 11, 1941, by Marshall Bartholomew, director, September 15, 1941, box 12, folder 92, Trips—South America, 1942, Family Collection, Record Group 4, Nelson A. Rockefeller Personal Papers, Series O, Washington, DC, files, RAC; Andrade Muricy, "Pelo mundo da música: O coral de universitários de Yale," *Jornal do Commercio*, July 9, 1941, BN. The three songs were "Couldn't Hear Nobody Pray," "There Is a Balm in Gilead," and "Battle of Jericho."

54. Luís da Câmara Cascudo, "Coral de estudantes da Universidade de Yale," *Diário de Notícias*, July 5, 1941.

55. Project authorization, sound recording project no. 6 (Concierto de musica popular), Records of the Department of Information, Regional Division, Coordination Committee for Brazil, General Records (E-99), 03.1, file folder Radio-Nall, folder no. 3, box 1270, Record Group 229, NARA; Kozinn, Alan Shulman's obituary (a New Friends of Rhythm cellist, composer, and arranger), in *New York Times*, July 13, 2002. Other helpful descriptions of the septet's music are "modern jazz music played in classical chamber music style" and "something neither jazz nor classical and yet somehow both, a world between." See *The Billboard: The World's Foremost Amusement Weekly* 59, no. 25 (June 28, 1947): 130; and Peter Aaron, review of the compact disc *The New Friends of Rhythm, 1939–1947 Performances*, in *Chronogram Magazine*, December 2007. Benny Goodman first played with an integrated band in 1938, and he is credited with being the first bandleader to do so. See Tackley, *Benny Goodman's Famous 1938 Carnegie Hall Jazz Concert*. For an excellent study of the Cold War jazz tours, see Von Eschen, *Satchmo*.

56. *Music in American Life*, no. 41, "Theatre," November 28, 1944 (produced and recorded), Records of the Department of Information, Records of the Radio Division, Radio Program Scripts, Mujeres de America—Muzak Continu-

ity Series, file folder Music in American Life, box 58, Record Group 229, NARA. The episodes ran for thirty minutes. The announcer used the English term *minstrels*.

57. Memo from Mary Winslow to Nelson Rockefeller, May 14, 1941, file folder Negroes, General Records, Central Files, Information, Science and Education, Race, box 411, Record Group 229, NARA; and memo from Mary Winslow to Nelson Rockefeller, July 24, 1941, file folder Negroes, General Records, Central Files, Information, Science and Education, Race, box 411, Record Group 229, NARA.

58. Brenda Gayle Plummer has written that the government did not send blacks to Latin America until after the war ended. See Plummer, *Rising Wind*, 100–101.

59. Project authorization, special project no. 68, Coordinating Committee for Brazil, file folder 03.1 b, Special Projects, Records of the Department of Information, Regional Division, Coordination Committee for Brazil, General Records (E-99), 03.1, Record Group 229, NARA.

60. The *Does Nature Prefer Blondes?* film appears many times in the archives, including "Propaganda Projects," document attached to memorandum from Philip Dunne to John H. Whitney, April 15, 1942, "Propaganda Films" file folder, General Records, Central Files, Information Motion Pictures, Plans-Policy-Procedure, Films, box 214, Record Group 229, NARA; "Motion Picture Section Planned Emergency Program for Immediate Action: Short Subject Ideas," December 13, 1941, p. 2, box 7, folder 56, Motion Picture Division, 1941–1945, Family, Record Group 4, Personal, O, Washington, DC, files, RAC; and "16 mm Films Being Distributed in Latin America" (n.d.), Nelson A. Rockefeller Personal Papers, box 7, folder 56, Family, Record Group 4, Personal, O, Washington, DC, files, RAC.

61. Memorandum from Richard Wilson (recipient unknown), March 13, 1942, pp. 15–16, folder (WW. Wilson. Film. *It's All True* [1993]. Research. Photocopies of 1930s–1950s Mercury docs, [4 of 10]); box 12, Papers 1930–2000; Richard Wilson—Orson Welles Papers, Special Collection, University of Michigan, Ann Arbor; project authorization, special project no. 61, Rio de Janeiro, January 28, 1943, file folder 03.1 (c), Projects (Summary), Records of the Department of Information, Regional Division, Coordination Committee for Brazil, General Records (E-99), 03.1, box 1271, Record Group 229, NARA; Tota, *Seduction*, 67–69, 79. Ayres de Andrade of the DIP's radio division informed Wilson about Brazil's monthly broadcasts to the United States.

62. Benamou, *It's All True*, 25–47, 329.

63. Examples of Welles's affinity with black themes and artistic circles included his directing of the all-black *"Voodoo" Macbeth* for the Federal Theatre Project in 1936, mentioned in chapter 4, and his theater adaptation of Richard Wright's *Native Son*. See Stam, "Orson Welles."

64. Benamou, *It's All True*, 25–45, 329.

65. See Filho, "O Turismo na Era Vargas e o Departamento de Imprensa e Propaganda—DIP"; and Benamou, *It's All True*, 46, 236–37.

66. See the documentary *It's All True: Based on an Unfinished Film by Orson Welles* (Paramount Pictures, a Les Film Balenciaga Production, 1993); Benamou,

It's All True, 213; and Stam, "Slow Fade to Afro," 18. Herivelto Martins was one of Welles's top consultants on the project. His son Pery Ribeiro (whom Benamou calls Pery Martins) was four years old when he participated in the film. Note: the English translation of the documentary's dialogue is my own and may be slightly different from the documentary's English subtitles.

67. Benamou, *It's All True*, 240. Welles would have combined the swanky with the street versions of Carnival in part by alternating musical scenes between Linda Batista, white Brazilian star of the elite Cassino da Urca, and Grande Otelo singing in the famous Praça Onze, favorite site for working-class samba revelers. Although they were in different venues, the editing-driven interaction would have made it appear that Batista and Otelo were, in fact, responding to one another. See Stam, "Orson Welles," 106; and Stam, *Tropical Multiculturalism*, 107–32.

68. Letter from V. Benício da Silva to Gustavo Capanema, October 12, 1941, Gustavo Capanema Papers, Code GC b Silva, V., rolo 6, fotograma 172, CPDOC/FGV.

69. "Concerning: Carnaval" report, p. 6, appendix pp. B, D, folder 7 (Films—It's All True), Box 17, the Welles mss., Orson Welles Collections, Lilly Library, Indiana University.

70. "Concerning: Carnaval" report, p. 13, Appendix pp. B, D–F, H, folder 7 (Films—It's All True), box 17, the Welles mss., Orson Welles Collections, Lilly Library, Indiana University. The term used in the report for the commercial music industry was *Rio's Tin Pan Alley*.

71. Folder WW. Wilson. Film. It's All True (1993). Scripts. Screenplay, 2/29/89, box 11, Papers 1930–2000, Richard Wilson-Orson Welles Papers, Special Collections, University of Michigan Library, Ann Arbor.

72. See the documentary *It's All True*. In the context of Welles's comments and of his description of the repressive nature of the Estado Novo, it is clear he felt that authorities were behind the attack. His quote is also cited and contextualized in Benamou, *It's All True*, 260–61.

73. See Stam, "Orson Welles," 109–10; and Siqueira, "É tudo verdade," 4–5.

74. Stam, *Tropical Multiculturalism*, 123. Similarly, US critics referred to Welles's 1940 theatrical adaptation of Richard Wright's *Native Son* as "communist propaganda."

75. See the documentary *It's All True;* and Benamou, *It's All True*, 259. Vargas had agreed to expand social benefits such as pensions to the *jangadeiros*.

76. Benamou, 55–59, 270–72.

77. Benamou, 47, 55–59, 199, 236–38, 270, 350n27; and see Stam, "Orson Welles," 109. Welles's role as ambassador actually caused some tension between him and RKO, as it slowed down production. RKO president Shaefer accused Welles of being more interested in his role with the OCIAA than with RKO. See Bender, "Film as an Instrument," 150.

78. Letter from Reg Armour to Phil Reisman, April 27, 1942, Folder WW. Wilson. Film. *It's All True* (1993). Research. Photocopies of 1930s–1950s Mercury docs (6 of 10), box 12, Richard Wilson-Orson Welles Papers, University of Michigan Library, Special Collections, Ann Arbor.

79. Bender, "Film as an Instrument," 151.

80. Stam, "Orson Welles," 98, 106–10, 151; and *Dicionário Histórico-Biográfico Brasileiro,* s.v. "A Manhã (1941)."

81. Stam, "Orson Welles," 97–98, 106.

82. Benamou, *It's All True,* 213–14, 235–37, 242, 265.

83. Benamou, 55, 141–43, 237–38, and 350n27. For an image of Welles in deep conversation with Foreign Minister Oswaldo Aranha and DIP head Lourival Fontes, see Tota, *Seduction of Brazil.*

84. For instance, in footage of Welles discussing the film, he repeatedly uses the term *voodoo* to describe candomblé ceremonies, and he tells a story about a black "voodoo witch doctor" wearing a feathered headpiece that visited him, suggesting he may have been cursed by the black visitor. See Paramount Pictures, *It's All True.*

85. "Brazil," file folder Reaction to Films, General Records, Central Files, Information Motion Pictures, Plans-Policy-Procedure, Films, box 214, Record Group 229, NARA.

86. Quoted in Freire-Medeiros, "Hollywood Musicals," 63–64.

87. "Brazil," file folder Reaction to Films, General Records, Central Files, Information Motion Pictures, Plans-Policy-Procedure, Films, box 214, Record Group 229, NARA.

88. *Saludos Amigos,* Disney Gold Classic Collection (Burbank, CA: Buena Vista Home Entertainment, 1943); *The Three Caballeros* (Walt Disney Productions, 1945).

89. "Brazil," file folder Reaction to Films, General Records, Central Files, Information Motion Pictures, Plans-Policy-Procedure, Films, box 214, Record Group 229.

90. Richard, introduction to *Censorship and Hollywood's Hispanic Image,* xxvii–xxviii, xxxvi, xxiv. *Brazil,* which starred Carmen's sister, Aurora, was released in 1944 by Republic and is described as "one of the MPSA's biggest successes." See Richard, *Censorship,* introduction, 285–86; and Castro, *Carmen: Uma biografia,* 387. The original poster reads "The Musical Love Story of Pan-America!" See the Internet Movie Database (IMDB), accessed August 1, 2010, http://www.imdb.com/title/tt0036670/.

91. Carmen Miranda was born in Portugal to Portuguese parents and immigrated to Brazil with her family as a baby.

92. Richard F. Behrendt, "The Other America," *Washington Post,* August 10, 1941; and Ninkovich, *Diplomacy of Ideas,* 41. Ninkovich states that the OCIAA and the State Department prioritized creating the Pan American buzz.

93. Bosley Crowther, "The Screen in Review," *New York Times,* March 10, 1941. *That Night in Rio* was Miranda's first acting role.

94. Castro, *Carmen,* 398.

95. Stam, *Tropical Multiculturalism,* 84–87; Roberts, "'Lady in the Tutti-Frutti Hat,'" 13; and Schpun, "Carmen Miranda," 459–60, 466–67.

96. Nona Baldwin, "The Samba Down in Rio: The Voodoo Dancers of Brazil Created a Rhythm for the Days of Carnival," *New York Times,* March 16, 1941. For a good analysis of Elsie Houston, see Seigel, *Uneven Encounters,* 166–78.

97. See Levine, *Brazilian Photographs of Genevieve Naylor;* and Fabris, *Portinari, pintor social.*

98. Brazil, Departamento de Imprensa e Propaganda, *Facts and Information about Brazil,* 21.

99. Brazil, Departamento de Imprensa e Propaganda, *Brazil in America,* 16.

100. Brazil, Departamento de Imprensa e Propaganda, *Facts and Information about Brazil,* 19–21.

101. Brazil, Departamento de Imprensa e Propaganda, *Brazil in America,* 16, 48. In the original, "trilogy" is misspelled as "triology." The white, black, and indigenous men whom the book references were João Fernandes Vieira Funchal, Henrique Dias, and Antônio Filipe Camarão, respectively.

102. Brazil, Departamento de Imprensa e Propaganda, *Facts and Information about Brazil,* 17–19, 21.

103. In his seminal book, *Black into White,* Thomas Skidmore argued that such whitening ideals largely fell out of favor after the First World War.

104. Brazil, Departamento de Imprensa e Propaganda, *Facts and Information about Brazil,* 20–21.

105. Brazil, Departamento de Imprensa e Propaganda, *Facts and Information about Brazil,* 18; and *Brazil in America,* 14 (italics mine).

106. Brazilian Ministry of Foreign Affairs, *Brazil, 1943: Resources and Possibilities* (Rio de Janeiro: Est. de Artes Gráficas, 1944), 78.

107. Historian Darlene Sadlier also mentions that the Estado Novo "aspire[d] to whiteness." See Sadlier, *Americans All,* 75.

108. Departamento de Imprensa e Propaganda, *Facts and Information,* 48. Critics of Orson Welles pined for the work of artists like Carlos Gomes. See Stam, "Orson Welles," 110.

109. Departamento de Imprensa e Propaganda, *Brazil in America,* 32–33. Micol Seigel has described maxixe as the "'oldest of the urban dances of Brazil,' and the 'immediate ancestor' of samba. . . ." See Seigel, *Uneven Encounters,* 72.

110. Brazil, Departamento de Imprensa e Propaganda, *Brazil in America,* 61.

111. See Vianna, *Mystery of Samba.*

112. The original phrase was "sem distinção de sexo." See "Decreto-Lei Nº 5.452, de 1º de Maio de 1943," accessed March 7, 2019, https://www2.camara. leg.br/legin/fed/declei/1940–1949/decreto-lei-5452-1-maio-1943–415500-publicacaooriginal-1-pe.html.

113. Brazilian Ministry of Foreign Affairs, *Brazil, 1943,* 513.

114. For a description of the law's impact on blacks in São Paulo, see Andrews, *Blacks and Whites in São Paulo,* 97–98, 147–48, and 291n100.

115. Focusing on the state of Bahia, Anadelia Romo also studies the ways that authorities and intellectuals framed black Brazilian culture and traditions as things of the past. See Romo, *Brazil's Living Museum.*

116. Barbara Weinstein advances a similar argument in *Color of Modernity.*

CHAPTER 7

1. Grossman, *Land of Hope;* Hirsch, *Making the Second Ghetto;* and Korstad and Lichtenstein, "Opportunities Found and Lost," 786–98.

2. The language of the executive order promoted equal opportunity in defense industry employment under federal contract regardless of race, religion, or national origin.

3. Fujitani, *Race for Empire*, 90–96.

4. There is debate and conflicting evidence about whether or not Lourival Fontes was fascist. Lúcia Lippi Oliveira has explained that Fontes remains an elusive figure in part because information about him is rather sparse. See Oliveira, "O intelectual do DIP," in Bomeny, *Constelação capanema;* and Tota, *Seduction of Brazil.*

5. Carone, *Brasil: Anos de crise,* 309–11; Sotero, "Representação política negra no Brasil pós-Estado Novo"; the quote is from French, *Brazilian Workers' ABC,* 92. For good descriptions of the redemocratization process, see Carone, *Brasil: Anos de crise,* 93–131; French, *Brazilian Workers' ABC,* 93–131; Levine, *Father of the Poor?,* 62–74; Gomes, *A invenção do trabalhismo,* 267–324; and chap. 2 in the seminal Skidmore, *Politics in Brazil,* 48–80.

6. *Diário de Notícias,* May 3, 1945, 3, Biblioteca Nacional.

7. Paulina Alberto offers a great analysis of both the ways that black activists and thinkers utilized the postwar discourse of democracy to demand equal citizenship rights and the charges of reverse racism against them. See Alberto, *Terms of Inclusion,* 151–95, 202. Antonio Sérgio Alfredo Guimarães discusses the impact of the war and Nazism on the racial rhetoric of democracy in Brazil. See Guimarães, *Classes,* 141–51.

8. See Araújo, *Memórias estudantis,* 35–36; and Carone, "A luta contra o Estado Novo," 104.

9. Quoted in Camargo, Araújo, and Simonsen, *Oswaldo Aranha,* 315.

10. Quoted in *Dicionário Histórico-Biográfico Brasileiro,* s.v. "Manifesto dos Mineiros."

11. French, *Brazilian Workers' ABC,* 93.

12. Quoted in Carone, "A luta contra o Estado Novo," 107.

13. Quoted in Edgard Carone's book of primary documents, *A terceira república,* 478. The other parties also discussed democracy in their proclamations; the UDN included an entire section on *Democracia* and its description of such in its 1945 program. See Carone, 426–27.

14. Carone, 486, 507. Carone shows how still other communists felt that in a show of true support, the official Communist Party of Brazil (PCB) should have dissolved itself along with Comintern in 1943. The majority of the active communist cells did not fit into this group.

15. See Levine, *Father of the Poor?,* 68.

16. See Carone, *A terceira república,* 533, 537.

17. Guimarães and Macedo, "Diário trabalhista," 161. Nascimento stated that he disagreed with Édison Carneiro on race and that the latter subordinated racism to class oppression. See Nascimento and Nascimento, *Africans in Brazil,* 37.

18. Sotero, *Representação política negra,* 253–55. For more on Carneiro, see Rossi, *O intelectual feiticeiro Edison Carneiro e o campo de estudos das relações raciais no Brasil;* and Nascimento, "O sexto sentido do pesquisador."

19. Gomes, *A invenção do trabalhismo.* The quote is Skidmore's in *Politics in Brazil,* 39–40.

318 | Notes

20. Frank McCann Jr. touches upon the rhetorical shift to Estado Nacional in McCann, *Brazilian-American Alliance,* 300. Ângela de Castro also addresses the Estado Nacional in *Invenção do trabalhismo,* 259–64. Robert Levine writes about Vargas attempting to woo the communists with Prestes's release in Levine, *Father of the Poor?,* 68. Levine also mentions the Estado Novo's language of democracy during this phase in Levine, 71. Marcondes Filho's speeches are a good place to locate the omnipresence of the term *democracy.* See a selection of his *Hora do Brasil* radio speeches during this period in Filho, *Trabalhadores do Brasil!*

21. See the program in its entirety in Carone, *A terceira república,* 455.

22. Moura, *História do Negro Brasileiro,* 77–79. See also Nascimento, *Sorcery of Color,* 138. As Nascimento points out, the period of redemocratization began what Roger Bastide identified as the third phase of black activism in Brazil. Historian Petrônio Domingues has determined 1945–64 to be the "second phase of the organized Black Movement in the Republic." See Domingues, "Movimento negro Brasileiro," 107–11.

23. Edilza Sotero touches upon Nascimento's political influence in the era of redemocratization. See Sotero, *Representação política negra.*

24. See Leite, . . . *E disse,* 142–44; and Alberto, *Terms of Inclusion,* 155–57. According to Leite, Vargas only responded to the Associação José do Patrocínio's requests fourteen months later.

25. Nascimento, *Sorcery of Color,* 139 (her translation); and Sotero, "Representação política negra," 72–79.

26. Manoel Antonio dos Santos, "Acabemos com isto!," *Alvorada,* March 1945.

27. Santos, "Acabemos com isto!"

28. Micol Seigel makes such an observation of black Brazilians during the 1930s. See Seigel, *Uneven Encounters.*

29. Leite, . . . *E disse,* 158.

30. Nascimento and Nascimento, *Africans in Brazil,* 28–29.

31. See *Dicionário Histórico-Biográfico Brasileiro,* s.v. "Diário trabalhista." Also quoted in Guimarães and Macedo, "Diário trabalhista," 145.

32. Guimarães and Macedo, "Diário trabalhista," 144–46; and Sotero, *Representação política negra,* 142–46. Nascimento's collaborators were Sebastião Rodrigues Alves, Ironides Rodrigues, and Aguinaldo Camargo.

33. Quoted in Guimarães and Macedo, "Diário trabalhista," 158–59. Mention of Aladir Custódio's work in the folklore movement, where he led the Center of Afro-Brazilian Culture with Solano Trindade and Corsino de Brito, is in Nascimento, *Sorcery of Color,* 144–45.

34. Quoted in Nascimento and Nascimento, *Africans in Brazil,* 38–39; and Sotero, "Representação política negra," 132–41.

35. Nascimento, *Sorcery of Color,* 146; Nascimento and Nascimento, *Africans in Brazil,* 39; and Sotero, 133–39.

36. Nascimento and Nascimento, *Africans in Brazil,* 29.

37. Nascimento, *Sorcery of Color,* 145. Although the UNE was by no means merely a student branch of the Communist Party, it did have, as UNE activist José Gomes Talarico later said, a strong leftist and communist presence. Scholar

Maria Paulo Nascimento Araújo also has written that some of the leaders were "notoriously linked" to the PCB. See Araújo, *Memórias estudantis*, 40.

38. Nascimento and Nascimento, *Africans in Brazil*, 29–30.

39. See Guimarães and Macedo, "*Diário trabalhista*," 161. The TEN also held another convention in Rio de Janeiro in 1946.

40. Alberto, *Terms of Inclusion*, 173.

41. Nascimento, *Sorcery of Color*, 148; and Alberto, *Terms of Inclusion*, 173–74. Alberto discusses the postwar role that social science and sociology played to debunk scientific racism. See Alberto, *Terms of Inclusion*, 181–95.

42. *Anais da Assembléia Constituinte*, 3, 25th Sess. (March 14, 1946), 409–10.

43. *Anais da Assembléia Constituinte*, 3, 25th Sess. (March 14, 1946), 409–10.

44. "Preconceito," in *Alvorada*, July 1946, 1.

45. Nascimento, *Sorcery of Color*, 146–48. The quote cited is her translation. Congressmen used the term "*casos concretos.*"

46. Quoted in Nascimento, *Sorcery of Color*, 266n104.

47. Constituição da República dos Estados Unidos do Brasil (de 16 de julho de 1934) Artigo 113; and Constituição da República dos Estados Unidos do Brasil (de 18 de setembro de 1946) Artigo 141. The text of all Brazilian constitutions can be accessed at http://pdba.georgetown.edu/Constitutions/Brazil/brazil.html. "Class" shared the same fate as "race" in the constitutional changes from 1934 to 1946.

48. See Nascimento and Nascimento, *Africans in Brazil*, 33–36; Andrews, *Blacks and Whites in São Paulo*, 184–85. The text of the bill in its entirety is in Bastide and Fernandes, *Brancos e Negros em São Paulo*, 304–5. Freyre's speech is mentioned in Maria Teresa, "Preconceito de côr," *Redenção*, December 30, 1950, 3.

49. Quoted in Andrews, *Blacks and Whites in São Paulo*, 184–85. The lack of blacks in congress to debate and vote on what would become the Afonso Arinos Law is discussed in Bastide and Fernandes, *Brancos e Negros em São Paulo*, 302, 304.

50. Quoted in Nobles, *Shades of Citizenship*, 109 (translation hers).

51. Quoted in Andrews, *Blacks and Whites in São Paulo*, 185, 318n10.

52. Quoted in Nascimento, *Sorcery of Color*, 150 (translation hers).

53. Bastide and Fernandes, *Brancos e Negros em São Paulo*, 315.

54. Quoted in Bastide and Fernandes, 307–9, 311, 315–16.

55. Quoted in Bastide and Fernandes, 307–8, 316.

56. Quoted in Andrews, *Blacks and Whites in São Paulo*, 185; and Nobles, *Shades of Citizenship*, 108–9 (translation his).

57. Nascimento and Nascimento, *Africans in Brazil*, 35–36; Nascimento, *Sorcery of Color*, 147–49; and Andrews, *Blacks and Whites in São Paulo*, 186. The quote from the *Manifesto* is cited in Nascimento, *Sorcery of Color*, 147. The new Lei Caó did not do much better than the Afonso Arinos Law for the first ten years of its existence. From 1989 to 1999, only two convictions in the entire country were reached under the Lei Caó. In the following decade, public prosecutors became more aggressive, filing multiple lawsuits charging racial discrimination. See Hensler, "Não Vale a Pena?," 267–346.

58. See Schrecker, *Many Are the Crimes*, 95–115. Earl Browder had testified before the HCUA in 1939 that he had made a false statement on his passport application. HCUA members and others mounted pressure to prosecute. The court sentenced Browder to four years and fined him $2,000, an unusually severe sentence for such an offense. See Schrecker, *Many Are the Crimes*, 95–96.

59. Davis's other objections to the MOWM included Randolph's emphasis on black, not interracial participation, and that no mention had been made of winning the war. See Horne, *Black Liberation/Red Scare*, 94–95, 102.

60. Horace R. Cayton, "Left-Wingers: Adopt New Technique in Present Struggle—Ignore Race Causes," *Pittsburgh Courier*, April 25, 1942.

61. Horne, *Black Liberation/Red Scare*, 92, 95. Dies's red-baiting of Frazier and Bethune, as well as the latter's response, is analyzed in "The Work of the Dies Committee," *Atlanta Daily World*, October 3, 1942; and "Mrs. Bethune Calls Dies' Accusations 'Malicious, Absurd,'" *Pittsburgh Courier*, October 3, 1942.

62. See Janken, *Rayford W. Logan*, 118–19. The military appropriations legislation was the Burke-Wadsworth Bill.

63. Quoted in Garfinkel, *When Negroes March*, 16.

64. See Weiss, *Farewell to Party of Lincoln*; Wolters, *Negroes and Great Depression*; and Sullivan, *Days of Hope*.

65. See Janken, *Rayford W. Logan*, 116–17.

66. *Atlanta Daily World*, May 31, 1941. Speaking about the postwar world, Logan said that blacks "must not be caught, as we were after the last World War, with little or no conception of a course of action."

67. Senate Committee on Appropriations, Military Establishment Appropriation Bill for 1941: Hearings before the Subcommittee on Appropriations, 76th Cong., 3rd Sess., May 14, 1940, 367.

68. House Committee on Military Affairs, Selective Compulsory Military Training and Service: Hearings Before the Committee on Military Affairs, 76th Cong., 3rd Sess., August 14, 1940, 578–79, 589–90.

69. Logan, "Crisis of Democracy," 344, 350–52.

70. *Chicago Defender (National Defender)*, September 21, 1940, 1.

71. Garfinkel, *When Negroes March*, 33–34; and A. Philip Randolph, "'Defense Rotten'—Randolph," *Pittsburgh Courier*, January 25, 1941.

72. Quoted in Garfinkel, *When Negroes March*, 34–35. On the death of the antilynching bill, see *New York Amsterdam News*, October 19, 1940.

73. A. Philip Randolph, "'Defense Rotten'—Randolph."

74. See Garfinkel, *When Negroes March*, 37–39, 56–61. Notably, the *Pittsburgh Courier*, which had not yet begun its famous "Double V" campaign, opposed the movement, although its CPNNDP partner Rayford Logan accepted the MOWM's invitation to participate in final negotiations with the administration. See Janken, *Rayford W. Logan*, 127–29. For an example of the *Courier's* take on the pitfalls of the march, see Marjorie McKenzie, "Pursuit of Democracy: Trek to Washington Presents Many Angles that Need Studying," *Pittsburgh Courier*, June 28, 1941.

75. *Chicago Defender*, June 28, 1941. The slogans are all reported in *New York Amsterdam Star-News*, June 28, 1941.

76. See Garfinkel, *When Negroes March*, 61.

77. J. Robert Smith, "Asks Pressure on Roosevelt," *New York Amsterdam Star-News,* April 11, 1942; *Pittsburgh Courier,* June 27, 1942; Garfield L. Smith Jr., "Randolph Prepares for New 'March,'" *Pittsburgh Courier,* December 26, 1942; and Alfred A. Duckett, "25,000 Roar Approval as Speakers Define 'Real Democracy,'" *Pittsburgh Courier,* June 27, 1942. Reverend S.T. Eldridge (proxy, Baptist Ministers' Alliance of Greater New York and Vicinity) made the statement about the "label on a bottle." Similar language was used at the following rally in Chicago, reportedly attended by 12,000. See, for example, George F. McCray, "12,000 in Chicago Voice Demands for Democracy," *Chicago Defender,* July 4, 1942.

78. *Pittsburgh Courier,* June 15, 1940. For Bethune's participation in the MOWM rally at Madison Square Garden, see Duckett, "25,000 Roar Approval." The *Chicago Defender* is among the journals that referred to Bethune as the "First Lady of Negro America." See Mary McLeod Bethune, "When Peace Comes . . . What? Mrs. Bethune Sees Labor Board Key to Job Bias Fight," *Chicago Defender,* February 17, 1945.

79. Quoted in Garfinkel, *When Negroes March,* 88–89.

80. A. Philip Randolph, "'Defense Rotten'—Randolph."

81. Garfinkel, *When Negroes March,* 60–61.

82. See Garfinkel, 49–53, 61.

83. See the full text of Executive Order 8802 at the government's Equal Employment Opportunity Committee's official website, accessed August 11, 2016, https://www.eeoc.gov/eeoc/history/35th/thelaw/eo-8802.html.

84. See Janken, *Rayford W. Logan,* 129–30.

85. Alvarez, *Power of the Zoot,* 38.

86. Quoted in Hart, "Making Democracy Safe," 64–65. For an analysis of Mexican American labor and the FEPC, see Daniel, *Chicano Workers.*

87. See Executive Order 8802.

88. Garfinkel, *When Negroes March,* 20, 194. For the entire text of Executive Order 9346, signed by FDR on May 27, 1943, see John T. Woolley and Gerhard Peters, *The American Presidency Project,* Gerhard Peters (database), accessed October 7, 2009, https://www.presidency.ucsb.edu/documents/executive-order-9346-establishing-committee-fair-employment-practice.

89. Quoted in Garfinkel, *When Negroes March,* 144–45. The riot that largely targeted Mexican Americans, who were clothed in zoot suits, took place in Los Angeles. Some blacks and Filipinos, also wearing zoot suits, were also attacked. See Alvarez, *Power of the Zoot,* 155–99.

90. Quoted in Hart, "Making Democracy Safe," 66–67. For an excellent overview of Mexican American and African American FEPC activism, see Foley, chapter 2 in *Quest for Equality,* 54–94.

91. Alvarez, *Power of the Zoot,* 38.

CONCLUSION

1. I borrow the term *age of decolonization* from historian Simeon Man, who shifts the focus of postwar history from Europe and North America to the hot wars for independence that occurred across Asia, and we can include Africa.

2. Pandolfi, introduction to *Repensando o Estado Novo*, 11.

3. Alves, *State and Opposition*.

4. Alberto, *Terms of Inclusion*, 151–81; Guimarães, *Classes*, 146–47.

5. Fischer, *Poverty of Rights*, 77–78; and Fischer, "Red Menace Reconsidered," 4.

6. Silva, *An Afro-Brazilian Woman's Story*, 41–44. Fischer shows that communists were among many groups who were active in the efforts to save favelas from removal between 1945 and 1964. She states that this history has been forgotten within communist, community, and academic circles. See Fischer, "Red Menace Reconsidered."

7. Guimarães, *Classes*, 166.

8. Alberto, *Terms of Inclusion*, 250, 269–71.

9. Alberto, "When Rio Was Black"; Hertzman, *Making Samba*, 230–31.

10. Antonio Guimarães has written that the dictatorship brought to an end the rights-based language of racial democracy that had prevailed since the end of the war. See Guimarães, *Classes*, 168.

11. See Dudziak, *Cold War Civil Rights*; and Von Eschen, *Satchmo Blows Up the World*.

12. Singh, *Black Is a Country*, 159–63.

13. See Sparrow, *Warfare State*; and Cowie, *Great Exception*.

14. Gore, *Radicalism at the Crossroads*, 144–51; and Davies, *Left of Karl Marx*, 131–66.

15. Singh, *Black Is a Country*, 164–67.

Bibliography

ARCHIVAL SOURCES

Arquivo Edgard Leuenroth, Campinas, São Paulo
    Fundo Edgard Leuenroth
Arquivo Nacional, Rio de Janeiro
    Fundo Góes Monteiro
Arquivo Público do Estado de São Paulo
    Departamento Estadual de Ordem Política e Social, São Paulo Files
Arquivo Público do Estado do Rio de Janeiro
    Delegacia Especial de Segurança Política e Social
Arquivo Público e Histórico do Município de Rio Claro, São Paulo
    Fundo Plínio Salgado
Centro de Documentação e Memória da Universidade Estadual Paulista, São Paulo
    Coleção Internacional Comunista, Fundo Astrojildo Pereira
Centro de Pesquisa e Documentação de História Contemporânea do Brasil, Fundação Getúlio Vargas, Rio de Janeiro
    Gustavo Capanema Papers
Hoover Institution, Stanford University
    Lawrence Dennis Papers
Library of Congress
    Rayford Whittingham Logan Papers
Lilly Library, Indiana University
    Orson Welles Collections
National Archives and Records Administration
    Department of State Records, Record Group 59
    International Conferences, Commissions, and Expositions Records, Record Group 43

Office of Inter-American Affairs Records, Record Group 229
Office of Strategic Services Records, Record Group 226
Raymond E. Murphy Collection on International Communism, 1917–1958,
Records of the Central Intelligence Agency, Record Group 263
US Joint Chiefs of Staff Records, Record Group 218
War Department General and Special Staffs Records, Record Group 165
Rockefeller Archive Center, New York
Nelson A. Rockefeller Personal Papers
Special Collections Library at the University of Michigan
Richard Wilson—Orson Welles Papers
Tamiment Library and Robert F. Wagner Labor Archives, New York University
Mark Solomon and Robert Kaufman Research Files on African Americans
and Communism

NEWSPAPERS, PERIODICALS, AND JOURNALS

Alvorada
Anauê!
Atlanta Daily World
Billboard: The World's Foremost Amusement Weekly
Chicago Daily Tribune
Chicago Defender
O Clarim da Alvorada
A Classe Operária
Cultura Política
Diário de Notícias
Jornal do Brasil
Jornal do Commércio
Los Angeles Sentinel
New York Amsterdam News
New York Times
A Ofensiva
Pittsburgh Courier
Senzala
A Voz da Raça
Washington Post

PRIMARY SOURCES, PUBLISHED

Allen, James S., and James W. Ford. *The Negroes in a Soviet America.* New
York: Workers Library Publishers, 1935.
Aranha, Oswaldo, and José Roberto de Macedo Soares. *A Revolução e a Amer-
ica: O Presidente Getúlio Vargas e a diplomacia (1930–1940).* Discurso e
Conferência Realizados, no Palácio Tiradentes, no dia 23 de Dezembro de
1940. N.p.: DIP, 1941.
Baker, Ella, and Marvel Cooke. "The Bronx Slave Market." *Crisis,* November
1935, 330–31, 340.

Brasil. Anais da Assembléia Constituinte de 1946.
———. Constituição da República dos Estados Unidos do Brasil de 16 de julho de 1934. Accessed June 20, 2010. http://pdba.georgetown.edu/Constitutions/Brazil.
———. Constituição da República dos Estados Unidos do Brasil de 18 de setembro de 1946. Accessed June 20, 2010. http://pdba.georgetown.edu/Constitutions/Brazil/brazil46.html.
———. Departamento de Imprensa e Propaganda. *Brazil in America*. Rio de Janeiro: Grafica Olimpica, 1942.
———. Departamento de Imprensa e Propaganda. *Facts and Information about Brazil*. Translated by Corey James Spencer. Rio de Janeiro: Department of Press and Propaganda, 1942.
———. Departamento Nacional de Propaganda. *20 anos de tragédia experiência: A verdade sobre a Rússia Soviética*. Rio de Janeiro: Departamento Nacional de Propaganda/Imprensa Nacional, 1938.
———. Departamento Nacional de Propaganda. *Exposição Nacional do Estado Novo*. Rio de Janeiro: Departamento Nacional de Propaganda, 1939.
———. Departamento Nacional de Propaganda. *O Brasil é bom*. Rio de Janeiro: Departamento Nacional de Propaganda/Agência Nacional, 1938.
———. Ministry of Foreign Affairs. *Brazil, 1943: Resources and Possibilities*. Rio de Janeiro: Est. de Artes Gráficas, 1944.
———. *Polícia política preventiva: Serviço de Inquéritos Políticos Sociais*. Rio de Janeiro: Departamento Federal de Segurança Pública, 1939.
Calhoun, Harold G., and Dorothy Calhoun. *Let Freedom Ring!* Washington, DC: US Government Printing Office, 1938.
Camargo, Joracy. *A Lei Áurea*. Rio de Janeiro: Departamento de Propaganda e Difusão Cultural, 1938.
Carneiro, Édison. "Situação do negro no Brasil." In *Estudos Afro-Brasileiros: Trabalhos apresentados ao 1º Congresso Afro-Brasileiro realizado no Recife, em 1934*, 237–41. Recife: Fundação Joaquim Nabuco: Editora Massangana, 1988.
Carone, Edgard. *A terceira república (1937–1945)*. 2nd ed. São Paulo: Difel, 1982.
Communist Election Platform, 1938: For Jobs, Security, Democracy, and Peace. New York: Workers Library Publishers, 1938.
Communist International. *VII Congress of the Communist International: Abridged Stenographic Report of Proceedings*. Moscow: Foreign Languages Publishing House, 1939.
———. *Theses, Resolutions and Manifestos of the First Four Congresses of the Third International*. Translated by Alix Holt, Alan Adler, and Barbara Holland. London: Ink Links, 1980.
Communist Party of the United States of America. *Communist Election Platform 1938: For Jobs, Security, Democracy and Peace*. New York: Workers Library, 1938.
Dennis, Lawrence. *The Coming American Fascism*. New York: Harper, 1936.
———. *The Dynamics of War and Revolution*. New York: Weekly Foreign Letter, 1940.

———. "Fascism in America." *Annals of the American Academy of Political and Social Science* 180 (July 1935): 62–73.

Dies, Martin. *Martin Dies' Story.* New York: Bookmailer, 1963.

———. *The Trojan Horse in America.* New York: Dodd, Mead, 1940.

Filho, Alexandre Marcondes. *Trabalhadores do Brasil!: Palestras do Ministro Marcondes Filho na Hora do Brazil, em 1942.* Rio de Janeiro: Revista dos Tribunais, 1943.

Fish, Hamilton, Jr. *Memoir of an American Patriot.* Washington, DC: Regnery Gateway, 1991.

———. "The Menace of Communism." *Annals of the American Academy of Political and Social Science* 156 (July 1931): 54–61.

——— (chairman), Carl G. Bachmann, Edward E. Eslick, and Robert S. Hall, *Investigation of Communist Propaganda: Report,* pursuant to H. Res. 220, 71st Cong., 3rd Sess., House Report no. 2290, January 17, 1931.

Foner, Philip S. *American Communism and Black Americans: A Documentary History, 1919–1929.* Philadelphia: Temple University Press, 1987.

Freyre, Gilberto. *Casa-grande & senzala: Formação da família brasileira sob o regimen de economia patriarchal.* 2nd ed. Rio de Janeiro: Schmidt-Editor, 1936.

Gellermann, William. *Martin Dies.* New York: John Day Company, 1944.

Gutiérrez, David. *Walls and Mirrors: Mexican Americans, Mexican Immigrants, and the Politics of Ethnicity.* Berkeley: University of California Press, 1995.

Haywood, Harry. *Black Bolshevik: Autobiography of an Afro-American Communist.* Chicago: Liberator Press, 1978.

———. *The Road to Negro Liberation.* New York: Workers Library Publishers, 1934.

Hitler, Adolf. *The Speeches of Adolf Hitler, April 1922–August 1939.* Vol. 1. Edited and translated by Norman H. Baynes. New York: Howard Fertig, 1969.

Kallen, Horace. *Culture and Democracy in the United States.* New York: Boni & Liveright, 1924.

League of the Struggle for Negro Rights. *Equality Land and Freedom: A Program for Negro Liberation.* New York: League of the Struggle for Negro Rights, 1933.

Leite, José Correia . . . *E disse o velho militante José Correia Leite.* 19th ed. rev. São Paulo: Noovha América, 2007.

Lenin, Vladimir. "Preliminary Draft Theses on the Agrarian Question for the Second Congress of the Communist International." In *Lenin's Collected Works,* 4th English ed., translated by Julius Katzer. Moscow: Progress Publishers, 1965.

Locke, Alain. "The Negro's Contribution to American Culture." *Journal of Negro Education* 8, no. 3 (July 1939): 521–29.

Loewenstein, Karl. *Brazil under Vargas.* New York: Macmillan, 1942.

———. "Militant Democracy and Fundamental Rights, 1." *American Political Science Review* 31, no. 3 (June 1937): 417–32.

———. "Militant Democracy and Fundamental Rights, 2." *American Political Science Review* 31, no. 4 (August 1937): 638–58.

Logan, Rayford W. "The Crisis of Democracy in the Western Hemisphere." *Journal of Negro Education* 10, no. 5 (July 1941): 344–52.

Luis Carlos Prestes: The Struggle for Liberation in Brazil. New York: Workers Library Publishers, 1936.

Meneses, Djacir. "Contribuição brasileira para a paz no mundo de amanhã." *Cultura política* 3, no. 31, Edição Extraordinária (August 1943): 330–39.

Morris, Vivian. "Bronx Slave Market," interview of Minnie Marshall, 1938. US Work Projects Administration, Federal Writers' Project Manuscript Division, Library of Congress. https://www.loc.gov/item/wpalh001468/.

Myrdal, Gunnar. *An American Dilemma: The Negro Problem and Modern Democracy.* New York: Harper, 1944.

Nascimento, Abdias do. "The Myth of Racial Democracy." In *The Brazil Reader: History, Culture, Politics,* edited by Robert Levine and John Crocitti, 379–81. Durham, NC: Duke University Press, 1999.

———, ed. *Teatro Experimental do Negro: Testemunhos.* Rio de Janeiro: GRD, 1966.

———. *Memórias do exílio.* São Paulo: Editora e Livraria Livramento, 1976.

Pinheiro, Paulo Sérgio, and Michael Hall. *A classe operária no Brasil, 1889–1939, Documentos.* Vol. 1, *O movimento operário.* São Paulo: Editora Alfa Omega, 1979.

Prado, Caio, Jr. *Evolução política do Brasil.* São Paulo: Revista dos Tribunais, 1933.

Prestes, Luís Carlos. *The Struggle for Liberation in Brazil.* New York: Workers Library Publishers, 1936.

Ramos, Arthur. *Guerra e relações de raça.* Rio de Janeiro: Departamento Editorial da União Nacional dos Estudantes, 1943.

Rauschning, Hermann. *Hitler Speaks: A Series of Political Conversations with Adolf Hitler on His Real Aims.* London: Thornton Butterworth, 1939.

———. *O Hitler me disse.* Rio de Janeiro: Edições Dois Mundos, 1940.

Ribeiro, Esmeralda, and Márcio Barbosa. *Frente Negra Brasileira: Depoimentos.* São Paulo: Imprensa Oficial do Estado de São Paulo, 2012.

Schuman, Frederick L. *Soviet Politics at Home and Abroad.* New York: Knopf, 1947.

Sección Sudamericana de la Internacional Comunista. *El movimiento revolucionário Latino Americano.* Buenos Aires: La Correspondencia Sudamericana, 1929.

Silva, Benedita da. *An Afro-Brazilian Woman's Story of Politics and Love.* As told to Medea Benjamin and Maisa Mendoça. Oakland: Food First Books, 1997.

Songs of the People. New York: Workers Library Publishers, 1937.

United States. *History of the Office of the Coordinator of Inter-American Affairs.* Washington, DC: US Government Printing Office, 1947.

———. Office of the Coordinator of Inter-American Affairs. *Brazil: Introduction to a Neighbor.* Washington, DC: US Government Printing Office, 1943.

US Congress. House. Committee on Military Affairs. *Selective Compulsory Military Training and Service: Hearings before the Committee on Military Affairs.* 76th Cong., 3rd sess., 1940.

———. House. *Investigation of Communist Propaganda, House Report 2290.* 71st Cong., 3rd sess., January 17, 1931.

———. House. Special Committee on Un-American Activities. *Investigation of Un-American Propaganda Activities in the United States.* 75th Cong., 1st sess., 1939.

———. Senate. Committee on Appropriations. *Military Establishment Appropriation Bill for 1941: Hearings before the Subcommittee on Appropriations.* 76th Cong., 3rd sess., 1940.

US Department of War. *Final Report: Japanese Evacuation from the West Coast, 1942.* Washington, DC: US Government Printing Office, 1943.

Vargas, Getúlio. *Dever do estado e defesa do regime.* Rio de Janeiro: Departamento Nacional de Propaganda, 1936.

———. *Discursos.* Rio de Janeiro: Departamento de Imprensa e Propaganda, 1944.

———. *A nova política do Brasil X: O Brasil na guerra.* Rio de Janeiro: Livraria José Olympio Editora, 1944.

———. *Ordem e democracia.* Rio de Janeiro: Departamento Nacional de Propaganda, 1936.

———. *Palavras aos brasileiros.* Rio de Janeiro: Departamento Nacional de Propaganda, 1936.

Works Progress Administration. *We Work Again.* Washington, DC: Works Progress Administration, 1937.

SECONDARY SOURCES

Acerbi, Patrícia. *Street Occupations: Urban Vending in Rio de Janeiro, 1850–1925.* Austin: University of Texas Press, 2017.

Adi, Hakim. *Pan-Africanism and Communism: The Communist International, Africa and the Diaspora, 1919–1939.* Trenton, NJ: Africa World Press, 2013.

Alberti, Verena, and Amilcar Araújo Pereira, eds. *Histórias do movimento negro no Brasil: Depoimentos ao CPDOC.* Rio de Janeiro: Pallas; CPDOC-FGV, 2007.

Alberto, Paulina L. "Para Africano Ver: African-Bahian Exchanges in the Reinvention of Brazil's Racial Democracy, 1961–63." *Luso-Brazilian Review* 45 (June 2008): 78–117.

———. *Terms of Inclusion: Black Intellectuals in Twentieth-Century Brazil.* Chapel Hill: University of North Carolina Press, 2011.

———. "When Rio Was Black: Soul Music, National Culture, and the Politics of Racial Comparison in 1970s Brazil." *Hispanic American Historical Review* 89, no. 1 (2009): 3–39.

———, and Jesse Hoffnung-Garskof. "'Racial Democracy' and Racial Inclusion: Hemispheric Histories." In *Afro-Latin American Studies: An Introduction,* edited by George Reid Andrews and Alejandro de la Fuente. Cambridge: Cambridge University Press, 2018.

Allen, Ernest. "When Japan Was Champion of the Darker Races: Satokata Takahashi and the Flowering of Black Messianic Nationalism." *Black Scholar* 24, no. 1 (1994): 23–46.

Almeida, Marly de, Érica Sarmiento da Silva, and Leandro Pereira Gonçalves, orgs. *Presos políticos e perseguidos estrangeiros na Era Vargas.* Rio de Janeiro: MAUAD X: Faperj, 2014.

Alvarez, Luis. *The Power of the Zoot: Youth Culture and Resistance during World War II.* Berkeley: University of California Press, 2009.

Alves, Jaime Ampara. *The Anti-Black City: Police Terror and Black Urban Life in Brazil.* Minneapolis: University of Minnesota Press, 2018.

Alves, Maria Helena Moreira. *State Opposition in Military Brazil.* Austin: University of Texas Press, 1985.

Amaral, Karla Cristina de Castro. "Getúlio Vargas—O criador de ilusões." Paper presented at the Núcleo de Pesquisa Publicidade, Propaganda e Marketing, XXV Congresso Anual em Ciência da Comunicação, Salvador/BA, September 4–5, 2002. Accessed May 12, 2010. http://www.intercom.org.br/papers/nacionais/2002/congresso2002_anais/2002_NP3amaral.pdf.

Anderson, Benedict. *Imagined Communities: Reflections on the Origin and Spread of Nationalism.* Rev. ed. New York: Verso, 1991.

Anderson, Carol. *Eyes off the Prize: The United Nations and the African American Struggle for Human Rights, 1944–1955.* Cambridge: Cambridge University Press, 2003.

Andrade, Oswald de. *Manifestos antropófagos e outros textos.* Edited by Jorge Schwartz and Gênese Andrade. São Paulo: Penguin Classics, Companhia das Letras, 2017.

Andreucci, Álvaro Gonçalves Antunes, and Valéria Garcia de Oliveira. *Cultura amordaçada: Intelectuais e músicos sob a vigilância do DEOPS, Módulo 6—Comunistas.* São Paulo: Arquivo do Estado/Imprensa Oficial, 2002.

Andrews, George Reid. *Blacks and Whites in São Paulo, Brazil, 1888–1988.* Madison: University of Wisconsin Press, 1991.

Appelbaum, Nancy, Anne MacPherson, and Karin Rosemblatt, eds. *Race and Nation in Modern Latin America.* Chapel Hill: University of North Carolina Press, 2003.

Aptheker, Herbert. *Marxism and Democracy: A Symposium.* New York: Humanities Press, 1965.

Araújo, Maria Paula Nascimento. *Memórias estudantis, 1937–2007 da fundação da UNE aos nossos dias.* Rio de Janeiro: Relume Dumará, 2007.

Asukile, Thabiti. "Joel Augustus Rogers: Black International Journalism, Archival Research, and Black Print Culture." *Journal of African American History* 95, no. 3–4 (Summer–Fall 2010): 322–47.

Azevedo, Thales de. *As elites de côr: Um estudo de ascenção social.* São Paulo: Companhia Editora Nacional, 1955.

———. *Democracia racial: Ideologia e realidade.* Petrópolis, Brazil: Editora Vozes, 1975.

Bacelar, Jeferson. "A Frente Negra Brasileira na Bahia." *Afro-Ásia*, Salvador, no. 17 (1996): 73–85.

Baldwin, Davarian L., and Minkah Makalani, ed. *Escape from New York: The New Negro Renaissance beyond Harlem.* Minneapolis: University of Minnesota Press, 2013.

Baraka, Amiri. *Blues People: Negro Music in White America*. New York: Harper Perennial, 1999.

Barbosa, Márcio. *Frente Negra Brasileira: Depoimentos*. São Paulo: Quilombhoje, 1998.

Barlow, William. *Voice Over: The Making of Black Radio*. Philadelphia: Temple University Press, 1999.

Bastide, Roger, and Florestan Fernandes. *Brancos e negros em São Paulo*. 2nd ed. São Paulo: Companhia Editora Nacional, 1959.

Bederman, Gail. *Manliness and Civilization: A Cultural History of Gender and Race in the United States, 1880–1917*. Chicago: University of Chicago Press, 1995.

Bekerie, Ayele. "African Americans and the Italo-Ethiopian War." In *Revisioning Italy: National Identity and Global Culture*, edited by Beverly Allen and Mary Russo, 116–33. Minneapolis: University of Minnesota Press, 1997.

Benamou, Catherine. *It's All True: Orson Welles's Pan-American Odyssey*. Berkeley: University of California Press, 2007.

Bender, Pennee. "Film as an Instrument of the Good Neighbor Policy, 1930s–1950s." PhD diss., New York University, 2002.

———. "Policies and Productions of the Motion Picture Division of the Office of the Coordinator of Inter-American Affairs." Paper presented at the symposium Imagining Latin America: United States Film Policy and Its Impacts during World War II, New York University, April 24, 1993.

Bendersky, Joseph. *A Concise History of Nazi Germany*. 4th ed. Lanham: Rowman & Littlefield, 2014.

Bertonha, João Fábio. "Entre Mussolini e Plínio Salgado: O fascismo Italiano, o Integralismo, e o problema dos descendentes de italianos no Brasil." *Revista Brasileira de História* 21, no. 4 (2001): 85–105.

Bindas, Kenneth J. *Swing, That Modern Sound*. Jackson: University of Mississippi Press, 2001.

Boaventura, Maria Eugenia. *A vanguarda antropofágica*. São Paulo: Ática, 1985.

Bomeny, Helena, ed. *Constelação Capanema: Intelectuais e políticas*. Rio de Janeiro: Ed. Fundação Getulio Vargas and Ed. Universidade de São Francisco, 2001.

Bonavides, Paulo, and Roberto Amaral. *Textos políticos da história do Brasil*. 3rd ed. Brasília: Senado Federal, 2002.

Borges, Dain. "Brazilian Social Thought of the 1930s." *Luso-Brazilian Review* 31, no. 2 (Winter 1994): 137–50.

———. "Puffy, Ugly, Slothful, and Inert: Degeneration in Brazilian Social Thought." *Journal of Latin American Studies* 25, no. 2 (1993): 235–56.

———. *The Family in Bahia, Brazil, 1870–1945*. Stanford, CA: Stanford University Press, 1992.

———. "The Recognition of Afro-Brazilian Symbols and Ideas, 1890–1949." *Luso-Brazilian Review* 32, no. 2 (1995): 59–78.

Borstelman, Thomas. *The Cold War and the Color Line: American Race Relations in the Global Arena*. Cambridge, MA: Harvard University Press, 2001.

Brinkley, Alan. *Voices of Protest: Huey Long, Father Coughlin, and the Great Depression.* New York: Vintage, 1983.

Briones, Matthew M. *Jim and Jap Crow: A Cultural History of Interracial 1940s America.* Princeton, NJ: Princeton University Press, 2013.

Brown, Nikki. *Private Politics and Public Voices: African American Women's Activism from World War I to the New Deal.* Bloomington: Indiana University Press, 2006.

Brown, Robert J. *Manipulating the Ether: The Power of Broadcast Radio in Thirties America.* Jefferson, NC: McFarland, 1998.

Buhite, Russell, and David Levy, eds. *FDR's Fireside Chats.* Norman: University of Oklahoma Press, 1992.

Bush, Roderick. *The End of White World Supremacy: Black Internationalism and the Problem of the Color Line.* Philadelphia: Temple University Press, 2009.

Butler, Kim D. *Freedoms Given, Freedoms Won: Afro-Brazilians in Post-Abolition São Paulo and Salvador.* New Brunswick, NJ: Rutgers University Press, 1998.

Caballero, Manuel. *Latin America and the Comintern, 1919–1943.* Cambridge, UK: Cambridge University Press, 1986.

Cabral, Sérgio. "Getúlio Vargas e a Música Popular Brasileira." In *Ensaios de Opinião: Getúlio Vargas,* vol. 2, 36–41. Rio de Janeiro: Inúbia, 1975.

Caldwell, Kia. *Health Equity in Brazil: Intersections of Gender, Race, and Policy.* Champaign: University of Illinois Press, 2017.

———. *Negras in Brazil: Re-envisioning Black Women, Citizenship, and the Politics of Identity.* New Brunswick, NJ: Rutgers University Press, 2006.

Callow, Simon. *Orson Welles, Volume 1: The Road to Xanadu.* New York: Viking, 1995.

———. *Orson Welles, Volume 2: Hello Americans.* New York: Penguin, 2007.

Camargo, Alexandre de Paiva Rio. "Mensuração racial e campo estatístico nos censos brasileiros (1872–1940): Uma abordagem convergente." *Boletim do Museu Paraense Emílio Goeldi, Ciências Humanas 1* 4, no. 3 (2009): 361–85.

Camargo, Aspásia, João Hermes Pereira de Araújo, and Mário Henrique Simonsen. *Oswaldo Aranha: A estrela da revolução.* São Paulo: Editora Mandarim, 1996.

Campbell, Courtney J. "Four Fishermen, Orson Welles, and the Making of the Brazilian Northeast." *Past and Present* 234, no. 1 (February 2017): 173–212.

Campos, André Luiz Vieira de. "The Institute of Inter-American Affairs and Its Health Policies in Brazil during World War II." *Presidential Studies Quarterly* 28, no. 3 (1998): 523–34.

Canedy, Susan. *America's Nazis: A Democratic Dilemma; A History of the German American Bund.* Menlo Park, CA: Markgraf Publications Group, 1990.

Caponi-Tabery, Gena. *Jump for Joy: Jazz, Basketball, and Black Culture in 1930s America.* Amherst: University of Massachusetts Press, 2008.

Carmody, Todd. "Sterling Brown and the Dialect of New Deal Optimism." *Callaloo* 33, no. 3 (Summer 2010): 820–40.

Carneiro, Maria Luiza Tucci, ed. *Minorias silenciadas: História da censura no Brasil.* São Paulo: Fapesp: Edusp, 2002.

————, and Boris Kossoy, eds. *A imprensa confiscada pelo DEOPS, 1924–1954*. São Paulo: Atiliê Editorial/Imprensa Oficial do Estado de São Paulo/ Arquivo do Estado, 2003.

————, Eliane Bisan Alves, Priscila Ferreira Perazzo, and Ana Maria Dietrich, eds. *Inventário DEOPS, Módulo I, Alemanha*. São Paulo: Arquivo do Estado, 1997.

————. "O Estado Novo, o Dops e a ideologia da segurança nacional," in *Repensando o Estado Novo*, edited by Dulce Pandolfi, 327–40. Rio de Janeiro: Ed. Fundação Getúlio Vargas, 1999.

————. *Livros proibidos, idéias malditas: O DEOPS e as minorias silenciadas*. São Paulo: Ateliê Editorial, 2002.

Carone, Edgard. *Brasil: Anos de Crise (1930–1945)*. São Paulo: Editora Ática, 1991.

————. "A luta contra o Estado Novo." *Perspectivas: Revista de ciências Sociais* 2 (1977): 97–112.

————. *Revoluções do Brasil contemporâneo (1922–1938)*. São Paulo: Difel, 1977.

————. "O Estado Novo no contexto internacional." In *Repensando o Estado Novo*, edited by Dulce Pandolfi, 17–20. Rio de Janeiro: Ed. Fundação Getúlio Vargas, 1999.

Carrion, Raul. "1922–1929: Os primeiros passos do Partido Comunista do Brasil." In *Contribuição à história do Partido Comunista do Brasil*, orgs. José Carlos Ruy and Augusto Buonicore, 57–66. São Paulo: Fundação Maurício Grabois/Anita Garibaldi, 2010.

Castelo, Cláudia. "Uma incursão no lusotropicalismo de Gilberto Freyre." *Blogue de História Lusófona* 6.1 (2011): 261–80.

Castro, Ruy. *Caermen: Uma biografia*. São Paulo: Companhia das Letras, 2005.

Caulfield, Sueann. *In Defense of Honor: Sexual Morality, Modernity, and Nation in Early-Twentieth-Century Brazil*. Durham, NC: Duke University Press, 2000.

Cavalari, Rosa Maria Feiteiro. *Integralismo: Ideologia e organização de um partido de massa no Brasil (1932–1937)*. Baúru, Brazil: Editora da Universidade do Sagrado Coração, 1999.

Chadarevian, Pedro. "Raça, classe e revolução no Partido Comunista Brasileiro (1922–1964)." *Política e Sociedade* 11, no. 20 (April 2012): 255–83.

Chauncey, George. *Gay New York: Gender, Urban Culture, and the Makings of the Gay Male World, 1890–1940*. New York: Basic Books, 1994.

Chazkel, Amy. "Beyond Law and Order: The Crônica, the City, and the Invention of the Underworld: Rio de Janeiro, 1889–1922." *Estudios Interdisciplinarios de América Latina y el Caribe* 12, no. 1 (January–June 2001): 79–106.

————, Daryle Williams, and Paulo Knauss, eds. *The Rio de Janeiro Reader: History, Culture, Politics*. Durham, NC: Duke University Press, 2016.

Cohen, Lizabeth. *Making a New Deal: Industrial Workers in Chicago, 1919–1939*. Cambridge: Cambridge University Press, 1990.

Cooper, Brittney C. *Beyond Respectability: The Intellectual Thought of Race Women*. Urbana: University of Illinois Press, 2017.

Cooper, Frederick, Thomas Cleveland Holt, and Rebecca J. Scott. *Beyond Slavery: Explorations of Race, Labor, and Citizenship in Postemancipation Societies.* Chapel Hill: University of North Carolina Press, 2000.

Costa, Emília Viotti da. *The Brazilian Empire: Myths and Histories.* Chicago: University of Chicago Press, 1985.

Cowan, Benjamin A. *Securing Sex: Morality and Repression in the Making of Cold War Brazil.* Chapel Hill: University of North Carolina Press, 2016.

Cowie, Jefferson. *The Great Exception: The New Deal and the Limits of American Politics.* Princeton, NJ: Princeton University Press, 2016.

Cramer, Gisela, and Ursula Prutsch. *Americas Unidas! Nelson A. Rockefeller's Office of Inter-American Affairs (1940–46).* Iberoamericana/Vervuert, 2012.

———. "Nelson A. Rockefeller's Office of Inter-American Affairs (1940–1946) and Record Group 229." *Hispanic American Historical Review* 86, no. 4 (2006): 785–806.

Crick, Bernard. *Democracy: A Very Short Introduction.* Oxford: Oxford University Press, 2002.

Cruz, Natalia dos Reis. "O integralismo e a questão racial: A intolerância como princípio." PhD diss., Universidade Federal Fluminense, 2004.

Cunha, Olívia Maria Gomes da. "Sua alma em sua palma: Identificando a 'raça' e inventando a nação." In *Repensando o Estado Novo,* edited by Dulce Pandolfi, 257–88. Rio de Janeiro: Editora FGV, 1999.

Dahlquist, Karl. "The Young Macpherson on the Transition into Socialism and the Rise of Fascism." *Canadian Journal of Political Science* 51, no. 2 (June 2018): 405–24.

D'Araújo, Maria Celina. *As instituições brasileiras da Era Vargas.* Rio de Janeiro: EdUERJ, 1999.

———. "Entre a Europa e os Estados Unidos: Diálogos de Vargas com seu diário." *Luso-Brazilian Review* 34, no. 1 (1997): 17–41.

Daniel, Cletus E. *Chicano Workers and the Politics of Fairness: The FEPC in the Southwest, 1941–1945.* Austin: University of Texas Press, 1991.

Daniel, G. Reginald. *Race and Multiraciality in Brazil and the United States: Converging Paths?* University Park, PA: Penn State University Press, 2006.

Davenport, Lisa. *Jazz Diplomacy: Promoting America in the Cold War Era.* Jackson: University Press of Mississippi, 2009.

Davies, Carol Boyce. *Left of Karl Marx: The Political Life of Black Communist Claudia Jones.* Durham, NC: Duke University Press, 2007.

Dávila, Arlene. *Sponsored Identities: Cultural Politics in Puerto Rico.* Philadelphia: Temple University Press, 1997.

Dávila, Jerry. *Diploma of Whiteness: Race and Social Policy in Brazil, 1917–1945.* Durham, NC: Duke University Press, 2003.

———. *Hotel Trópico: Brazil and the Challenges of Decolonization (1950–1980).* Durham, NC: Duke University Press, 2010.

Davis, Angela. *Women, Race, and Class.* New York: Random House, 1981.

Davis, Darién J. *Avoiding the Dark: Race and the Forging of National Culture in Modern Brazil.* Aldershot, UK: Ashgate, 1999.

Degler, Carl N. *In Search of Human Nature: The Decline and Revival of Darwinism in American Social Thought.* New York: Oxford University Press, 1991.

———. *Neither White nor Black: Slavery and Race Relations in Brazil and the United States.* New York: Macmillan, 1971.

Degras, Jane. *The Communist International: 1919–1943 Documents.* Vol. 2. London: Oxford University Press, 1960.

———. *The Communist International: 1919–1943 Documents.* Vol. 3. London and New York: Routledge, 2014.

Denning, Michael. *The Cultural Front: The Laboring of American Culture in the Twentieth Century.* London: Verso, 2000.

Dietrich, Ana Maria. *Nazismo tropical?: O Partido Nazista no Brasil.* São Paulo: Todas as Musas, 2012.

Dinerstein, Joel. *Swinging the Machine: Modernity, Technology, and African American Culture between the World Wars.* Amherst: University of Massachusetts Press, 2003.

Doherty, Thomas. *Projections of War: Hollywood, American Culture, and World War II.* New York: Columbia University Press, 1993.

Domingues, Petrônio. "'Constantemente derrubo lágrimas': O drama de uma liderança negra no cárcere do governo Vargas." *Topoi* 8, no. 14 (January–June 2007): 146–71.

———. "'O caminho da verdadeira emancipação': A Federação dos Negros do Brasil." In *Experiências da emancipação: Biografias, instituições e movimentos sociais no pós-abolição (1890–1980),* 157–84. São Paulo: Selo Negro, 2011.

———. "O 'messias' negro? Arlindo Veiga dos Santos (1902–1978)." *Varia Historia* 22, no. 36 (July/December 2006): 517–36.

———. *Uma história não contada: Negro, racismo e branqueamento em São Paulo no pós-abolição.* São Paulo: Senac, 2003.

———. "Movimento Negro Brasileiro: Alguns apontamentos históricos." *Tempo* 12, no. 23 (2007): 103–4.

———. "Os 'Pérolas Negras': A Participação do negro na Revolução Constitucionalista de 1932." *Afro-Ásia* 29/30 (2003): 199–245.

———. "'O recinto sagrado': Educação e antirracismo no Brasil." In Flávio Gomes and Petrônio Domingues, *Da nitidez e invisibildade: Legados do pós-emancipação no Brasil,* 274–82. Belo Horizonte: Fino Traço, 2013.

———. "'Este samba selvagem': O Charleston na arena transatlântica." In Flávio Gomes and Petrônio Domingues, *Da nitidez e invisibildade: Legados do pós-emancipação no Brasil,* 177–201. Belo Horizonte: Fino Traço, 2013.

———. "O mito da democracia racial e a mestiçagem no Brasil (1889–1930)." *Diálogos Latinoamericanos* 10 (2005): 126–27.

Dorr, Kirstie A. *On Site, in Sound: Performance Geographies in América Latina.* Durham, NC: Duke University Press, 2018.

Dudziak, Mary. *Cold War Civil Rights: Race and the Image of American Democracy.* Princeton, NJ: Princeton University Press, 2000.

Dulles, John. *Anarchists and Communists in Brazil, 1900–1935.* Austin: University of Texas Press, 1973.

———. *Brazilian Communism: 1935–1945.* Austin: University of Texas Press, 1983.

Dzidzienyo, Anani. *The Position of Blacks in Brazilian and Cuban Society*. Rev. ed. London: Minority Rights Group, 1979.

Edwards, Brent Hayes. *The Practice of Diaspora: Literature, Translation, and the Rise of Black Internationalism*. Cambridge, MA: Harvard University Press, 2003.

Fabris, Annateresa, ed. *Portinari amico mio: Cartas de Mário de Andrade a Cândido Portinari*. Campinas, Brazil: Mercado de Letras–Autores Associados/Projeto Portinari, 1995.

———. *Portinari, pintor social*. São Paulo: Perspectiva; Editora da Universidade de São Paulo, 1990.

Fausto, Boris. *A Concise History of Brazil*. 2nd ed. Translated by Arthur Brakel. New York: Cambridge University Press, 2014.

Fenerick, José Adriano. "Nem do morro, nem da cidade: As transformações do samba e a indústria cultural, 1920–1945." PhD diss., Universidade de São Paulo, 2002.

Fernandes, Florestan. *The Negro in Brazilian Society*. Translated by Jacqueline Skiles. New York: Columbia University Press, 1969.

———. *A integração do negro na sociedade de classes*. 2 vols. São Paulo: Globo, 2008.

Ferrara, Miriam. "A imprensa negra Paulista (1919–1963)." *Revista Brasileira de História* 5, no. 10 (March/August 1985): 197–207.

———. *A imprensa negra Paulista, 1915–1963*. São Paulo: FFLCH-USP, 1986.

Ferreira, Marieta de Moraes. "Os anos rebeldes do tenentismo." *Revista de História* 1, no. 1 (July 2005): 46–51.

Ferreira, Ricardo Franklin. *Afro-descendente: Identidade em construção*. Rio de Janeiro: São Paulo, 2004.

Ferris, Williams R. "Sterling Brown 1901–1989." In *The Storied South: Voices of Writers and Artists*, 104–10. Chapel Hill: University of North Carolina Press, 2013.

Filho, João dos Santos. "O turismo na Era Vargas e o Departamento de Imprensa e Propaganda—DIP." *Cultur: Revista de Cultura e Turismo* 2, no. 2 (July 2008): 103–15.

Fischer, Brodwyn. *A Poverty of Rights: Citizenship and Inequality in Twentieth-Century Rio de Janeiro*. Stanford, CA: Stanford University Press, 2008.

———. "The Red Menace Reconsidered: A Forgotten History of Communist Mobilization in Rio's Favelas, 1946–1956." *Hispanic American Historical Review* 94, no. 1 (2014): 1–33.

Fitzgerald, David Scott, and David Cook-Martin. *Culling the Masses: The Democratic Origins of Racist Immigration Policy in the Americas*. Cambridge, MA: Harvard University Press, 2014.

Flanagan, Hallie. *Arena: The History of the Federal Theatre*. New York: B. Blom, 1965.

Foley, Neil. *Quest for Equality: The Failed Promise of Black-Brown Solidarity*. Cambridge: Cambridge University Press, 2010.

Foner, Philip S., and James S. Allen. *American Communism and Black Americans: A Documentary History, 1919–1929*. Philadelphia: Temple University Press, 1987.

Foner, Philip, and Herbert Shapiro. *American Communism and Black Americans: A Documentary History, 1930–1934*. Philadelphia: Temple University Press, 1991.

Freire-Medeiros, Bianca. "Hollywood Musicals and the Invention of Rio de Janeiro, 1933–1953." *Cinema Journal* 41, no. 4 (Summer 2002): 52–67.

———. *O Rio de Janeiro que Hollywood inventou*. Rio de Janeiro: Jorge Zahar, 2005.

French, John. *The Brazilian Workers' ABC: Class Conflict and Alliances in Modern São Paulo*. Chapel Hill: University of North Carolina Press, 1992.

———. *Drowning in Laws: Labor Law and Brazilian Political Culture*. Chapel Hill: University of North Carolina Press, 2004.

Freyre, Gilberto. *The Masters and the Slaves: A Study in the Development of Brazilian Civilization*. Translated by Samuel Putman. New York: Knopf, 1963.

———. *New World in the Tropics: The Culture of Modern Brazil*. New York: Knopf, 1959.

———. *Order and Progress: Brazil from Monarch to Republic*. Translated by Rod W. Horton. Berkeley: University of California Press, 1986.

Friedman, Max Paul. *Nazis and Good Neighbors: The United States Campaign against the Germans of Latin America in World War II*. Cambridge, UK: Cambridge University Press, 2003.

de la Fuente, Alejandro. "Myths of Racial Democracy: Cuba, 1900–1912." *Latin American Research Review* 34, no. 3 (1999): 39–74.

———. *A Nation for All*. Chapel Hill: University of North Carolina Press, 2001.

Fujitani, Takashi. *Race for Empire: Koreans as Japanese and Japanese as Americans During World War II*. Berkeley: University of California Press, 2011.

Gallicchio, Marc. *The African American Encounter with Japan and China: Black Internationalism in Asia, 1895–1945*. Chapel Hill: University of North Carolina Press, 2000.

Gambini, Roberto. *O duplo jogo do Getúlio Vargas: Influência americana e alemã no Estado Novo*. São Paulo: Edições Símbolo, 1977.

Garfinkel, Herbert. *When Negroes March: The March on Washington Movement in the Organizational Politics for FEPC*. Glencoe, IL: Free Press, 1959.

Gerstle, Gary. *American Crucible: Race and Nation in the Twentieth Century*. Princeton, NJ: Princeton University Press, 2001.

Gertz, René. *O Fascismo no Sul do Brasil*. Porto Alegre: Mercado Aberto, 1987.

Gilmore, Glenda Elizabeth. *Defying Dixie: The Radical Roots of Civil Rights, 1919–1950*. New York: Norton, 2009.

Gilroy, Paul. *One Nation under a Groove: The Cultural Politics of Race and Racism in Britain*. Minneapolis: University of Minnesota Press, 1990.

Ginio, Ruth. *French Colonialism Unmasked: The Vichy Years in French West Africa*. Lincoln: University of Nebraska Press, 2008.

Gleason, Philip. *Speaking of Diversity: Language and Ethnicity in Twentieth-Century America*. Baltimore: Johns Hopkins University Press, 1992.

Gomes, Adildo Soares. "Cabo Verde e a Segunda Guerra Mundial: A importância geoestratégica do arquipélago na política externa Portuguesa (1939–1945)." Master's thesis, Universidade Nova de Lisboa, 2011.

Gomes, Ângela de Castro. *História e historiadores*. São Paulo: Fundação Getúlio Vargas, 1996.

———. *A invenção do trabalhismo*. São Paulo: Vértice; and Rio de Janeiro: Instituto Universitário de Pesquisas do Rio de Janeiro, 1988.

Gomes, Flávio. *Negros e política (1888–1937)*. Rio de Janeiro: Jorge Zahar Editor, 2005.

———, and Anamaria Fagundes. "'Idiossincrasias cromáticas': Projetos e propostas de 'imigração negra' no Brasil republicano." In *Da nitidez e invisibilidade: Legados do pós-emancipação no Brasil*, 208–19. Belo Horizonte: Fino Traço, 2013.

Goodman, James. *Stories of Scottsboro*. New York: Pantheon, 1994.

Gore, Dayo. *Radicalism at the Crossroads: African American Women Activists in the Cold War*. New York: New York University Press, 2011.

———, Jeanne Theoharis, and Komozi Woodard, eds. *Want to Start a Revolution? Radical Women in the Black Freedom Struggle*. New York: New York University Press, 2009.

Graham, Jessica. "A virada antirracista do Partido Comunista do Brasil, a Frente Negra Brasileira, e a Ação Integralista Brasileira na década de 1930." In *Políticas da raça—Experiências e legados da abolição e da pós-emancipação no Brasil*, Petrônio Domingues and Flávio Gomes orgs., 353–76. São Paulo: Selo Negro Edições, 2014.

Graham, Richard. *Patronage and Politics in Nineteenth-Century Brazil*. Stanford, CA: Stanford University Press, 1990.

Green, Adam. *Selling the Race: Culture, Community, and Black Chicago, 1940–1955*. Chicago: University of Chicago Press, 2007.

Greenberg, Cheryl Lynn. *"Or Does It Explode": Black Harlem in the Great Depression*. Oxford: Oxford University Press, 1991.

———. *To Ask for an Equal Chance: African Americans in the Great Depression*. Lanham, MD: Rowman & Littlefield, 2009.

Griffin, Roger. *The Nature of Fascism*. London: Pinter, 1991.

Grossman, James. *Land of Hope: Chicago, Black Southerners, and the Great Migration*. Chicago: University of Chicago Press, 1989.

Guimarães, Antonio Sérgio Alfredo. "Racial Democracy." In *Imagining Brazil*, edited by Jessé Souza and Valter Sinder, 119–40. Lanham, MD: Lexington Books, 2005.

———. *Classes, raças e democracia*. São Paulo: Editora 34, 2002.

Guimarães, Antonio Sérgio Alfredo, and Márcio Macedo. "*Diário trabalhista* e democracia racial negra dos anos 1940." *Dados* 51, no. 1 (2008): 143–82.

Guimarães, Manoel Luiz Salgado. "Nação e Civilização nos Trópicos: O Instituto Histórico Geográfico Brasileiro e o projeto de uma história nacional." *Revista Estudos Históricos, América do Norte* 1, no. 1 (1988): 5–27.

Guimarães, Valéria Lima. *O PCB cai no samba: Os comunistas e a cultura popular, 1945–1950*. Rio de Janeiro: Governo do Rio de Janeiro, Arquivo Público do Estado do Rio de Janeiro, 2009.

Gutierrez, David. *Walls and Mirrors: Mexican Americans, Mexican Immigrants, and the Politics of Ethnicity*. Berkeley: University of California Press, 1995.

Hall, Jacqueline Dowd. "The Long Civil Rights Movement and the Political Uses of the Past." *Journal of American History* 91 (March 2005): 1233–63.

Hall, Kermit, and John Patrick. *The Pursuit of Justice: Supreme Court Decisions that Shaped America*. Oxford: Oxford University Press, 2006.

Hall, Stuart, Jessica Evans, and Sean Nixon, eds. *Representation: Cultural Representations and Signifying Practices*. London: SAGE Publications, 2003.

Hanchard, Michael. "Identity, Meaning, and the African-American." *Social Text*, no. 24 (1990): 31–42.

———. *Racial Politics in Contemporary Brazil*. Durham, NC: Duke University Press, 1999.

———. *The Spectre of Race: How Discrimination Haunts Western Democracy*. Princeton, NJ: Princeton University Press, 2018.

Hanson, Joyce. *Mary McLeod Bethune and Black Women's Political Activism*. Columbia: University of Missouri Press, 2003.

Harris, Lashawn. "Marvel Cooke: Investigative Journalist, Communist and Black Radical Subject." *Journal for the Study of Radicalism* 6, no. 2 (Fall 2012): 91–126.

Harris, Stephen. *Harlem's Hellfighters: The African-American 369th Infantry in World War I*. Dulles, VA: Potomac Books, 2003.

Hart, Justin. "Making Democracy Safe for the World: Race, Propaganda, and the Transformation of U.S. Foreign Policy during World War II." *Pacific History Review* 73, no. 1 (February 2004): 49–84.

Hayashi, Brian. *Democratizing the Enemy: The Japanese American Internment*. Princeton, NJ: Princeton University Press, 2004.

Hendrickson, Mark. *American Labor and Economic Citizenship: New Capitalism from World War I to the Great Depression*. New York: Cambridge University Press, 2013.

Helwig, David. *African American Reflections on Brazil's Racial Paradise*. Philadelphia: Temple University Press, 1992.

Hensler, Bejamin. "Não Vale a Pena? (Not Worth the Trouble?): Afro-Brazilian Workers and Brazilian Anti-Discrimination Law." *30 Hastings International and Comparative Law Review* 267 (Spring 2007): 267–346.

Hertzman, Marc A. *Making Samba: A New History of Race and Music in Brazil*. Durham, NC: Duke University Press, 2013.

Higham, John. *Strangers in the Land: Patterns in American Nativism, 1860–1925*. New Brunswick, NJ: Rutgers University Press, 1955.

Hilliard, Robert L., and George L. Hall. *Radio Broadcasting: An Introduction to the Sound Medium*. New York: Hastings House, 1967.

Hilton, Stanley. *Hitler's Secret War in South America: German Military Espionage and Allied Counterespionage in Brazil*. Baton Rouge: Louisiana State University Press, 1981.

Hine, Darlene Clark, William Hine, and Stanley Harrold. *The African American Odyssey. Vol. 2: Since 1865*. Upper Saddle River, NJ: Pearson Education, 2006.

Hirsch, Arnold. *Making the Second Ghetto: Race and Housing in Chicago, 1940–1960*. Cambridge, UK: Cambridge University Press, 1983.

Hobbs, Allyson. *A Chosen Exile: A History of Racial Passing in American Life.* Cambridge, MA: Harvard University Press, 2014.

Hobsbawn, Eric. *Nations and Nationalism since 1780: Programme, Myth, Reality.* New York: Cambridge University Press, 1993.

Hofbauer, Andreas. *Uma história de branqueamento ou o negro em questão.* São Paulo: Editora UNESP, 2006.

Holt, Thomas. *Children of Fire: A History of African Americans.* New York: Hill and Wang, 2011.

———. "Marking: Race, Race-Making, and the Writing of History." *American Historical Review* 100, no. 1 (February 1995): 1–20.

———. *The Problem of Freedom: Race, Labor, and Politics in Jamaica and Britain, 1832–1938.* Baltimore: Johns Hopkins University Press, 1991.

———. *The Problem of Race in the 21st Century.* Cambridge, MA: Harvard University Press, 2002.

———. Foreword to *Race and Nation in Modern Latin America,* edited by Nancy Appelbaum, Anne MacPherson, and Karin Rosemblatt, vii–xiv. Chapel Hill: University of North Carolina Press, 2003.

Hordge-Freeman, Elizabeth. *The Color of Love: Racial Features, Stigma, and Socialization in Black Brazilian Families.* Austin: University of Texas Press, 2015.

Horne, Gerald. *Black Liberation/Red Scare: Ben Davis and the Communist Party.* London: Associated University Press, 1994.

———. *Black Revolutionary: William Patterson and the Globalization of the African American Freedom Struggle.* Champaign: University of Illinois Press, 2013.

———. *The Color of Fascism: Lawrence Dennis, Racial Passing, and the Rise of Right-Wing Extremism in the United States.* New York: New York University Press, 2006.

———. *Race Woman: The Lives of Shirley Graham Du Bois.* New York: New York University Press, 2002.

———. *Race War! White Supremacy and the Japanese Attack on the British Empire.* New York: New York University Press, 2005.

Horsman, Reginald. *Race and Manifest Destiny: The Origins of American Racial Anglo-Saxonism.* Cambridge, MA: Harvard University Press, 1981.

Hutchinson, George. *Harlem Renaissance in Black and White.* Cambridge, MA: Harvard University Press, 1996.

Ignatieff, Michael. *Blood and Belonging: Journeys into the New Nationalism.* New York: Farrar, Straus, and Giroux, 1993.

Irons, Peter. *Justice at War.* New York: Oxford University Press, 1983.

———, ed. *Justice Delayed: The Record of the Japanese Internment Cases.* Middletown, CT: Wesleyan University Press, 1989.

It's All True: Based on an Unfinished Film by Orson Welles. DVD. Directed by Richard Wilson. Hollywood, CA: Paramount Pictures/Les Film Balenciaga Production, 1993.

Jackson, Walter. *Gunnar Myrdal and America's Conscience: Social Engineering and Racial Liberalism, 1938–1987.* Chapel Hill: University of North Carolina Press, 1990.

Jacobson, Matthew. *Whiteness of a Different Color: Immigrants and the Alchemy of Race*. Cambridge, MA: Harvard University Press, 1998.

Jambeiro, Othon, Amanda Mota, Andrea Ribeiro, Clarissa Amaral, Cassiano Simões, Eliane Costa, Fabiano Brito, Sandro Ferreira, and Suzy dos Santos. *Tempos de Vargas: O rádio e o controle da informação*. Salvador: Ed. UFBA, 2004.

James, C. Boyd. *Garvey, Garveyism, and the Antinomies in Black Redemption*. Trenton, NJ: Africa World Press, 2009.

James, C. L. R. *A History of Pan-African Revolt*. Washington, DC: Drum and Spear Press, 1969.

James, Winston. *Holding Aloft the Banner of Ethiopia: Caribbean Radicalism in Early Twentieth Century America*. New York: Verso Books, 1999.

Janken, Kenneth Robert. *Rayford W. Logan and the Dilemma of the African-American Intellectual*. Amherst: University of Massachusetts Press, 1993.

———. *White: The Biography of Walter White, Mr. NAACP*. New York: New Press/Norton, 2003.

Johnson, John. *Latin America in Caricature*. Austin: University of Texas Press, 1980.

Kalfatovic, Martin R. *The New Deal Fine Arts Projects: A Bibliography, 1933–1992*. Metuchen, NJ: Scarecrow Press, 1994.

Kallen, Horace. *Culture and Democracy in the United States*. New York: Boni & Liveright, 1924.

Karepovs, Dainis, and José Castilho Marques Neto. "Os Trotskistas brasileiros e suas organizações políticas (1930–1966)." *História do Marxismo no Brasil: Partidos e organizações dos anos 1920 aos 1960*. Vol. 5, edited by Marcelo Ridenti and Daniel Aarão Reis. Campinas, Brazil: Editora da Unicamp, 2007.

Kelley, Robin D. G. *Freedom Dreams: The Black Radical Tradition*. Boston: Beacon Press, 2002.

———. *Hammer and Hoe: Alabama Communists During the Great Depression*. Chapel Hill: University of North Carolina Press, 1990.

———. *Race Rebels: Culture, Politics, and the Black Working Class*. New York: Free Press, 1994.

———. *Thelonious Monk: The Life and Times of an American Original*. New York: Free Press, 2009.

Kirby, John. *Black Americans in the Roosevelt Era: Liberalism and Race*. Knoxville: University of Tennessee Press, 1980.

Klein, Marcus. *Our Brazil Will Awake! The Acção Integralista Brasileira and the Failed Quest for a Fascist Order in the 1930s*. Amsterdam: Centre for Latin American Research and Documentation, 2004.

Klinkner, Philip, and Rogers Smith. *The Unsteady March: The Rise and Decline of Racial Equality in America*. Chicago: University of Chicago Press, 1999.

Kornweibel, Theodore, Jr. *Seeing Red: Federal Campaigns against Black Militancy, 1919–1925*. Bloomington: Indiana University Press, 1998.

Korstad, Robert, and Nelson Lichtenstein. "Opportunities Found and Lost: Labor, Radicals, and the Early Civil Rights Movement." *Journal of American History* 75, no. 3 (1988): 786–811.

Kössling, Karin Sant'Anna. "Os afro-descendentes na Ação Integralista Brasileira." *Revista Histórica* 14 (2004): 19–24.

Kühl, Stefan. *The Nazi Connection: The American Eugenics Movement and the Racial Policies of German National Socialism*. Oxford: Oxford University Press, 1994.

Kwak, Nancy. *A World of Homeowners: American Power and the Politics of Housing Aid*. Chicago: University of Chicago Press, 2015.

Laclau, Ernesto. *On Populist Reason*. London: Verso, 2005.

Lake, Marilyn, and Henry Reynolds. *Drawing the Global Colour Line: White Men's Countries and the International Challenge of Racial Equality*. Cambridge, UK: Cambridge University Press, 2008.

Larkins, Erika Robb. *The Spectacular Favela: Violence in Modern Brazil*. Berkeley: University of California Press, 2015.

Lauerhauss, Ludwig, Jr. *Getúlio Vargas e o triunfo do nacionalismo brasileiro*. Belo Horizonte and São Paulo: Editora Itatiaia and Editoria da Universidade de São Paulo, 1986.

Lauerhass, Ludwig, and Carmen Nava, eds. *Brazil in the Making: Facets of National Identity*. Lanham, MD: Rowman & Littlefield, 2006.

Leal, Maria das Graças de Andrade. *Manuel Querino entre letras e lutas*. São Paulo: Annablume, 2009.

Leal, Victor Nunes. *Coronelismo, enxada e voto (O município e o regime representativo no Brasil)*. São Paulo: Editora Alfa-Omega, 1976.

Lesser, Jeffrey. *Immigration, Ethnicity, and National Identity*. Cambridge: Cambridge University Press, 2013.

———. *Negotiating National Identity: Immigrants, Minorities, and the Struggle for Ethnicity in Brazil*. Durham, NC: Duke University Press, 1999.

Leuchtenburg, William E. *The FDR Years: On Roosevelt and His Legacy*. New York: Columbia University Press, 1995.

———. *Franklin D. Roosevelt and the New Deal, 1932–1940*. New York: Harper & Row, 1963.

Levin, Michael. *Marx, Engels, and Liberal Democracy*. New York: St. Martin's Press, 1989.

Levine, Robert. *The Brazilian Photographs of Genevieve Naylor, 1940–1942*. Durham, NC: Duke University Press, 1998.

———. *Father of the Poor?: Vargas and His Era*. Cambridge, UK: Cambridge University Press, 1998.

———. *The Vargas Regime: The Critical Years, 1934–1938*. New York: Columbia University Press, 1970.

Lewis, David L. *When Harlem Was in Vogue*. New York: Vintage Books, 1982.

Lima, Aruã Silva de. "Comunismo contra o racismo: Autodeterminação e vieses de integração de classe no Brasil e nos Estados Unidos (1919–1939)." PhD diss., Universidade de São Paulo, 2015.

Lopes, Nei. *O samba na realidade*. Rio de Janeiro: Codecri, 1981.

Loviglio, Jason. *Radio's Intimate Public: Network Broadcasting and Mass-Mediated Democracy.* Minneapolis: University of Minnesota Press, 2005.

———. "Memória histórica: A Frente Negra Brasileira." *Revista de Cultura Vozes, Petrópolis* 83, no. 3 (May/June 1989): 332–42.

Luca, Tania Regina de. "A produção do Departamento de Imprensa e Propaganda (DIP) em acervos norte-americanos: Estudo de caso." *Revista Brasileira de História* 31, no. 61 (2011): 271–95.

MacDonnell, Francis. *Insidious Foes: The Axis Fifth Column and the American Home Front.* New York: Oxford University Press, 1995.

Maio, Marcos Chor. *Nem Rotschild nem Trotsky: O pensamento anti-semita de Gustavo Barroso.* Rio de Janeiro: Imago Editora, 1991.

———. "Tempo controverso: Gilberto Freyre e o Projeto UNESCO." *Tempo Social* 11, no. 1 (May 1999): 111–36.

———. "UNESCO and the Study of Race Relations in Brazil: Regional or National Issue?" *Latin American Research Review* 32, no. 2 (2001): 118–36.

Makalani, Minkah. *In the Cause of Freedom: Radical Black Internationalism from Harlem to London, 1917–1939.* Chapel Hill, NC: University of North Carolina Press, 2014.

Martius, Karl Friedrich von, and José Honório Rodrigues. "Como se deve escrever a história do Brasil." *Revista da História da América*, no. 42 (1956): 433–58.

Maxwell, William J. *New Negro, Old Left: African-American Writing and Communism between the Wars.* New York: Columbia University Press, 1999.

McCann, Bryan. *Hello, Hello Brazil: Popular Music in the Making of Modern Brazil.* Durham, NC: Duke University Press, 2004.

McCann, Frank, Jr. *The Brazilian-American Alliance, 1937–1945.* Princeton, NJ: Princeton University Press, 1973.

———. "Brazil and World War II: The Forgotten Ally. What Did You Do in the War, Zé Carioca?" *Estudios interdisciplinarios de América Latina y el Caribe* 6, no. 2 (1995). Accessed June 1, 2014. http://eial.tau.ac.il/index.php/eial/article/view/1193/1221.

McClain, Charles, ed. *The Mass Internment of Japanese Americans and the Quest for Legal Redress.* New York: Garland, 1994.

McDonald, William Francis. *Federal Relief Administration and the Arts: The Origins and Administrative History of the Arts Projects of the Works Progress Administration.* Columbus: Ohio State University Press, 1969.

McDonogh, Gary W., ed. *The Florida Negro: A Federal Writers' Project Legacy.* Jackson: University Press of Mississippi, 1993.

McDuffie, Erik S. *Sojourning for Freedom: Black Women, American Communism, and the Making of Black Left Feminism.* Durham, NC: Duke University Press, 2011.

McKenzie, Kermit E. "The Soviet Union, the Comintern and World Revolution: 1935." *Political Science Quarterly* 65, no. 2 (June 1950): 214–37.

McNeil, Genna Rae. *Groundwork: Charles Hamilton Houston and the Struggle for Civil Rights.* Philadelphia: University of Pennsylvania Press, 1983.

MacPherson, C. B. *The Real World of Democracy.* New York: Oxford University Press, 1972.

Man, Simeon. *Soldiering through Empire: Race and the Making of the Decolonizing Pacific.* Oakland: University of California Press, 2018.

Matory, J. Lorand. *Black Atlantic Religion: Tradition, Transnationalism, and Matriarchy in the Afro-Brazilian Candomblé.* Princeton, NJ: Princeton University Press, 2005.

Meade, Teresa, and Gregory Alonso Pirio. "In Search of the Afro-American 'Eldorado': Attempts by North American Blacks to Enter Brazil in the 1920s." *Luso-Brazilian Review* 25, no. 1 (1988): 85–110.

Mesquita, Gustavo Rodrigues. "O projeto regionalista de Gilberto Freyre e o Estado Novo: Da crise do pacto oligárquico à modernização contemporizadora das disparidades regionais do Brasil." Master's thesis, Universidade Federal de Goiás, 2012.

Miceli, Sérgio. *Intelectuais e classe dirigente no Brasil (1920–1945).* São Paulo: Difel, 1979.

Mills, Charles. *The Racial Contract.* Ithaca, NY: Cornell University Press, 1999.

Mills, Quincy T. *Cutting along the Color Line: Black Barbers and Barbershops in America.* Philadelphia: University of Pennsylvania Press, 2013.

Mitchell, Sean. *Constellations of Inequality: Space, Race, and Utopia in Brazil.* Chicago: University of Chicago Press, 2018.

Mitchell-Walthour, Gladys. *The Politics of Blackness: Racial Identity and Political Behavior in Contemporary Brazil.* Cambridge: Cambridge University Press, 2018.

Molina, Natalia. *How Race Is Made in America: Immigration, Citizenship, and the Historical Power of Racial Scripts.* Berkeley: University of California Press, 2014.

Mota, Carlos Guilherme. *Ideologia da cultura brasileira (1933–1974): Pontos de partida para uma revisão histórica.* São Paulo: Ática, 1997.

Motta, Rodrigo Patto Sá. *Em guarda contra o perigo vermelho: O anticomunismo no Brasil (1917–1964).* São Paulo: Editora Perspectiva, 2002.

Mouffe, Chantal. *The Democratic Paradox.* London: Verso, 2000.

———. "Feminism, Citizenship and Radical Democratic Politics." In *Feminists Theorize the Political,* edited by Judith Butler and Joan Scott, 369–84. New York: Routledge, 1992.

Moura, Clovis. *História do negro brasileiro.* São Paulo: Editora Ática, 1989.

———. *Dialética radical do Brasil negro.* 2nd ed. São Paulo: Fundaçõ Maurício Grabois: Anita Garibaldi, 2014.

Moura, Gerson. *Autonomia na dependência: A política externa brasileira de 1935 a 1942.* Rio de Janeiro: Editora Nova Fronteira, 1980.

———. *Relações exteriores do Brasil (1939–1950): Mudanças na natureza das relações Brasil-Estados Unidos durante e após a Segunda Guerra Mundial.* Brasília: Fundação Alexandre de Gusmão, 2012.

———. *Tio Sam chega ao Brasil: A penetração cultural americana.* São Paulo: Brasiliense, Coleção tudo é História, 1986.

Mullen, Bill V. *Un-American: W. E. B. Du Bois and the Century of World Revolution.* Philadelphia: Temple University Press, 2015.

Murray, Pauli. *Song in a Weary Throat: Memoir of an American Pilgrimage.* New York: Harper & Row, 1987.

Naison, Mark. *Communists in Harlem during the Depression*. Urbana: University of Illinois Press, 1983.

Nascimento, Abdias do, and Elisa Larkin Nascimento. *Africans in Brazil: A Pan-African Perspective*. Trenton, NJ: African World Press, 1992.

Nascimento, Ana Carolina Carvalho de Almeida. "O sexto sentido do pesquisador: A experiência etnográfica de Edison Carneiro." Master's thesis, UFRJ, 2010.

Nascimento, Elisa Larkin. *The Sorcery of Color: Identity, Race, and Gender in Brazil*. Philadelphia: Temple University Press, 2007.

Needell, Jeffrey. "Identity, Race, Gender, and Modernity in the Origins of Gilberto Freyre's *Oeuvre*." *American Historical Review* 100, no. 1 (February 1995): 51–77.

———. *A Tropical Belle Époque: Elite Culture and Society in Turn-of-the-Century Rio de Janeiro*. Cambridge: Cambridge University Press, 1987.

Nesbitt, Francis Njubi. *Race for Sanctions: African Americans against Apartheid, 1946–1994*. Bloomington: Indiana University Press, 2004.

Ng, Wendy. *Japanese American Internment during World War II: A History and Reference Guide*. Westport, CT: Greenwood Press, 2002.

Ngai, Mae. *Impossible Subjects: Illegal Aliens and the Making of Modern America*. Princeton, NJ: Princeton University Press, 2004.

Nicodemo, Thiago L. "State-Sponsored Avant-Garde and Brazil's Cultural Policy in the 1940s: Candido Portinari and Gilberto Freyre in the USA." *Revista Landa* 5, no. 1 (2016): 350–79.

Ninkovich, Frank. *Diplomacy of Ideas: US Foreign Policy and Cultural Relations, 1938–1950*. Cambridge, UK: Cambridge University Press, 1981.

Nobles, Melissa. *Shades of Citizenship: Race and Census in Modern Politics*. Stanford, CA: Stanford University Press, 2000.

Oliveira, João Pacheco de. "Pardos, mestiços, ou caboclos: Os índios nos censos nacionais no Brasil (1872–1980)." *Horizontes Antropólogicos* 3, no. 6 (October 1997): 61–84.

Oliveira, Lúcia Lippi. *O Brasil dos imigrantes*. Rio de Janeiro: J. Zahar, 2001.

———, Mônica Pimenta Velloso, and Ângela de Castro Gomes. *Estado Novo: Ideologia e poder*. Rio de Janeiro: Zahar Editores, 1982.

———. "O intelectual do DIP: Lourival Fontes e o Estado Novo." In *Constelação Capanema: Intelectuais e políticas*, edited by Helena Bomeny. Rio de Janeiro: Editora FGV; Universidade de São Francisco, 2001.

Oliveira, Rodrigo Santos de. "A evolução dos estudos sobre o integralismo." *Estudos Ibero-Americanos* 36, no. 1 (2010): 118–38.

Oliveira, Valéria Garcia de. "A música, o DEOPS e o ideal revolucionário (1924–1950)." In *Cultura amordaçada: Intelectuais e músicos sob a vigilância do DEOPS, Modulo VI—Comunistas*. São Paulo: Arquivo do Estado/Imprensa Oficial, 2002.

Omi, Michael, and Howard Winant. *Racial Formation in the United States*. 3rd ed. New York: Routledge, 2014.

O'Shaughnessy, Nicholas. *Selling Hitler: Propaganda and the Nazi Brand*. London: Hurst, 2016.

Ortiz, Renato. *Cultura brasileira e identidade nacional*. São Paulo: Brasilense, 1985.

Otovo, Okezi T. *Progressive Mothers, Better Babies: Race, Public Health, and the State in Brazil, 1850–1945*. Austin: University of Texas Press, 2016.

Owensby, Brian P. *Intimate Ironies: Modernity and the Making of Middle-Class Lives in Brazil*. Stanford, CA: Stanford University Press, 1999.

Painter, Nell Irvin. *Creating Black Americans: African-American History and Its Meanings, 1619 to the Present*. New York: Oxford University Press, 2007.

Pallares-Burke, Maria Lúcia Garcia. *Gilberto Freyre: Um vitoriano dos trópicos*. São Paulo: Editora Unesp, 2005.

Pandolfi, Dulce, ed. *Repensando o Estado Novo*. Rio de Janeiro: Ed. Fundação Getúlio Vargas, 1999.

Paschel, Tianna. *Becoming Black Political Subjects: Movements and Ethno-Racial Rights in Colombia and Brazil*. Princeton, NJ: Princeton University Press, 2016.

Payne, Charles. *I've Got the Light of Freedom: The Organizing Tradition and the Mississippi Freedom Struggle*. Berkeley: University of California Press, 1995.

Pereira, Amilcar Araujo. "'O Mundo Negro': A constituição do movimento negro contemporâneo no Brasil (1970–1995)." PhD diss., Universidade Federal Fluminense, Niterói, 2010.

Pereira, João Baptista Borges. *Cor, profissão e mobilidade: O negro e o radio de São Paulo*. São Paulo: Livraria Pioneira Editora, Editora da Universidade de São Paulo, 1967.

Peretti, Burton W. *Jazz in American Culture*. Chicago: Ivan R. Dee, 1997.

Perry, Keisha-Khan. *Black Women against the Land Grab: The Fight for Racial Justice in Brazil*. Minneapolis: University of Minnesota Press, 2013.

Pfeffer, Paula. *A. Philip Randolph: Pioneer of the Civil Rights Movement*. Baton Rouge: Louisana State University Press, 1990.

Pincus, Steven, and William Novak. "Political History after the Cultural Turn." In *Perspectives on History*, May 1, 2011. Accessed March 10, 2016. https://www.historians.org/publications-and-directories/perspectives-on-history/may-2011/political-history-after-the-cultural-turn.

Pinheiro, Paulo Sérgio. *Estratégias da ilusão: A revolução mundial e o Brasil, 1922–1935*. 2nd ed. São Paulo: Companhia das Letras, 1991.

Pinto, Aguiar Costa. *O negro no Rio de Janeiro: Relações de raça numa sociedade em mudança*. 2nd ed. Rio de Janeiro: Editora Universidade Federal do Rio de Janeiro, 1998.

Pinto, Regina Pahim. "O movimento negro em São Paulo: Luta e identidade." PhD diss., Universidade de São Paulo, 1993.

Plant, Rebecca Jo. *Mom: The Transformation of Motherhood in Modern America*. Chicago: University of Chicago Press, 2010.

Plummer, Brenda Gayle. *Black Americans and U.S. Foreign Affairs, 1935–1960*. Chapel Hill: University of North Carolina Press, 1996.

———. *Rising Wind: Black Americans and U.S. Foreign Affairs, 1935–1960*. Chapel Hill: University of North Carolina Press, 1996.

———. *Window on Freedom: Race, Civil Rights, and Foreign Affairs, 1945–1988*. Chapel Hill: University of North Carolina Press, 2003.

Prestes, Anita Leocádia. "A conferência dos Partidos Comunistas da América do Sul e do Caribe (Moscou, Outubro/1934) e os Levantes de Novembro de 1935 no Brasil." *Crítica Marxista* 22 (May 2006): 132–53.

———. *Da insurreição armada, 1935. À "União Nacional," 1938–1945*. São Paulo: Editora Paz e Terra, 2001.

Putnam, Lara. *Radical Moves: Caribbean Migrants and the Politics of Race in the Jazz Age*. Chapel Hill: University of North Carolina Press, 2013.

Querino, Manuel R. *O colono preto como fator da Civilização Brasileira*. Bahia: Imprensa Oficial do Estado, 1918.

———. *Costumes africanos no Brasil*. Edited with a preface by Arthur Ramos. Rio de Janeiro: Civilização Brasileira, 1938.

Raphael, Alison. *Samba and Social Control: Popular Culture and Racial Democracy in Rio de Janeiro*. New York: Columbia University Press, 1980.

Rebelo, Apolinário. *Jornal "A Classe Operária": Aspectos da história, opinião e contribuição do Jornal Comunista na vida nacional*. São Paulo: Anita Garibaldi, 2003.

Record, Wilson. *The Negro and the Communist Party*. Chapel Hill: University of North Carolina Press, 1951.

Redles, David. *Hitler's Millennial Reich: Apocalyptic Belief and the Search for Salvation*. New York: New York University Press, 2005.

Reed, Merl. *Seedtime for the Modern Civil Rights Movement: The President's Committee on Fair Employment Practices, 1941–1946*. Baton Rouge: Louisiana State University Press, 1991.

Reich, Cary. *The Life of Nelson A. Rockefeller: Worlds to Conquer, 1908–1958*. New York: Doubleday, 1996.

Richard, Alfred Charles, Jr. *Censorship and Hollywood's Hispanic Image: An Interpretive Filmography, 1936–1955*. Westport, CT: Greenwood Press, 1993.

Roberts, Shari. "'The Lady in the Tutti-Frutti Hat': Carmen Miranda, a Spectacle of Ethnicity." *Cinema Journal* 2, no. 23 (Spring 1993): 3–23.

Robinson, Cedric. *Black Marxism: The Making of the Black Radical Tradition*. Chapel Hill: University of North Carolina Press, 1983.

———. *Forgeries of Memory and Meaning: Blacks and the Regimes of Race in American Theater and Film before World War II*. Chapel Hill: University of North Carolina Press, 2012.

Rodrigues, Ana María. *Samba negro, espoliação branca*. São Paulo: Editora Hucitec, 1984.

Rodrigues, R. Nina. *As raças humanas e a responsabilidade penal no Brasil*. Bahia, 1894.

———. *O animismo fetichista dos negros baianos*. Rio de Janeiro: Ministério da Cultura: Fundação Biblioteca Nacional, 2006.

Rolinson, Mary G. *Grassroots Garveyism: The Universal Negro Improvement Association in the Rural South, 1920–1927*. Chapel Hill: University of North Carolina Press, 2007.

Romo, Anadelia A. *Brazil's Living Museum: Race, Reform, and Tradition in Bahia*. Chapel Hill: University of North Carolina Press, 2010.

Rossi, Gustavo. *O intelectual feiticeiro Edison Carneiro e o campo de estudos das relações raciais no Brasil.* Campinas: Ed. Unicamp, 2015.

Ruy, José Carlos, and Augusto Buonicore, orgs. *Contribuição à história do Partido Comunista do Brasil.* São Paulo: Fundação Maurício Grabois/Anita Garibaldi, 2010.

Sadlier, Darlene. *Americans All: Good Neighbor Cultural Diplomacy in World War II.* Austin: University of Texas Press, 2012.

Sandroni, Carlos. *Feitiço decente: Transformações do samba no Rio de Janeiro (1917–1933).* Rio de Janeiro: Jorge Zahar Ed.: Ed. UFRJ, 2001.

Santos, Sales Augusto dos. "Historical Roots of the 'Whitening' of Brazil." Translated by Laurence Hallewell. *Latin American Perspectives* 29, no. 1 (2002): 61–82.

———. "Who Is Black in Brazil? A Timely or a False Question in Brazilian Race Relations in the Era of Affirmative Action?" Translated by Obianuju C. Anya. *Latin American Perspectives* 33, no. 4 (2006): 30–48.

Savage, Barbara. *Broadcasting Freedom: Radio, War, and the Politics of Race, 1938–1948.* Chapel Hill: University of North Carolina Press, 1999.

Schneider, Alberto Luiz. "Iberismo e luso-tropicalismo na obra de Gilberto Freyre." *História da historiografia* 10 (2012): 77–82.

Schpun, Mônica Raisa. "Carmen Miranda: Uma star migrante." *Revista de Antropologia* 51, no. 2 (2008): 451–71.

Schrecker, Ellen. *Many Are the Crimes: McCarthyism in America.* Boston: Little, Brown, 1998.

Schwarcz, Lilia Moritz. *The Spectacle of the Races: Scientists, Institutions, and the Race Question in Brazil, 1870–1930.* Translated by Leland Guyer. New York: Hill and Wang, 1999.

———. "A Mestizo and Tropical Country: The Creation of the Official Image of Independent Brazil." *Revista Europea de estudios Latinoamericanos y del Caribe* 80 (April 2006): 25–42.

Schwartzman, Sheila. *Humberto Mauro e as imagens do Brasil.* São Paulo: Editora UNESP, 2004.

Seigel, Micol. *Uneven Encounters: Making Race and Nation in Brazil and the United States.* Durham, NC: Duke University Press, 2009.

Selig, Diana. "Celebrating Cultural Diversity in the 1920s." Special issue, "Reinterpreting the 1920s," *OAH Magazine of History* 21, no. 3 (July 2007): 41–46.

Sentinelo, Jacqueline Tondato. "O lugar das 'raças' no projeto de nação da Ação Integralista Brasileira." *Revista espaço acadêmico* 108 (May 2010): 145–52.

Serratto, Edgar Bruno Franke. "Estudos sobre o Integralismo e seus momentos." Paper presented at Associação Nacional de História—ANPUH XXIV Simpósio Nacional de História 2007.

Seyferth, Giralda. "Racismo e o ideário da formação do povo no pensamento brasileiro." *Cadernos PENESB*, no. 4 (2002): 13–32.

Shaw, Lisa. *The Social History of the Brazilian Samba.* Farnham, UK: Ashgate, 1999.

Sheriff, Robin. *Dreaming Equality: Color, Race, and Racism in Urban Brazil.* New Brunswick, NJ: Rutgers University Press, 2001.

Shirts, Matthew. "Socrates, Corinthians, and Questions of Democracy and Citizenship." In *Sport and Society in Latin America: Diffusion, Dependency, and the Rise of Mass Culture,* edited by Joseph L. Arbena, 97–112. Westport, CT: Greenwood Press, 1988.

Silva, Carla Luciana. *Onda Vermelha: Imaginários anticomunistas brasileiros (1931–1934).* Porto Alegre: EDIPUCRS, 2001.

Silva, Nelson do Valle, and Barbosa, Maria Ligia de Oliveira. *População e estatísticas vitais. In.: Estatísticas do século XX.* Rio de Janeiro: IBGE, 2006.

Singh, Nikhil Pal. *Black Is a Country: Race and the Unfinished Struggle for Democracy.* Cambridge, MA: Harvard University Press, 2004.

Siqueira, Servelo. "É tudo verdade: Política, samba e racismo no filme brasileiro de Orson Welles." *Folha de São Paulo,* Folhetim, December 2, 1984.

Skidmore, Thomas. *Black into White: Race and Nationality in Brazilian Thought.* Oxford: Oxford University Press, 1974.

———. *Brazil: Five Centuries of Change.* Oxford: Oxford University Press, 1999.

———. "The Historiography of Brazil, 1889–1964: Part 1." *American Historical Review* 55, no. 4 (November 1975): 716–48.

———. "The Historiography of Brazil, 1889–1964: Part 2." *American Historical Review* 56, no. 1 (February 1976): 81–109.

———. *Politics in Brazil, 1930–1964: An Experiment in Democracy.* 40th anniversary ed. Oxford: Oxford University Press, 2007.

———. "Racial Ideas and Social Policy in Brazil, 1870–1940." In *The Idea of Race in Latin America, 1870–1940,* edited by Richard Graham, 7–36. Austin: University of Texas Press, 1990.

Sklaroff, Lauren Rebecca. *Black Culture and the New Deal: The Quest for Civil Rights in the Roosevelt Era.* Chapel Hill: University of North Carolina Press, 2009.

Smith, Christen. *Afro-Paradise: Blackness, Violence, and Performance in Brazil.* Champaign: University of Illinois Press, 2016.

Smith, Jennifer. *An International History of the Black Panther Party.* New York: Garland, 1999.

Sodré, Jaime. *Manuel Querino: Um herói da raça e classe.* Salvador, 2001.

Soihet, Rachel. *A subversão pelo riso: Estudos sobre o carnaval carioca da Belle Époque ao tempo de Vargas.* Rio de Janeiro: Fundação Getúlio Vargas Editora, 1998.

Solomon, Mark. *The Cry Was Unity: Communists and African Americans, 1917–1936.* Jackson: University Press of Mississippi, 1998.

Sotero, Edilza Correia. "Representação política negra no Brasil pós-Estado Novo." PhD diss., Universidade de São Paulo, 2015.

Souza, Marcilene Garcia de. "Ações Afirmativas, cotas para negros nos concursos públicos federais e os desafios para sua efetividade." Paper presented at the Latin American Studies Association Annual Conference, San Juan, Puerto Rico, May 30, 2015.

Sparrow, James T. *Warfare State: World War II Americans and the Age of Big Government.* Oxford: Oxford University Press, 2013.

Stam, Robert. "Orson Welles and the Power of Blackness." *Persistence of Vision* 7 (1989): 219–44.

———. "Slow Fade to Afro: The Black Presence in Brazilian Cinema." *Film Quarterly* 36, no. 2 (Winter 1982–83): 16–32.

———. *Tropical Multiculturalism: A Comparative History of Race in Brazilian Cinema and Culture*. Durham, NC: Duke University Press, 1997.

Stepan, Nancy Leys. *The Hour of Eugenics: Race, Gender, and Nation in Latin America*. Ithaca, NY: Cornell University Press, 1991.

Stewart, Catherine A. *Long Past Slavery: Representing Race in the Federal Writers' Project*. Chapel Hill: University of North Carolina Press, 2016.

Stuckey, Mary E. *Defining Americans: The Presidency and National Identity*. Lawrence: University Press of Kansas, 2004.

Sullivan, Patricia. *Days of Hope: Race and Democracy in the New Deal Era*. Chapel Hill: University of North Carolina Press, 1996.

Susman, Warren. *Culture as History: The Transformation of American Society in the Twentieth Century*. New York: Pantheon Books, 1984.

Tackley, Catherine. *Benny Goodman's Famous 1938 Carnegie Hall Jazz Concert*. Oxford: Oxford University Press, 2012.

Tannenbaum, Frank. *Slave and Citizen: The Negro in the Americas*. New York: Knopf, 1946.

Taylor, Brennen. *UNIA and American Communism in Conflict, 1917–1928: An Historical Analysis in Negro Social Welfare*. Pittsburgh, PA: University of Pittsburgh Press, 1984.

Taylor, Ula Y. *The Veiled Garvey: The Life and Times of Amy Jacques Garvey*. Chapel Hill: University of North Carolina Press, 2002.

Telles, Edward. *Race in Another America: The Significance of Skin Color in Brazil*. Princeton, NJ: Princeton University Press, 2004.

Tidwell, John Edgar, and Steven C. Tracy. *After Winter: The Art and Life of Sterling A. Brown*. Oxford: Oxford University Press, 2009.

Tolbert, Emory J. *The Universal Negro Improvement Association in Los Angeles: A Study of Western Garveyism*. Ann Arbor, MI: University Microfilms International, 1983.

Tota, Antonio Pedro. *O amigo Americano: Nelson Rockefeller e o Brasil*. São Paulo: Companhia Das Letras, 2014.

———. *The Seduction of Brazil: The Americanization of Brazil during World War II*. Translated by Lorena B. Ellis. Austin: University of Texas Press, 2009.

Trindade, Hélgio. *Integralismo: O fascismo brasileiro na década de 30*. Porto Alegre, Brazil: Difel/UFRGS, 1974.

Turner, Joyce Moore. *Caribbean Crusaders and the Harlem Renaissance*. Urbana: University of Illinois Press, 2005.

Twine, France Widdance. *Racism in a Racial Democracy: The Maintenance of White Supremacy in Brazil*. New Brunswick, NJ: Rutgers University Press, 1998.

Van Rijn, Guido. *Roosevelt's Blues: African American Blues and Gospel Songs on FDR*. Jackson: University Press of Mississippi, 1997.

Vasconcellos, Gilberto. *A ideologia curupira: Análise do discurso integralista*. São Paulo: Brasiliense, 1977.

Velloso, Mônica Pimenta. "Os intelectuais e a diversidade cultural." In *Getúlio Vargas e Seu Tempo*, orgs. Raul Mendes Silva, Paulo Brandi Cachapuz, and Sérgio Lamarão, 149–51. Rio de Janeiro: BNDES, 2004.

Vianna, Hermano. *The Mystery of Samba: Popular Music and National Identity in Brazil*. Translated by John Charles Chasteen. Chapel Hill: University of North Carolina Press, 1999.

Vianna, Marly de Almeida, ed. *Pão, terra e liberdade: Memória do movimento comunista de 1935*. Rio de Janeiro and São Carlos: Arquivo Nacional, Universidade Federal de São Carlos, 1995.

Vincent, Theodore. *Black Power and the Garvey Movement*. Baltimore: Black Classic Press, 2006.

Von Eschen, Penny. *Race against Empire: Black Americans and Anticolonialism, 1937–1957*. Ithaca, NY: Cornell University Press, 1997.

———. *Satchmo Blows Up the World: Jazz Ambassadors Play the Cold War*. Cambridge, MA: Harvard University Press, 2004.

Wagley, Charles, ed. *Race and Class in Rural Brazil*. Paris: UNESCO, 1952.

Wall, Cheryl. *Women of the Harlem Renaissance*. Bloomington: Indiana University Press, 1995.

Warren, Donald. *Radio Priest: Charles Coughlin, the Father of Hate Radio*. New York: Free Press, 1996.

Washburn, Patrick. *A Question of Sedition: The Federal Government's Investigation of the Black Press during World War II*. New York: Oxford University Press, 1986.

Weber, Mark. "Swiss Historian Exposes Anti-Hitler Rauschning Memoir as Fraudulent." *Journal of Historical Review* 4, no. 3 (Fall 1983): 378–80.

Weinstein, Barbara. *The Color of Modernity: São Paulo and the Making of Race and Nation in Brazil*. Durham, NC: Duke University Press, 2015.

———. "Slavery, Citizenship and National Identity in Brazil and the United States South." In *Nationalism in the New World*, edited by Don Doyle and Marco Antonio Pamplona, 248–71. Athens: University of Georgia Press, 2006.

———. "Racializing Regional Difference: São Paulo versus Brazil, 1932." In *Race and Nation in Modern Latin America*, edited by Nancy Appelbaum, Anne Macpherson, and Karin Rosemblatt, 237–62. Chapel Hill: University of North Carolina Press, 2003.

Weisberger, Bernard A., ed. *The WPA Guide to America: The Best of 1930s America as Seen by the Federal Writers' Project*. New York: Pantheon, 1985.

Weiss, Holger. *Framing a Radical African Atlantic: West African Intellectuals and the International Trade Union Committee of Negro Workers*. Leiden, Netherlands: Brill Academic Publishers, 2013.

Weiss, Nancy. *Farewell to the Party of Lincoln: Black Politics in the Age of FDR*. Princeton, NJ: Princeton University Press, 1983.

West, Michael Oliver, William G. Martin, and Fanon Che Wilkins. *From Toussaint to Tupac: The Black International since the Age of Revolution*. Chapel Hill: University of North Carolina Press, 2009.

Whitaker, Robert. *On the Laps of Gods: The Red Summer of 1919 and the Struggle for Justice That Remade a Nation*. New York: Crown Publishers, 2008.

Whitman, James Q. *Hitler's American Model: The United States and the Making of Nazi Race Law*. Princeton, NJ: Princeton University Press, 2017.

Widener, Daniel. *Black Arts West: Culture and Struggle in Postwar Los Angeles*. Durham, NC: Duke University Press, 2010.

Williams, Daryle. *Culture Wars in Brazil: The First Vargas Regime, 1930–1945*. Durham, NC: Duke University Press, 2001.

Williams, Erica Lorraine. *Sex Tourism in Bahia: Ambiguous Entanglements*. Champaign: University of Illinois Press, 2013.

Wolcott, Victoria. *Remaking Respectability: African American Women in Interwar Detroit*. Chapel Hill: University of North Carolina Press, 2001.

Woll, Allen. *The Hollywood Musical Goes to War*. Chicago: Nelson-Hall, 1983.

———. *The Latin Image in American Film*. Rev. ed. Los Angeles: UCLA Latin American Center Publications, University of California, 1980.

Wolters, Raymond. *Negroes and the Great Depression: The Problem of Economic Recovery*. Westport, CT: Greenwood Publishing, 1970.

Woodley, Jenny. *Art for Equality*. Lexington: University Press of Kentucky, 2014.

Wu, Ellen. *The Color of Success: Asian Americans and the Origins of the Model Minority*. Princeton, NJ: Princeton University Press, 2013.

Young, Robert. "The Linguistic Turn, Materialism and Race: Toward an Aesthetics of Crisis." *Callaloo* 24, no. 4 (Winter 2001): 334–45.

Zuburan, M. Angélica. "Narrativas étnico-raciais e de gênero na campanha ao monumento da 'Mãe Preta': Pedagogias da imprensa negra (O Exemplo, 1920–1930)," VII Simpósio Nacional de História Cultural: Escritas, Circulação, Leituras e Recepções, 2014.

Zumoff, Jacob. *The Communist International and U.S. Communism, 1919–1929*. Chicago: Haymarket Books, 2015.

Index

Abbott, Robert, 12
abolition, 6, 10, 22, 55, 225, 239, 245: commemorations of, 54, 61, 65, 102, 123, 137, 153, 244. *See also* cinquentenário.
Ação Integralista Brasileira (AIB, or Brazilian Integralist Action), 106, 112–18, 123–124, 126–27
Additional Act, 232
Afonso Arinos Law, 26, 31, 245–49, 259, 261
African Blood Brotherhood for African Liberation and Redemption (ABB), 35, 37–39
Afro-Brazilian Congress, 30, 45, 55, 162.
Afro-Brazilian Democratic Committee, 240–41
Alabama Supreme Court, 61
Alfinete, O, 14
Aliança Nacional Libertadora (ANL, or National Liberation Alliance), 50, 62–65, 70, 89, 96, 97
Alien Registration Act, 250
Allen, James S., 40, 57–58, 82
Allied nations: Brazilian dictatorship and, 6, 174, 177–79, 230; CPUSA and, 250; Hitler's reference to, 107, 202; ideology of, 237; loyalty concerns of, 173; Nogueira on, 242; racial justice and, 236; racial utopia and, 206; racism and, 228; Roosevelt's equal opportunity for

all and, 203; and segregation in Brazil, 192
Alvorada, 236, 242–43
Alves, Sebastião Rodrigues, 240–241
Amaral, Raul Joviano do, 236
American Civil Liberties Union, 158
American Council of Learned Societies (ACLS), 198
American Federation of Labor, 75
American Negro, The (pamphlet), 40
American Negro Labor Congress (ANLC), 37, 41–42
Americans All, Immigrants All, 148, 163
America's Town Meeting of the Air, 147, 160
Amos 'n' Andy, 145–46
Anauê!, 117, 123
Andrade, Almir de, 179, 180–81
Andrade, Oswald de, 17
Anglo-Saxonism, 10–11
"Anthem of the Poor Brazilian," 28, 64, 95
antilynching: anticommunism and, 68, 76–79, 88; bills on, 41, 123, 130–31, 254, 257. *See also* lynching
anti-Semitism, 114, 118, 242
Arabs, 110
Aranha, Oswaldo, 180, 183, 217, 231
Argentina, 209, 223
Armstrong, Louis, 212
army officers (Brazilian tenentes), 17, 252

353

United Nations Educational, Scientific and
  Cultural Organization (UNESCO), 184
Universal Negro Improvement Association
  (UNIA), 16, 36–40
University of Chicago Roundtable, 147
University of São Paulo (USP), 232, 264
urbanization, 33–34
US-Mexican War, 186
USS West Virginia, 206
US Supreme Court, 11, 13, 111, 157, 159

Vagalume, 152
Vargas, Getúlio: AIB and, 116; authoritarianism of, 262, 263; communism and,
  31, 50, 52, 60, 66, 69–70, 89; state
  cultural production during regime of,
  139, 141–42, 149–50, 212, 214–15,
  217; Estado Novo and, 89, 218,
  230–31, 234, 236; fascism and, 122–23,
  126, 133, 135–36; immigration laws
  and, 114, 223; labor laws and, 21, 103,
  106; national culture and, 19; PTB and,
  240; neutrality of, 172, 175; race and
  democracy and, 179–81, 91, 94–96,
  184; self-promotion by, 225; and vow
  to end corruption, 46
Vasconcelos, José, 183
Venezuela, 44, 195, 253
Versailles, 15
Vianna, Alfredo da Rocha, 169
Vianna, Ferreira, 160
Vianna, Hermano, 23, 225
Vianna, Oliveira, 112
Viany, Alex, 214, 217
Villa-Lobos, Heitor, 209, 224
Volusia, Eros, 221

voting rights, 68, 92, 116, 158, 160, 232
Voz da Raça, A, 48, 98, 123, 124, 126

Wagner Act, 70
Wall Street, 119
War Department (US), 189–90, 251
Ward, Theodore, 167
Warner Bros. Studios, 210, 218
Weimar Republic, 108, 124
Welles, Orson, 26, 165, 194, 212–18, 224
Welles, Sumner, 203, 206
We Work Again, 163–66
white cultural mediators: demarginalization
  and, 194, 261; US-Brazil wartime
  cultural exchange and, 210–11, 217,
  219, 221, 226; state cultural production
  and, 138, 145, 147, 153, 169, 171
whitening. See branqueamento
Whiteman, Paul, 170
White, Walter, 42, 76, 79, 98, 146, 191,
  254
Whitley, F.L., 189
Whitman, James, 110–11, 123
Whitney, John "Jock", 212, 219
Wilson, Elizabeth, 215
Wilson, Richard, 215
Wilson, Woodrow, 15
Winslow, Mary, 197, 210
Woll, Matthew, 75
Workers Party of America (WP), 35, 37
Works Progress Administration (WPA), 136,
  140, 149, 158, 163–65, 167, 252

Yale Glee Club, 209

Zumbi, 55, 61

Founded in 1893,
UNIVERSITY OF CALIFORNIA PRESS
publishes bold, progressive books and journals
on topics in the arts, humanities, social sciences,
and natural sciences—with a focus on social
justice issues—that inspire thought and action
among readers worldwide.

The UC PRESS FOUNDATION
raises funds to uphold the press's vital role
as an independent, nonprofit publisher, and
receives philanthropic support from a wide
range of individuals and institutions—and from
committed readers like you. To learn more, visit
ucpress.edu/supportus.